Set Lighting Technician's Handbook

Film Lighting Equipment, Practice, and Electrical Distribution

Harry C. Box

Second Edition

Focal Press

Boston Oxford Johannesburg Melbourne New Delhi Singapore

D0754071

Focal Press is an imprint of Butterworth–Heinemann.

Copyright © 1997 by Butterworth–Heinemann
 ℞ A member of the Reed Elsevier group.
All rights reserved.

 Recognizing the importance of preserving what has been written,
Butterworth–Heinemann prints its books on acid-free paper whenever possible.

Library of Congress Cataloging-in-Publication Data
Box, Harry C.
    Set lighting technician's handbook : film lighting equipment,
    practice, and electrical distribution / by Harry C. Box. -- 2nd ed.
        p.   cm.
    Includes index.
    ISBN 0-240-80257-8 (alk. paper)
    1. Cinematography--Lighting.   I. Title.
TR891.B68   1996
778.5'343--dc20   96-24075
                                                         CIP

British Library Cataloguing-in-Publication Data
A catalogue record for this book is available from the British Library.

The publisher offers special discounts on bulk orders of this book.
For information, please contact:

Manager of Special Sales
Butterworth-Heinemann
313 Washington Street
Newton, MA 02158-1626
Tel: 617-928-2500
Fax: 617-928-2620

For information on all Focal Press publications available, contact our
World Wide Web home page at http://www.bh.com/fp

10 9 8 7 6 5 4 3 2

Printed in the United States of America

To my mother and father

Contents

List of Tables

List of Appendices

Preface

Terminology

Imagine that your mother visits you on the set. You introduce her to the gaffer, who she says seems like a nice fellow, that is, until he starts giving orders: "Hang a baby. Kill the midget and have two blondes standing by for the martini."

The set lighting profession uses volumes of peculiar-sounding technical terms. In this book, terms are explained the first time they are used, and can also be found in the glossary. You will find, however, that the same equipment has different names from country to country, city to city, and studio lot to studio lot. An *Obie* light is called a *basher* in England. In Jamaica a scrim is known as a *strainer*, while here we often simply call it *wire*. A wall sled is called a *Grumpy* at Paramount Studio (the name that people around the lot bestowed on its inventor). There are even a few common terms that are difficult to use in polite conversation.

People who work in rental houses will act as if you are out of your mind if you call something by a different name than that with which they are familiar. This can be frustrating when working out of town with a new rental house.

To make matters even more unpredictable, terms change over time and are constantly being invented and evolving. I've adopted the terms that, in my experience, are most universally used, but you will no doubt run across many other names that do not appear here.

The correct terms for the head of the camera and lighting departments are Director of Photography or Cinematographer. To some, the abbreviation DP is objectionable for various reasons (DP also stands for Displaced Person, the label given refugees after World War II). Having acknowledged this fact, I am going to go ahead and use DP anyway as a matter of convenience in writing and reading. Readers should be aware, however, that for many Directors of Photography, the use of the abbreviation in conversation does not show proper respect for the title.

Acknowledgments

I am indebted to many individuals for their generous contributions to this book: Darryl Murchison, whose discussions during the early stages of writing helped set the book on course; Michael Skinner, who generously shared his expertise helping me unravel the vagaries of the NEC; Doug Pentek, Earl Gilbert, Larry Parker, Cyrus Yavneh, Russ Brandt, Dean Bray, Frieder Hochheim, Herb Breitling, Michael Kaiping, Scott Toland, and Jon Bart, all of whom read and improved sections of the book;

Richard Mula and Pete Romano, who shed much light on the subject of underwater lighting; Frank "The Dinosaur" Valdez and Gary Scalzo, who lent their expertise to the section on rigging; and Vance Trussell, whose suggestions and ongoing interest and encouragement were invaluable to me.

I also gratefully acknowledge the many manufacturers who provided technical information, photographs, and illustrations. The manufacturers are listed in Appendix H. I also thank Doug Pentec and Carly Barber of Hollywood Rental and Robert Guzman of Concept Lighting for the use of their rental equipment in creating the art work.

I would like to extend a special note of thanks to the illustrators, Shawn Murphy and Lisa Cyr, who may well have been inking drawings on their wedding night in order to make the publication deadline.

My very greatest thanks, love, and appreciation go to Joan Box for her loving attention to my split infinitives and for her unending support.

Finally, thanks to my family, to Dana, and to other close friends for their support in the writing of this book.

Additional Acknowledgments for the Second Edition

There is a great deal of new material in this edition and more people to acknowledge for their contributions to its research. I would like to thank Eric King, who shared his expertise on HMIs and electronic ballasts. I owe a debt of gratitude to Chris Barratt, without whose generosity and vast experience I could not have created the new section on generator troubleshooting. I also thank Bernie Kret at Strand, who helped with the new section on electronic dimmers. I lastly would like to praise the talents of John Huey, who created additional art work for this edition.

CHAPTER 1

Set Basics: Your First Barbecue

The technical aspects of filmmaking — film stocks, cameras, lighting, sound, effects — all involve a myriad of small details that, taken as a whole, seem impossibly complex. As with any craft, to become a master requires years of experience and exposure to many different situations. It has been my experience, however, that no single piece of equipment or procedure or technique is really complicated; there is no one thing that cannot be explained and understood in less than ten minutes. Making movies is the artful application of millions of relatively simple details. This book helps with some of those details, describing procedures that save time and promote safety, clarifying aspects of the craft that are confusing and often misunderstood, and supplying a wealth of information about the hundreds of gadgets of which lighting technicians are so fond.

Starting with the basics, we begin with a summary of the role of the lighting crew on a film set.

Job Descriptions of the Lighting Crew

The electric, grip, and camera departments fall under the direction of the *director of photography* (DP). The *gaffer* and *key grip* are the DP's lieutenants. The gaffer is the head of the electric department and is in charge of the lighting crew. The gaffer's crew consists of the *assistant chief lighting technician*, known as the *best boy electric* or *second electrician*. Under the best boy are the set *electricians*, also called *lamp operators* or *third electricians*.

Director of Photography

Q: How many directors does it take to screw in a light bulb?
A: "One. No, two. No, no, one . . ."

The director of photography (DP) is the director's right hand; he or she is the one who helps the director make all the hard decisions. It is the DP's responsibility

1

to create on film what the director and DP have envisioned for each scene; to evoke the proper time, place, and atmosphere with the lighting; and to help choose the camera angles that will be most effective in telling the story. The DP chooses the lighting sources, balancing realism against the dramatic potential of more stylized effects, as called for by the script and the director. The DP has a say in the design and color of the sets and the wardrobe, and in the selection of locations. The DP helps the director decide how each scene is to be covered and what overlap the various camera angles will provide for the editor. In choosing the camera angles, the DP must maintain proper screen direction (a responsibility shared with the script supervisor) and lighting continuity between setups. The DP usually shoots tests prior to the beginning of photography. He or she may experiment with various lighting effects, with different gel colors, with a special lab process or different filter combinations — looking for a combination of effects that will accomplish the special requirements of the script. The DP may also conduct his or her own research prior to production to ensure the accuracy and authenticity of a period and to inspire ideas for the cinematography.

The DP holds a position of immense responsibility, creatively and financially. A producer depends on the DP not only for the photographic quality of the film, but also for maintaining the production schedule. The DP always faces conflicts, in meeting both his or her own aspirations for the photography and in meeting the demands of the film's schedule and budget. The lighting crew fights the DP's battles on the frontlines. Their ability to light the set quickly and efficiently directly affects the DP's ability to produce good work and maintain the production schedule.

Gaffer

The gaffer is the *chief lighting technician* (CLT). He or she works directly with the DP to implement the lighting plan and to help achieve the photographic look of the film. The DP, gaffer, and key grip attend preproduction meetings together and scout the locations where filming is to take place. They discuss the DP's approach to each scene and determine what lighting preparations and equipment are required.

On the set, the gaffer is responsible for the execution of the lighting scheme, the organization and operation of the lighting crew. The DP typically expresses his or her goals as to the mood and the motivating sources of light for the scene, and the f-stop at which he wants to shoot. The DP and the gaffer discuss the lighting. The DP may have specific lamps in mind or may leave it to the gaffer to translate general ideas into specifics. The gaffer then instructs the crew, and sees to the exact placement and focus of each light to accomplish the DP's instructions. Typically, once the gaffer has executed the lighting, the DP will "sweeten" to taste, with a few adjustments.

The gaffer must have a very strong eye for lighting and a solid knowledge of which lights to use to create any desired effect. As the lighting starts to come together, the gaffer functions as the director of photography's second pair of eyes. The gaffer is always on the lookout for problems — inadequate light, overexposure, hot spots, ugly shadows, and so on. Together the director of photography and gaffer look for ways to make the scene look more interesting. A first rate gaffer has a critical eye for the balance of light and shade, the modeling of facial features, and the separation of foreground from middle ground and background. The gaffer, carrying light meters on a belt, often stands next to the DP at the camera to view and measure the light hitting the subject and consult with him or her on issues of fill ratio and balance of exposure.

A very important part of the gaffer's job is organizing and running the operation. He or she must constantly be cycling through the many tasks at hand, pushing forward the progress of each project, keeping an eye on the performance of the lighting crew, thinking ahead so that power and lights are readily at hand for each shot, and forestalling delay by maintaining constant vigilance over every possible need.

The gaffer should never have to leave the immediate area in which the action is being filmed. He or she must rely on the crew to be near at hand to make lighting adjustments and to run for equipment when it is needed. If, during filming, it is necessary to clear the set, the grips and electricians remain just outside the set, near the door, during the takes. Because the lighting crew is always under time pressure, an electrician who stays near the action, listens, and thinks ahead can do a lot to help the gaffer improve the speed and efficiency of filming.

Best Boy Electric

The best boy electric is the gaffer's chief assistant. He or she is in charge of personnel and equipment for the electrical department — a vital role in the smooth running of the lighting crew. The best boy's duties include scouting the locations with the gaffer, making scouting notes and creating light plots with the gaffer when necessary, compiling the list of equipment needed, supervising the load-in (loading electrical equipment into the truck at the rental house before the first day of production), organizing the equipment and supplies in the truck, supervising the removal and return of equipment from the truck at each location, keeping track of inventory and damage, and supervising the load-out after the last day of production. At each location, the best boy plans the routing of the feeder cable and supervises the distribution of electrical power to the lights. In addition to the equipment inventory, the best boy keeps track of gels and expendables; coordinates equipment orders, returns, subrentals, and special orders; and is in charge of hiring and laying off extra electricians when needed. The best boy supervises the electrical crew's start-up paperwork and time cards.

During filming, the best boy helps make sure electricians are positioned where they are needed, ensuring that everyone doesn't wander off to graze at the craft service table or flirt with the makeup department — at least, not all at once. The best boy also repairs or exchanges broken equipment, changes burned-out bulbs, maintains equipment, and keeps the truck organized for easy access to equipment.

The best boy is the first person an electrician goes to if he or she has a complaint. A chain of command operates on the set; an electrician should not speak directly with the production manager or the director. If necessary, the best boy will take up the issue with the gaffer. It is then the gaffer's responsibility to engage in diplomacy and to fight for the needs of the electrical crew. There are always enough opinions on a set. It is preferable that the lighting crew be noticed for their good work, not for their remarks.

Most importantly, the best boy is the emissary of the electrical department, communicating and negotiating with other departments, with the fire marshal, and with rental houses and other equipment suppliers. A best boy who maintains good relations with each department can get cooperation when it is needed. For example, when the best boy needs to put a light on the roof of a building, the locations team must make the necessary contacts to secure that spot. When the best boy needs some extra equipment delivered quickly, his or her relationship with the transportation department and the contact at the rental house comes into play. The best boy's diplomacy is key.

Electricians

Electricians are affectionately known as *juicers* or *sparks* and are officially titled *set lighting technicians* or *lamp operators*. The electrician's primary responsibility is placing and focusing lights according to the wishes of the gaffer. At each location, the electricians unload and reload the lighting equipment from the trucks, run cabling, and run the distribution of electrical power for the lights. They may be asked also to provide power for other departments — hair, makeup, camera, sound — however, the transportation department usually provides power for all vehicles. On the set, electricians are responsible for safely securing lights and stands during use; manipulating the intensity, direction, color, and quality of light; wiring practical lamps (such as table lamps and wall sconces), switches, and wall outlets on constructed sets; and anticipating the needs of the gaffer so that equipment is at hand when needed.

There is a Zen to the job of the lamp operator. An experienced lamp operator handles the equipment with deft speed and smoothness, an economy of movement that comes with familiarity. His or her focused concentration is on two things — the activities of the lighting crew and the behavior of the light. He or she is constantly attentive to the gaffer and DP, and to fellow electricians who might need a hand. Simultaneously, the electrician is aware of the light falling, blasting, leaking, and spilling onto the faces and the surfaces around the set. Through the exchange of a few words, hand signals, or by clairvoyance, the electrician grasps the gaffer's intention and manipulates the lamp to create the desired effect.

It should be added that movie electricians are very rarely licensed journeyman or master electricians. They are not qualified to wire buildings or work on power lines. Their job is lighting movies.

Grip Department

Q: How many grips does it take to screw in a light bulb?
A: Grips don't change light bulbs. That's electric.

Nonelectrical lighting equipment is handled by our brothers and sisters in the grip department. (A grip is affectionately called a *hammer*.) Silks, flags, reflector boards, rigging, dollies and dolly track, cranes, jib arms, and so on are all in the domain of gripology. Lights, dimmers, and generally things with plugs are the domain of the juicers. You could say that the electricians do the lighting, and the grips do the shading. Each time an electrician sets up a light, a grip should be right next to him or her with a *grip package*, which includes a C-stand and a complement of flags and nets that may be needed in front of the light. On nonunion jobs, grips are usually in charge of placing sand bags on the light stands, providing ladders, and leveling large stands when they are placed on uneven ground. On union jobs in LA, the electricians handle their own ladders, sandbags, and rigging hardware such as pipe clamps. Grips handle gel and diffusion when it is used on a frame or when it is applied to windows. An electrician applies the gel and diffusion when it goes directly on a light.

Grips are responsible for the safety of the rigging, and they are often called upon to rig support for lighting equipment. Speed-rail grids, wall spreaders, trapezes, and similar rigs are built by the grips. When lights are to be hung from an overhead grid or rigged to the wall of the set, the grips will generally rig the support. An electrician then plugs the light in, focuses it, etc. When large lights are mounted on a high platform, on top of parallels, or in the basket of a crane such as a Snorkelift or Condor, the grips rig and secure the light or light stand. When an interior night scene needs to be shot during daylight hours, the grips will often be called upon to build big black tents around the windows to create darkness outside while providing space for lights outside the building.

The head of the grip department is the *key grip*. The key grip supervises the grips in the same way that the gaffer supervises the electricians. He or she works with the gaffer, supporting the gaffer's lighting needs.

The key grip's chief assistant is the *best boy grip*. The best boy grip functions in the grip crew in the same way that the best boy electric does in the electrical crew.

The *dolly grip* is in charge of operating the dollies and cranes: laying and leveling dolly track, moving the camera smoothly to exact marks and with precise timing, and booming the camera up and down. Grips also rig support for the camera when it is placed in unusual places, such as on the hood of a car.

The Company

A film crew is composed of freelance artists, technicians, and administrators who are brought together by the production company when the production is ready to be mounted. The producer and director select the department heads: the DP, production designer, sound mixer, editor, and so on. Each department head usually brings his or her own staff onto the production. The DP recommends a gaffer, key grip, camera operator, and camera assistants with whom he or she prefers to work. The gaffer, in turn, recommends electricians he or she knows and trusts.

Each production brings new faces, new locations, and new circumstances, and yet you can count on certain constants in relationships between electricians and the other departments.

Production Staff

The crew is officially hired by the producer. Although the gaffer usually brings electricians onto the crew, once an electrician is offered a job, it is the producer with whom he or she signs the deal memo, or contract. Paychecks are handled by the accounting department or by a payroll company.

The duties of the *unit production manager* (UPM) include preparing the script breakdown and production schedule, establishing and controlling the budget, supervising the selection of locations, overseeing daily production decisions such as authorizing overtime and making schedule changes due to weather, and managing all the off-set logistics, including housing, meals, transportation, permits, security, and insurance.

The *production coordinator* assists the production manager. His or her duties include booking the crew and cast, booking and returning equipment, ordering expendables and supplies, making deals for locations and services, monitoring petty cash, distributing production information to the various departments, coordinating and distributing the shooting schedule, and keeping the budget. The production manager and production coordinator work out of the production office, making frequent visits to the set.

Assistant Directors

The *assistant director* (1st AD) runs the set. He or she coordinates the actions of every department and the cast, plans the day's schedule, approves the call sheet (which is usually prepared by a second assistant director), keeps everyone informed about the shots, and plans ahead to minimize the amount of time used for each setup. The AD must stay informed of any potential delays or problems and facilitate, coordinate, and motivate the actions of the crew, solving problems before they occur. He or she is responsible for keeping the production moving and on schedule on an hour-to-hour basis.

The ADs are responsible for coordinating the actions of all the departments. For example, if an electrician needed some furniture moved in order to place a light and the set decorator was nowhere in sight, the 1st or 2nd AD would take the matter in hand.

The AD staff take care of the actors: coordinating their schedules, ushering them through makeup and wardrobe, and to and from the set. The AD also directs the background action, supervises crowd control, and determines safety precautions during stunts or complicated setups. The AD calls out "Rolling" just before the cameras roll and "Cut" after the director calls "Cut." It is the nature of the job that the AD has to tell everybody what to do all the time. One shouldn't hold it against him or her, though; a good AD can make the difference between a 12-hour day and a 16-hour day.

The AD is aided by a 2nd AD, and both in turn are helped by 2nd 2nd ADs and a squad of production assistants (PAs). You can usually enlist the help of a PA for any odd job that presents itself; just ask the 2nd ADs if they can spare one.

Script Supervisor

Details such as the hand in which an actor holds his beer, at what point in the scene he puts out his cigarette, and whether his shirt sleeves are rolled up or not are observed and noted by the *script supervisor*. For this reason it is vital for her to be able to see the action on every take; if you stand in her way, you risk being jabbed by her sharp little pencil. The script supervisor also keeps track of the scene and take numbers, lenses used, shot scale, movement, eyeline direction, good takes, flawed takes (and reason), line changes (including adlibs and mistakes), etc. The gaffer will sometimes have the best boy take detailed notes on the placement of the lights, especially if the scene may need to be replicated at another time. The script supervisor can provide the best boy with the applicable scene numbers for his notes.

Camera Department

The camera department is made up of the DP, camera operator, 1st assistant, 2nd assistant, and a loader. The *first camera assistant* (1st AC) is responsible for keeping the camera in focus, making lens changes, threading the film, and maintaining the camera. The 1st AC never leaves the camera's side.

From time to time the 1st AC calls on the lighting crew to help get rid of stray light hitting the lens. (When a light shines directly into the lens, it causes a flare on the image.) The AC and the grips watch for "hits" during setup and rehearsal.

The *second camera assistant* (2nd AC) and *loader* aid the 1st AC with lens changes, magazine changes, film loading, and paperwork. Almost all camera equipment runs on batteries, but a 2nd AC will need power to run a video monitor or to charge batteries. When a director is using a video monitor, it quickly becomes habit to supply power to the monitor as soon as the camera is placed. Similarly, a stinger should be supplied for the dolly at all times.

Sound Department

The *sound mixer* oversees the recording of audio, monitors the sound levels, and is generally responsible for the quality of the sound recording. The sound mixer is the one person on the set who is lucky enough to perform his or her job from a sitting position. He or she can usually be found reading the paper at the sound cart.

The *boom operator* is the person who actually positions the microphone within range of the actors, either by holding it on a pole over their heads, by wiring them with radio mikes, or by planting hidden microphones on the set. When a power cable must cross the microphone cable, he or she will run it under the microphone cable so it doesn't restrict the boom's movement.

The boom operator has to contend with shadows cast onto the actors and backgrounds by the microphone and boom pole. Boom operators are very good at analyzing the lighting and sometimes have to go through all sorts of contortions to avoid casting shadows. Very often setting a topper on one or two lights eliminates shadows cast onto the back wall. Flat-on hard light from the direction of the camera tends to throw mike shadows onto the back wall. Snooting the light so that it only lights the face, or raising it higher so the light is angled downward, then topping the light, can eliminate the problem. Steep, top-down lighting tends to throw microphone shadows down across the actor's clothes. Sometimes the lighting is such that a boom microphone simply cannot be used, and the sound department must accommodate by using other methods.

The sound department has a vested interest in good placement of the generator. Even with baffles to deaden it, engine noise can still be a nuisance. Ballasts and dimmers usually hum, and can become a concern for sound. Place them as far from the microphones as possible (preferably in another room or outside). If you wear a pager, don't forget to put it on silent (vibrate) mode.

The sound department sometimes needs AC power for the sound cart or for the cue light system (red rotating warning lights that indicate that a sound take is being recorded). When video playback is used, the video playback engineer also may need power. This power must be a clean line of 120-volt (V) alternating current (AC). Dimming, light cues, and effects create line noise. It is best if the sound cart be powered off separate utility power. All crew members must check with an electrician before plugging in their own electrical equipment; mistakenly plugging a monitor into a 240V outlet or a DC outlet, for example, would provide an unexpected fireworks display.

Locations

A script might call for a city street, department store, hospital, church, factory, private residence, prison, airport terminal, office building, hotel lobby, or post-apocalyptic tundra. Many settings can be more easily (and cheaply) filmed at an existing real site than recreated on the studio stage or lot. Whatever the case, the locations department finds, secures, and coordinates the film's locations.

When on location any questions or problems pertaining to the building or grounds (such as access to locked rooms or access to circuit breaker panels) are handled by the building engineer through the locations coordinator. The locations coordinator obtains permission to place lights in unorthodox places, such as on a roof. Care must be taken not to damage the floors, walls, or garden. When a house has hardwood floors, for example, the grips and electricians can put rubber crutch tips on the legs of the stands and ask that layout board be put on the floors to protect them.

Transportation

The drivers (usually Teamsters) are responsible for operating and maintaining all the production vehicles. In addition to the "production van" (usually a 40 ft. truck that carries all the lights), transportation usually provides stake-bed trucks (with hydraulic lift gate), pick-up trucks, or "dualies" to the grip and electric departments. These are particularly useful on location when equipment needs to be shuttled to several sites in one day, or must be dispersed over a large area. Drivers may also be dispatched to make runs, including to return equipment to or make pickups from suppliers. It is a good idea for the best boy to give the transportation coordinator as much advance warning as possible, as needs arise.

Art Department

Q: How many art directors does it take to screw in a light bulb?
A: Does it have to be a light bulb? I've got a really nice candelabra we could use.

Construction builds the sets, *set dressing* decorates the set with items not handled by an actor, while the *props department* is responsible for anything that is handled by an actor. Wall lamps, practicals, lanterns, and so forth are provided and placed by the set decorators. Wiring them is taken care of by an electrician.

Hair, makeup, wardrobe, stunts, special effects, first aid, craft service, and catering are the remaining departments on the set with which electricians need to consult from time to time. It pays to stay on good terms with every department.

Block, Light, Rehearse, Shoot

Progress on the set is measured in *setups*. A feature film crew may shoot 20 to 30 setups per day. The assistant director tries to schedule the shots so that all the shots in a scene in which the camera is looking in one direction, requiring one particular lighting setup, are shot together at one time. When possible, wider master shots are photographed first, establishing the lighting for the scene. Closer coverage, which usually requires refinements to the master setup, follows. Once coverage from one direction is complete, the AD calls, "Turning around," "Moving on," or "Next setup," and the camera is moved around to shoot the other way. The crew then relights the scene for the new camera angle. Once a scene is completed, the AD calls, "New deal," the company clears out the set, and the director and actors block out the next scene on the schedule.

Although it is convenient when the shots can be scheduled in an efficient order for lighting, the AD may have other priorities. Shot order may be arranged to give precedence to, for example, a particularly difficult performance or a stunt that will destroy part of the set.

The standard procedure for filming each new scene has four steps: block, light, rehearse, and shoot. First the director, DP, and actors block the entire scene (plan the staging). During blocking rehearsal, the set is usually cleared so that the actors and director can work without distraction. The director and principal actors are called the *first team*. The DP, gaffer, and key grip watch the rehearsal to determine lighting needs and constraints. The 2nd AC marks the actors' positions with tape at their feet.

Once the scene has been blocked, the actors are sent to makeup, and the DP begins lighting. Often, the lighting crew has already roughed in some of the lights during a prelight. The actors are replaced by costumed *stand-ins*, who act as models for the gaffer and DP while the lights are placed. The stand-ins are known as the *second team*. The camera crew sometimes rehearses complicated camera moves using the stand-ins to avoid dulling the performances of the principal actors with technical rehearsals.

Once the lighting is in place, the AD calls the first team back to the set for final rehearsal. He calls, "Quiet please. Rehearsal's up." The actors run through the scene with the camera and sound crew to iron out any remaining problems. The AC gets final focus marks; the dolly grip gets marks for the camera moves. After one or two rehearsals, the scene is ready to shoot.

Final rehearsals may take place while the electricians and grips are still adding final touches to the lighting. As a courtesy to the actors and director, everyone works quietly while the actors are on the set.

To save time between setups, electricians may begin lighting a new part of the set while the rest of the crew is filming, but before the camera rolls. When the AD calls, "Hold the work," he expects the work to stop immediately.

When it is time for cameras to roll, the AD calls, "Picture's up," followed by "Roll sound." Second ADs and set PAs, who are equipped with walkie-talkies, echo "Rolling" in every part of the set. Everyone remains absolutely silent once "Roll sound" is called. Be careful not to stand in an actor's eyeline. It distracts an actor to see a technician standing directly in his line of sight (staring blankly at him) while he or she is trying to perform. When the take is finished, the AD broadcasts, "That's a cut" on the walkie-talkie, at which time work can resume.

The AD makes other announcements, such as the following:

"*Going again right away.*" The electrical crew may not have time to resume work because a second take will be rolling immediately.

"*Hold the roll.*" There has been a momentary delay. It cues the sound mixer to stop rolling tape while the problem is fixed.

"*That's lunch, one half-hour.*"

"*Abby Singer is up.*" The Abby Singer is the second to last shot of the day. It was named for (former) assistant director Abbey Singer, who always had "just one more shot" after the last shot of the day.

"*Martini is up.*" The martini is the last shot of the day. (Your next shot will be out of a glass.)

"*That's a wrap.*" This announcement is made after the last shot of the day has been successfully completed. Electricians then begin wrapping — taking down the lights, coiling the cable, and loading the truck. When filming will resume in the same place on the following day and the equipment can simply be left where it is, it is a "walk away."

"*MOS.*" This phrase means that sound will not be recorded for the shot. The term comes from the early days of sound. It is an acronym for minus optical stripe.

"*Fire in the hole!*" This is announced before a shot in which there will be gunfire or explosions. Be prepared for a loud noise to follow.

CHAPTER 2

Preproduction Planning:
Lighting Package, Expendables, and Personal Tools

Preproduction Planning

One of the first responsibilities of the gaffer during preproduction is to prepare an equipment list (equipment and expendables lists are given in Appendix J and K). To come up with a complete equipment list, the gaffer needs to have pretty clear ideas about how each scene will be lit. In scouting the locations and looking at the sets, the gaffer, key grip, and DP are confronted with the particular challenges they'll need to address. The gaffer reads the script carefully, making notations and raising questions for the DP. He discusses scenes with the DP. The input of the director, production designer, and costume designer will often steer important lighting decisions.

Production Meetings

At every stage of planning the gaffer is considering three things: equipment, personnel, and time.

Equipment: What basic equipment will be needed to light the scenes? Which scenes will require special equipment (e.g., condor cranes, xenon spot lights, and the like)? Will the transportation department need to furnish extra vehicles on particular days to move equipment from place to place?

Personnel: How many extra electricians will be needed to operate this special equipment, or to prerig or wrap-out cabling and equipment? Are there days on the schedule that are particularly difficult, or large locations that will require extra hands?

Time: What prerigging time will be required to achieve efficiency during shooting? What wrap time will be required? Can the shooting be realistically accomplished in the time allotted for it in the schedule? What workable solutions can the gaffer suggest to the assistant director and UPM?

Additionally, the gaffer and DP coordinate with the production designer to determine what special considerations should be given to the lighting in designing the sets. Designers are generally very conscious of lighting and will design the sets with windows in places that will make good lighting; however, looking over the designer's plans will forestall impediments to the lighting and may inspire ways to incorporate the DP's lighting ideas into the design.

During preproduction the gaffer and DP also discuss how to approach the material. What is the mood and style of the film? When will the shots be fairly conventional, and when will there be steadicam shots that reveal every corner of a room, requiring that all lights be hung above or outside the set? What gel colors will be needed? What film stocks will be used? Will the lighting be at a low level or a high level? Each of these questions affects the equipment the gaffer will need.

Scouting Locations

The director, assistant director, and department heads scout each location in a group, discussing how the scenes will be played out. The DP and gaffer formulate a rough idea of how they will light each space. The best boy takes notes, which include: lighting plots, special rigging required, special equipment required, cable routing, generator placement, location of the staging area, and placement of the production van. If the lighting is complex he may also want to make notes on the placement of windows and doors in each room, as well as wall sconces or chandeliers that may be seen on camera. If possible, he also notes the geography of the furniture and blocking of the actors. These notes will be invaluable during future discussions.

During the scout the DP, gaffer, and key grip are constantly working out plans to adapt the space for lighting. Parallels may need to be built outside the windows to support large lights. Wall spreaders or other lighting support may need to be rigged near the ceiling. Windows may need to be gelled or tented.

In addition to absorbing this information, the best boy needs to determine his routes of access to each set for cabling. He must carefully ascertain where the generator can be placed so as to be as close to the set as possible without causing sound problems, and how the feeder cables can be run to the set without entering into the shots. If a tie-in is a possibility, he inspects the power boxes to determine their suitability. If house circuits may be used, he locates and examines the breaker box to determine its capacity and the layout of circuits. He locates the light switches for sconces and house lights. He coordinates with the locations manager and the contact at the location to gain access to locked rooms, or to arrange for lights to be placed on neighboring property or on the roof. He must find the service entrance through which to bring in carts and equipment without encountering stairs. He must locate the elevators. If large numbers of fluorescent lights will be needed, he must get a count of the number of tubes to be ordered. In short, he must fully think through the lighting needs at each location and prepare for all contingencies.

Once the locations have been scouted, the gaffer and best boy look over the production schedule; evaluate personnel, equipment, and time requirements; and appraise the production department of their needs. It is helpful to create a calendar that outlines when extra workers and equipment will be required.

Equipment Package

The load-in is the first day of work for an electrician on a feature film. It is the first day the electrician puts his or her hands on the lights.

The best boy supervises the check-out and load-in, making sure the order is correctly filled and that all the equipment is in full working order. The check-out must be extremely thorough. Even at the best rental houses, you cannot assume that all the equipment will be in perfect working order or leave the counting to someone else. At the completion of filming, any broken or missing items will be charged as "lost and damaged." There are an infinite number of ways circumstances can conspire to foul things up: Orders are often changed at the last minute, special equipment may be coming from more than one rental house, etc. Almost always a few items will require maintenance or be miscounted by the rental house, so count and check the equipment carefully. The equipment package for a medium size feature film takes two days for three electricians to prep and load into a 40-ft. truck.

Lights. In film we call them lights, lamps, fixtures, or heads. Theater electricians call them instruments or luminaries. Each light should be tested at check out. Take the time; you do not want to discover problems on the set when production is in full swing. Once you establish a routine for checking lights, it takes very little time to check all the items listed in Checklists 2.1 and 2.2.

Stands. There are many different kinds of light stands, from short to very tall, from light-weight to heavy steel. All types of stands are covered in detail in Chapter 4. The stand check-out Checklist 2.3 enumerates the check-out procedure.

Electrical Distribution System. Lighting a set can require heavy loads of electricity. When shooting on location, where necessary electrical service is not available, the production is powered by one or more generators that are designed to run quietly and produce the quantities of power needed. Electricity is fed to the lights through the distribution system. Electricity and distribution are covered in detail in Chapters 8 through 10. The check-out Checklist 2.4 gives a brief description of the components of the distribution system, with some notes of things to watch for during the check-out.

Loading the Production Van

When shooting on location, the lighting crew works out of the production van, or grip truck. Depending on the size of the production, the vehicle may be anything from a cargo van to a 10-ton truck, to a fully customized, 40-ft. 18-wheeler. A fully equipped production van like the one shown in Figure 2.2 is complete with dual generators mounted on the tractor. The truck comes equipped with shelving for the lights, brackets on the doors to hold stands, a large hydraulic lift gate, one or more side doors with stairs, interior lighting, and a well-organized design. Smaller 5- and 10-ton trucks have jockey boxes underneath both sides of the truck that carry cable and sandbags. Larger trucks have doors along the length of the belly that can hold a substantial quantity cable and distribution equipment.

Figure 2.1 Complete scrim set with box. The set includes, from left to right, a half double, half single, two doubles, a single, and a set of gel frames.

Checklist 2.1 Fresnel and Open-Face Tungsten Lamps

☐ Check that each light is complete. Each must have a full set of scrims, a scrim box or bag, and barn doors. Count scrims. A complete five-piece set includes two doubles, one single, one half-double, one half-single, and one gel frame (Figure 2.1).

☐ Barn doors. Check fit. Check for floppy doors. Most gaffers prefer four-leaf doors to two-leaf. Doors should be fitted with safety chain.

☐ Plug in each fixture and turn it on to check the bulb and the switch. Make sure you have any needed connector adapters. Wiggle the cord at the switch and lamp housing to ferret out any intermittent discontinuity (a problem with power cord or lamp base contacts).

☐ Check flood spot mechanism for smooth, full travel. Observe the beam as it changes. An uneven or odd-shaped beam is evidence of an improperly aligned bulb, or a bent or damaged reflector.

☐ With power off, open the fixture and check the condition of the reflector. Especially with hot-burning lights such as baby-babies, or baby-juniors, the reflector can get cooked by prolonged use when tilted steeply downward. The reflector must be properly aligned, unbent, clean, and in good condition.

☐ Inspect the bulb for blisters and bulges — evidence that the bulb has been mishandled and burn-out is imminent.

☐ Check that the lens is clean and free of cracks. A little dust buildup on the lens will cut light output in half.

☐ Check that the T-handle threads properly. The threads sometimes get stripped.

☐ Check that the tilt lock knuckle holds the light firmly. The cork disks at the swivel point wear out and occasionally need to be replaced.

Checklist 2.2 HMI Lamps

- ☐ Each unit should be complete with scrim set, barn doors, lens set (PARs only), two head feeder cables, ballast, and power feeder cable (Figure 3.26). With units using large-size Socapex connectors, a j-box is also needed to connect the head feeders to one another.

- ☐ Barn doors. Check for floppy doors, bad fit, or missing barn door safety chain.

- ☐ Hook-up and turn on each light using both head feeders. Inspect head cables for bent pins or misthreaded connectors, cuts in insulation, and loose strain relief collar at connector. Check READY and ON indicator lights on head and ballast.

- ☐ Allow several minutes to reach full output. Using a three-color color temperature meter, measure the color temperature and green/magenta shift of each unit. Mark these measurements on a piece of white camera tape and tape it to the bail of the light. Also include the date and the unit number.

- ☐ Number each head, ballast, and globe box so that the same head, globe, and ballast are always used together.

- ☐ Check flood spot mechanism for smooth, full travel. An uneven or odd-shaped beam is evidence of an improperly aligned bulb, or a bent or damaged reflector.

- ☐ Watch for unstable arcs. If in question, use a welder's glass to observe the bulb.

- ☐ You may want to check for ground faults and leakage current from the head and from the ballast. Current leaking to the lamp housing or ballast casing will give you a nasty shock if you become well grounded (such as when standing in wet grass). This is rarely a problem with new equipment, but often occurs with older, poorly maintained equipment. You can run into this problem if the wires in the head feeder cables are crossed, or if there is a short in the cable, the head, or the ballast.

- ☐ You may also want to test the restrike capability of the light by turning it off, and attempting a restrike after 15 seconds. If the light will not restrike, try again once every 60 seconds to see how long you have to wait. Note: Repeated unsuccessful ignition attempts will discolor the inside of the bulb; don't overdo it.

- ☐ Inspect the bulb for blisters and bulges — evidence that burn-out is imminent.

- ☐ If the ballast uses a fuse, get a couple of spares.

- ☐ Check that the lens is clean and uncracked. Dust on the lens cuts light output in half.

- ☐ Check that the T-handle threads properly. The threads sometimes get stripped.

- ☐ Check that the tilt lock knuckle holds the light firmly. The cork disks at the swivel point wear out and occasionally need to be replaced.

Checklist 2.3 Stands

- ☐ Raise each stand to full extension. Check for binding and corrosion. Test lock of each T-handle.
- ☐ Inspect for bent or broken braces, or loose or missing brace bolts.
- ☐ Crank stands and motorized stands should be tested by raising and lowering the stand with a sand bag on the top. The weight is necessary to prevent the stand's inner mechanism from binding up when lowered.
- ☐ Pneumatic tires should be fully inflated and should roll smoothly.
- ☐ Check that the wheel swivel locks, brace hinges, collars, and so on operate properly.

Checklist 2.4 Cable and Distribution

- ☐ Main disconnect. The main disconnect or bull switch is a high-amperage (200 or 400 A), fused switch box used as a main on/off switch for power to the set. Be sure that at least one spare fuse is included.
- ☐ Feeder cable. Heavy-gauge (4/0 or 2/0), single-conductor cable used to run power from the power source to the set. Check lug and pin connectors for bent or broken ends. Inspect cable for cuts in the insulation showing exposed copper.
- ☐ Deuce boards. Fused remote switches which subdivide current into 200A subcircuits. Stock spare fuses.
- ☐ Banded cable, stage extensions, Bates cable and stage extensions (porcelains). Types of heavy extension cable that carry power to various areas of the set and to high-amperage lights. Check for melted, overheated plastic on connectors. Check for bent or broken pins. Check for gashes in cable insulation.
- ☐ Edison boxes, or gang boxes, plug into the larger feeder cable to provide a number of Edison outlets. Stock replacement fuses.
- ☐ Stingers. Edison extension cord. Used to carry power to medium and small lights (2000 W and less). Check connectors for melted or blackened plastic. Test any suspicious looking ones.

A head cart (Figure 2.3) is a customized cart with large pneumatic tires and sturdy shelves onto which a variety of the most commonly used lights are packed. The cart shown also carries a variety of stands (or gel rolls).

Head carts provide convenience and mobility during shooting and expedite loading and unloading. You typically have at least two carts, one for tungsten units, for example, the other for HMIs. When the truck travels, the carts are simply secured in the aisle. Lights are packed tightly and neatly onto the shelves of the carts, and onto the shelves of the truck, grouped according to size. Once the lights are packed, the best boy labels the shelves of the carts and the truck to show where each type of light is kept. It is helpful to include the number of lights on each shelf. This makes it easy to conduct an inventory fast at the end of a day's shooting. Before the truck travels,

Figure 2.2 A 40-ft. production van with two tractor-mounted generators. Note that stands are mounted on the rear doors. The small door on the side provides access to 12ks. (Photo courtesy of Hollywood Rental, Sun Valley, CA.)

Figure 2.3 Pictured here are a "tungsten cart" (holding a crate of Peppers, and shelving for a variety of tungsten lamps and slots for stands, a "distro cart" containing crates of splitters and adaptors, and a cable cart (far right).

Figure 2.4 The crate cart carries various types of electrical expendables and rolls of gel or stands (as shown here). (Courtesy of Backstage Studio Equipment, Sun Valley, CA.)

the lights are secured with rubber bungy cords. Large lights — 5k and 10k fixtures and large HMIs — are kept on the floor of the truck along with HMI ballasts.

The electric crew typically also has a milk crate cart for stinger crates, practical bulbs and wiring devices, dimmers, a gel crate, expendables, and rolls of gel (Figure 2.4).

One or more cable dollies (Figure 2.5) also are typically part of the equipment package. Cable dollies can be stowed in the aisle of the truck during travel, convenient for keeping cable ready to be wheeled out. Similarly, a doorway dolly can be used (Figure 2.6).

When packing the truck, be sure you provide immediate access to equipment that is routinely needed. Don't bury your distribution boxes under cable or behind big lights. Put spare items (fluorescent tubes, spare globes) on the top shelves, along with fixtures that are seldom called for. During night shooting, reserve a special spot for the items that will be packed away last — the work lights and associated cable and distribution.

The workbox — a wooden chest of drawers — is usually secured inside the truck. It is used to store spare bulbs, electrical expendables, tools, paperwork, and supplies.

Figure 2.5.   A cable cart. (Courtesy of Backstage Studio Equipment, Sun Valley, CA.)

Figure 2.6   Cable or large lights are moved from place to place on a doorway dolly.

Expendable Supplies

Expendables (see also checklist Appendix L) are supplies that are purchased and used up in the course of production. In addition to equipment inventory and check-out, the best boy and electricians use prep days for organizing and prepping expendables, cutting gels for the lights, and completing any similar tasks to get everything ready for the first day of shooting.

Gels and Diffusion

Gels are used for three purposes: (1) to correct the color of one light source to match that of another (tungsten correction, daylight correction, carbon arc correction, and fluorescent correction gels), (2) to alter the color of a source to create an effect (theatrical or effects gels), and (3) to reduce the intensity of a source without altering its color (neutral-density gels). Diffusion media soften light. Gels come in wide rolls and in sheets. They can be applied to lights or windows or put in frames that are placed in front of the light source.

Cuts of gel are kept in a crate or box, sectioned according to size and color (Figure 2.7). This practice makes gel fast and easy on the set, and ultimately saves gel because less is wasted. Precut color correction gel and diffusion in squares of 6 in., 8 in., 10 in., and 12 in., and a couple cuts of 20 in. and 24 in. (A 6-in. square fits inside the barn doors of units 1k or smaller. An 8-in. square fits studio babies and baby juniors. The 10-in. and 12-in. sizes fit inside the doors of regular juniors and outside the doors of lamps 650 watts and smaller. The larger cuts of gel fit on the outside of the doors of 2ks, 1200 HMIs, and PAR lights.) Anything larger than 24 in. can be gelled using a frame supplied by the grips.

The best way to cut gel from the roll is to use a template. Cut a 24 x 48 in. piece of 1/2 in. plywood and score it with grooves 1/4 in. deep, making the grid pattern of 6-, 8-, 10-, and 12-in. squares. The matte knife blade slices down the grooves and makes cutting gel very fast and easy. The smaller cuts can be made from the scraps left over from the larger cuts. Once the gel is cut and organized, the gel crate finds a home on the cart, where it will remain close at hand during shooting. Assorted rolls of gel may be kept on the head cart, and the remaining rolls are stored in boxes on the truck.

Electrical Expendables

A production may or may not require all of the items described here. During prep these items are organized in the drawers of a work box, into crates on the milk crate cart, and into boxes on the shelves of the truck. Label each drawer, crate, and box with its contents. A large capacity toolbox with drawers makes an excellent storage place for all the small expendable items. You can also keep gel swatch books, special tools, and meters in the tool box. The tool box fits right on the milk crate cart (see Figure 2.7).

Black wrap   A durable, black foil used on hot lights to control spill and to shape the beam. It is available in rolls of 12 in. (50 ft.), 24 in., and 36 in. (25 ft.). White-wrap is also available.

Figure 2.7 Cut gel and diffusion are marked with permanent marker and stored according to size and type in a sectioned milk crate.

Clothespins Nicknamed *C-47s* or *bullets*. Used to attach gels and diffusion to the lights.

Rubber matting Matting used to cover power cables where they cross doorways and other traffic areas. It comes in rolls 24 in. wide, up to 100 ft. long.

Sash cord White cotton rope. Used for tying cable to pipe, among other things. Commonly used weights are #6, #8, and #10.

Trick line and mason line #4 weight nonstretch rope. Trick line is black. Mason line is white. It comes in handy for odd jobs, such as making stinger tie-strings and power cord hangers.

Bungy cords and S-hooks Black rubber bungy cords come in various sizes and should be ordered to fit the shelves of the truck and carts.

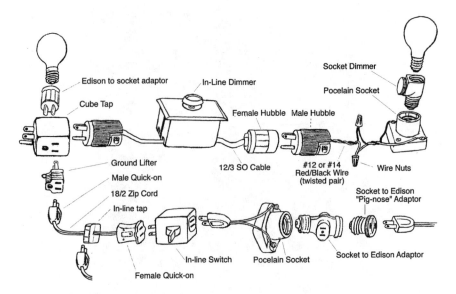

Figure 2.8   Electrical supplies.

Cube taps   Used for plugging several low-amperage lights into one outlet. General Electric makes a cube-shaped tap from which the device gets its name, but any connector that serves the same function may be called a cube tap (15 A max). See Figure 2.8.

Ground plug adapter   Used to adapt grounded plugs to ungrounded outlets found in older houses. Also called a cheater, ground lifter, or two-to-three adapter. See Figure 2.8.

Quick-on plugs   Small, low-amperage Edison sockets and plugs that can be connected to #18 zip cord quickly without tools. Quick-on plugs provide a speedy way to rig small lamps. See Figure 2.8.

Add-a-taps or in-line taps   A female Edison that can be spliced onto a piece of #18 zip cord without cutting the cord. See Figure 2.8.

Zip cord   Light 18-gauge household lamp cord used for rigging practicals and other small lights. See Figure 2.8.

Wire nuts   Insulated cap used to splice two bare wires together. See Figure 2.8.

Dimmers   Household dimmers of 600W and 1000W are commonly used to dim small lights and practicals. See Figure 2.8.

Porcelain sockets   Lamp sockets (medium screw base, E26) are used to mount light bulbs in set pieces and soft boxes. Use porcelain sockets, as photo bulbs will melt a plastic socket. See Figure 2.8.

Socket dimmers   A socket dimmer (150 W max) screws in between the lamp socket and the light bulb, allowing the bulb to be dimmed. See Figure 2.8.

In-line switches   When rigging practical lights in sets, it is sometimes handy to have a plug-in, 15A switch on the line. See Figure 2.8.

Hubble Edison   The best boy stocks male and female Hubble Edison plugs to re-place the plugs on stingers and power cords when they burn out. See Figure 2.8.

#12 copper wire   The best boy may want to have rolls of black, white, and green #12 wire, which is handy for wiring special lights and devices. A twisted pair of red/black wire is commonly used also. See Figure 2.8.

Buss fuses   Spare buss fuses for deuce boards and bull switches are usually provided by the rental company.

Gang box fuses   20A BAF buss fuses. Essential replacement fuses for gang boxes. Gang box fuses blow quite frequently, so be sure to have plenty on hand.

Splitter fuses   60A fuses used in in-line fuses on 100A to two 60A Bates splitters.

Electrical tape   Tape used for insulating wire splices. It comes in a variety of colors (red, white, blue, black, and green) and is handy for color-coding cables and spider boxes.

Gaffer's tape   Heavy 2 in. fabric-based tape that rips cleanly in the direction of the weave. It is used to tape just about everything.

Paper tape   Tape that has less adhesion than gaffer's tape. Black 2 in. paper tape is handy for masking light. It has less of a tendency to pull the paint off walls than gaffer's tape.

White camera tape   1 in. and 2 in. tape used for labeling equipment.

Snot tape   A sticky film that is handy for mounting gels in gel frames (3M transfer tape).

Best boy paint   White, heat-resistant paint used to repaint the reflective surfaces of soft lights without altering the color of the light emitted.

Dulling spray   A spray applied to shiny surfaces to tone down reflective glints.

Streaks and tips   Colored hair spray used to tone down or black out surfaces that are too bright. It is water soluble, washes off easily after filming, and comes in shades of auburn, beige, black, blond, brown, gray, pink, silver, and white.

Practical bulbs   Bulbs used in practical lamps, usually household (medium screw base) bulbs. Various types are used, among them photoflood bulbs, household bulbs, floodlights, spotlights, and small fluorescents. Specifics appear in Chapter 7 and Appendix E.1.

Fluorescent bulbs   Optima 32 (tungsten) and Vitalite (daylight) tubes replace fluorescent tubes in offices and commercial buildings where the existing fluorescents are not correct for photography.

Spare flashlight bulbs   Replacement bulbs for electricians' flashlights.

Batteries   AA for flashlights and pagers. AAA for light meters. Disk batteries for DM73 voltage/continuity meter. 9V for amp probe and light meters.

Cotter pins   Used when hanging lights to prevent the receptacle from slipping off the pin.

Visqueen heavy plastic sheet   Used to protect equipment and electrical connections from rain, precipitation, dew, dust, and sand. Comes in 100-ft. rolls, 20 ft. wide (folded to 5 ft.).

Crutch tips   Put on the legs of stands to protect floors. Sizes: 3/4 in. for small stands, 1-1/4 in. for large stands.

Refracil   A heat-resistant cloth, similar to asbestos, that will not burn when a hot light is placed on it. It protects ceiling and wall surfaces from heat damage.

Bailing wire   Stiff wire, also called stove pipe wire. Can be used as a barn-door safety, although grip chain is preferable.

Preparations may include the following:

Set box   The best boy will often prepare a set box, which is kept close to the action at all times, and contains all the commonly needed items: tape rolls, zip cord and quick-ons, cube taps, dimmers, and a supply of clothespins.

Tape rolls   Put together a selection of tape rolls on a loop of sashcord: one roll each of 2 in. gaffer's tape, 2 in. black paper tape, and white camera tape. Snot tape should also be readily available. The electrical tape rolls (all colors) go together on a separate rope.

Practical bulbs   Mark and organize practical bulbs so their wattages and type are easily readable. Label the boxes. Insert (foamcore) dividers in a couple of milk crates. Stock compartments with various types and wattages to keep near the set. PH-bulbs (211, 212, and 213) do not have their rating printed on the top of the bulb. It is helpful to mark the top of these bulbs with a permanent marker: one dot for 211, two dots for 212, and three dots for 213.

Zip cord stingers, porcelain sockets   Put together a number of zip cord stingers (zip cord fitted with quick-on plugs). They will come in handy when wiring practical lamps.

Homemade boxes   Homemade lighting fixtures, such as softboxes, are wired by an electrician. Soft box construction is discussed in Chapter 6.

Tools and Personal Gear

Tool Belt

Carry all the tools and supplies you will need on a tool belt (Figure 2.9). Include the following:

Leather work gloves   Cowhide or equivalent. Used for handling hot lights and dirty cable and hardware. Clip them onto your belt when you're not wearing them.

Clothespins   Keep a dozen or so on your belt. Figure 2.9 shows an inverted C-47 (a C-74), which is handy to pull hot scrims out of lights.

Screwdriver   Carry a flat-head screwdriver and a Phillips screwdriver or, better, a single screwdriver with a reversible tip: flat-head on one side, Phillips on the other.

Utility knife with retractable blade   For cutting gels, foamcore, rope, and so on.

Scissors   Small, sharp scissors are often handy for making more careful cuts of gels, etc.

Flashlight   Electricians frequently find themselves working in the dark. When dealing with electricity, you always need to see what you are doing. Small, rugged, focusable flashlights are very popular and easy to carry on your belt.

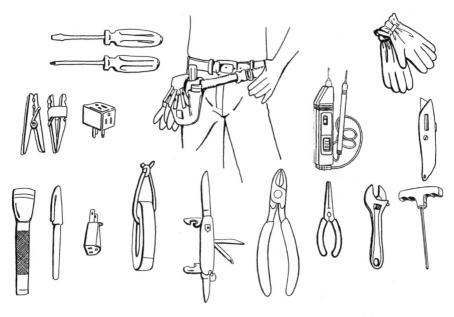

Figure 2.9 Tools and supplies carried on an electrician's tool belt.

Permanent marker For labeling gels, fixtures, connectors, cables, and so forth.

Ballpoint pen For taking notes, filling out paperwork, taking down phone numbers, etc.

Ground plug adapter When on location it's good to keep a couple cheaters in your pouch.

Cube taps Keep a supply of two or three on you.

Gaffer's tape Loop sash cord through the tape, and attach it to your belt with a carabineer. If the roll is too bulky, you can make a "tape cube." Fold about 9 in. of tape onto itself, then continue to wind tape around until you have about 5 or 6 ft. of it wound onto the strip. The tape cube can go in your back pocket.

Knife A sharp knife with a retractable blade is useful for cutting rope, gel, card, and foamcore.

Wire snips Used primarily for cutting wire for practical lamps and making wire splices.

Crescent wrench An adjustable wrench is used to adjust the friction of a bail, tighten a pipe clamp, and perform countless other jobs. The jaws must be large enough to fit a 3/4 in. bolt. You can find 6 in. crescent wrenches with an extra wide jaw, which are ideal. An 8 in. wrench is bulky, and a standard 6 in. crescent wrench is not quite big enough.

Speed wrench Ratcheted 3/8 in. square wrench for securing sister-lugs (square-headed set screws) onto bus bars.

Needle-nose pliers Used for pulling hot scrims out of a light, small repairs, etc.

T-handle Allen wrench   A 3/16 in. Allen wrench with a long insulated T-handle is used for tightening the set screws on sister-lugs inside a spider box.

Voltmeter/continuity tester   Used to check line voltage (120V, 208V, or 240V) and to check for voltage drop. Used to locate broken connections in power cords. A continuity tester tests for burnt-out bulbs and fuses.

Circuit tester   Plugs into an Edison outlet and tells you if the line is hot. Also indicates if the polarity and grounding are correct.

Line sensor   Device that indicates if a wire has current flowing through it by sensing the magnetic field.

Best Boy's Kit

Some less frequently needed items that are handy to have in a tool box are as follows:

- Full set of screw drivers, including a small flat-head screw driver with a very narrow tip (needed when repairing light fixtures), a super large flat-head, and a right-angle screw driver (for working inside small fixtures).
- Vice grips: Small needle-nose vice grips are handy for repairs and wiring jobs. Large crescent vice grips are useful for getting a grip on a tight pin connector.
- Soldering iron and solder
- Metric Allen wrenches: For repairing stands, among other things.
- English Allen wrenches
- Cordless drill with flat head, Phillips head, and drill bits.
- Hammer
- Tape measure
- Pens and pencils
- Extra strong glue
- Amp probe: Essential equipment of the best boy electric.
- Circuit finder: This device tells you which outlets are on the same breaker and which breaker they are on.
- Fluke memory multimeter or equivalent: This is a sophisticated (and expensive) meter with many special functions, including the ability to monitor Hertz rate over a period of time and read out the high, low, and average reading.
- Lamp socket adapters: The best boy will often stock socket adapters in his tool box. Medium (E26) to mogul (E39) screw base adapters and miniature to medium screw base adapters are handy to adapt to or from nonstandard bulb and socket sizes.
- Edison/lamp socket adapters: Allows you to make a lamp screw base into an Edison outlet or to adapt an Edison outlet into a lamp base (see Figure 2.8).
- GFI circuit breakers with Edison outlets: When filming around water, GFI breakers are used to detect leakage current in a fixture.
- Variac fuses: Variac fuses rarely blow, but it is wise to stock a couple for each type of variac being used.
- Screw-socket fuses: 20A house fuses for older residence locations.
- T-handles: Lock-down knuckle on stands and fixture bails — keep a selection of sizes of T-handles in your tool box in case one breaks or goes missing.

Personal Gear

Electricians get dirty; jeans, a T-shirt, and sneakers are normal apparel. Weather permitting, it is advisable to protect your legs and arms with long pants and a shirt. Be prepared for the weather. In southern California you might need only sunscreen, a baseball hat, sunglasses, and a jacket and jeans for after sunset, but be prepared for all weather conditions. When shooting on location, bring a full rain suit, boots, cold-weather jacket, hat and gloves, and a change of clothes in case you get wet. Also consider the terrain. Hiking boots or work boots are often desirable.

You might want to keep the following personal gear in your duffel bag:

- sunscreen
- lip ointment
- mosquito repellent
- ear protection (disposable earplugs or head gear for when firearms are used)
- eye protection (goggles or safety glasses): the special effects department usually supplies eye protection to everyone who is needed near the action during explosions and stunts

Grip Equipment

Grips and electricians work together closely, and it is important to have a working knowledge of grip equipment. A brief description of common pieces of equipment follows.

Shiny Boards

Shiny boards   A 42 x 42 in. silver-covered board that mounts on a junior stand. Reflectors are used to bounce light, usually sunlight. They can be panned, tilted, and locked into position. They normally have a hard side that reflects a hard squarish patch of light, and a soft side that reflects a slightly broader, less intense, area with soft edges. Also called shiny boards.

2 x 2 ft. shiny board   Similar to the larger ones, but this uses a baby stand.

Mirror boards   A mirror board is a shiny board with a mirror surface. Quite a bit heavier than shiny boards, it gives off a very bright, sharply delineated square of light.

Combo stand   A stand with a junior receptacle (1-1/8 in. female), used for shiny boards or lights.

Low combo stand   A short combo stand (36 in. instead of the standard 48 in.). Also called a low boy junior.

Overhead Sets

Overhead set   A large frame with one of several types of material stretched across it. Overhead sets are used on exteriors to shade the action (see Figure 2.10). Standard sizes are 20 x 20 ft., 12 x 12 ft., and 6 x 6 ft. An overhead set includes a single net (which cuts light by a half stop), a double net (cuts a full stop), a silk (diffuses light, softens shadows), and a solid made of black duvetyne (shades action completely). A set may also include a griffolyn, a silver, a gold, grid cloth, or diffusion.

Griffolyn (griff)   A nylon/plastic sheet that is white on one side and black on the other. When stretched in an overhead frame, the white side provides a big bounce source for exterior fill; the black side absorbs light for negative fill (Figure 2.11).

Silver and gold lamé   A silver is a reflective silver fabric used as a large, strong exterior bounce source. A gold has a reflective gold side to create a golden bounce light. They are stretched on a frame.

Medium roller, high roller, and hi-hi roller stands   A stand that has a 4-1/2 in. gobo head suitable for holding an overhead frame. Usually also has a receptacle for a junior stud. Comes in various sizes. A hi-hi makes it possible to get lights and grip equipment as high as 20 ft. in the air.

Carts

The grips typically have a grip cart (called a taco cart). The cart holds C-stands, apple boxes, wedges, cup blocks, and cribbing, as well as providing drawers for hardware and expendables, and space for milk crates (which hold mounting hardware). A flag box attaches to the front and holds 2 x 3 ft. and 18 x 24 in. flags, nets, and silks. Grip clips are also found on the taco cart.

A 4-by cart holds 4 x 4 ft. flags, nets, silks, and bounce boards. Grips may have an additional large-wheeled flag box to hold large cutters and additional flags, nets, and silks.

Figure 2.10   A 20 x 20 ft. overhead silk reduces and softens direct sunlight.

Figure 2.11 A white griffolyn can be used as a giant soft bounce source. Gold and silver lamé give even stronger light.

Items Kept on the Carts

C-stands (Century stands) A stand used to hold just about everything, from flags, nets, and silks to tree branches, bead board, and lights that have a 5/8 in. baby receptacle. The standard height is 53 in. A hi-boy is 73 in. high, and a low-boy is 26 in. high.

Flags Black Duvatyne fabric stretched over a metal frame and used to cut a selected portion of a light beam. Common sizes include 18 x 24 in., 24 x 36 in., and 4 x 4 ft.

Nets Bobbinet stretched over a metal frame and used to reduce the strength of a selected portion of a beam of light. Common sizes include 18 x 24 in., 24 x 36 in., and 4 x 4 ft.

Silks White silk stretched over a metal frame and used to reduce and soften a beam or light. Common sizes include 18 x 24 in., 24 x 36 in., and 4 x 4 ft. Thinner silks, called half silk and quarter silk, are also available.

Frames Empty metal frame onto which diffusion and gel is mounted (using snot tape) in order to diffuse or color a beam of light. Common sizes include 18 x 24 in., 24 x 36 in., 3 x 3 ft., and 4 x 4 ft.

Cukes and celo cukes   A cuke is a piece of 1/4 in. plywood with holes cut in it in random shapes. It is used to break up a beam of light into a pattern. A celo cuke uses a painted wire mesh instead of plywood to give a more subtle effect. Common sizes include 18 x 24 in., 24 x 36 in., and 4 x 4 ft.

Cutters   Long narrow flags used to create shadows or to cut the light. Common sizes include 10 x 42 in., 18 x 42 in., and 24 x 72 in.

Dots and fingers   Very small flags and nets used to make very small cuts.

Flex arm   A jointed, lightweight arm used to support small flags (postage stamps, fingers, and dots).

Apple boxes   Solidly constructed, internally reinforced plywood boxes used for everything imaginable. They come in a variety of sizes: full, half, quarter, and a pancake. A wall plate mounted on a pancake is useful to position a light on the floor. Apple boxes are also used to raise cable connections off the ground when water or moisture is present.

Cup blocks   Wooden blocks that are placed under the wheels of light stands for leveling on uneven ground and to prevent stands rolling.

Foamcore holder   A device used to mount foamcore and bead board on a C-stand. A vice grip clamps two 6 x 6 in. plates around the bead board. The baby stud provides a means of attaching it to the C-stand. Also known as a duck bill or platypus.

Grip clips   Metal spring clamps, usually kept on a loop of rope hung on the taco cart. They are sometimes referred to by their size number. A #1 grip clip will clamp onto objects that are up to 1 in. thick, a #2 up to 2 in., and a #3 up to 3 inches.

Mounting Hardware

Mounting hardware provides either a baby stud or a junior receptacle for mounting a light in just about any position imaginable: mounted to a pipe, ceiling, wall, floor, pillar, or false ceiling or outstretched on an arm, camera, or dolly. The typical grip package has a good selection of hardware available to accommodate any situation. Mounting equipment includes c-clamps, furniture clamps, chain vice grips, mafer clamps, gator clamps, junior and baby offsets, junior drop downs, stud adapters, nail-on plates, and putty knives with baby studs. The use of stands and mounting equipment is covered in detail in Chapter 4.

Dollies

Doorway dolly   A small, steerable dolly. Although designed as a simple camera platform, a doorway dolly is great for moving sand bags. Electricians use them for cable and large lights.

Western dolly   Similar to a doorway dolly but bigger.

Camera Dollies   The camera is mounted on a dolly for moves during takes and for general ease in moving between shots. Dollies feature a hydraulic boom arm and a heavy smoothly controllable chassis. Dollies generally run on a track, although a smooth floor will do.

Wedges Triangular wooden blocks used to level dolly track, keep doors open, and so on. Kept in a milk crate.

Cribbing Blocks of 2 x 4 in. used to level dolly track. Kept in a milk crate.

Other Grip Equipment

Ladders A-frame ladders are available in heights of 4, 6, 8, 10, and 12 ft., and extension ladders are 24 ft. tall. They are also referred to by the number of steps (four-step, eight-step, and so on). Use only wooden or fiberglass ladders when handling electrical equipment. Aluminum ladders conduct electricity and are unsafe.

Parallel set Similar to scaffolding, but simpler and quicker to assemble. A parallel set provides a high platform for lights or the camera. Comes in 6-ft. sections, with 18 ft. the maximum.

Ratchet straps Nylon straps with a ratchet tightening device, commonly used to secure camera- and light-mounting equipment to automobiles, to secure a stand on scaffolding, or to secure similar rigging.

Sandbags Dead weight to stabilize stands. Shot bags are filled with lead shot and are therefore smaller per pound. Bags come in various sizes from 5 lb. up to 50 lb.; 15- and 35-lb. bags are normally used to secure light stands.

Stair blocks Blocks of 2 x 4 in., assembled in a stair shape to provide increments of adjustment for raising furniture by a small amount.

Furniture pad A packing blanket with a multitude of uses. Furniture pads are used to protect floors from being scratched by stands. Also called sound blankets, they are used to deaden live rooms.

Other equipment carried on the grip truck may include a water cooler, sun/rain umbrella, ice chest, shovels, rakes, brooms, trash can, traffic cones, pickax, sledgehammer, and fire extinguishers.

Grip Expendables

Safety chain Also called grip chain or sash chain. In addition to barn door safety, safety chain is used for such tasks as chaining the legs of a stand to a high platform.

Automatic tape gun (ATG) A dispenser for snot tape. Used to attach gels to windows and gel frames.

Bead board Styrofoam 3/8, 1/2, or 1 in. thickness. Comes in 4 x 8 ft. sheets. It is used to bounce light and gives off a softer and weaker light than foamcore.

J-lar tape Clear 2 in. tape used to repair ripping gel and to stop gel from rattling in frames or on windows.

Chalk Used to mark dolly marks on floor.

Duvetyn   Thick, black canvas-like cloth used for obstructing light in a multitude of applications, such as blacking and tenting windows and covering distracting objects. It comes in 50-yd. rolls.

Foamcore   An extremely lightweight bounce board made from 1/4 in. foam reinforcement glued between two sheets of white, glossy card stock. Foamcore also comes with flat black on one side and is available in 4 x 8 ft. sheets.

Hardware   Includes drywall screws for mounting wall plates, staples, pushpins, nails, bolts, nuts, and so on for general construction.

Lumber   It is useful to stock lumber in a variety of sizes and forms. For example, 1 x 3 in. (batten) board is used to build soft boxes; 2 x 4 in. and 2 x 6 in. boards are used for wall spreaders. Plywood may be laid on the floor to make a dance floor for smooth dolly moves.

Rope   Manila hemp (rough brown rope) in 1/4 in., 3/8 in., and 1/2 in. thicknesses. Among the many uses, 1/4 in. is used for tag line and guy wires.

Show card   Thick card stock, usually white on one side and black on the other, used to bounce light or to absorb it. Show cards come in a range of colors, including silver.

Silicone spray   A dry lubricant used on dolly track.

Tracing paper   Vellum 1000H translucent paper used to white-out windows. Available in rolls.

CHAPTER 3

Lighting Fixtures

Light fixtures come in all shapes and sizes. The design of the fixture, bulb, lens, reflector, and accessories determines the nature of the beam, and provides some methods of controlling it. A fixture's beam characteristics — such as brightness, focusability, evenness, punch, softness, size, shape, and color — dictate its function in our lighting arsenal. Each type of fixture has specific advantages in certain applications, and there are tricks to using each. In this chapter we will concentrate on the most common types — fresnels, softlights, open face, area lights, pars, HMIs, and fluorescents. Chapter 11 describes ellipsoidal spotlights, par cans, xenon lights, and more specialized and exotic fixtures.

Tungsten Lights

The Incandescent Filament

Incandescent fixtures, commonly called *tungsten lights*, create light by running current through a tungsten filament until it glows, that is, until it is heated to incandescence. They can be powered by either AC or DC. Since tungsten filaments burn most efficiently at a color temperature of 3200K (Kelvin degrees), tungsten-balanced color motion picture films are designed to reproduce colors accurately when lit at 3200K color temperature. Note that color temperature, expressed in degrees Kelvin, is a measure of the color output, not actual operating temperature. Daylight-balanced films are designed to reproduce colors accurately when lit with light having a color temperature of 5600K, or daylight.

Tungsten light and daylight include every color across the color spectrum, and are therefore said to have a *continuous spectrum*. The graph of spectral power distribution (Figure 3.1) compares the distribution of energy across the spectrum of a tungsten source to that of daylight. Daylight is much stronger in the blue end of the spectrum, and tungsten light is much stronger in the red end. (Color balance and color correction are explained in detail in Chapter 6.)

Figure 3.1 Spectral Power Distribution graphs (SPD). These graphs illustrate the distribution of energy over color spectrum for four primary light sources. Incandescent lamps are strong in the yellow orange and red, and weak in blue and violet. As color temperature increases the curve shifts towards the blue spectral band.

In contrast, daylight is stronger on the blue end of the spectrum. Shown here are spectral distribution for:
(A) clear noon sky (10,000K),
(B) clear north sky (7000K),
(C) sun plus sky (6500K),
(D) overcast sky (6800K), and
(E) direct sun (5600K).
Incandescent and daylight sources have continuous spectrum as shown by their smooth spectral distribution curves.

HMI and fluorescent sources do not have a continuous spectrum. An HMI has a multiline spectrum (correlates to 5500K) which appears to the eye much the same as daylight. Note that generally the HMI graph has a similar distribution as line C or E on the daylight graph.

The fluorescent graph shows a standard cool white bulb (correlates to 4500K). Note that most of its energy comes from narrow peaks. The color rendition of this bulb will be poor.

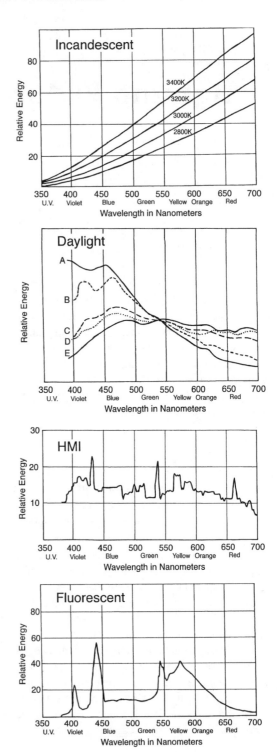

Tungsten Halogen versus Standard Tungsten Bulbs

A *tungsten halogen* bulb is a type of incandescent bulb that contains special regenerative elements to prevent blackening on the sides of the globe. The regenerative elements carry the evaporated tungsten, which is responsible for the blackening, back to the filament where it is reused, thereby increasing the life of the bulb. For the regenerative process, called the *halogen cycle*, to occur, a high temperature (at least 250°C) must be maintained inside the globe, and for this reason, tungsten halogen globes tend to be compact and are made of quartz, which can withstand the high temperature. In the old days, large 10k lamps contained a cleaning agent that had to be manually swished around the inside of the globe between uses to clean off the tungsten blackening.

The standard type of globe used in each fixture is listed in Appendix A. There are often alternatives to the standard type: a bulb with a different wattage or color temperature, or one that uses frosted instead of clear glass (see Table E.3).

Fresnels

The Fresnel fixture (pronounced *frenel*) is designed to create a relatively even field of light with adjustable intensity and field size, making it a flexible light with which to work. For these reasons, it is the most commonly used fixture in film and television (Figure 3.2). Figure 3.7 illustrates some Fresnel fixtures that every electrician must be able to identify.

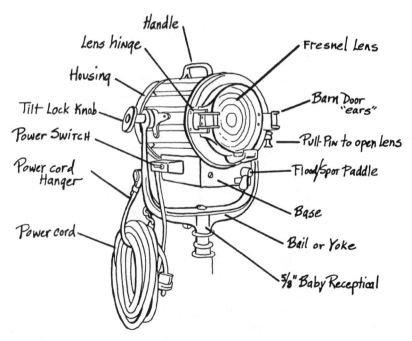

Figure 3.2   Anatomy of a Fresnel fixture.

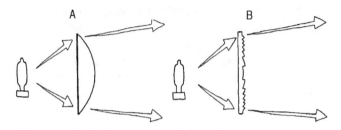

Figure 3.3 (A) A plano-convex lens. (B) A Fresnel lens.

The light is named for its Fresnel lens, which bends the diverging rays of light emitted by the bulb into a controlled beam of light. The Fresnel lens has the same light-bending characteristics as a standard plano-convex lens, but the Fresnel's design compresses the convex curve into jagged steps (Figure 3.3), making it lighter and thinner so that it retains less heat.

Inside the housing, the globe and spherical reflector are mounted together and can be moved toward or away from the lens by an exterior adjustment knob. Moving the globe and reflector toward the lens *floods* the beam, increasing its spread and decreasing its intensity (Figure 3.4A). Moving the globe and reflector away from the

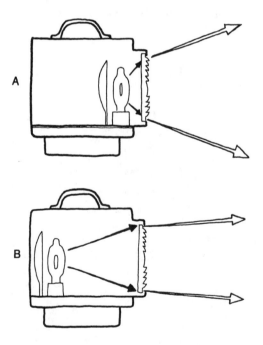

Figure 3.4 (A) A Fresnel lamp and reflector in flood position. Rays are refracted into a wide beam. (B) A Fresnel is spot position. The lamp and reflector are positioned so that the rays are concentrated into a tighter, more intense beam.

lens *spots* the beam, making it narrower and more intense (Figure 3.4B). The adjustable focus makes it quick and easy to obtain the desired intensity or beam width.

Fresnel Beam

To anticipate how the light will behave when an actor walks through it, the electrician must have a three-dimensional mental picture of the beam's shape and intensity, the manner in which intensity falls off towards the edges, and how varying the amount of spot or flood changes these characteristics. In describing the photometric qualities of a fixture, the terms *field* and *beam* are often used (Figure 3.5). A polar distribution graph (Figure 3.6) gives a clear picture of the shape of the beam intensity and how it changes from flood to spot.

At full flood the beam is relatively even across a 40° sweep, then falls off quickly towards the edges. Note that in full flood the beam has no central hot spot; the field is very even. As the lamp is spotted-in, the beam narrows and gets brighter in the center, falling off rapidly on either side. At full spot the usable portion of the beam is narrow, about a 10° angle. The term *throw* refers to the distance from the lamp to the subject. A lamp in spot position has a greater throw; it will illuminate the subject to the same brightness at a much greater distance. Table A.14 gives the intensity at any distance for a variety of fixtures.

These are terms for the light manufacture's sales literature; they rarely are mentioned on set, but in practice electricians use these concepts all the time. For example, let's say a large room is to be lit using several lights spaced evenly along one wall of the room. In order to make the light intensity even across the whole room, the lamps are set at full flood, and the edge of the *beam* of each light is feathered into that of the next. The beams overlap slightly at the 50% point, creating an even 100% intensity across the entire space.

Photometric data provided by manufacturers denotes the range of spot and flood achieved by each light by giving the beam angle at the two ends of the range. A typical Fresnel has a range from about 10° to 45° or 50°. (Such data may also be expressed by giving the beam diameter and peak intensity, in foot-candles, at various distances from the fixture.) Table A.13 gives the beam diameter at various distances for given beam angle.

Figure 3.5 The field defines the usable light — the area of light in which the intensity is at least 10% of the peak value. The beam is defined as the area of light in which the intensity is at least 50% of the peak value. The *hot spot* is the brightest spot within the beam. The terms *beam angle* and *field angle* refer to the angle of the beam and field, respectively, from the fixture.

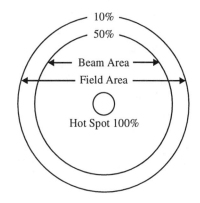

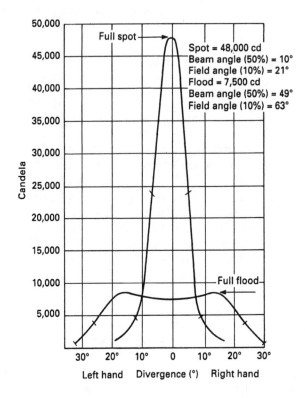

Figure 3.6 A polar distribution graph shows light intensity across the diameter of a field of light. The upper tick marks denote the beam angle (the "working" light); the lower tick marks denote the field angle (the "usable" light). In flood position the light offers virtually even intensity across the wide spread of the beam; in spot position beam intensity falls off rapidly outward from the central hot spot. Note: cd is an abbreviation for candela or candle power. It is a measure of brightness: cd = footcandles x (distance)^2.

The Globe and Its Installation

Bulbs are referred to by a three-letter code that is assigned by the American National Standards Institute (ANSI). For example, a typical 1k Fresnel uses an EGT bulb. ANSI codes are listed with other specifications in Appendix A.

Most larger Fresnels used in motion picture work have a bipostal lamp base. Smaller lamps, such as the 200W FEV, have a bayonet base. Bulbs are listed by base type in Table E.3. Figure 3.8 shows how to open up various models of lights to get at the globe.

On small units, the bulb simply plugs straight into the lamp base and is held in place by friction. When removing the bulb from this type of base, be careful not to break the glass off its porcelain base. Firmly grasp the porcelain base and wiggle the globe out. Do not handle the glass. On lights of 2000W and larger, a screw in the

Baby 1,000 Watt Type 407	Junior 2,000 Watt Type 412	Senior 5,000 Watt Type 415	Tener 10,000 Watt Type 416	"Big Eye" Tener 10,000 Watt Type 4241
Baby-Baby 1,000 Watt Type 2831	Baby Junior 2,000 Watt Type 4131	Baby Senior 5,000 Watt Type 4191	Baby Tener 10,000 Watt Type 4181	20K 20,000 Watt Type 4251
200 Watt (Left to Right) Types 2901, 2351 and 2801	Betweenie 300 Watt Type 3131	Tweenie 650 Watt Type 4821	Baby 1,000 Watt Type 3081	8" Junior 2,000 Watt Type 5291

Tiny　Mini　Midget

Pepper 100W/200W	Pepper 200W	Pepper 300W	Pepper 420W	Pepper 650W	Pepper 500W/1k

Figure 3.7　Fresnel fixtures.

fixture's lamp base tightens the base around the pins of the bulb. With this type of base, the globe comes out freely when the thumb screw is loosened.

The position of the bulb relative to the reflector is critical to the proper operation of the light. The filament of the bulb sits precisely at the focal point of the reflector. Therefore, if the bulb is not seated properly, or the reflector is bent, the lamp's performance is drastically reduced.

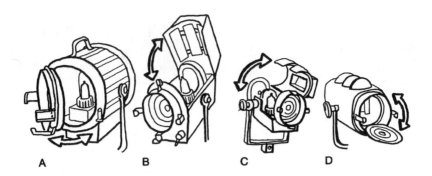

A   B   C   D

Figure 3.8   Four common ways to access the inside of a Fresnel fixture. (A) With most lights of 1000W and larger, the lens door swings open on a hinge. (B) On a baby-baby, the top of the housing swings back on a hinge at the back of the fixture. (C) The top of a pepper's housing swings open to one side. (D) The lens of a midget is held in place by a spring.

Tilt Angle

To ensure proper heat dissipation, manufacturers recommend that Fresnels be hung with the base down. Each type of globe has a limit to the amount it can be tilted on its side without shortening the life of the globe. For example, a senior (a 5k Fresnel fixture) should burn with the bulb oriented within 45° to vertical. In addition to damaging the bulb, a 2000W baby junior light hung at an extreme downward tilt will melt the reflector. In practice, tilt angle is only a concern with lights that have large, expensive globes. Small lights are hung in whatever manner is required.

Fresnel Accessories

Each Fresnel should always be accompanied by barn doors and a set of scrims in a scrim box or scrim bag. A typical equipment package also includes snoots and at least one focal spot in various sizes to fit the various lights.

Scrims

A *scrim* is a stainless steel wire screen used to reduce the intensity of the light. A single scrim has a loose wire weave, is identified by its green ring frame, and cuts the intensity of the light by approximately a half-stop. A double scrim has a tighter weave, is identified by its red ring frame, and cuts the light by approximately one full stop. A standard set of scrims includes a single, two doubles, a half-single, a half-double, and a gel frame. Quarter scrims and graduated scrims are also available for some fixtures.

Half scrims affect just one-half of the beam. A bottom-half double can be used to even out the intensity of the light as the subject moves closer to the fixture (Figure 3.9). It reduces the light falling on objects close to the light, bringing the light level down to that of objects farther from the light.

Figure 3.9 A bottom-half scrim is used to even out intensity as the subject moves closer to the light fixture.

A gel frame can be used to hold light gels or diffusion for short spans of time; however, because of the heat close to the lens, many lights will melt gels mounted in the gel frame. Similarly, hot scrims will melt the gel in a gel frame (and make a big gooey mess on the scrim). Therefore, gels and diffusion materials are often attached to the barn doors, where the heat is less intense.

Appendix A lists the appropriate scrim size for various lighting fixtures.

Barn Doors

Barn doors provide the most basic control over the placement of the edges of the beam of a Fresnel or open-face fixture. Because the doors are so close to the fixture, the cut is fairly soft (Figure 3.10).

Barn doors typically have two large leaves and two smaller triangular ones. When the bigger doors are horizontal, they are said to be "Chinese"; when they are vertical, we call them "English." By closing the two large leaves into a narrow slit and folding the small leaves out of the way, you can make a narrow slash. The slash can be horizontal — for an eye light, for example — or turned diagonally to make a slash across a background.

Snoot

When a very confined, narrow, circular beam is desired, replace the barn doors with a snoot. Snoots come in various sizes, from wide (called a *top hat*) to very narrow (*stovepipe*). Some snoots are fitted with four rings with different aperture sizes so that you can adjust the beam width (Figure 3.11).

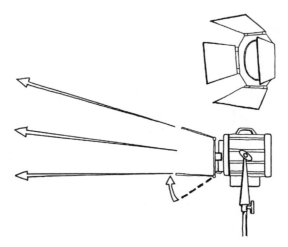

Figure 3.10 Barn doors contain the light, putting a straight edge on the beam.

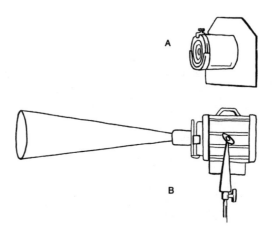

Figure 3.11 (A) A snoot with multiple aperture rings allows some flexibility in beam width. (B) A snoot confines the beam to a narrow circle.

Focal Spot

A focal spot essentially changes a Fresnel into a spotlight. The focal spot lens assembly creates a narrow, bright, even circle. Like an ellipsoidal reflector spotlight, a focal spot has framing shutters. It accepts design patterns called gobos and mattes, which can be projected and focused onto the scene. It has interchangeable lens tubes — wide beam and narrow beam. It also comes with a gel ring to add color gels (Figure 3.12).

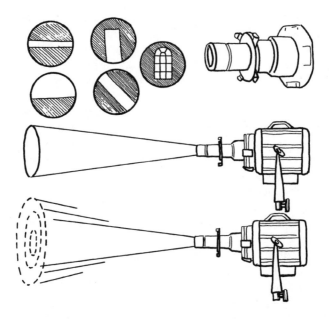

Figure 3.12 A focal spot. The four framing shutters can be pushed into the beam to form hard cuts in any shape: a narrow slit for an eye light, a rectangle to frame a doorway, a straight-line cut, or a diagonal slash, for example. It can also project gobo patterns. The gobo fits into a slot on the barrel. The beam can be focused to create hard edges or defocused to soften them.

Shutters

Shutters are like heavy-duty venetian blinds; they have rows of parallel slats that open and close. The shutter is mounted on the front of the light (Figure 3.13).

The shutter can be controlled to smoothly reduce the amount of light getting to the subject. Shutters are handy when the light level needs to change during a shot. Care must be taken to avoid projecting a venetian-blind pattern on the subject. Keep the light some distance from the subject, and use diffusion material between the two. Be watchful also for a vertical shift in the position of the beam as the shutters are closed. Shutters are frequently used to create a lightning effect; a sudden flash can be produced by opening and quickly closing the shutter. Use appropriate caution; the shutters will warp from the heat buildup if kept closed for too long.

Dedolight

Strictly speaking, Dedolights, manufactured by Dedotec USA, Inc., are not Fresnel fixtures. They are small, compact, 100W and 150W fixtures that use two specially designed lenses in an assembly that is more efficient than a Fresnel and that provides a hard, adjustable beam with exceptionally even light across the field (Figure 3.14).

The special lens assembly gives the fixture an unusually wide range of adjustment (from 40° in full flood to 2.5° in full spot) and unusual punch for long throw. A 100W Dedolight has roughly the same light output as a 300W Fresnel. The lights are so small, lightweight, and unobtrusive that they can easily be hidden in the set.

The lights have various accessories, including barn doors, gel frames, lightweight mounting hardware, suction mounts, camera clamps, and a focal-spot-like projection attachment. The projection attachment allows extremely precise control of the beam. It can be shuttered in on a beer label, for instance, providing a hard edge cut with no color fringing or softness around the edges. For this reason, the lights are useful in tabletop setups and miniature work.

The 100W Dedolights run on 12V. The 150W version runs on 24V. The power supplies power three, four, or five lights at a time. There are three power settings on the power supply for each light: high (3300K, maximum light output), medium (3200K, medium light output), and low (about 3000K, lower light output). The lights can also be powered directly off battery.

The Dedocool is a 250W tungsten-balanced light designed for lighting small areas when a great deal of light is needed, for an extremely high shutter speed, for example. Used at close range, the light can provide 220,000 FC at 8 to 12 in., while giving off very little heat. Insects, plants, food, plastics, paper, and other such items that would be adversely affected by the heat of any other source of this intensity can be filmed using this light. A cooling fan at the back of the fixture is necessary to cool

Figure 3.13 Shutters on a 10K Fresnel. (Equipment courtesy of Hollywood Rental, Sun Valley, CA).

Figure 3.14   The refined beam of a 100W Dedolight. (Photo courtesy of Dedotec USA, Inc., Lodi, NJ).

the bulb. The special power supply keeps the fan running for a short time after the light is turned off to cool the light. If the light is unplugged hot, damage to the fan can result.

Soft Lights

Soft lights (Figure 3.15) are designed to produce soft, shadowless light. Instead of using a lens, the light from the long tubular globes is directed into a white concave reflector.

Because the light is indirect, bounced off a diffuse white surface, and exits through a relatively large aperture, the resulting light is soft and has a wide, even, uncontrolled spread. Soft lights are commonly used for fill. Table A.2 (Appendix A) provides soft light specifications.

Because soft lights use indirect light, they produce far less light per watt than Fresnels. Most soft lights have multiple globes, each switched individually, making it easy to increase or reduce the light's intensity. Figure 3.16 shows the egg crate and snoot, which can also be used to contain and control soft light. Soft lights don't generally have scrims, but you can improvise by inserting a baby scrim between the base and the white reflector surface, sandwiched with the egg crate and held in place with a grip clip.

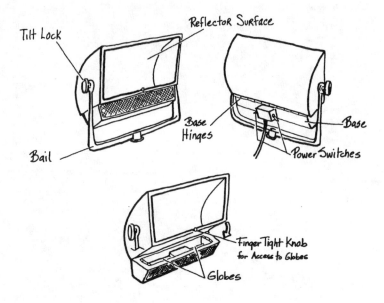

Figure 3.15 Anatomy of a 2k zip soft light. (Equipment courtesy of Hollywood Rental, Sun Valley, CA.)

To maintain maximum intensity and proper color temperature, the white reflector must periodically be cleaned or repainted. When repainting the interior surface, use best boy white paint. Best boy white reflects light without changing the color of the light, and it withstands high temperatures. If regular white paint is used, it will appear off-color.

To gain access to the globes, loosen the finger screws that lock the basket to the reflector and hinge the base open. The globes are double-ended and are held in place in a spring-loaded porcelain base. To install the globe, insert one end and push back the spring until the other end can slide in.

Area Lights

Scoop Lights and Sky Pans

Scoops (Figure 3.17F) and *sky pans* (Figure 3.17H) are very simple lights that have been around since incandescent lights were first used in motion pictures. They consist of an exposed bulb mounted in a large white reflector. Scoops are 1k or 2k; sky pans can be 2k, 5k, or 10k.

Sky pans are used for general illumination over a large area or for lighting scenic paintings, backdrops, or backings, which must be lit evenly from side to side and

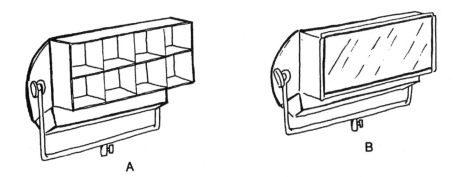

Figure 3.16 Soft light accessories. (A) Egg crate. This black, metal grid helps control spill and also reduce the overall intensity of the light. It is a good idea to keep an egg crate with each soft light because they are used frequently. (B) Diffuser frame (shown here placed on the front of a snoot). This square gel fits in the front of the unit to hold colored gels or diffusion. (Equipment courtesy of Hollywood Rental, Sun Valley, CA.)

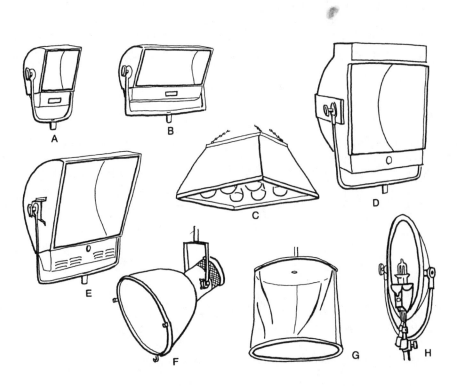

Figure 3.17 Soft lights and area fixtures. (A) 400W, 650W mini, or 750W Baby soft light; (B) 2k Zip; (C) six-light chicken coop; (D) 8k Super Softlight with 1k globes; (E) 1k, 2k, or 4k soft light; (F) scoop; (G) Space Light; (H) sky pan.

from top to bottom. The light can be made softer and more even by employing a frame of spun glass diffusion. The gel frame fits into a metal skirt that one attaches to the face of the light.

Chicken Coops and Space Lights

The *chicken coop* (Figure 3.17C) hangs on a chain and uses six 1000W silver bowl globes. The globes are silvered on the bottom to prevent direct hard light from shining downward. Chicken coops and space lights are commonly hung throughout a very large set to fill the space with a general soft overhead illumination. A *space light* (Figure 3.17G) consists of six 1k nook lights configured like spokes of a wagon wheel, pointing down into a silk cylinder. At the bottom is a round diffusion ring to which a diffusion material or gel can be clipped.

Open-Face Lights

As the name implies, open-face lights do not have a lens and are therefore slightly brighter per watt than a Fresnel. However, their light is less even, and they are harder to control (Figure 3.18).

Open-face fixtures can be divided into four categories: prime fixtures, broads and nook lights, cyc strips and ground rows, and portable fixtures. Figure 3.19 illustrates open-face lights with which an electrician must be familiar. Table A.3 (Appendix A) lists their specifications.

Prime Fixtures

Prime open-face fixtures (Figure 3.19 A–E) have a round face and an adjustable reflector for flood/spot control, and they come with barn doors and a scrim set. The flood/spot mechanism alters the globe's position relative to the reflector. When the globe is close to the reflector, the reflector sends out a wide beam; when the globe is pulled away from the reflector, it reflects a narrower beam. They are durable lights with a relatively high intensity per watt, and they are much more controllable than

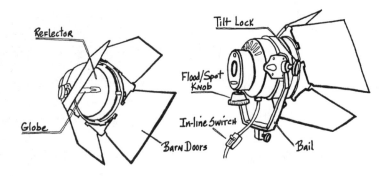

Figure 3.18 Anatomy of a blonde 2k open-face fixture. (Equipment courtesy of Hollywood Rental, Sun Valley, CA.)

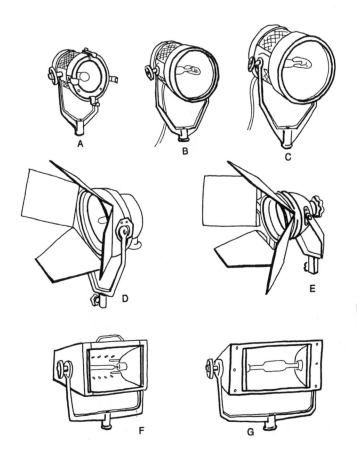

Figure 3.19 Open-face fixtures. (A) 650W Teenie-Weenie, (B) 1k Mickey, (C) 2k Mighty, (D) 2k Blonde, (E) 1k redhead, (F) 1k broad, (G) 1k or 2k nook light. (Equipment courtesy of Hollywood Rental, Sun Valley, CA.)

broads and nook lights. They are also relatively lightweight; all sizes mount on a baby stud.

Open-face prime fixtures are often bounced into a white surface such as foamcore to create soft light. Note that open-face lights tend to burn very hot and can melt a foamcore bounce board or destroy a flag if it is placed too close to the light. Think twice before rigging a light close to set pieces, and allow ventilation above the fixture.

Broads and Nook Lights

Broads and nook lights (Figure 3.18 F and G) consist of little more than a long, double-ended bulb and a curved or V-shaped silver reflector. Nook lights are small and light, and can be easily hidden in the set. Because broads and nook lights create raw, hard light, they tend to be used for jobs such as throwing light on a background or illuminating a soft box. They are also handy as work lights.

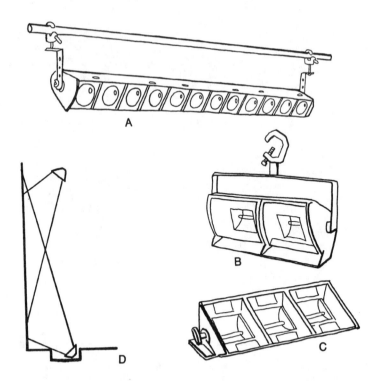

Figure 3.20 Cyc lighting. (A) Border light. (B) Two-light far cyc (also made in strips of many lights and in groups of four). (C) Ground row cyc strip (comes in strips of 1, 2, 3, 4, 6, 8, 9, and 12 or more lights). (D) The typical cyc lighting method lights the cyc evenly from top to bottom.

Cyc Strips, Ground Rows, and Borders

A cyc strip is a row of open-face lights having a specially shaped reflector used to illuminate a *cyclorama*, or *cyc*, evenly from top to bottom and from side to side. Cyc strips come in either short strips of 1, 2, 3, or 4 lights or longer strips of 6, 8, 9, or 12. The larger strips are wired in groups to provide three or four separate circuits for different colored gels, with one circuit of several lights per color (Figure 3.20).

A four-circuit cyc strip might have the three primary colors of light — red, green, and blue — and either a white circuit or a second blue circuit. (Blue gel absorbs more light than the other colors and is therefore weaker.) By mixing the primary colors using dimmers on each circuit, the cyc can be made any color or can take on a gradation of colors from top to bottom.

Cyc strips are positioned on the floor, called a *ground row*, or in a trench below floor level, pointing up at the cyc, and they are hung from pipes or *battens* in front of or behind the cyc, pointing down at it. The angle of the strip and its distance from the cyc are critical for achieving even lighting from top to bottom.

Strips of PAR lights, called *border lights*, are also used to light cycs and curtains. PARs have a better throw and a tighter, more intense beam, which is sometimes needed on a very tall cyc to carry light into the center of the cloth.

Light Kits

Screw Base Fixtures

The Lowel K5, Desisti Pinza, and other similar fixture provides a regular screw socket that can be fitted with a photoflood (or any other type of medium screw base bulb) of up to 500W. Because K5 kits are lightweight and can be easily hung, clamped, dangled, or taped to walls and ceilings, they are easy to rig. Fitted with R-40 mushroom floods and hoods (Figure 3.21), they can create nice pools of light from above. (Photoflood and mushroom flood bulbs are discussed in detail in Chapter 7.)

Stick-Up Kits

A stick-up is a very small open-face light that can be taped or clipped into the smallest of places. It can be fitted with a 100W or 200W, 120V bayonette base bulb or with a 100W, 12V bulb. The latter is ideal as a dome light in an automobile because it can run off the car battery (Figure 3.22).

Because a stick-up is so small and light, it can be taped in place or hung on pushpins. When the light is placed against a surface, insulate the surface with a double or triple layer of refracil heat-resistant cloth. You can wrap a piece of black wrap around the back of the fixture to act as barn doors.

Portable Light Kits

Portable open-face lights are normally used by small, mobile camera crews for documentary, industrial, and promotional video and film work. The lights come in kits with a full complement of accessories, including adaptive, lightweight mounting hardware and lightweight stands. The units are small and usually draw 1000W or less (Figure 3.23).

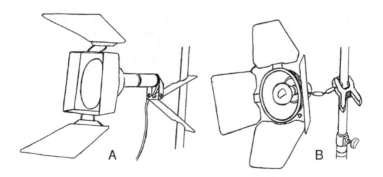

Figure 3.21   (A) Molite or Lowel K5: a R-40 bulb with attachable barn doors. (B) A Pinza reflector lamp that takes photoflood bulbs.

Figure 3.22 The stick-up illustrated is 3 in. tall and weighs 9 oz. with its 9-ft. power cord. It comes with a wire framed for securing gels and diffusion. (Photo courtesy of Great American Market, Hollywood, CA.)

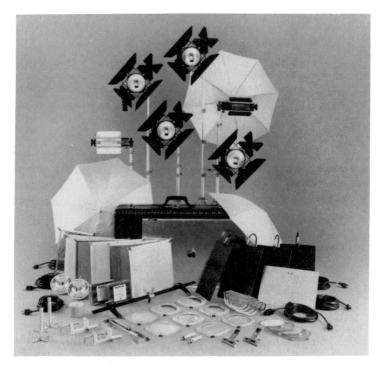

Figure 3.23 Lowel open-face lighting kit with accessories. The solo kit shown includes two Toto lights, four Omni lights, scrims, special barn doors, silver umbrellas, flags with flexible shafts, scissor clamps, c-clamps, a space clamp (special furniture clamp), a door-top hanger, a cucaloris, diffusion glass, a spare globe case, power cords and extensions, reflector boards, white bounce boards, and more. (Photo courtesy of Lowel-Light Manufacturing, Brooklyn, NY.)

Lightweight, portable soft lights are also available. Compact fixtures can illuminate only a limited area, but they can be useful to supplement heavier lighting equipment.

The quality of the light can be manipulated using gel frames to alter color or to diffuse the light. Because the raw light from an open-face fixture is often hard and unattractive, cinematographers often seek to soften the source. Bouncing the units into silver umbrellas provides a large, yet lightweight, source of soft light.

PAR Lights

Parabolic aluminized reflector (PAR) lights are sealed-beam lamps. That is, the globe, lens, and reflector are one permanently sealed unit, like a car headlight (Figure 3.24).

PAR bulbs are typically mounted in clusters of individually directable, individually switched lamps, with 1 to 12 or more lights to a cluster. They are referred to by the number of lights in the cluster: for example, a four-light, six-light, or, most common, nine-light. (Table A.4 in Appendix A list the common types.) Globes are made in various beam widths: wide flood, medium flood, narrow spot, and very narrow spot. PAR lamps tend to have an elliptical beam rather than a circular one. A PAR lamp can be turned in its fixture to orient the beam as required.

PAR lights tend to burn very hot and can melt a foamcore bounce board or destroy a flag if it is placed too close to the light. Be careful when rigging a light close to set pieces, and be sure to allow ventilation above the fixture.

There are a number of types of PAR globes that are appropriate for different situations. The term *FAY light* is often used to refer generally to any fixture using PAR-36 globes, and not necessarily the FAY type specifically (Figure 3.25 A and B; Table E.6). "FAY" bulbs are daylight-balanced PAR-36 globes (5000K, 650W per bulb, 4-1/2 in. diameter). FAY dichroic bulbs are used for daylight fill. Though HMIs can also fulfill this objective, FAY lamps still offer an inexpensive alternative for exterior lighting. FCX and FCW are medium- and wide-beam versions of a tungsten-balanced PAR-36 globe (3200K, 650W).

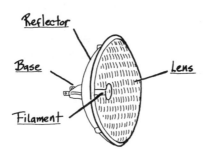

Figure 3.24 Anatomy of a PAR lamp.

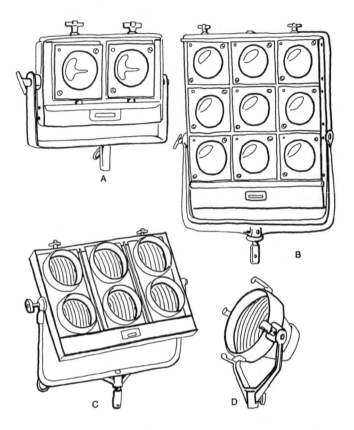

Figure 3.25 PAR Fixtures. (A) Two-light FAY (650W per light). (B) Nine-light FAY (650W per light). (C) Six-light PAR (1k per light). (D) 1k PAR.

The term *PAR light* usually refers to 1k PAR fixtures that use PAR-64 lamps (1000W, 3200K, 8 in. diameter; Figure 3.25 C and D). Again, the globe may be wide flood (WF), medium flood (MF), narrow spot (NSP), or very narrow spot (VNSP). These lamps have a lot of punch; they can throw fairly long distances or over a fairly wide area. The light they produce is very hard and unpleasant when used directly on faces. *Maxi-brute* is a common name for a nine-light using PAR-64 globes. Table E.5 (Appendix E) lists specifications for all common types.

HMI Lights

HMI lights are a highly efficient source of daylight-balanced light (5600K or 6000K, depending on the globe manufacturer). They are used when mixing with natural daylight. An HMI puts out about four times as much light as a tungsten light of the same wattage — 85 to 108 lumens per watt of electricity, compared to 26 lumens per watt for tungsten halogen bulbs. This is partly because an incandescent bulb expends 80% of its energy creating heat (infrared wavelengths), whereas HMIs convert that same percentage of its energy into usable illumination. As a result, HMIs operate at much cooler temperatures, making them more comfortable to work under and better for lighting temperature-sensitive subjects, such as animals and food (not to mention actors).

HMI lights use a ballast connected between the AC power source and the lamp head. The component parts of an HMI are the head, the head cable, the ballast, and in most cases a separate ballast cable (Figure 3.26). Standard HMIs run on AC power only (a couple of notable exceptions are described later).

There are two types of ballasts: magnetic, which are standard, and electronic (also called square-wave or flicker-free), which are becoming more and more com-

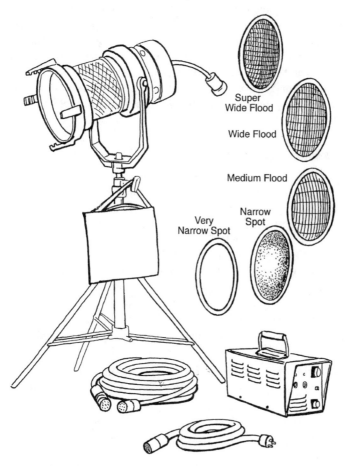

Figure 3.26 LTM 1200 HMI PAR head, head cable, ballast cable, ballast, scrims, lens case, and set of spreader lenses.

mon. With a magnetic ballast, the camera must be crystal-controlled and must be run at one of a number of specific frame rates. More about this shortly.

There are five types of HMI fixtures: Fresnels, sealed beam PARs, single-ended (non-sealed-beam) PARs, soft lights, and battery-powered sun guns. Specifications for HMI fixtures appear in Tables A.5, A.6, A.7, and A.8 in Appendix A.

HMI Fresnels

Small Fresnels of 200W, 575W, and 1200W are commonly used as interior direct light or bounce light when daylight color balance is needed. They are equivalent in function to a tweenie, a baby, and a junior, respectively. These sizes have the advantage of plugging into a standard household outlet when necessary. Medium size HMI Fresnels of 2500W, 4000W, and 6000W are used in much the same manner as 5k and 10k tungsten units — to light large interiors, to double as sunlight, to provide fill on exteriors, or to provide key light and backlight on night exteriors.

Large HMI Fresnels — 12k and 18k — have replaced the carbon arc as the workhorse large light. A necessary part of almost any equipment package, the 12ks are used for fill on day exterior shots. To cover wide exterior night shots, they are often mounted to an 80 ft. arm (they can light up an entire city block). Another common application is making sunlight effects through windows both on location and inside the studio. They may be put through diffusion or bounced to create a large, bright soft source.

HMI (Sealed-Beam) PARs

PAR lights are more efficient than Fresnels, and they deliver a strong punch of light with a long throw. They come with a case of three or four spreader lenses (Figure 3.26 and Table A.6).

The beam of an HMI PAR is elliptical, not circular. The shape varies with the lens used. The medium and wide flood lenses create a more oblong beam than the others. Take, for example, the LTM 1200 PAR. A narrow or very narrow lens gives about a 12° beam width and an 8° beam height. Medium and wide lenses create a much wider ellipse: Medium gives 22° × 9°, wide 53° × 22° (about 2-1/2 times as wide as it is high). The pebbled lens (very wide flood) gives a circular beam with about a 64° spread. On some fixtures the entire housing can be rotated so that the oblong beam can be oriented to any angle. Alternately, you can simply turn the lens.

HMI Single-Ended (Nonsealed-Beam) PARs

Single-ended HMI PARs have a similar appearance to HMI PAR lights, but instead of using a sealed-beam globe they use a single-ended HMI globe mounted in front of a highly efficient parabolic reflector, and the globe does not have a sealed lens. UV-protective glass covers the front of the unit, and spreader lenses are also used (see Table A.6).

Because the single-ended globe is not mounted horizontally, but on the optical axis of the reflector, and because of the compatibility of the relatively small arc with the shape and coating of the reflector, single-ended HMI lamps can deliver several times the light of even HMI PAR lights. A 2500 PAR with a spot lens is so intense that a piece of wood 4 ft. from the fixture will begin to smoke in a matter of minutes. With 4k and 6k Pars this sometimes gets to be a problem. PAR lights also work well as a bounce source to create soft light (but be sure to use wide or extra-wide lens or you'll melt or burn the bounce surface).

Again, the lenses affect both beam shape and angle. The very narrow and narrow spot lenses give a circular beam of 6° and 8°. The medium and wide flood lenses give a wide elliptical beam of 27° × 11°, and 60° × 25°, respectively. The super-wide flood gives a circular beam of about 54°. To turn an oblong beam, the operator rotates the lens.

HMI Soft Lights

As with incandescent soft lights, the globe of an HMI soft light is aimed into a white concave reflector. The bounced light and large aperture create a soft, even field of daylight-balanced light. The HMI soft light, of course, produces much greater quantities of light than an incandescent (see Table A.8).

HMI Sun Guns

A sun gun is a small (125W, 200W, 250W, or 400W) light powered by a 30V nickel-cadmium battery, usually in the form of a battery belt (Figure 3.27, Table A.7).

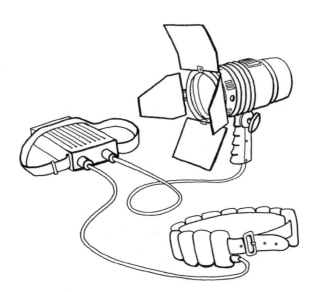

Figure 3.27 This HMI sun gun takes a 250W SE HMI globe and has a color temperature of 5600K. It operates on a 30V battery belt and is adaptable to a 24V car-type battery.

The light has a hand grip as well as a mounting stud. Sun guns are sometimes employed in remote locations where power is not available — in a cave in the mountains of Mexico — and in situations where the expediency of a battery-powered light takes priority — in a moving vehicle or on a moving elevator, for example.

Although the 30V nicad belt batteries are supposed to last as long as an hour, rented batteries rarely keep the light going for more than 20 to 25 minutes. When battery-powered lights are to be relied on over the course of a whole scene or a whole day, it is necessary to have many batteries on hand. They must be fully charged overnight (8 hours), and it helps to have them "topped-off" again within an hour prior to use.

HMI Operation

Setup

The ballast circuit breakers should be off or the ballast unplugged while connecting or disconnecting head cables. The breakers should remain off while plugging in the power (Figure 3.28).

Head cable connectors (Socapex or VEAM) have multiple pins and a threaded collar that screws onto their receptacle. Use the keyway to orient the plug into the socket. VEAM connectors for 575W, 1200W, 2500W, and 4000W fixtures are all identical, except that the keyway is oriented differently. To tell the cables apart many manufacturers and rental houses color code the connectors or cables as follows:

Green	575
Yellow	1200
Red	2500
Blue	4k

Be sure to tie a tension relief so that the weight of the head cable does not pull on the connector, especially with larger lights that have heavy head cables.

Junction Boxes

The large Socapex connectors used on some head feeders can only be connected to a panel-mounted receptacle and not to another head cable. A junction box (j-box) provides a means of connecting one head cable to another.

Striking

Once the head cable is connected to the head and ballast, plug in the ballast and switch on the circuit breakers. With 12k and 18k lamps, place the bulb in full spot position before pushing the ON switch. This backs the bulb away from the lens so that the lens does not crack from thermal shock. Also, in the (rare) event that the globe explodes during warm-up, the chance of shattering the lens is minimized. When 12k bulbs do explode, they often go within the first five or ten minutes of ignition or reignition.

Before pushing the ON switch, call out "Striking" to warn people that the light is about to be ignited. HMIs have ON/OFF switches on both the head and the ballast,

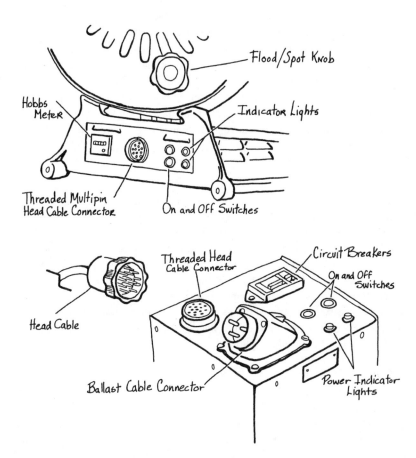

Figure 3.28 Anatomy of an HMI head and ballast. (Equipment courtesy of Hollywood Rental, Sun Valley, CA.)

and most models can be turned on and off from either place. When you press the ON switch, the ballast briefly sends a high-voltage ignition charge to the head, and this makes a sparking sound.

The igniter circuit provides an ignition charge of 5000V to 17,000V, depending on the size of the globe. The ignition charge creates a brief arc between the electrodes in the globe. Once the flow of electrons is initiated, the ballast brings the voltage down to the operating level and regulates the current.

Once sparked, the HMI will begin to emit light. From a cold state it takes one to three minutes for the substances in the globe to vaporize. At the same time, lamp voltage, lamp current, luminous flux, and color temperature are all reaching their nominal values.

When a globe is hot from prior use, a much higher ignition voltage is necessary (25,000V to 65,000V). Very often the ballast will not be able to produce sufficient voltage to accomplish a hot restrike, and you have to wait a couple of minutes for the globe to cool before it will light again. When hot gases inside the globe are under greater pressure, high resistance is created between the electrodes. Much higher voltage is necessary to ionize the pressurized gap between the electrodes. The electronics of most newer ballasts take this into account and have better hot restrike performance. An old magnetic ballast may not have sufficient voltage to generate an arc until the lamp has cooled.

Troubleshooting

If an HMI will not work, first double-check all the obvious possibilities. Are the ballast breakers turned on? Are the cables connected properly? Is a bulb installed? Is the HMI plugged into the proper voltage? (Some are 120V, others are 208V, 220V, or 240V.) If the HMI still doesn't work, isolate the problem; is it the head cable, the head, the globe, the ballast, or the power? Isolating the problem requires a logical, methodical approach. If the problem is hidden, you may have to change out each component before you find the problem. In the worst case there is more than one faulty part conspiring to confuse things. You can eliminate possibilities by temporarily borrowing a ballast and head cables that are known to work; this will usually get you to the heart of the problem quickly.

Problems with the Head

If the indicator light shows that there is power at the head but nothing happens when you press the button, or if the HMI shuts itself off when tilted down, it is likely that the lens door is slightly loose, allowing the UV protection microswitch to shut off the unit. Check that the door is tightly closed, even when the light is tilted forward. You may need to adjust the rod on the microswitch so that the switch engages. Once in a great while, the microswitch becomes overheated, breaks, and must be replaced.

If the light makes a striking sound but will not take, the problem is most likely with the globe, igniter circuit, or internal cables. If the globe is hot from prior use, it is very likely that the globe simply needs a minute to cool before it will restrike.

As globes gets older, they have more difficulty striking. As the electrodes wear away and the gap between them becomes wider; the igniter has to generate sufficient voltage to bridge the gap. You may have to try several times before the globe takes. Wait 20 seconds between strikes. It is time to replace the globe when its electrodes have worn down so far that the igniter can no longer induce an arc.

When using an electronic ballast, be wary about repeatedly attempting to strike a bad head. (See Electronic Ballasts.)

With 12k lamps, if the light makes a loud buzz and arcing sound when you attempt to strike, but does not take, check the high-voltage cables and lamp cables. The lamp cables connect the lamp to terminals at the base of the lamp holders. The high-voltage igniter cables run from the base of the lamp holders to the igniter circuit in the base of the head (Figure 3.29).

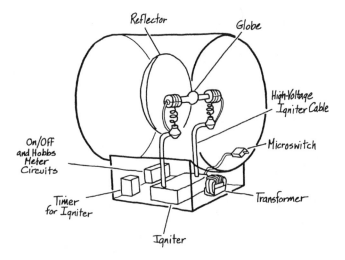

Figure 3.29 Interior anatomy of an HMI head.

If the lamp cables are hanging close to a metal part (such as the reflector), the start-up charge may arc. This deprives the bulb of the necessary start voltage and burns away the lamp cables over time. When installing the globe, position lamp cables so they have plenty of clearance and will not arc to the reflector or lamp housing. If you find a lamp cable that is partially burnt (blackened, fraying strands of cable), do not use that globe until the lamp cables have been replaced.

Another cause of HV cable burnout is overheating. The cables can get jostled around and the terminal screws loosened, causing overheated contacts, which eventually burn right through the igniter cables or lamp cables. Check and tighten the terminals each day when the lights are getting moved around a lot.

Problems with the Ballast

Some magnetic 12k ballasts have a selector switch that must be set at the appropriate input voltage (208V or 240V). Improper input voltage selection can cause trouble in striking and operating the light. The Cinemills ballast has an internal patch panel instead of a selector switch. To check or change the input voltage selection, remove the front panel of the ballast and repatch the plugs inside. Some ballasts are self-regulating, and require no adjustment to be used with 208V or 240V power.

Ballast hum is normal; nonetheless, it is the electrician's duty to remedy any annoyance to the sound mixer. It is best to place HMI ballasts in a separate room from the start. When one ballast is particularly noisy, exchange it with a new one. In the meantime, placing sandbags above and below the ballast helps dampen vibration. Building a tent with furniture pads also helps, but do not block ventilation.

If a magnetic ballast starts to buzz, it can be a symptom of low input voltage. When operating on a low input voltage, the ballast has to draw more current to provide the needed voltage to the head. This can cause overheating and nuisance circuit breaker trips. Check the line voltage.

Problems with the Head Cable

If the indicator lights are on at the ballast and off at the head, and you get absolutely no response from the head when you try to strike it, the problem is most likely in the cable or the ballast. A bad contact in the head cable connector or damaged wire in the line are common culprits. Dirty connector pins may also be at fault, in which case the pins should be blown out with compressed air and cleaned with contact cleaner. Swap the head feeder for a new one to see if it is malfunctioning. (Note: The neon indicator lights in the head sometimes burn out. The light is often integral to the switch and it is an expensive part for the rental house to replace, so you can't always count on them being in working order.)

When the head cables are checked out at the rental house — and periodically during shooting — check for missing screws on the strain-relief part of the connectors. If the strain-relief clamp comes loose, the connections inside can get pulled out and twisted. Also look for damaged insulation along the length of the cable. Treat head cables with care; avoid dragging them across pavement or throwing them on the ground because this can bend the connectors, making them impossible to connect. Never run head cables where heavy equipment and vehicles will run over them; this will damage the wires inside, causing endless headaches later on.

The pins and keyway are oriented differently for different sizes of HMIs and for the products of different manufacturers. Check that you are using the right head cable. The keyway orientation normally prevents you from using the wrong kind of connector, but if the connector is forced into place, it may appear to be connected. Again, color-coding similar-looking head cables by wattage helps avoid this.

Problems with Flicker

Flicker is one of the most aggravating problems you can have because it can occur from a number of different causes. Most commonly it is due to a bad connection in the distribution system, but sometimes it is due to a wandering arc in the globe, improper voltage, bad power cable connection, or faulty head cable. An intrepid and dauntless electrician is needed to track down the actual cause of the flicker.

First, let me stress that we are now talking about **visible** flicker. It is a common misconception that a visible "flicker" in the light is cause for concern about the generator's Hertz regulator. Electricians are generally aware that to avoid flicker HMIs require a precisely regulated Hertz rate; however, one must realize that this type of "flicker" is a pulsation recorded *on film only*—it is not visible to the eye on set. (More about this horror later under Flicker-Free Solutions: Square Wave.)

Visible, random, intermittent flicker is almost always caused by a bad connection in the distribution system, head feeder, or ballast feeder cable. In the worst case, a bad contact in the power feeder or distribution cable can cause the light to stop working altogether. Try to determine if more than one light is being affected; if so, what part of the distribution do they share? Are they on the same 100A whip (bad Bates plug)? Are they on the same leg (loose connection on that phase)? If a neutral connector is lose in the distribution, all phases will flicker.

When using Bates cable, check for loose-fitting pins and hot connectors and black pitting on the hot pin of the power feeder. Use your dikes or a pin-splitter to spread the pins if the pin is squished together. Contact cleaner also works miracles to restore dirty pins. When working in dirt, dust, or sand over an extended time it is a good idea to give the HMI connectors a cleaning every week or so. Blow out dirt with compressed air, and clean the pins and receptacles with contact cleaner.

A visible ongoing pulsation or a flutter in the light is evidence of a wandering or unstable arc in the globe. Arc instability may be due to the nonhorizontal orientation of the globe or to a defective globe. For example, some 1200W PAR globes develop a wandering arc when the inner globe is positioned on a tilt. Arc instability may also be due to excess current on the electrodes, which points to faulty voltage regulation by the ballast or to improper input line voltage. Excess current wears down electrodes at an accelerated pace, aging the globe before its time. Before discarding a globe as unstable, check it by using a different ballast.

The condition of the arc can be checked by viewing the globe through a welding glass. Because of the other lights in use, a wandering or fluttering arc may not be apparent to the eye when looking at the subject onto which the light is falling, but it will register on film. The problem becomes clearly apparent when you observe the arc in the globe. This is harder to do with Fresnels because you can't see through the lens very clearly. Do not attempt to view the bulb directly.

Momentary spikes or flashes in an HMI, other than during the warm-up period, may be an indication that the Hertz rate of the generator is jumping (magnetic ballasts only). The generator's frequency meter may not detect very short, erratic frequency pulses. Measure the current with a frequency meter that has a high sampling rate to determine if the governor in the generator is faulty.

Flicker-Free Solutions: Square-Wave Ballasts

Standard Magnetic Ballasts

The light intensity of an HMI increases and decreases 120 times a second — twice every AC cycle. This fluctuation is not visible to the eye but will be captured on film as a steady pulsation if the camera is not in precise synchronization with the lights. To avoid capturing light pulsation on the filmed image, you must (1) use a crystal-controlled camera, (2) run the camera at one of a number of specific frame rates, and (3) use a line current that is maintained at exactly 60 Hz.

The frame rate must divide evenly into 120 in order for the film to receive the same amount of light in each exposure (120, 60, 40, 30, 24, 20, 15, 10, etc.). Safe frame rates at any shutter angle are listed in Tables D.1 to D.4 (Appendix D). At any of these frame rates, the camera motor must be crystal-controlled. A wild or non-crystal-controlled camera cannot be used with magnetic HMI ballasts.

Standard ballasts will also create light pulsation on film if the AC Hertz rate is not precisely controlled. The Hertz rate for any power line can be checked by using an in-line frequency meter or by measuring the light's flicker rate with a photosensitive Cinecheck frequency meter pointed at the HMI head itself (magnetic ballast only). Rental companies can supply a frequency meter with their equipment. Additionally, most generators have built-in frequency meters.

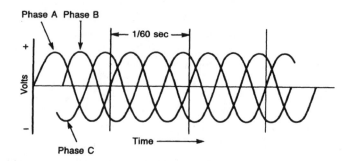

Figure 3.30 With three-phase power, the peak of each leg is a third of a cycle out of sync with the last, creating six peaks in each cycle. At 60 Hz, that amounts to 360 peaks per second, which is high enough frequency to be flicker-free at any frame rate.

Three-Head, Three-Phase Solution

One way to get around the HMI pulsation problem when operating at off speeds or with a wild camera and with magnetic ballasts is to use three standard HMI ballasts connected to three heads, each powered from a different leg of a three-phase source. Because the three phases peak a third of a cycle apart, when taken together the three lights have an actual frequency of 360 peaks per second (3 × 120 = 360). At this frequency, the camera will not detect the pulsation (Figure 3.30).

The lights must be bounced or mounted close together and placed far enough from the subject not to create separate shadows. The light created will be flicker-free at any frame rate.

Square-Wave Electronic Ballasts

Square-wave ballasts eliminate the flicker problem. They allow you to film at any frame rate, at changing frame rates, and with a wild camera (Figure 3.31).

When filming an action sequence — explosion or a car crash, for example — some of the cameras will shoot at a high shutter speed — slow-motion. To give the DP the flexibility to choose any speed, the light output from the HMIs must be made constant.

A square-wave ballast maintains a virtually constant output of light over the whole AC cycle by squaring off the curves of the AC sine wave. The changeover period is so brief that the light is virtually continuous (Figure 3.32).

Unfortunately, the square wave causes the globe, igniter, and other parts of the head to make a high-pitched whistle. The head becomes a resonating chamber, amplifying the noise and projecting it out toward the set and the microphones. To make the ballasts quiet when recording dialogue, electronic ballasts are fitted with a switch to change between *flicker-free* operation and *silent operation*. In the silent mode, a special circuit electronically rounds off the sharp corners of the square wave, which eliminates the noise (Figure 3.32E).

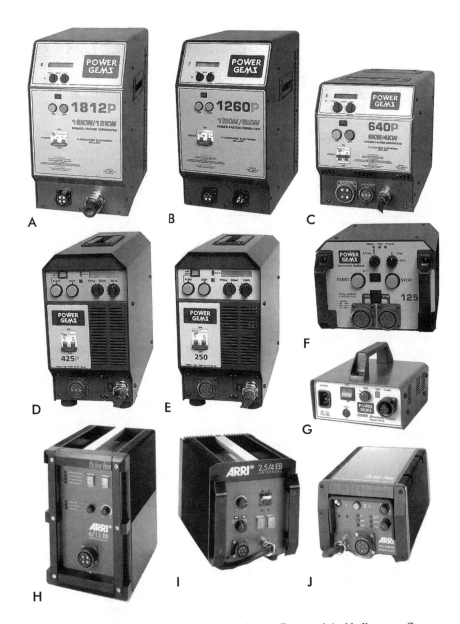

Figure 3.31 Electronic Flicker-free Ballasts. Power Gems and Arri ballasts are *Constant Power* ballasts. Most models are dual-wattage with auto-sensing. On Power Gems (A) 18k/12k, (B) 12k/6k, (C) 6k/4k, (D) 4k/2.5k, (E) 2500/1200W controls include: Start and Stop momentary switches, breakers, dimmer pot, Silent/Flicker-free selection switch, and liquid crystal operation/diagnostic display. The 1200W/575W model (F) has a wattage selection switch and separate output connectors for 575 and 1200W lamps. G is a 200W ballast. A–D above are power factor corrected models. Arri ballasts shown are (H) 12k/6k, (I) 4k/2.5k, and (J) 1200W/575W. Arri also makes electronic ballasts for their 200W and 125W fixtures, and a power factor corrected 18k/12k model.

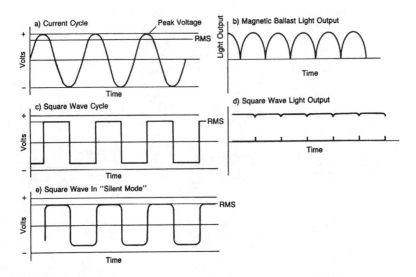

Figure 3.32 The normal sinusoidal 60-Hz current cycle of a magnetic ballast (A) creates a fluctuating light output, (B) requiring that the camera frame rate be synchronized with the light fluctuations to obtain even exposure from frame to frame. The refined square-wave signal of an electronic ballast (C) creates virtually even light output, (D) rendering the fixture flicker-free. The sharp corners of the normal square-wave signal create noise in the head. When operated in the silent mode (E), the ballast electronically rounds off the corners of the square wave.

In the silent mode, a square-wave ballast provides flicker-free light at frame rates up to about 34 frames per second (fps), and in flicker-free mode, up to 10,000 fps. Make sure that all ballasts are set to the same setting.

The shape of the globe contributes to the intensity of the buzz. Globes with elliptical envelopes tend to be noticeably quieter than the square type. Wolfram, for example, makes the quieter rounded globes (Figure 3.33). Head manufacturers and globe manufacturers are both in the process of developing quiet igniter and globe parts matched for use with electronic ballasts.

Square-wave ballasts completely process and regulate the input power, and as a result, they offer additional advantages and features including:

- light weight; a lot less backache than their ship-anchor magnetic counterparts.
- wide tolerance for voltage and Hertz rate discrepancies. Variation of up to ± 10% in voltage or line frequency has no adverse effect on operation.
- "dimming" capability. By controlling current, the ballast can dim the lamp 50%, or about one stop of light. At 50% power, a globe's color temperature will be 75K to 200K higher (bluer) than normal.
- increased light output (5%).
- increased globe life (as much as 20%).

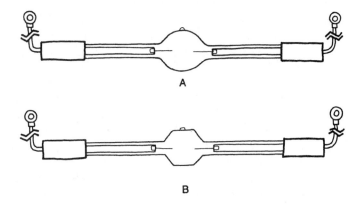

A

B

Figure 3.33 An elliptical globe (A) is less noisy than the squarer design (B) when operated with a square-wave power source.

In addition, modern *constant power* electronic ballasts are able to regulate not just lamp current, but lamp power, enabling the ballast to compensate for changing lamp voltage as a lamp ages. Constant power means the lamp has stable, optimal color temperature that remains uniform regardless of lamp age or line voltage. Constant power designs are also less prone to overheating than constant current ballasts (in situations where line voltage is low, current can become excessive).

The more sophisticated electronic ballasts (like those shown in Figure 3.31) incorporate self-diagnostic messages on an display or warning lights. After shutdown the display will identify the problem: an overheated power module, improper input voltage, a short in the output circuits, current on the ground wire, a misconnected cable — everything but a readout of the gaffer's blood pressure. If the ballast shuts off, be sure to check the display before rebooting the ballast.

Power Factor Correction Circuits

European electrical codes now require the use of power factor correction with mains power, but it is not required in the United States. Almost all manufacturers now include power factor correction on 12k/18k ballasts (for these high-current units, power factor becomes not just desirable but necessary to protect the electronics from extremely high currents and overheating). However, the added weight, cost, and complexity of power factor correction makes it a less popular option on smaller units. For most applications it is of no consequence; however, when large numbers of 4k and 6k ballasts are to be used, power factor correction may be advisable.

Because of its heavily capacitive front-end components, an electronic ballast puts current and voltage out of phase with one another. As a result, it typically has a power factor of 0.7 or less, meaning the ballast has to draw at least 30% more power than it uses. Some types of rectifiers also create spike currents that can reach 2.5 times those of the equivalent sinusoidal waveform. This happens because the capacitors are only charging at the peak of the sine wave. This creates extremely high loads on the service or generator and can interfere with the generator's voltage regulator and can even burn out the alternator. To contend with spike currents the generator needs to be oversized to at least twice the size of the load. Spikes may also affect other units running on the same service.

Also associated with low power factor and irregular waveform are return currents that build up on the neutral wire. With uncorrected square-wave ballasts, 65 to 80% of the current does not cancel out between phases, even when all hot legs are evenly loaded. This means that when operating a lot of large lights, the neutral wire will need to be doubled or even tripled to carry the additive current (see Power Factor, Chapter 8).

A power factor correction circuit realigns the waveform, and induces a smoother waveform. Power factor correction circuits successfully increase the power factor to as much as 0.98. The ballast uses power more efficiently and minimizes return current and line noise and also reduces heat, thereby increasing reliability. Table 3.1 lists power consumption for three prominent makes.

Troubleshooting

The development of electronic ballasts with features such as constant power output, sophisticated diagnostic and protection circuits, and power factor correction is the result of years of ballast manufacturers struggling to master reliability. The older, simpler electronic ballasts are susceptible to blowing electronic parts. For example, repeated hot stabs can burn out the inrush resistor that protects the front-end rectifier bridge diodes and capacitors during start-up. The most common repairs to older electronic ballasts revolve around damage to input rectifiers, vented (blown) capacitors, open inrush resistors or blown power module fuses — all caused by high inrush current. To protect the inrush resistor, be sure to turn off the main ON/OFF switch or breaker after use, and make sure it is off before plugging in the power cord.

Another common repair on older ballasts is damage to the output transistors (IGBTs and FETs) caused by a short or arc path in the head or head cable. A shorted igniter circuit can burn out ballast after ballast. In some cases the ballast will continue to work even though internal parts are damaged. The result is that other parts overheat and short out, and the repair bill and turnaround time keep going up.

Newer ballasts include back-end protection circuits — a sensor shuts it off if it senses a short. This protects the ballast but it doesn't lower the blood pressure of the gaffer who is waiting for that light to come on. As a precondition to operation, sophisticated ballasts demand that the head and cables be in good condition, with no shorts in the power line or ground, and a continuous ground.

Once an electronic ballast craps out, there is seldom anything you can do but replace it. Nothing inside an electronic ballast is user-serviceable; you have to leave it to a qualified electronics technician. For this reason preventative steps become all the more important. There are many things electricians can do to prevent a failure. The main one is to *treat the equipment like an electronic device*. Electronic ballasts must be handled gently, and be thoroughly protected from heat, moisture, condensation, precipitation, dirt, sawdust, and so on. They cannot be left baking on a hot beach or outside overnight in the dew. Magnetic ballasts are just about bullet proof, being

Table 3.1 Electronic Ballast Power Consumption

	Lightmaker AC/DC	*Lightmaker AC/DC*	*B & S (Arri, Sachtler)*	*Power Gems (LTM, Strand, Leonetti)*	
	DC Amps	*AC Amps*	*AC Amps*	*AC Amps*	
				240V Input	*120V Input*
200	3A, 120V	5.1A, 120V		1.5A @ 240V	3A @ 120V
575	8A, 120V	10A, 120V	9A, 120V	5A @ 240V 3A @ 240V w/pfc	10A @ 120V
1200	17A, 120V	20A, 120V	18A, 120V	8.3A @ 240V 5.6A A 240V w/pfc	17A @ 120V
2500	27A, 120V	39A, 120V	32A, 120V	16A @ 240V 11.5A @ 240V w/pfc	32A @ 120V
4000	42A, 120V	56A, 120V	52A, 120V	25.7A @ 230V 18A @ 240V w/pfc	51A @ 120V
6000	65A, 120V	75A, 120V	41A, 120V	41A @ 240V 27A @ 240V w/pfc	
12,000	120A, 120V	145A, 120V	81A, 240V	80A @ 240V 52A @ 240V w/pfc	
12/18k			61A/91A, 240V	53A/79A, 240V w/pfc	

w/pfc = Unit with power factor correction

made mostly of copper and iron. They can take all kinds of abuse, both physical and electrical, without failing. Electronic ballasts are made of circuit boards, relays, capacitors, and transistors; and although they have rugged casings and use heavy, commercial-grade components, electronic ballasts cannot be treated like magnetic ballasts. The electrician must enter a solid-state frame of mind when handling this equipment.

Ballast Electronics

A magnetic ballast is a very simple device. Input power is routed through the main breakers to a choke coil that is connected between the main input and the lamp. The coil may be tapped in several places to provide for various input voltages and to provide high start-up voltage. Capacitors are also included to compensate for the inductance of the coil, and to restore unity power factor. The coil provides the start-up charge for the igniter circuit, then acts as a choke, regulating current to the lamp once the light is burning. Power from the coil is routed to the main contactors (which are controlled by a low-voltage control circuit) and to the igniter circuit wire.

An electronic ballast is quite a bit more complicated (Figure 3.34). There are three primary stages to a square-wave ballast. The first stage –– the DC intermediate circuit — converts power to DC. As a preliminary, power flows from the mains supply through the circuit breakers and earth leakage detection circuit to the RF mains filter. This filter restricts the flow of noise back onto the supply service. Contactors K1 and K2 and the startup resistor form a circuit that charges the capacitors before the power electronics are activated at startup. The input rectifier and capacitors then convert the current to DC — the input rectifier inverts the negative half of the AC cycle, and the capacitors level it out to one continous positive DC voltage.

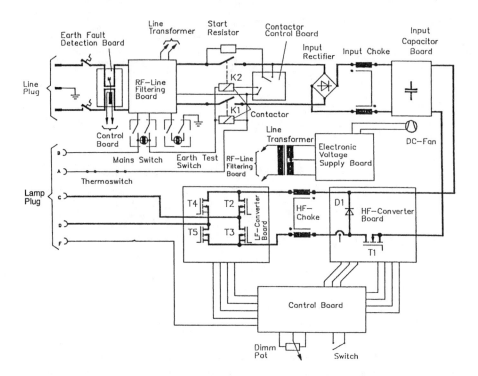

Figure 3.34 Block diagram of an 2500W electronic ballast. Courtesy Arri Lighting, New York, and B & S Elektronische Gerate GmbH, Germany.

The second and third stages are referred to as the power electronics or power modules. The second stage is a step down or buck converter (HF-converter board and HF-choke) that draws a constant current from the DC intermediate stage, then precisely regulates current flow to the final power electronics. Actual current flow is constantly monitored by the control board and adjusted by controlling the high frequency (20kHz) duty cycle of transistor T1. It is this circuit (T1, D1, and HF-choke) that allows a constant power ballast to maintain a lamp at optimum color and output performance as lamp voltage increases with age.

The final stage (LF converter board) serves as an invertor, turning the DC current into an AC square wave using four specialized transistors (insulated gate bipolar transistors, or IGBTs). The IGBTs switch back and forth in pairs (T4 and T3, then T2 and T5), reversing the polarity at a frequency controlled by the control board. (Frequency is not referenced to the line Hertz rate. Thus, an electronic ballast is not affected by a generator that is slightly off speed.) Power for the control boards is provided by a transformer and voltage supply board circuit.

Whether the ballast is electronic or magnetic, there are seven wires that run through the head feeder to the head (except in some Arri ballasts that get away with six). They are: two (thicker) power wires, *VOH* (voltage out hot), and *VOR* (voltage out return); a *ground wire*; the *igniter's power* line; and three 15V logic signal wires: *switch common* (15V from ballast), *On momentary* (remote On switch at the head), and *safe on* (which is wired to the microswitch in the lens door and to the OFF switch on the head. Both switches must be closed for the main contactors in a magnetic ballast to close (in the case of an electronic ballast, the power modules act as an electronic circuit breaker).

In the head, VOH and VOR run directly to the terminals of the globe. The ground wire is connected to the lamp housing. The igniter's power line and VOR are connected to the primary step-up transformer of the igniter circuit. This transformer steps voltage up to about 5000V. From there current runs through a spark gap to a secondary transformer, which boosts voltage up to the starting voltage of the lamp, on the order of 17kV. When the operator pushes the strike button two things happen: The contactors in the (magnetic) ballast are closed [in an electronic ballast the control board turns on the power control circuits (FETs and IGBTs)], which apply voltage to VOR and VOH, and a 200V to 350V strike voltage is sent to the head on the igniter power line.

Taking it in extreme slow motion, the strike sequence happens as follows: The ignition voltage climbs from zero, increasing until the voltage potential is sufficient to bridge the spark gap. When a spark bridges the gap, a very high voltage start charge is delivered to the electrodes of the lamp from the secondary transformer. After 1 to 1.5 seconds a timer circuit removes igniter power from the circuit. Once the flow of electrons is initiated in the bulb, the ballast starts to hold back current. The lamp arc stabilizes and voltage rises to normal operating value.

The spark gap is set to deliver the proper strike voltage for the bulb. To some extent increasing the spark gap can improve hot restrike characteristics because it increases strike voltage; however, adjusting the spark gap involves special tools and an experienced technician—the parts are fragile and extremely small. Too narrow a gap will produce insufficient voltage to arc the bulb; with too wide a gap the voltage will not bridge the spark gap.

The lamp is turned off when the SAFE ON line is interrupted — either by the lens door microswitch, or by the OFF button on the head or ballast. This opens the main contactors in a magnetic ballast or shuts off the power control circuits in an electronic ballast.

AC/DC Flicker-Free HMI Ballasts

Lightmaker makes flicker-free, solid-state ballasts that operate on either AC or DC power. Ballasts come in all standard sizes, from 200W up to 18,000W. Lightmaker ballasts work with all brands of HMI lights; however, head cables differ from manufacturer to manufacturer, so a head cable pigtail adapter is needed to connect the head cable to the ballast. The rental house handling the equipment should provide all the needed adapters. For optimum performance, the voltage must be within 5V of the ballast's voltage rating.

Most LTM heads require a simple internal modification to work with Lightmaker ballasts. The modification should have been made in the rental house or by the manufacturer. Double-check with the rental house when you pick up the equipment.

The amperage requirements for Lightmaker equipment are not what you might expect. See Table 3.1 for load calculations. All sizes of AC/DC ballasts use 120V input power. DC ballasts are not required to be grounded when they are using a DC source, but if multiple DC ballasts are used, the grounds should be bonded together. When operated on AC power, all HMI ballasts must be grounded.

DCI Lamps and Ballasts

Direct current iodide (DCI) lamps were introduced in 1993 by L.P. Associates. Like a xenon bulb, a DCI lamp uses DC current. It creates a constant, flickerless light and therefore has no light pulsation problem. DCI lamps have many of the same characteristics as HMIs: 5600K color temperature, cool operating temperature, high luminous efficiency, bright light output, and hot restrike capability. DCIs have a dimming capability, like HMI electronic ballasts, but unlike them DCIs operate silently and are flicker-free at any frame rate. DCI lamps are made in sizes from 500W to 10,000W that match the dimensions of corresponding HMI lamps: 750 or 1000 DCI (575 HMI), 1500 DCI (1200 HMI), 3000 DCI (2500 HMI), 5000 DCI (6000 HMI), and 10,000 DCI (12,000 HMI). With a simple modification to the lamp holder, standard HMI fixtures can use DCI lamps by operating on a special DCI power supply. The small, lightweight power supplies take AC input power and deliver DC power to the lamp. On L.P. Associates' 750W and 1500W fixtures with the power supply and igniter built into the housing on the base of the light, there is no separate ballast and feeder cable.

Operating characteristics, such as lamp warm-up time, the need for care in handling and cleaning the lamp, lamp installation with nipple pointed forward, the use of UV emission safeguards, and lamp life (200 to 300 hours), are the same as for standard HMI lamps. Unlike HMIs, DCI lamps have a positive electrode (anode) and a negative electrode (cathode). Installing the lamp with correct polarity is critical to proper operation; therefore, the diameter of the positive end is slightly larger, requiring that one lamp holder on a standard HMI fixture be enlarged for use with a DCI lamp. To prevent an AC ballast from being connected to a DCI lamp, the feeder cable connectors are also different.

Like other electronic power supplies, DCI ballasts have a fairly low power factor, and with 120V ballasts there is return current on the neutral (see Chapter 8).

HMI-Type Lamps

HMI (Mercury [Hg] medium-arc iodide, Osram), HMI/SE (single-ended, Osram), MSR (medium source rare earth, single-ended, Philips), GEMI (General Electric metal iodide), CID (compact indium discharge, Thorne UK), CSI (compact source iodine, Thorn UK),[1] DAYMAX (made by ICL), and BRITE ARC (Sylvania) are trade names of lamps in the HMI family registered by the various manufacturers.

---

[1] CID and CSI are used in stadium lighting. CID (5500K) are also used in small sungun fixtures and have the same color characteristics as HMI globes.

They all consist of two tungsten-coated electrodes surrounded by mercury vapor and other metal halides held in a quartz envelope. The flow of electrons switches electrons in the gas from one highly excited state to another, releasing energy in the form of visible and UV light. While the mercury is responsible for most of the light output, an optimal mix of halides of rare earth metals in the mercury vapor brings a balance of color output. The result is a quasi-continuous *multiline spectrum*, meaning that the color is made up of narrow peaks of various wavelengths rather than a continuous spectrum, which closely resembles the makeup of daylight and renders colors faithfully on film. There are three kinds of HMI globes: single-ended, double-ended, and PAR globes (Figure 3.35).

Single-Ended Globes

The design of single-ended (SE) globes allows for greatly improved efficiency when mounted axially and used with a bright reflector, as in SE PAR fixtures. They are also used mounted vertically in newer models of Fresnel fixtures. Single-ended globes of 575W and larger can generally be burned in any orientation. The design and short overall length of SE globes make it easy for them to restrike while hot.

Double-Ended Globes

HMI Fresnels and soft lights use double-ended globes. The range of sizes is shown in Figure 3.35. Double-ended globes of 4k and larger must be burned with their arc within 15° of horizontal; never tip these larger HMIs on their side.

PAR Globes

Some models must be operated in a horizontal orientation, others can operate in any orientation. The sealed lens/reflector envelope provides UV protection, but manufacturers recommend that an additional spreader lens be used as a second protection, in case the lens envelope breaks. Only some PAR bulbs are made to extinguish automatically if the lens envelope is broken.

Relamping HMI Heads

Before relamping a light, be sure that the breakers are off, the fixture is unplugged, and the lamp is completely cooled. HMI bulbs build up internal pressure when in use. It is dangerous to handle them when hot; if broken, they will explode, sending shards of hot quartz in all directions.

The golden rule when relamping any fixture is never to touch the quartz envelope with your fingers and never to allow moisture or grease to come into contact with the bulb. Even a light smudge of finger grease will cause a hot spot on the quartz envelope, which weakens the quartz and causes the envelope to bubble. When the globe loses its shape, the globe's photometric and structural properties are compromised and the globe could explode. HMI globes are too expensive to handle carelessly. At this writing, a 12k HMI globe is priced at around $1200! When an HMI globe explodes, it shatters the lens and destroys the lamp holder and reflector, bringing the total loss to a staggering sum. Always handle globes with a clean and dry rag, with clean cotton gloves (editor's gloves), or with the padding in which the globe is

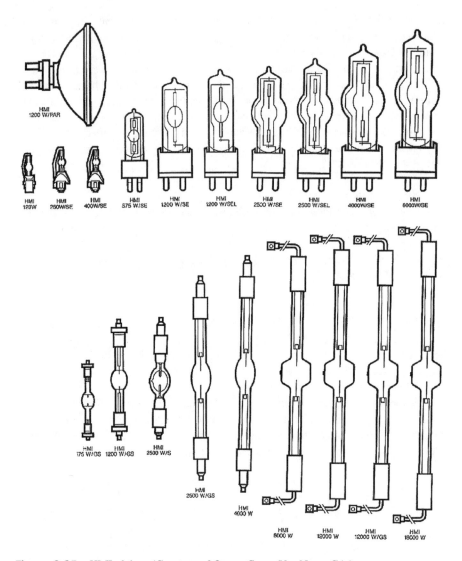

Figure 3.35 HMI globes. (Courtesy of Osram Corp., Van Nuys, CA.)

packed. Make it a practice to clean the globe once it is mounted in the fixture. Use a presaturated alcohol wipe or isopropyl alcohol and a clean lint-free tissue.

Double-ended HMI globes have metal ends that are laid into the lamp holder. HMIs of 2500W and larger have clamps that close around the globe ends and are tightened with a screw. Finger screws, Allen screws, nuts, or standard screws are used. HMI globes of 6k, 12k, and 18k have connection wires that have to be attached to terminal screws on the base of the lamp receiver. Globes of 575W and 1200W are

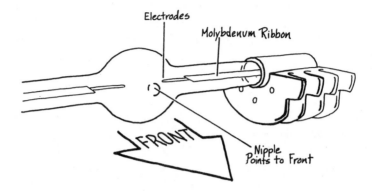

Figure 3.36 Proper installation of an HMI globe. Notice that the ribbon is horizontal and the nipple is oriented outward (it may also be oriented upward). Connections are tight. HMI globes should be cleaned with an alcohol-impregnated cloth as a part of daily maintenance. (Equipment courtesy of Hollywood Rental, Sun Valley, CA.)

held in a U-shaped receiver. Their ends are threaded and are tightened in place with knurled nuts. The 200W globe has a knife plug, a flat tab that slides into the connectors on the base and is locked in place with tightening screws.

Insert double-ended globes into the fixture with the molybdenum ribbon horizontal so that it does not block light returning from the reflector (Figure 3.36).

Orient the nipple on the bulb upward or outward toward the lens, not downward or toward the reflector. The nipple should always be above the arc to prevent a cold spot from forming where chemicals in the globe enclosure may condense and interfere with the burning cycle.

Be sure the globe's contact pins are tightly secured in place. Contamination in the contacts or a loose contact will impair proper cooling. A bad contact, evidenced by pitting and discoloration on the contact pins, causes premature lamp failure. A loose HMI globe may also vibrate.

With some SE PAR fixtures, it is impossible to install or remove the globe without handling it by the glass. Great care must be taken to avoid breaking the glass where it attaches to its ceramic base. Wiggle the globe gently along, not across, the axis of the pins; any stress across the axis can very easily snap the quartz. The better single-ended PAR fixtures provide a globe release. When the knob is loosened, the globe can be inserted and removed with ease.

Color Temperature
Factors that affect the color output of HMIs are the type of globe (5600K or 6000K), the number of hours the globe has been used, lamp cooling, and the regulation of the power by the ballast. It is good practice, especially with HMIs larger than 2500W, to match heads to ballasts and number and label both the head and the ballast

with the color temperature and the amount of green that the light emits. For example, a head and ballast would be labeled "#1, 5500K, +2, 5/13/96." This indicates ballast 1, which is matched to head 1, 5500K color temperature, has a +2 CC of green on the date shown.

Globe Life

When an HMI globe is brand new it will often show a very high color temperature (10,000K to 20,000K). This is sometimes accompanied by some arc instability, causing flicker. You may want to "burn-in" the globe before filming starts, or color correct the lamp. During the first couple hours of use, the color temperature comes down quite quickly to the nominal value (5600K or 6000K) and the arc stabilizes. Thereafter the color temperature changes over the life of the globe at the rate of 0.5K to 1K per hour, depending on conditions. The color temperature decreases because as the gap between electrodes increases, more voltage is required to maintain the arc, and as the voltage increases, the color temperature decreases. For safety reasons, manufacturers recommend that globes not be used for more than 125% of their rated service life. As the bulb ages, changes in the quartz glass envelope make the globe increasingly fragile.

Lamp Cooling

You can overheat a lamp and cause damage to the reflector or lens by pointing the lights at an extreme up or down tilt. Also, if the light receives inadequate ventilation, the color temperature will shift toward green and blue.

Ultraviolet Emissions

All HMI globes produce light that has harmful amounts of UV radiation. Skin and retinal burns can result from direct exposure to the light. For this reason, a special housing and protective lens must be used. UV rays are reduced to a safe level when the light passes through the glass lens or when the light is indirect, bouncing off the inside walls of the fixture, for example. HMIs always have a safety switch that shuts off the globe if the lens door is opened or if the lens breaks. You can get a nasty burn very quickly by tampering with these safety features or by using broken or homemade equipment that doesn't have them.

A damaged or poorly made fixture that leaks direct UV radiation can, and has, caused skin burns, retinal burns, and even skin cancer. If prolonged proximity is unavoidable, as when operating a 12k in a condor, and you start to feel some burning on your skin, place a flag to block radiation from the fixture.

Mercury

HMI globes contain very small amounts of mercury, which is poisonous. If a globe breaks, take sensible precautions to prevent ingestion of toxic chemicals. Keep chemicals off your hands. Wash your hands. Dispose of broken and burnt-out bulbs in an appropriate place. Normally burnt-out globes must be returned to the rental house for inventory.

Carbon Arc Lights

From the early days of motion pictures, when film stocks were very slow and a lot of light was required for a good exposure, up to the 1970s, when HMI lights were developed, carbon arc lights were the only lights capable of doing the job. Larger carbon arcs put out about as much light as a 12k HMI. Arc lights run exclusively on DC power. When only AC power is available, a *rectifier* must be used to convert the power to DC.

Arc lights operate as follows: An electrical (DC) arc formed in free air between positive and negative carbon electrodes slowly burns away the positive carbon. The resultant gas fuels an extremely bright flame at the tip of the negative carbon, which licks upward toward the positive carbon. Both carbon electrodes slowly burn away during use and must be fed continually by a motor to maintain the proper gap between them. A carbon arc has greater lumen efficiency (lumens per watt) than incandescent lamps: about 46 lumens per watt compared to 26 for tungsten lamps. The studio arc light is a large Fresnel designed and used exclusively for filmmaking (Figure 3.37).

Table A.9 lists some specifications for studio arc lights. Today studio arc lights have been replaced by HMIs. Arc lights require a full-time operator because the carbons must be changed every 30 minutes and must be shut off whenever possible to save the carbons and prevent excess heating. The phrase, "Lights, camera, action," comes from the days when the lights were turned on immediately before each take. Arcs are noisy and make smoke. They aren't widely used except when the unique quality of their light is desired. An arc light makes very defined shadows and is used to simulate hard sunlight or moonlight. Many gaffers believe that its quality and color are the most pleasing of all sources.

Fluorescent Lights

Until relatively recently cinematographers regarded fluorescent lighting as a minefield of photographic headaches, virtually incompatible with motion picture photography. Fluorescents were associated with ghoulish green skin tones, poor color rendering, anemic light output, noisy humming ballasts, and the same shutter speed restrictions that exist with HMIs.

It took the innovations of a determined gaffer and his best boy to overcome these obstacles. Freider Hochheim and Gary Swink designed fixtures, ballasts, and lamps tailored to the needs of film production. Their company, Kino Flo, Inc., continues to make groundbreaking advances in the photographic applications of fluorescent technology. Various manufacturers now offer stand-mounted fluorescent fixtures with high-frequency, flicker-free ballasts (Table A.10), which operate with commercially available lamps. Kino Flo makes their own lights, which are high output and color correct (Table A.11). Cinematographers have discovered the positive qualities of fluorescent lights: lightweight fixtures that put out soft, controllable light that wraps around the features and creates a pleasing eye light. They can easily be built into sets when a fluorescent environment is called for, but can also be used purely as a low profile, soft lighting instrument.

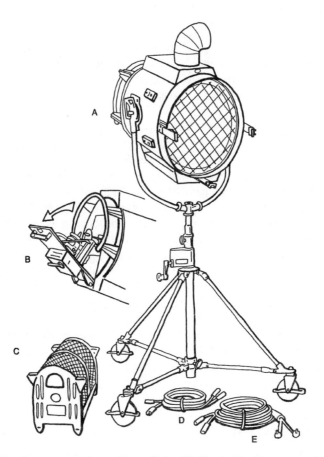

Figure 3.37 Components of a studio arc light: (A) Head with chimney attached. (B) Access to the carbons and internal mechanisms is gained by folding out the back of the unit. (C) Power grid. (D) Head cable. (E) Grid cable with lug connectors. (Equipment courtesy of Mole-Richardson Co., Hollywood, CA.)

High-Frequency Ballasts

High-frequency ballasts bypass the problem of intensity fluctuation by converting a 60-Hz input frequency to between 20,000 and 40,000 Hz. The period of time between the off and on pulse of each cycle is so short that the illuminating phosphors do not decay in light output. The phosphors are essentially flicker-free. When shooting on constructed sets, such ballasts are used for built-in fluorescent light fixtures. However, when filming in older locations, existing banks of fluorescents will usually not have electronic high-frequency ballasts, and therefore fewer shutter speeds and shutter angles can be used. Commercial electronic ballasts are becoming more common. In a modern installation, open up the fixture to check the ballast type.

Color-Correct Fluorescent Tubes

Duro-test manufactures standard tubes suitable for color photography, Optima 32 (3200K) and Vita-lite (5500K). Unlike other commercial manufacturers, these tubes incorporate wide-band phosphor crystals and produce close to correct color rendering. Fluorescent fixtures (other than Kino Flo) typically use these tubes. When filming in a location with ceiling fluorescents, the lighting crew will typically replace all the existing fluorescent tubes with color-correct tubes.

Kino Flo

Kino Flo makes fluorescent lighting systems specifically for film production work, utilizing various types of lamps, fixtures, and ballasts (See Table A.11, Appendix A). Kino Flo tubes are specially designed to be used with Kino Flo high-output ballasts. The Kino Flo KF55 (5500K) and the KF32 (3200K) broad-spectrum fluorescent lamps are engineered to correspond to the spectral sensitivity curves of color film emulsions. Kino Flo tubes mix wide-band and narrow-band phosphor crystals with rare earth elements. The phosphor blend displays a complete spectrum of light (Color Rendering Index of 95) and no green spike when operated with Kino Flo high-output ballasts.

Optima 32s, which have very little green when powered by a conventional ballast, will require magenta correction when powered with a Kino Flo high-output ballast. High-output ballasts overdrive the fluorescent tube, which raises the color temperature and green output.

Kino Flo also supplies special green and blue tubes for lighting green and blue screens. Red, pink, and yellow tubes are also available, which are great for decorating a set with neon-like lines of light. Kino Flo tubes are safety-coated to make the lamps more durable and to ensure that no glass fragments, mercury, or harmful phosphors will be released if the lamp should break. Table E.2 (Appendix E) lists all Kino Flo tubes. Figure E.1 illustrates base types.

Kino Flo ballasts run at high frequency (25kHz), resulting in flicker-free operation at any frame rate or shutter setting. The lights turn on instantly, even when cold, requiring no warm-up time. Kino Flos can be dimmed about one stop on a variac dimmer. Kino Flo dimming ballasts can reduce output to 3% without flicker. (You cannot use an electronic SCR dimmer or household resistance-type dimmer with a fluorescent light.) Kino Flo ballasts are lightweight and run silently.

Kino Flo 120V Systems

Portable Fixtures   Kino Flo fixtures come in various configurations and sizes: four-bank systems, double-bank systems, and single systems each have their own corresponding ballast and head cable (Figure 3.38).

All fixtures come in 4-ft., 2-ft., and 15-in. sizes. Each fixture is equipped with a lightweight egg-crate louver that controls the spread (and slightly reduces the intensity) of light. The fixture has a snap-on mounting plate for attachment to a C-stand (Figure 3.39), but because the fixtures are lightweight, they can also be taped or stapled into place.

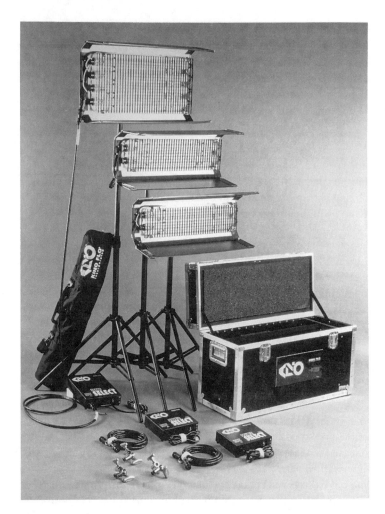

Figure 3.38 Kino Flo "Interview Kit" illustrates the 2-ft. four-bank, and double-bank fixtures with stands, mounting adapters, and traveling case.

Wall-O-Lite   The Wall-o-lite is an amazingly bright fixture with ten 4-ft. lamps and a built-in ballast (Figure 3.40).

It puts out about as much light as a 2.5 HMI Fresnel bounced. This fixture has proved especially useful for lighting matte screens (green screens or blue screens). It creates a broad, even light, which is necessary for matte work. Kino Flo provides green (560 nanometer) or blue (420 nanometer) tubes that are extremely bright in a selected part of the spectrum and will fully saturate the matte color. Up to 50 Wall-o-lite fixtures can be jumpered together and controlled on a single three-position remote switch (10 lamps/OFF/5 lamps).

Figure 3.39 The removable mounting plate.

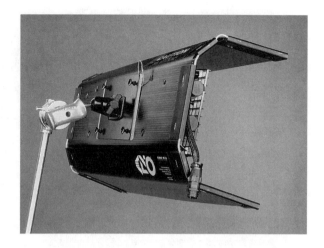

Figure 3.40 Wall-o-lite.

Figure 3.41 Rear-lit blue screen for matte photography.

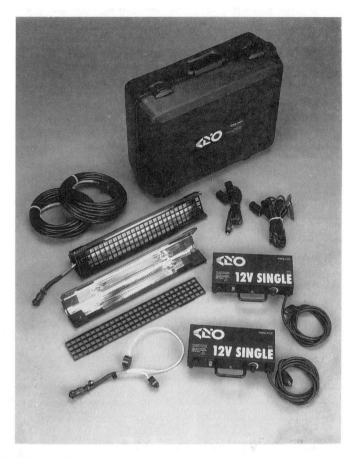

Figure 3.42 12V DC single kit; 15-in. fixture, 12V DC ballast, cigarette lighter adapter, and clip-on car battery cables.

Big Foot Fixtures Kino also makes 8 ft. and 6 ft. fixtures that run on the high-output *Mega-ballast*. Double- and single-tube fixtures are available.

Studio Fixtures The Kino Flo studio fixtures (Image 80, 40, and 20) are designed for studio applications and green and blue screen work. They are yoke-mounted with metal housings and built-in ballasts. They come in 8-tube (4-ft.), 4-tube (4-ft.) and 4-tube (2-ft.) fixtures.

Trans-Panel System Figure 3.41 shows the Kino Flo trans-panel lighting system. This system of modular 12-tube panels creates a wall of even, bright light for back-lighting a translight or blue-screen.

The system is powered from a master controller, which can control up to 44 panels. The controller can dim the panels up to four stops with no change in color output. A translight hung as close as 3 ft. in front of the panels will be evenly illumi-

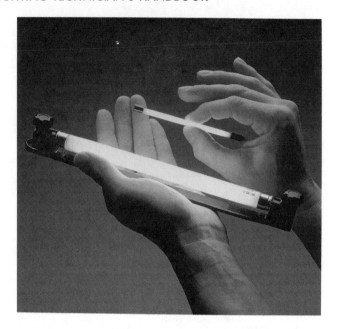

Figure 3.43 Nine-inch Mini-flo (reflector and door removed) and 4-in. micro-flo tube Kino Flo lights. (Photos courtesy Kino Flo, Inc., Sun Valley, CA)

nated to about 640FC. For blue screen work, an 8-ft. separation is recommended. KF55 lamps (420 nanometer) are used to light a rear-transmission blue screen.

12V DC Kits: 12V Single, Mini-Flo, and Micro-Flo

Kino Flo makes a variety of 12V DC fixtures that can run on battery power or a 12V transformer power supply (120V AC or 220V AC).

12-Volt Single The 12V single ballast can power T-12, T-10, or T-8 lamps, ranging in size from 15 in. up to 4 ft. (Figure 3.42).

In a car or elevator where AC power is not available, you can run any of the standard Kino fixtures from a 12V DC battery. With the proper adapter cables, you can power a standard four-bank fixture from four 12V ballasts. The 9-, or 15-in. lamps are ideal in a night-time car scene to give the appearance of dashboard light. The Kino Flo 12V kit includes two 15-in. single-tube fixtures, dimmable ballasts, all the usual accessories, cigarette lighter connector, and spring clamps to connect to a car battery.

Mini-Flo and Micro-Flo The 12V Mini-Flo system is a 9-in. lamp with a corresponding fixture, ballast, and head cable. The Micro-Flos are tiny 6-in. and 4-in. tubes, thinner than a pencil (either tungsten or daylight) (Figure 3.43).

Their size makes them uniquely suited for many special applications, such as to light a face inside a space suit helmet. They are commonly used for tabletop and miniature photography.

Using Kino Flo Fixtures

The component parts of each fixture (fixture with barn doors, reflector, egg-crate louver, lamp harness, and tubes) can be disassembled and employed as needed (Figure 3.44): bare tubes (taped under a bar counter, for example), bare tubes taped to a reflector for greater light output, or the assembled fixture with or without the egg-crate louver, depending what takes priority, control of side spill or maximizing light output.

Bare tubes can be neatly mounted to a surface using plastic cable ties and adhesive cable tie mounts (and staples), or by applying double-stick tape to the tube.

You can order a special Y-splitter, which splits a four-bank cable (or two-bank cable) into single harnesses, so you can mount tubes end to end, for example. Be sure to order additional single harnesses and cables with the splitter.

Ballast Features

Standard Ballasts Kino Flo standard ballasts (4-Bank, Double, and Single) provide a three-position toggle selection switch (all lamps/off/half the lamps).

Select Ballasts Kino Flo *Select* ballasts (4-Bank, Double-bank, and Single) feature an additional high-output/standard-output toggle switch. Use the high-output setting for 4-ft lamps and the standard setting for 2-ft. and 15-in. lamps. Operating 2 ft. and 15 in. lamps in the HO setting will cause the color temperature and green output to be higher. The Select ballast also features more advanced electronics than the standard ballast, which gives it more reliable and consistent performance.

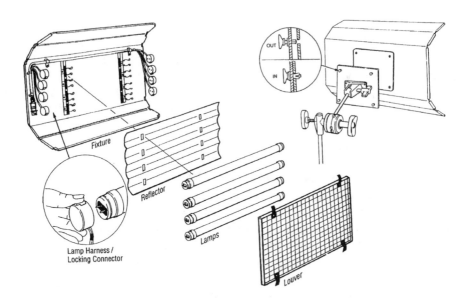

Figure 3.44 The component parts of the portable Kino Flo fixtures and how they fit together. (Photos courtesy of Kino Flo, Inc., Sun Valley, CA.)

Dimming Ballasts Kino Flo *Dimming ballasts* (4-Bank, Double-Bank, and Single) feature a slider to adjust light output in a full range with no change in color temperature. A *trim* adjustment allows you to set and return to a particular setting easily, and to turn the lamp on at a preset level. Dimming ballasts provide a jack for attachment of a remote cable. Multiple dimming ballasts can be wired to and controlled by a standard dimmer board.

Slimline Select and Mega-Ballast The Kino Flo *Slimline Select* powers single-pin 6-ft. and 8-ft. tubes. The Kino Flo *Mega-ballast* powers 6-ft. and 8-ft. fixtures only (4-Bank, Double-Bank, and Single).

Troubleshooting

From time to time one or more tubes in a fixture will not light. The problem could be in the ballast, the lamp harness, or the lamps. The best way to proceed is as follows:

1. Double check that the ballast is hot — plugged into a live 120V AC service.
2. Check that the extension is properly connected at the ballast and harness.
3. Check that the harnesses are properly secured to the tubes and that the head cables are fully connected at both ends. Harness connectors are color-coded; the same color must be on both ends of the lamp.
4. Switch the ballast to full ON position. Note which lamps do not work, and try another ballast. If the same lamps still do not fire, change out those lamps. If the lamps still do not fire, change out the harness.

When renting Kino Flos in large numbers, it is prudent to include a few extra back-up four-bank ballasts (one for every 12 systems). Newer Kino Flo ballasts have a latch-up feature to protect the solid state circuitry from abuse during operation. However, many older style ballasts are still in circulation. Single and double systems generally do not require back-up ballasts.

Kino Flo portable fixtures are made with wire barn-door "hinges" (the flexible metal rods at the corners of the doors), which are made to be disposable. If one breaks, it can be easily replaced by removing the end screw, pulling out the broken wire, and replacing it with a length of good wire.

Some Additional Notes About Fluorescent Lights

Effect of Temperature

Fluorescent lamps are sensitive to extremes of temperature. Standard fluorescents are designed for operation above 50°F. Fluorescents operating on high-frequency ballasts will operate in temperatures below freezing. With all fluorescents, even those operating on high-output ballasts, the operating temperature affects both the color and the intensity of the light. In freezing conditions, the high-intensity ballast can get the tube started, but it takes a few minutes for the tube to reach the proper color and output. In hot temperatures, or if the tubes are enclosed in an unventilated space, the color may wander toward the blue-green end of the spectrum, and additional color correction may be needed.

Effect of Voltage Shifts

Voltage shifts do not appreciably affect the color temperature of fluorescents. If the voltage is *too* low, however, the light will go out completely or will not start. A 10% decrease in power will yield a 10% decrease in light output.

Calculating Power Needs

Fluorescent lights are generally of nominal wattage and therefore pose no special power demand concerns. However, when a large number (hundreds) of fluorescent lights are to be powered, one must keep in mind some additional factors. The wattage rating on a fluorescent tube is the power consumed by the tube alone. The ballast typically consumes an additional 10% to 20%. Thus, a 40W tube actually consumes as much as 48W of power (20% of 40 = 8, 40 + 8 = 48). In addition, power factor must be taken into account (reactive current and power factor are explained in Chapter 8).

CHAPTER 4

Stands and Rigging

We constantly need to hang lights in awkward places, so naturally, over the years, ways have been devised to secure a light almost anywhere.

Stands

Stands come in two basic types. *Baby* stands (on the East Coast they call them *750* stands) have 5/8 in. stud that fits into the baby receptacle found on most lights of baby-2k or smaller (Figure 4.1).

Junior stands (East Coast *2k* stands) have a 1-1/8 in. receptacle that takes the junior stud found on larger lights (see Figure 4.3). Stands of both types come in short, "low boy" versions as well as the standard height with two-risers or three-risers. Stands may be made of aluminum, which is lightweight, or of steel, which is stronger.

Baby Stands

The most versatile baby stand for location work is a steel three-riser stand with a mountain leg (See Figure 4.1). The legs can be quickly retracted by loosening the T-handle on the top collar and pulling up. The mountain leg makes it easy to level the stand when it is placed on uneven ground, on a stair, over the edge of a curb, or leaning against a set wall (Figure 4.2).

Rolling Stand   Baby rolling stands are convenient when working in the studio on a level surface. Many rolling stands have brakes that snap into a locked position.

Blade Stand   Blade stands are extremely lightweight, which is their one advantage. They are also somewhat flimsy and unstable. They are best used with small lights. It is wise to stabilize a lightweight stand by hanging a small shotbag on the lower T-handle.

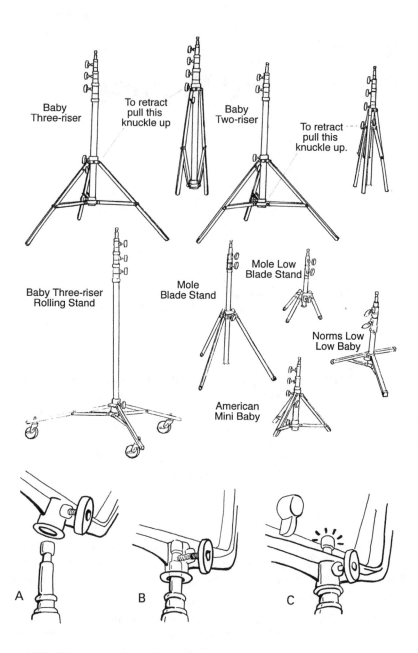

Figure 4.1 To retract the legs of most stands, loosen the upper tie-down knob and pull the legs up and in. With some stands the legs retract by loosening the bottom tie-in knob and sliding that collar upward. A 5/8 in. baby stud inserts into the receptacle on a fixture (A). When mounting the light, the stud should be flush with the receptacle and not stick through. This ensures that the T-handle is engaging the indent of the stud (B). Also some lights (notably the baby junior) will not tilt properly if the stud sticks through (C).

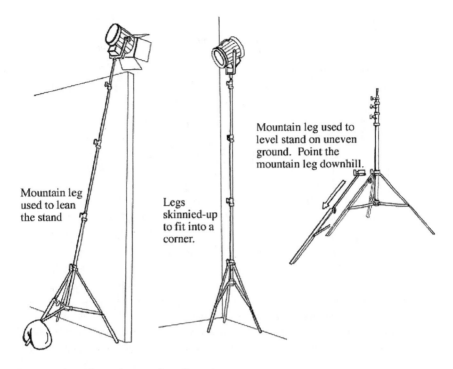

Figure 4.2   Alternative stand configurations.

Low Stands   When you need a light placed low, a mini-baby (22 to 50 in.) or preemie (31 to 70 in.) stand comes in handy. Table 4.1 lists the basement and top floor for many common stands.

Junior Stands

Combo   The junior combo stand is so named because it was designed to handle both lighting units and reflector boards. Larger fixtures, Studio 2k and larger, have a 1-1/8 in. junior stud. A typical two-riser combo has a maximum height of 11 ft. A three-riser combo has a maximum height of 14 ft. Figure 4.3 illustrates the junior stand and some common stand accessories: the baby pop-up stud, the angled drop-down offset, and the baby spud adapter.

Low Boy   The minimum height of a typical combo stand is 48 in. If the light must be lower than that, you need a low boy junior stand, which has a minimum height of around 33 in. If you need to mount a light lower than 33 in., you'll have to use a turtle stand or T-bone.

T-Bones and Turtle Stands   A T-bone is simply a metal T fitted with a junior receptacle (Figure 4.4). A T-bone can be nailed or screwed into place in green beds or on parallels.

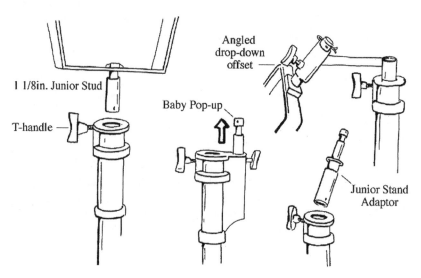

Figure 4.3 The 1-1/8 in. junior stud fits into the receptacle on the stand. The T-handle should engage the indented part of the stud. Some stands have a baby pop-up, which allows the junior stand to support either a baby or junior fixture. An angled drop-down offset allows a light or reflector to hang lower than the lowest height of the stand. The 45° angle holds the light away from the stand. In the absence of a baby pop-up, as stand adapter can be used.

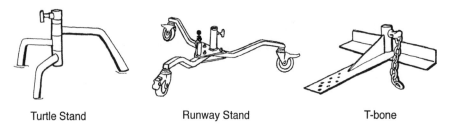

Turtle Stand   Runway Stand   T-bone

Figure 4.4

It sits flat on the floor, providing a low position for larger lights. A turtle stand is nothing more than three legs joined in the center to a junior receptacle. Matthew's C+ stand has removable legs, which serve as a turtle stand. The riser section of the C+ stand can be used as a stand extension. Matthews and other manufacturers also make wheeled turtle stands. Matthews calls theirs a *runway* stand.

Mombo Combo   A mombo combo is a very substantial, four-riser, steel stand with a very wide base (no wheels), which allows a maximum height of more than 26 ft.

Table 4.1 Stands

Name	Type	Risers	Min Height	Max	RM Leg	Brand
Low Baby Stands						
Runway Base Only		0	11"	11"		Matthews
Mini Preemie	St	2	20"	39"		Matthews
Preemie baby	Al	2	31"	5'10"		Matthews
Mini Baby	St/Al	2	22"	50"	X	American
Low Low Baby	Al	2	20"	3'3"		Norms
Low Hefty Baby	Al	2	33"	5'7"		Norms
Baby Stands						
Steel Maxi	St	3	34"	10'		Matthews
Beefy baby standard	Al	2	37"	8'3"		Matthews
Beefy baby 3-riser	Al	3	45"	12'	X	Matthews
Baby 2-riser	St/Al	2	40"	9'4"	X	American
Baby 3-riser	St/Al	3	44"	12'5"	X	American
Baby Light 2-riser	Al	2	44"	9'4"		Norms
Baby Light 2-riser	St	2	52"	10'6"		Norms
Hefty Baby 2-riser	Al	2	47"	9'10"	X	Norms
Hefty Baby 3-riser	Al	3	50"	12'10"	X	Norms
Low Jr. Stands						
Low Boy	St	2	33"	6'9"	X	Matthews
Low Boy	Al	2	37"	6'9"	X	Matthews
Low Combo 1-riser	St	1	29"	4'0"	X	American
Low Combo 2-riser	St	2	32"	5'6"	X	American
Low Combo 2-riser	St	2	33"	5'7"	X	American
Low Boy		2	36"	5'8"	X	Norms
Junior Stands						
Combo	St	2	48"	11'	X	Matthews
Sky High	St	3	52"	14'	X	Matthews
Mombo Combo	St	4	76"	27'	X	Matthews
Light Duty Combo	St	2	48"	10'5"	X	American
Heavy Duty 2-riser	S	2	50"	11'3"	X	American
Heavy Duty 3-riser	St	3	51"	14'3"	X	American
Alum Combo 2-riser	St/Al	2	48"	10'3"	X	American
Alum Combo 3-riser	St/Al	3	51"	13'9"	X	American
Mombo Combo	St	4	5'8"	23'5"	X	American
Standard		2	54"	11'2"	X	Norms
Sky High		3	58"	13'	X	Norms
Sky High	Al	3	61"	13'	X	Norms

Notes: RM leg stands for Rocky Mountain leg. St/Al means the stand has steel legs and aluminum risers.

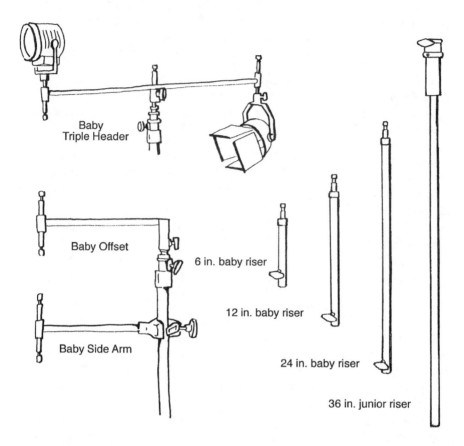

Baby Triple Header

Baby Offset

6 in. baby riser

12 in. baby riser

Baby Side Arm

24 in. baby riser

36 in. junior riser

Figure 4.5 Offsets, side arms, double-headers, and triple-headers are available in baby and junior sizes (babies are shown here).

Offsets, Side Arms, Extensions, and Right Angles

Offsets Figure 4.5 shows various types of baby offsets that can be used to put the position of the head out away from the stand.

They are useful when some obstruction, such as furniture or a set piece, prevent the stand from being placed under the light. Note that an offset or side-arm puts the stand off its center of balance. Use sandbags on the legs to counterweight.

Risers

Risers come in many sizes, typical sizes would be 6, 12, 18, and 24 in. A riser is a handy piece of hardware when a light mounted to a plate or clamp is not quite high enough. A 36 in. junior stand extension essentially adds an additional riser to a stand. It can also be inserted into the receptacle on the dolly or the crane when a light is to ride with the camera.

Using Stands

- See Chapter 2, Checklist 2.3, for check-out procedure.
- "Righty tighty, lefty loosey." Lock-off knobs (T-handles) tighten when turned to the right (clockwise) and loosen when turned to the left.
- Extend the top riser first. If you extend the second riser first, you will raise the first riser out of your reach, and you'll look like a bonehead. One exception, if the light is heavy for the stand, you can add strength to the stand by not using the first riser, or only using part of it.
- Bag any raised stand. A good rule of thumb is one sandbag per riser. If the light is extended all the way up on a three-riser stand, you would use three bags. Place the sandbags on the legs so that the weight rests on the stand, not on the floor. If the grips are busy with other things, take care of it yourself.
- Get help when needed. As a rule, use two people to head up any light 5k or larger. Depending on the height of the stand and the awkwardness of its position, heading-up a 12k or Dino can require three or even four people. Don't hesitate to round up the other electricians and grips when you need them. It is poor judgment to bite off more than you can chew. A heavy light can get away from you and cause injury and damage. Moreover, handling large lights alone will tire you out before the day is over and, in a short time, is likely to lead to back and knee problems. I know too many people in their mid and late thirties who have done permanent damage by abusing themselves when they were younger. Lifting equipment is not a contest; the lighting crew works as a team.

Crank-Up and Motorized Stands

Crank-up stands provide a mechanical advantage needed for raising heavy lights. Table 4.2 gives the weights and weight capacities of crank-up and motorized stands. They have a chain-, cable-, or screw-driven telescoping extension system with a crank and clutch, so that the crank will not reverse and spin out of control under weight. Do not crank up a stand without some kind of weight on it, as this can cause problems in the inner mechanisms.

The Cine-Vator, Molevator, and similar motorized stands power the telescoping mechanism with an electrical motor that is operated by a single up/down toggle switch (Figure 4.6).

These stands can handle the heaviest lights made (up to 300 lbs.). The motor is usually 115V AC (at about 6 A) but can be 115V DC, 220V AC, or 220V DC.

- When rolling a large light on a crank stand or motorized stand, push the stand from the back with the swivel locks on the two rear tires unlocked and the front tire locked. Steer by pushing the back wheels left or right. If you put two tires in front, they can catch in a rut and the whole stand will tip over.
- When the stand is in place, prevent the stand from rolling by swiveling each wheel straight out from the stand and locking each swivel. Additionally, wedges in the tires and cup blocks under the tires will prevent them from turning (grip department).

Table 4.2   Weight Capacities of Crank-Up and Motorized Stands

	Floor	Ceiling	Capacity	Type
American				
Roadrunner 220	4'2"	11'3"	220 lbs.	Crank
Big Fresnel Lamp Stand (BFL)	4'2"	12'6"	300 lbs.	Motor
Matthews				
Lite Lift	4'1"	8'6"	85 lbs.	Crank
Crank-O-Vator	4'11"	12'	150 lbs.	Crank
Low Boy Crank-O-Vator	3'2"	5'5"	150 lbs.	Crank
Super Crank	5'9"	12'6"	200 lbs.	Crank
Cine-Vator	4'6"	12'	300 lbs.	Motor
Mole Richardson				
Folding Crank-up Litewate Stand	4'5"	10'	—	Crank
Molevator	5'1"	11'1"	250 lbs.	Motor

- Before raising the stand, make sure it is totally leveled with cup blocks, wedges, and apple boxes if necessary (grip department).
- Use your strong arm to turn the crank to raise and lower the light. Never release the clutch without having a good grip on the crank. If the crank gets away from you, there is a good chance you will not be able to get hold of it again before the lamp hits you in the head. There is also a good chance you'll hurt yourself trying to grab hold of the spinning crank. If you lose control, let go of the clutch and get out of the way of the light.

Grip Stands

For the most part, the grips' stands are used for flying overhead sets and setting flags, nets, and diffusion frames and so on. However, in special situations they are needed as light stands.

C-Stands

Q: How do you drive an electrician crazy?
A: Lock him in a small room with a C-stand.

The Century stand is a versatile, all-purpose, rigging gadget that is the centerpiece of the grip's equipment. Its component parts are like parts of an erector set, and rigging C-stands is a little-appreciated art form. Given enough C-stands and enough time, a grip could build a scale model of the Eiffel Tower. When a C-stand is used as a light stand, however, it becomes the electrician's responsibility (Figures 4.7 and 4.8).

We are straying into the domain of gripology. However, knowing grip techniques will save you much embarrassment; grips like nothing better than to heckle an electrician who is making a mess of a grip job.

- Place the longest leg under the extended arm. This helps stabilize the stand. Always sandbag the legs when putting weight on an extended arm (Figure 4.7).
- Work with gravity, not against it. When you are standing behind the stand with the arm pointing away from you, the knuckles should be on your right. In this way, when weight is put on the arm, gravity pulls the grip head clockwise, which tightens it. If the knuckle is on the left, the weight will eventually loosen the knuckle, and the whole rig will collapse (very bad form).
- Avoid configurations in which the back end of the arm sticks out, especially at eye level; it could hurt someone. There is almost always an alternative configuration that eliminates the hazard. If it's unavoidable, place a tennis ball or styrofoam cup on the end of the arm so people will see it.
- Place the sand bag on the top leg so that the weight is on the leg and not resting on the ground.

Figure 4.6 A Cine-Vator stand. (Photo courtesy of Matthews Studio Equipment, Burbank, CA.)

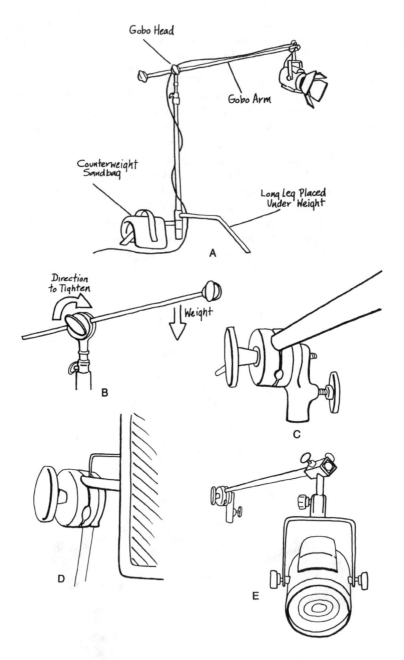

Figure 4.7 (A) A C-stand supporting a light fixture. (B) Orient the knuckle so that gravity tightens it (righty tighty). (C, D) The grip head accepts various sizes: a 5/8 in. hole for the gobo arm or a baby stud, a 3/8, 1/2, or 1/4 in. hole for nets and flags. (E) The light fixture shown uses a bar clamp adapter (used on furniture clamps) to attach the gobo arm. (Equipment courtesy of Concept Lighting, Sun Valley, CA.)

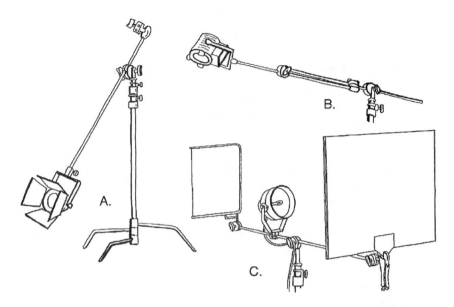

Figure 4.8 Some special uses for C-stands. (A) To place the lights in a low position. (B) To arm the lights out of action. Here (C) two gobo arms are coupled together. A bounce card like this uses a single stand to support the light, bounce card, and a net.

- Always place the C-stand on the "off-stage side" of the light — the outside, as viewed from the camera. This helps keep grip equipment out of the movie.
- When a lot of torque is placed in the gobo head, configure the stand so that the flag rests on the T-handle. Do not rely on the strength of the grip head alone.
- Take wind into account. When setting 4-by frames or flags in a wind, use a larger stand with a wide base, such as a combo stand. A C-stand does not handle big flags or frames well in any kind of wind.

Medium, Hi, and Hi-Hi Rollers

A medium roller stand is slightly taller than a junior combo, about 14 ft. maximum, and has wheels, which makes it easy to move around. The wheels have brakes that should be locked once the stand is placed. In addition to a junior receptacle, roller stands typically provide a 4 in. grip head for mounting overhead frames, large flags, and other grip gear. A hi-hi roller is especially useful when height is required; it has a maximum height of 20 ft.

Booms

Boom poles allow a fixture to be suspended over or behind the actors in places where it could not be mounted by other means. Booms vary in size and strength. The small ones mount on a baby stand and provide about a 4-ft. arm with almost as much counterweight length. The larger ones mount on a junior stand, have more length and more counterweight, and provide either a junior or a baby mount for the light. Sand-bags can be added for additional counterweight.

Stand Maintenance

Modern stands are made of stainless steel and aluminum. Stainless steel stands are extremely weather resistant. A well-made stand will not rust or corrode. When stands get muddy, they should be cleaned so that dirt does not get inside between the risers. Wipe each riser down with a rag or towel. If a riser starts to bind, lubricate with silicone spray.

Occasionally the Allen screws that secure the bonnet castings and the riser cast-ings to the tube parts of a stand get loose and the castings come off. It is a simple matter to push the castings back into place and tighten down the Allen screws. Be sure to keep the castings tight. If the casting comes off while you are raising a light, the riser will separate from the stand and you'll wind up balancing the light on a pole like an acrobat does with tea cups.

Rigging Hardware

Baby and Junior Nail-On Plates

A *nail-on plate*, also called a *wall plate* or *pigeon plate* (Figure 4.9), mounts to a surface with screws.

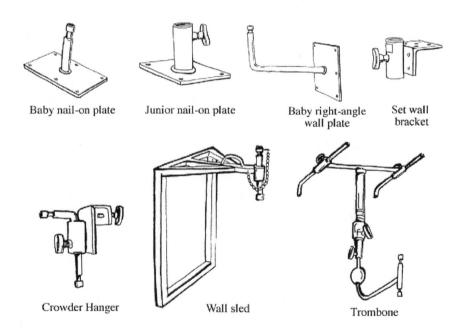

Baby nail-on plate	Junior nail-on plate	Baby right-angle wall plate	Set wall bracket

Crowder Hanger　　　　Wall sled　　　　Trombone

Figure 4.9 Plates and hangers for set walls.

Use a cordless electric drill with a Phillips bit and wood screws or drywall screws. The plate can be mounted to a horizontal surface, a wall, or a ceiling, but be sure you are screwing into something solid. If you are screwing into a set wall (usually 1/4 in. plywood), you will need to place a piece of cribbing on the other side of the wall to give the screws something to hold to.

The grips usually prepare several apple boxes with nail-on plates. When mounted on an apple box, a nail-on plate provides a stable lighting position that is handy for setting a light on the floor or on a counter top.

Set Wall Mounts

See Figure 4.9.

Set Wall Bracket   A set wall bracket is a right-angle plate that mounts to any right-angle corner, such as the top of a flat.

Crowder Hanger   A crowder hanger fits over the top of a door or on a 2-x 4 in. beam. It can be used with a baby adapter that provides two mounting positions, one above and one below the hanger.

Edge Plate Bracket   An edge plate bracket is similar to a crowder hanger. It is used to mount lights to the side edge of a green bed.

Wall Sled   A wall sled is suspended on rope from the top of a set wall. The weight of the light holds the sled in position against the wall without screws or tape. Wall sleds are made with either a junior or a baby mount.

Trombone   Like the crowder hanger, a trombone also fits over the top of the set, but it is adjustable to any width of wall. It provides an adjustable drop-down position for the light. Use a rubber ball on the telescoping arm to prevent it from scraping the wall. A trombone can have either a junior or a baby mount.

Clamps

C-Clamp   C-clamps (Figure 4.10) come in various sizes: 4, 6, 8, and 12 in. Each one has two baby studs or a 1-1/8 in. junior receptacle welded to it. The feet are either round and flat, or squared off. The squared metal clamps are designed for mounting to pipes.

With any of the clamps shown, to prevent puncturing or marring the beam and to increase the surface area of the clamp, insert two pieces of 1×3 in. cribbing between the clamp and the surface. Wrap the cribbing in duvatyne when it is important not to scratch the finish.

A common problem when mounting lights to a C-clamp on top of the set wall is that the light cannot be tilted down far enough. Use the angled stud on a C-clamp to get around this problem.

Furniture Clamp and Bar Clamp   A furniture clamp, or bar clamp, holds itself in place by applying pressure on either side of the beam to which it is attached. Furniture clamps come in various sizes (6, 12, 18, 24, and 36 in.); standard bar clamps

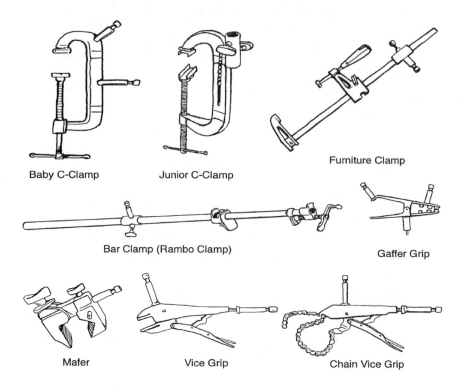

Baby C-Clamp   Junior C-Clamp   Furniture Clamp

Bar Clamp (Rambo Clamp)   Gaffer Grip

Mafer   Vice Grip   Chain Vice Grip

Figure 4.10 Clamps.

are 48 in., all of which are adjustable. Furniture clamps can be used to put lights on top of set walls, suspend them from ceiling beams, or mount them to furniture. As with C-clamps, use cribbing to increase the surface area of the clamp and to protect the surface to which you attach the clamp.

Gaffer Grip   A gaffer, or gator, grip is a spring clamp with rubber teeth. It is used to mount smaller lights to doors, pipes, and furniture.

Mafer   A mafer (pronounced *mayfer*) is a very strong and versatile mount, a favorite clamp-type mount. A cammed screw mechanism closes and opens the rubber-lined jaws. It can attach to any round surface from 5/8 in. to 2 in. in diameter and any flat surface from 1/16 in. to 1 in. thick. The baby stud snaps into place with a spring-loaded lock. The removable stud can be exchanged for accessories, such as a flex arm, a double-header offset arm, or a right-angle baby stud.

Vice Grip   The adjustable width of a vice grip provides a strong grip. As with any vice grips, the clamp is released by pressing the unlocking handle.

Chain Vice Grip A chain vice grip provides a very solid mount to any pipe up to 6 in. in diameter. It is used to mount a light to a pipe or small pillar. It is also often used to secure a stand to a standing post to hold the stand when there is no room to spread the legs. To make sure that the vice grip does not open, wrap tape around the handle after the chain vice grip is in place.

Grids and Green Beds

Pipe Clamp Pipe clamps (Figure 4.11) are used when hanging lights from an overhead pipe or grid. Pipe clamps come with a safety pin attached to the clamp with a safety chain. The cotter pin prevents the receptacle from slipping off the stud. Always use the safety pins when hanging lights.

In some instances it is possible to mount small lights to plumbing pipe on location, but be sure the pipe is not too soft, or you could rupture it. Wrap the pipe with a small piece of duvetyn to prevent the clamp from chipping the paint. Do not mount lights to fire sprinkler system pipes. It is against fire codes and a bad idea. If you rupture the pipe, it can flood the set.

Telescoping Stirrup Hanger To get a light lower than the height of the grid, use a telescoping hanger to lower it to the desired height. Hangers have a stirrup to which you attach a pipe clamp. They are also made with baby or junior receptacles instead of a stirrup.

Greens and Bazookas In most studio sound stages, wooden catwalks called *greens* or *decks* are suspended above the set to provide lighting positions. Along the edge of the greens, at 18 in. interval, are holes onto which a junior stud fits. A light may be inserted directly into this receptacle, or a *bazooka* can be inserted into the hole. A bazooka is like a one-riser stand with no legs. An L-shaped bracket fits over the catwalk's hand rail to support it.

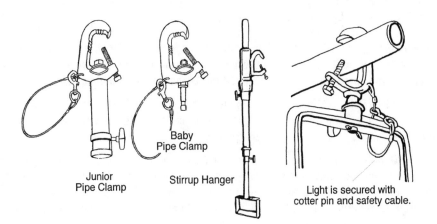

Junior
Pipe Clamp

Baby
Pipe Clamp

Stirrup Hanger

Light is secured with
cotter pin and safety cable.

Figure 4.11 Pipe clamps.

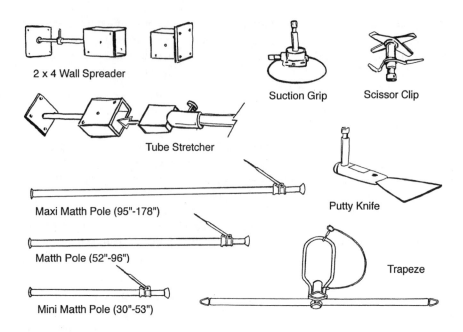

2 × 4 Wall Spreader

Suction Grip

Scissor Clip

Tube Stretcher

Maxi Matth Pole (95"-178")

Putty Knife

Matth Pole (52"-96")

Trapeze

Mini Matth Pole (30"-53")

Figure 4.12 Location rigging equipment.

Location Rigging Hardware

Wall Spreader and Tube Stretcher Wall spreaders (Figure 4.12) support lights by exerting pressure against two opposite walls or the floor and ceiling. A 2 × 4 in. or 2 × 6 in. piece of lumber creates the span. The hardware mounts to either end of the lumber and uses a threaded post to apply pressure against the walls. Lumber must be cut to fit the particular span needed.

A wall spreader can create a secure overhead beam of up to about 16 ft. from which lighting fixtures can be hung. With a long span be sure the hardware is aligned with wall studs, and screw the wall spreaders to the wall. A *tube stretcher* essentially adapts a wall spreader for use with speed-rail pipe instead of lumber.

Matth Pole A matth pole, or pole cat, is a smaller, lighter duty version of a wall spreader, especially useful in doorways or narrow halls. A Matth pole can support lightweight fixtures and grip equipment.

Suction Grip Suction grips of 4 or 6 in. can be used to affix small lighting units to nonporous surfaces, such as a window or a car hood. These grips generally use a cam to create the suction; they are not as strong as the larger pump-type grips. Suction grips come with baby studs only and should be limited to use with smaller lights.

Scissor Clip   A scissor clip is used to mount a light to the metal supports of a dropped ceiling. The scissor closes over the metal strips that support the ceiling tile. It is tightened in place by turning the 5/8 in. stud. Cables can be dressed above the ceiling or clipped to the metal strips with small grip clips.

Putty Knife   A putty knife can be wedged in a windowsill or door frame. It provides a baby stud for a small light fixture.

Trapeze   A trapeze is used to dead hang a light of any size from a rope. It provides a junior receptacle. Eyelets at each end of the trapeze are provided for guy wires, which prevent the light from turning once in position.

CHAPTER 5

Lighting Objectives and Methods

We've talked a lot about equipment. Let's put hardware aside for the moment and discuss the bigger question of what we want to accomplish with lighting and how we go about it. What are the considerations the Director of Photography (DP) and gaffer keep in mind when they make lighting decisions? To begin we'll look at some technical considerations: how to take and interpret light meter readings, how to use and control contrast, how to use the zone system to understand the placement of light and dark values, and what factors affect our working lighting levels for a given scene.

With these technical questions out of the way, we'll examine the conceptual basis the DP and gaffer use to generate ideas and devise schemes for lighting each scene. Each lighting decision begins with the consideration of four basic objectives: mood, visibility, naturalism, and composition. We arrive at the placement of each light, its direction, color, softness, and strength by considering how we wish to fulfill these objectives for a given lighting setup. Finally, we will look at lighting method: lighting the actor and lighting the scene.

A Brief Overview of Cinematography

An incident light reading can be expressed one of two ways, in foot-candles (FC) or in f-stops. Thinking in foot-candles has advantages when working with the lights, but ultimately it is the f-stop that is set on the camera, and most DPs think of their exposure range in terms of stops.

Foot-Candles

A light reading expressed in foot-candles is an absolute measurement of light level. A light reading expressed in f-stops depends on additional variables. A light meter, such as the digital Spectra Professional IV (Figure 5.1), tells you the intensity of light in foot-candles (Figure 5.2 shows the foot-candle scale). This meter also gives the reading as a working f-stop, taking into account the film ISO and shutter speed.

The advantage of working in foot-candles rather than f-stops is that a gaffer very quickly learns how many foot-candles he will get from a given light at a given

A

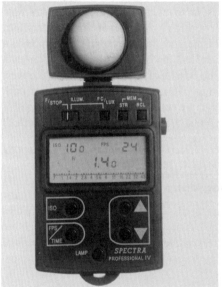

B

Figure 5.1 Light meters. (A) Spectra Professional incident light meter and (B) Spectra Professional IV digital/analog light meter. The latter reads incident or reflected light directly in f-stops and photographic illuminance in foot-candles or lux, with a range from 0.1 to 70,000 FC. (Photos courtesy of Spectra Cine, Inc., Burbank, CA.)

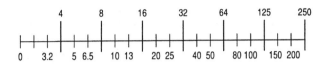

Figure 5.2 Actual numerical increments between standard foot-candle readings.

Figure 5.3 The actual numerical increments between f-stops.

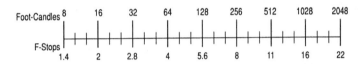

Figure 5.4 Comparison of foot-candles to f-stops with 320 ASA film.

distance (Table 5.1 lists some approximate data. Table A.14 is a more comprehensive list). If he is lighting to a given FC level, he will always call for the right light for the job. F-stops, on the other hand, do not correspond directly with light level. F-stop depends on a number of other variables — how the film stock is rated, what filters are being used, the frame-rate, and so on. It is not as straightforward to know what light fixture will give a particular f-stop.

F-Stops

F-stop settings are inscribed on the aperture ring of the lens of the camera by the manufacturer in standard increments: 1, 1.4, 2, 2.8, 4, 5.6, 8, 11, 16, and 22, as shown in Figure 5.3. The lower the f-stop, the larger the aperture, and the more light passes through the lens.

A light meter gives the f-stop by taking into account the film speed and exposure time. (For normal filming at a crystal sync speed of 24 fps, and with a standard 180° shutter, the exposure time is 1/48th of a second.) Many meters (e.g., Minolta) only read out in f-stops.

The f-stop scale in Figure 5.4 shows how foot-candles compare with f-stops for 320 ISO film. As you can see, the foot-candles double with each f-stop.

Each incremental f-stop cuts the light by a half. f/4 lets half as much light through as f/2.8, so it takes twice as many foot-candles at f/4 (64 FC) to get the same exposure as at f/2.8 (32 FC). Table 5.2 correlates f-stop to foot-candle level for all film speeds.

Table 5.1 Relative Strengths of Various Light Sources

Source	fc spot	fc flood
Direct Sunlight		6400–8600
Skylight on an overcast day		450–1800
Brute Arc at 30'	9000	1190
12k HMI at 30'	8250	500
9-lite PAR 64 at 30'	NS lens 3600	WF lens 450
2500 HMI PAR at 30'	NS lens 2880	WF lens 247
4000 HMI Fresnel at 30'	2305	247
10k at 30'	2465	460
5k baby senior at 30'	655	110
PAR 64 at 30'	VNS lens 560	MF lens 150
2k Junior at 20'	1000	130
1k baby at 20'	440	45
2k zip soft light at 10'		100
650 pepper at 10'	528	110
750 soft at 10'		30
200 Mini at 10'	195	25
100 pepper at 10'	55	23

Taking Readings with an Incident Light Meter

Incident light meters measure the amount of light falling on the face of the light meter. A *hemispherical light collector*, or *photosphere* (commonly known as "the ball"), collects light from the sides, top, and bottom as well as from the front. The reading is taken by holding the meter up in the position of the subject. When the ball faces the camera, the meter gives an average reading of the total amount of light falling on the subject as viewed from the camera.

Alternatively, by pointing the ball at the light source, you can read the amount of light from that source. However, keep in mind that when light hits the subject from the side or back, relative to the camera, less light is reflected toward the camera than when that light hits the subject from the front. Making allowance for this, the reading of a side-light can be accurately taken by turning the meter, splitting the angle toward camera.

When reading the output of individual lights, some cinematographers replace the hemispherical collector with a flat disk collector. The flat disk reads only light coming from the front. The disk is also used when photographing flat art work, such as a painting or front-lit titles.

Table 5.2 F-Stop versus Footcandles for Various Film Speeds

Incident light in footcandles
Frame rate: 24 fps
Exposure time: 1/50 sec (180 degree shutter opening)

ASA	f/1.4	f/2	f/2.8	f/4	f/5.6	f/8	f/11
25	100	200	400	800	1600	3200	6400
50	50	100	200	400	800	1600	3200
64	40	80	160	320	640	1250	2500
100	25	50	100	200	400	800	1600
125	20	40	80	160	320	640	1250
160	16	32	64	125	250	500	1000
200	13	25	50	100	200	400	800
320	8	16	32	64	125	250	500
400	6.4	13	25	50	100	200	400
500	5	10	20	40	80	160	320

When taking a reading, use your free hand to shade unwanted light off the photosphere. If you were reading the intensity of frontal lights, you would shade off any light coming from high backlights. The facial tones are not affected by the light hitting the back of the hair and shoulders, and if you do not shade the meter from the backlights, the reading will be incorrect. Backlight would be measured separately.

You can get an impression of the relative strengths of various lights, key and fill, for example, by shading the photosphere from one source, usually the key, and noting the change in the reading. You would use this technique to determine the *contrast ratio*.

When the reading is halfway between two numbers, it is called a *split*. For example, a 2.8/4 split would be halfway between f/2.8 and f/4. Increments between stops are also commonly expressed in thirds of a stop, so you might say "one third stop closed from a 4" to indicate that the aperture is one third of the way toward 5.6.

The use of terms such as *warm* and *cool* can cause confusion. To the gaffer, *warm 4* means that there is slightly more light than a 4 — the aperture is a high-side 4. To the camera assistant, a *warm 4* could mean to open the aperture from a 4, which would increase the light — a low-side 4. Establish common terminology with the people you're working with, and use clear language. Double-check if you are not sure what someone means.

f-Stops for the Electrician

When setting a light, an increase of one stop means doubling the light output. The gaffer might tell the electrician to "remove a double," "spot it in a double's worth," or "move the light in one stop closer." An experienced electrician can approximate by eye.

Contrast Ratio

Contrast ratio is used when the key light is angled so that the actor's face takes on a light side — the key side —and a shadow side — the fill side. The *contrast ratio* is the ratio of brightness of one to the other. The exposure is set for the key side. The darkness of the fill side greatly influences emotional tone of the image.

The *fill light* typically comes from the direction of the camera and fills in the whole face. The *key light* hits selected parts of the face, favoring one side. Therefore, to determine the contrast ratio you compare the light on the key side, which is key plus fill, to the shadow side, which is fill alone:

key + fill : fill alone

If key plus fill reads 120 FC and fill alone reads 60 FC, the contrast ratio is 120:60, or 2:1. A 2:1 ratio has a one-stop difference between key plus fill and fill alone. A 2:1 ratio is relatively flat, a typical ratio for ordinary television productions. It provides modeling while remaining bright and void of noticeably strong shadows. With a two-stop difference, or 4:1 ratio, the fill side is distinctly darker and paints a more dramatic, chiaroscuro style. For most normal situations, the contrast ratio is kept somewhere between 2:1 and 4:1. A three-stop difference, or 8:1 ratio, puts the fill side in near darkness, just barely leaving detail in the shadow areas. A bright, sunny day typically has between a 6:1 and 9:1 ratio, requiring the addition of fill light to lower the contrast ratio.

Contrast Viewing Glasses

A contrast viewing glass is a dark-tinted glass that typically hangs around the gaffer's neck like a monocle. By viewing the scene through the glass, the gaffer can evaluate the relative values — highlights and shadow areas. The glass darkens the scene so that the highlights stand out clearly, and shadow areas sink into exaggerated darkness. The glass helps evaluate if a particular highlight is too bright or a shadow too dark. On the other hand, if nothing stands out when viewed through the contrast glass, the scene has gotten too flat and monotonic; you might want to reduce the fill level, flag or net light off the backgrounds, and find places to add highlights. Contrast glasses are available in various strengths which are meant to approximate the contrast characteristics of different film stocks. The glass becomes ineffective when it is held to the eye long enough for the eye to adjust to it. Encircle the glass with your hand so that your hand forms a light-tight seal around your eye. Use the rest of your hand to shade the contrast glass from flare. You can also evaluate contrast without the aid of a contrast glass by doing it the old-fashioned way, by squinting.

Gaffers also frequently use a contrast glass to check the aim of the lights. By positioning oneself on the actors' marks, a gaffer can center the aim of the light fixtures (without blinding oneself) by viewing each light through the dark glass. Similarly, a contrast glass is used to view the movement of clouds in front of the sun on days with intermittent cloud cover.

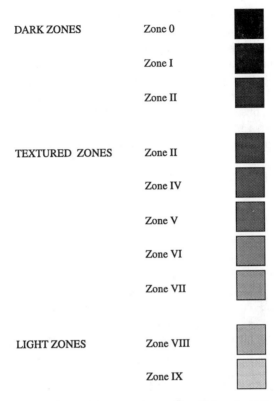

DARK ZONES	Zone 0
	Zone I
	Zone II
TEXTURED ZONES	Zone III
	Zone IV
	Zone V
	Zone VI
	Zone VII
LIGHT ZONES	Zone VIII
	Zone IX

Figure 5.5 The eleven values of the zone system. Zone X is pure white. It is not shown here. (From Chris Johnson, *The Practical Zone System: A Simple Guide to Photographic Control.* Boston: Focal Press, 1986, p. 31. Reproduced with permission of Focal Press.)

Film Latitude and the Zone System

The human eye can see detail in a much wider range of contrast than film emulsion. Although a person looking at a scene may see detail in every shadow and every highlight, on film anything too dark or too bright relative to the chosen exposure starts to lose definition as it approaches the extremes of the film's latitude. Details disappear into obscurity, and objects become either more and more bleached out, or increasingly lost in blackness.

It is helpful to think of the tones in a black-and-white picture. Between pure black and pure white there is a range of *values*, shades of gray that define the picture. The goal in choosing the exposure and in illuminating the scene is to place those values so that they will be rendered on film as the cinematographer has envisioned them.

Ansel Adams, the American still photographer, invented the zone system as a tool for understanding how the values in a scene will be rendered on film. There are eleven zones, as shown in Figure 5.5. Zone 0 is pure black and zone X is pure white. Each zone is one stop lighter than the last.

The range of brightness and darkness in which film emulsion can capture an image is known as its *latitude*. Each film emulsion has its own latitude characteristics within this ten-stop range. Cinematographers must therefore be familiar with the response of different film stocks.

Zone V, middle gray, is a very important value for determining exposure. Middle gray is 18% reflective and is commonly called *18% gray*. An incident light meter works by defining this midpoint in the latitude of the film. It gives an exposure reading that will make a middle-gray object appear middle gray on screen. When you define the exposure of middle gray, all the other values fall into place (to the extent of the film's latitude). On the outer edges of the exposure latitude, the image begins to lose detail and textured areas become less defined until, at the extremes of the scale (zones I and IX), no detail is visible and (zones 0 and X) only pure black and pure white.

Zone Appearance on Film

0   Total black. With a film stock that holds blacks well, the blacks on the edge of the frame merge with the black curtains surrounding the screen.

I   Threshold of tonality, but with no texture.

II   First suggestion of texture. Deep shadows represent the darkest part of the frame that still shows some slight detail.

III Average dark materials and low values, showing adequate texture.

IV   Average dark foliage, dark stone, or sun shadow. Normal shadow value for white skin in sunlight.

V   Middle gray (18% reflectance). Clear northern sky near sea level, dark skin, gray stone, average weathered wood.

VI   Average white skin value in sunlight or artificial light. Light stone, shadows on snow, and sunlit landscapes.

VII Very light skin, light gray objects, average snow with acute side lighting.

VIII Whites with texture and delicate values. Textured snow, highlights on white skin.

IX   White without texture, approaching pure white. Snow in flat sunlight.

X   Pure white. Spectral reflections, such as sun glints or a bare light bulb.

The way the cinematographer lights the set and sets the exposure determines the various values of the scene. Normally the actor's face is lit at exposure (though there are lots of situations where underexposure or overexposure are also appropriate and perhaps more expressive). The intensity of backlights, kicker lights, backgrounds, practical lights, windows, and so on must be manipulated to place their relative intensity in the zone desired. A spot meter can be used to measure and compare reflective values, but with practice one mostly balances levels by eye.

To give a practical example, suppose that the exposure outside a room with windows is five stops brighter than inside the room. If the aperture is set for the interior exposure, all details in the exterior portion of the image will fall into zone X and will be completely bleached out; the edges of the windows will likely get "blownout," with soft fringes around them. A compromise somewhere between the exterior and the interior exposures is not much better; the interior will still be very dark and muddy (zone III) and the exterior will be hot (zone VIII). The lighting must bring the outside and the inside exposures closer together.

To look natural, the exterior should be brighter than the interior, but by two or three stops, not by five. To close the gap you could reduce the exterior exposure two stops by gelling the windows with .6 neutral-density gel; you could light the inside, bringing it up to a level that is two stops less than the outside exposure; or you could combine these techniques.

Negative film stocks tend to have greater latitude in overexposure than they do in underexposure. As a general rule, a neutral-gray object can be overexposed by as much as four stops and underexposed by up to about three stops before it becomes lost, either washed out or lost in dark shadow.

Reversal film stocks have the opposite response; they have greater latitude in underexposure, and they lose definition faster in overexposure. Reversal stocks tend to be more contrasty and have less latitude in general than negative stocks. Similarly, video cameras have narrow latitude; typically detail is well rendered only within a four- or five-stop range.

Spot Meters

A spot meter (Figure 5.6) is a reflected light meter with a very narrow field of acceptance (less than 2°). An incident meter reads the amount of light hitting the light meter, and a reflected meter reads the amount of light reflected back from the subject.

The reading depends on the reflectance of the object as well as the amount of light. From behind the camera, the DP or gaffer can sight through the meter and pick

Figure 5.6   Minolta Spotmeter F. (Photo courtesy of Minolta Corp., Cypress, CA.)

Table 5.3 Spot Meter Readings. Reflectance and f-Stops

	O	I	II	III	IV	V	VI	VII	VIII	IX	X

Aperture Setting	f-stop	O	I	II	III	IV	V	VI	VII	VIII	IX	X
1.0		—	—	—	.5	.7	1.0	1.4	2.0	2.8	4	>5.6
1.4		—	—	.5	.7	1.0	1.4	2.0	2.8	4	5.6	>8
2.0		—	.5	.7	1.0	1.4	2.0	2.8	4	5.6	8	>11
2.8		.5	.7	1.0	1.4	2.0	2.8	4	5.6	8	11	>16
4		.7	1.0	1.4	2.0	2.8	4	5.6	8	11	16	>22
5.6		<1.4	1.4	2.0	2.8	4	5.6	8	11	16	22	>32
8		<2.0	2.0	2.8	4	5.6	8	11	16	22	32	>44
11		<2.0	2.8	4	5.6	8	11	16	22	32	44	>64
16		<4	4	5.6	8	11	16	22	32	44	64	>88
22		<5.6	5.6	8	11	16	22	32	44	64	88	>128

out any spot in the scene she wants to measure. By taking readings of various areas of the scene, she can compare the exact reflectances of face tones, highlights, and shadows.

Digital spot meters typically display readings in either f-stops or EV (exposure value) units. Some meters display readings only in EV units; the corresponding f-stop is found using the conversion dial on the meter. Table 5.3 shows how spot meter readings correspond to reflectance. The f-stops listed down the left side of the table represent the aperture setting on the camera lens. The zones across the top of the table indicate the actual reflectance, which corresponds to spot meter readings taken off various areas of the composition.

EV units are handy because they put reflectance value on a linear scale in one-stop increments. Each EV number represents a one-stop difference in value from the last. It eliminates the mental gymnastics involved in counting on the f-stop scale. For example, if a skin tone reads f/8, and a highlight reads f/45, how many stops brighter is the highlight? Before you start counting on you fingers, let's ask the same question in EV: The skin tone reads EV 10, the highlight EV 15; it's easy, the difference is five stops. You can even set the ASA on the spot meter so that EV 5 represents the f-stop on the lens. By so doing you calibrate the meter to read out in zones; EV 0–10 equal zones 0–X. EV readings are not affected by the shutter speed setting of the meter, only the ASA.

A great many DPs rely almost exclusively on their spot meter for light readings. Knowing that the reflectance of average Caucasian skin is about zone VI and one stop lighter than 18% gray (zone V), the DP can base his f-stop on a spot reading taken off an actor's face or his own outheld fist. The DP makes the necessary one-stop compensation mentally.

When reading the reflectance of white skin, the reading will be a half to one and a half stops brighter than the setting on the lens. Brown and olive skin falls around zone V, and dark brown and black skin values fall between zone II and IV. When lighting and exposing black skin, the shininess of the skin plays a larger role in determining the light value than it does with lighter skin. Reflective glints off black skin may range up into zone VI or higher. There is a tremendous range of tonal values in human skin that the cinematographer observes and takes into account. You can find out the exact reflectance of a particular actor by comparing the reading of the face to that of a gray card or one's own hand.

A spot meter is particularly handy for measuring naturally luminescent sources, such as television screens, table lamps, illuminated signs, stained glass windows, neon lights, or the sky during sunrise and sunset. It is also handy for getting readings on objects that are inaccessible or far away.

Light Level

A single parameter that greatly affects all of a gaffer's major decisions is the amount of light the DP will want to film a scene. One DP I have worked with likes to shoot ASA 50 film at a f/4 or f/5.6, requiring a light level of 400 to 600 foot-candles. To do this requires many large HMI units, heavy 4/0 cable, many large power plants, and lots of hard-working hands. Another DP shoots ASA 500 film with a very low f-stop, requiring only about 32 foot-candles of illumination. For this the biggest light needed is a 2k or baby, and the biggest cable is banded #2 cable. The choice of light level affects everything: what lights will be ordered, the power requirements, and the time and manpower needed.

Film Speed

A DP's choice of film stock depends on many factors, including the subject matter of the film, the director's ideas about how it should look, the types of locations, the need for matching with other stocks (matte work and opticals), and his own style of lighting and personal preferences about grain and color.

As illustrated in the examples above, the *speed* of the film, or ISO (also termed ASA or EI) is the primary determinant of light level. A high-speed film emulsion is very light sensitive and requires little light to gain an exposure. Slower film stocks require more light but have less apparent grain, finer resolution, and more deeply saturated colors.

The choice of film stock also affects the look of the lighting. If a slow film stock is used in an interior scene, a fairly drastic increase in light level is required, virtually replacing all natural light with brighter artificial sources. The large lights must very often be hung above the set, giving limited realistic lighting angles. Faster film stocks and lenses enable a more subdued lighting approach with fewer and smaller artificial lights brought to bear. The small lights are easier to hide, allowing more realistic angles for the light. The cinematographer can use existing light to a greater extent.

Optimizing Lens Characteristics

Lenses tend to have the greatest clarity and definition in the middle of the f-stop scale, between f/4 and f/8. Some loss of quality occurs at the ends of the scale. For this reason, many cinematographers ask for sufficient foot-candles to work in the center of the scale. Also, because lens characteristics change very slightly at different f-stops and for simplicity of lighting, DPs often prefer to shoot all the shots for a particular sequence at the same f-stop.

Depth of Field

Depth of field is the amount of depth that will appear in focus. As the iris is opened up to lower f-stops, the depth of field decreases. (Depth of field also decreases with an increase in the focal length and with a decrease in the subject's distance to the lens).

Depth of field is directly proportional to the f-stop. If the DP wants shallow focus with a given lens, he needs to use a low f-stop (f/2 or f/2.8), and therefore low light levels. If he wants to have lots of depth, he needs a higher f-stop, necessitating higher light levels. Thus the depth of field also affects the size and type of lighting fixtures used to light the scene.

Varying Exposure Time

When the camera is operated at high speed for slow-motion photography, the exposure time is decreased and the aperture must be opened up to compensate. For example, when filming a car stunt at night with multiple cameras, the working light level must be high enough to accommodate a lower f-stop setting on high-speed cameras. An f/4 (uncompensated) would force a camera running at 120 fps to expose at under an f/2. This could be accomplished with the use of super-speed lenses, which open up to about f/1.4, but could not be accomplished with many standard lenses (which typically open up to between f/2 and f/2.8), or zoom and telephoto lenses, which are slower still. Similarly, if the shutter angle is reduced, the exposure time is reduced.

When shutter speed or shutter angle are not standard, everyone must be very clear when giving f-stops as to whether the f-stop compensation has been taken into account. When giving the f-stop, you would say it is an "f/4 on the lens," meaning that the compensation has been taken into account. If not, you should say you are giving an uncompensated reading.

Genesis of Lighting Ideas

If ten world-class DPs each planned the lighting for a particular room, each of the ten lighting schemes would be different from the rest, as different as the mind and imagination of its creator. There can be no set prescription for "good lighting"; it is not the object here to present formulas. In fact, a gaffer or DP who always lights by formula or habit undervalues the potential impact of the lighting. The psychological effect of the script is played out not only through the dialogue and acting, but also in the lighting and camera work. Good lighting comes from the ability to visualize how light can underscore the drama and mood of a written scene. Mood is perhaps the most powerful contribution of lighting to a motion picture. It starts in the DP's imagination. He looks at the room he is going to light, and returns in his mind to the script: the events, the emotions, the personalities that inhabit the space in the story. In collaboration with the director and production designer, he arrives at a sense of what each scene should feel like. The lighting may be gritty and hyper-realistic, slick and clean, high-tech and stylish, or lush and glamorous. It may be naturalistic, or it may be stylized and theatrical. He is seeking conceptual ideas that will inspire his approach to the lighting.

- What color and quality of light support the character's inner emotional state, and what light sources could be introduced in the scene to motivate that light on the actor or in the room?
- How should the audience experience this character — radiant with charisma, frazzled and imperfect, strong and determined, or what?
- What are the conditions, the weather, the time of day? Are they dictated by the script? If not, does the tone of the scene suggest an approach to take?
- How is light treated by the character in the story? Would she invite sunlight to pour into the room like butterscotch, or would she close it out, leaving us in a musty dark room, the sunlight seeping around the edges of thick curtains?
- Does light connect the central character to his surroundings or does it isolate him? Is he surrounded with glowing human faces with whom he might interact, or anonymous figures who leave him alone and alienated?
- Where does the arc of the story take us? How does the space change in appearance and feel from one part of the film to the next? Is it a long day's journey into night, an emergence from darkness into light, or what? How will each scene in this progression be augmented?

The lighting does not necessarily follow a literal interpretation of the script's mood. It can be ironic — a miserable lonely person faced with a beautiful sunny day. This might be more compelling than giving the character a dull rainy afternoon to mope about, especially if the writer uses irony as a device elsewhere.

There are infinite creative possibilities that wed the lighting to the story. New ideas constantly suggest themselves from the dialogue, the setting, the actual location. Even the props, the set dressing, and the characteristics of the actors themselves can contribute to lighting ideas. Very often on location scouts the natural fall of the light lends itself to a particular scene, stimulating ideas for how that feeling can be recreated. A set painter's work light might be doing something interesting quite by accident.

Imaginative previsualization of each scene, based on story-driven concepts, stimulates an inexhaustible supply of lighting ideas. It brings variety to the cinematography and avoids a monotonous, formulaic approach. It offers the DP and gaffer a cohesive vision, which will result in creative, effective, and appropriate lighting design.

Lighting Objectives

What else are we thinking about as we face an unlit set, before we can name and place the particular lights we will use? Take a moment to consider the overall objectives of lighting.

Visibility (or Selective Visibility)

A film without sound is called a silent movie. A film without light is called radio. Obviously, you must have light to expose the film. Exposure and contrast are two essential elements of selective visibility in cinematography. Much of the artistry of cinematography is in the control of lightness and darkness throughout the film's latitude, selectively exposing objects and characters to appear bright and glowing, slightly shaded, darkly shaded, barely visible, or completely lost in darkness, as desired.

Equally important is the direction of light. One of our first concerns is how we will light the actor's face. What angle of light shall we use to reveal the face? How much of the face do we wish to reveal? Where does the actor stand? Which way will he face?

Naturalism

Lighting helps set the scene; it locates the scene in time and space. The quality and direction of the light and the sources it implies are part of what makes a scene convincing. Often unconsciously, we recognize lighting that portrays time, season, place, and weather conditions. The lighting is evocative of the way the air feels and smells—whether it is musty or clear, cool or hot, humid or dry.

In lighting a scene, the DP strives to evoke as much about the place and time as he can imagine. The crew won't necessarily shoot a given scene at the time specified in the script. In fact, day scenes are often shot at night, and night scenes during the day. To create natural-looking lighting and to keep things consistent, one must control the existing sources and utilize or invent techniques to recreate realistic, natural lighting using artificial sources.

The opposite of natural lighting is lighting that *gives away* the artificial setting to the audience: when multiple shadows are cast on the walls and floor by an actor, when a lamp or wall sconce casts its own shadow, when you can trace the diverging rays of light back to a lamp outside a window, when "direct sunlight" comes into a room at different angles at each window.

Composition

Lighting is used as a means of emphasis and delineation. It helps separate the layers of the three-dimensional world on the flat, two-dimensional screen. It can also create purely graphic effects that contribute to the design of the composition.

Emphasis

In some situations the DP will need to selectively emphasize characters or elements, letting the lighting direct the eye within the frame. For example, imagine a wide shot looking down over the congregation in a large church. The shot immediately conveys the grandeur of the ceremony, but without further help our eye wanders without a focus. An increased light level surrounding the figures at the front of the church draws the eye to our hero and heroine making their vows at the altar. The light falls off a little on peripheral figures.

Separation

When the three-dimensional world is telescoped onto a piece of celluloid and projected onto a flat screen, our natural stereoscopic ability to detect depth is lost. The cinematographer can reemphasize depth in the image by accentuating the outlines of characters and objects, contrasting the brightness and color of the different layers, and by moving the camera, which reveals depth with the relative motion of different planes.

A common problem is that when foreground and background share the same value they blend together. Suppose we are shooting a courtroom drama. The district attorney (DA) has brunette hair and is wearing a dark blue suit. The courtroom is paneled in dark wood, and the reporters and onlookers in the audience are wearing dark gray and black suits. The DA's dark hair will blend into her dark surroundings, making it hard to say just where her head stops and everything else starts.

The cinematographer may choose to remedy this with a strong backlight that creates a rim around her hair and shoulders to separate her from the background. The amount of backlight needed depends on the reflectance of the subject and how pronounced an effect is desired. Suppose the public defender is a dapper, blond-haired fellow sporting a cream linen jacket. He will require little or no backlight to separate him from the dark background, but a small amount of backlight might be used if the DP wants to glamorize the character with highlights in his hair. If we were to measure the intensity of the backlight, the light might be one stop under the key light. The dark hair of the DA will absorb light like a sponge, so her backlight would be set one or two stops over the key light.

There was a time in movie history when a bright glamorous backlight was an accepted convention. Today audiences tend to recognize it as artificial. Strong backlight can still look natural if it is well motivated; otherwise, it has to be subtle. Perhaps the DA's kicker could be motivated by a shaft of sunlight. A bright window in the background of the shot often helps in this type of situation; it provides a sense of source.

Backlight is not the only way to create separation. The cinematographer might choose to separate the foreground, middle ground, and background simply by lighting them to contrasting levels of brightness. The dark-haired DA could be separated by lightening the background behind her. Because the DP does not want to lose the sense of solemn darkness in the audience, he might choose to throw a shaft of sunlight across just one or two rows of the dark suits. The gaffer places the shaft so that it will line up behind the DA in a pleasing composition. A light dose of smoke in the air gives substance to the translucent shaft of light, leaving the audience in atmospheric dimness behind it. The DA's dark head of hair stands against lighter values, nicely separated and defined.

Depth

Another important compositional element is depth. A composition that includes surfaces at various distances receding into the distance increases the shot's sense of perspective and scale. If the shot includes some sense of space beyond the plane of the facing wall, outside a window or through an open doorway into other rooms, the gaffer can create planes of light and dark that recede deep into the picture. Depth offers nice opportunities for interesting lighting and composition.

Graphic Effect

A DP often wants light that simply creates graphic shapes or lines that enhance or distort shapes in the scenery. He might throw a diagonal slash across the background, a pattern of moving foliage, a window frame, a venetian blind, or use objects in the set dressing to create irregular shadows.

Lighting a textured surface at an oblique angle emphasizes the texture of the surface. The wall of a corrugated metal building appears as a pattern of vertical lines, a brick wall becomes a pattern of regular rectangles. Breaking up the background with textured light goes a long way toward creating an exciting image from one that would otherwise be dull.

Time Constraints

One final objective that has been conveniently ignored up until now is to work within the time frame permitted by the production schedule. In an ideal world, the DP can devote planning and attention to all the objectives previously discussed. In real life, however, speed often becomes the top priority, and the lighting has to be designed accordingly. There is little time to contemplate stylistic concerns; it is simply a matter of getting the scene lit fast and making it look as good as possible. The lighting crew spends all its energy trying to get out of the fire and back into the frying pan.

The speed of the lighting depends a great deal on the complexity of the DP's approach. One cinematographer might light a scene beautifully with a single soft source. Another might have a very detailed, painstaking approach, using dozens of fixtures and lighting practically every person and every object on the set individually, which takes much more preparation time.

Speed also depends on the gaffer's and best boy's planning and the flexibility of the rigging. With thoughtful planning and some prerigging time, the time spent on lighting during shooting can be quite minimal, and yet the lighting can still be complex. Without proper planning and a flexible rigging design, much time is wasted (rerouting cable, rigging and hanging new lights, and so on), stress is higher, more effort is expended, and the lighting can become rushed and sloppy.

The Process of Creating Natural Lighting

Many DPs have said that the best lighting is usually the simplest; with each additional light, you add at least one new problem. Two carefully placed lights usually give far better results than lighting a subject with five or six lights. DPs strive to find lighting that is deliberate, clean, and simple.

This is not to say that a DP will never use dozens, or even hundreds, of lights to illuminate a scene. A scene may call for many small pools of light. Each light is controlled and serves a distinct purpose. As an actor walks through the room, he may pass through twenty lights, but at any one moment no more than two or three sources are illuminating him.

Motivating Light Sources

It is sometimes helpful for the DP and gaffer to designate what the motivating sources of light are for a scene. These sources may be real or imagined; identifying them gives the DP and gaffer a starting point, a quality of light to emulate. Ostensibly, a scene could be lit by direct sunlight pouring through the windows, by soft light filtering through a skylight, by candles on a dining room table, by a table lamp and wall sconces, by moonlight, by torchlight, by the light of an instrument panel (in an airplane, a car, a spaceship, a submarine, etc.), by a flashing neon sign outside the window of an urban apartment, by the flashing lights of an ambulance, by the headlights of a passing car, or by the flickering glow of a bonfire on a beach. If the DP has previsualized the scene, he will already know what type of light source is appropriate. Now, taking into account the specific blocking, architecture of the set, and placement of practical lights in the set he will determine which source will act as key light on the actors face, which source might motivate lighting on the background, and which source he might use to motivate backlights.

Reinforcing the Motivating Source

A source may be shown on screen — a table lamp, for example — or may simply be suggested, a flashing neon sign, for example. In either case, the actors are illuminated either by the source itself or by lighting fixtures that strengthen the effect of the motivating source.

In most cases if the source is bright enough to provide illumination for the actors, it will appear too bright itself. For example, suppose an actor is sitting on a couch beside a table lamp. If we rely solely on the lamp to provide the exposure on the actor's face, the lamp will be greatly overexposed. Conversely, if we dim down the lamp to look natural (zone VIII), the actor's face will be too dark. The actor's face therefore needs to be illuminated separately by a source that mimics the soft, golden quality of the table lamp. This also affords us the opportunity to "cheat" the key light where it will look best on the actor's face. What matters is that the quality of the light — of the key source in particular — be that of a realistic and plausible lighting source and that the general direction of the light have continuity and not shift between camera angles. A diffused Fresnel aimed around the front of the lamp would serve this purpose. Care must be taken not to let light spill onto the lamp itself or to let the lamp cast a shadow from the Fresnel, as this would destroy the illusion of light originating from the lamp.

It is nice if the director, production designer, and DP consider the movement of the actors in relation to the placement of lighting sources. Light naturally influences behavior. For instance, a patch of sun moves across my living room floor during the afternoon, and my cat moves every 15 minutes to keep up with it. People also gravitate to light to read, work, and talk to one another. The lighting will therefore directly affect the blocking, and vice versa.

When no plausible sources exist to light the actors, as in a dark bedroom at night, a little dramatic license must be taken. The idea is to create a look that is psychologically palatable to the audience, if not wholly realistic. One approach to lighting a supposedly unilluminated night scene is to create a low base level of nondirectional blue light and underexpose it. Then, very selectively, add chips and slivers of light, and perhaps use subtle backlight to define the contour of the actor where he disappears into dark shadow. The success of such an effect is a delicate matter requiring an experienced eye and good judgment.

Establishing the Key Light

The first light to establish is the key light. The key light typically establishes the exposure for the scene. All the other lights — fill light, backlight, practicals, scenery lighting, and so on — are set relative to the key light. The key is the strongest light on an actor's face. It may cover a large area — the sun, for example, is one of the larger key lights — or it may cover only the immediate area around the motivating source. If the set is large, a number of different sources will be key lights in different areas of the set. For example, as an actress moves from a window to a sofa that is in front of a fireplace, she walks out of the soft, blue, window light and into the warm, flickering firelight.

The shape of a face is revealed to the eye by the way light falls on the curves and planes of features. Tonal variations, the shading and shadows, are what tell our brain the shape of an object. Certain features can be emphasized or de-emphasized by the placement of the lights. Often a DP's efforts are focused on de-emphasizing trouble spots, such as a double chin or sunken eyes. We may hide a double chin by keeping the light high and the chin in shadow.

The placement of the key light and the angles at which light strikes the subject greatly affect the associations evoked in the audience. Yet no particular meaning is necessarily associated with a given angle of light. Do not be limited by pedantic assumptions — a low light always denotes something sinister, or that the classic key position bestows glamour. Lighting is a subjective matter. The art of the gaffer and DP is to respond to the context of the moment being photographed.

Rembrandt Cheek-Patch Lighting

The conventional key light position is at 45° above and 45° to one side of the actor (Figure 5.7).

This position throws the shadow of the nose across the opposite side of the face, leaving a patch of light on the cheek. This patch is known as the *Rembrandt cheek*

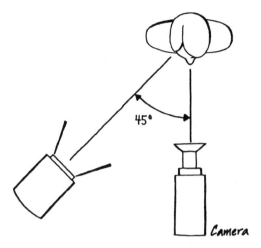

Figure 5.7 Conventional key position, 45° above and 45° to one side of the actor.

patch, after portraits by the seventeenth-century Dutch painter. This lighting angle puts light in both eyes and models the nose, lips, chin, and cheeks nicely. It is considered the most natural key light position. It is very important to realize, however, that every actor has a different face: One has a large nose; another has a broad face or a chin that sticks out or droops. Some have deeply set eyes that are difficult to get light into, or hair that interferes with the light, or wrinkles they wish their public not to see. The DP responds to these differences in the treatment given to each face; the 45° rule quickly becomes academic.

Most often the key is somewhere between 0 and 90° from a frontal position to the subject and between 0 and 45° above the subject's head; however, it can come from any direction that will reveal at least some of the features of the face: from below, from high overhead or high to the side, and even from a three-quarter back/side position.

Side Light

A direct side light at eye level puts one whole side of the face in shadow. When this half-light effect is desired, the best position for the key light is not at 90° to the face, but slightly less than 90°. At 90°, the cheek on the key side of the face tends to make an unattractive shadow. By bringing the light slightly forward of 90°, the shadow disappears, and the result is a pleasing half-light effect. It models the face nicely and gives a pronounced sense of contrast and direction. Light does not fall on the far eye. If desired, fill light or eye light may be added to put a glint in both eyes.

A nice addition to a side light key is to wrap the light around onto the far cheek with a very subtle soft source in a three-quarters frontal position on the same side as the key with little or no additional fill. The result, a very soft, high-contrast side light, gives an appealing gradation of tones across the face. This look came into vogue in

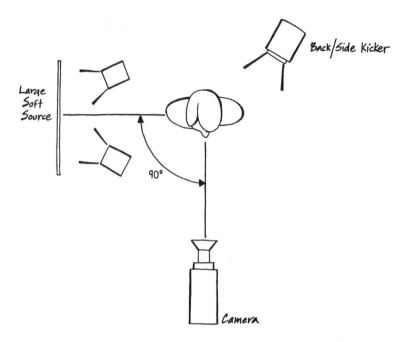

Figure 5.8   Soft side light with opposite side kicker.

the nineteen eighties in testimonial commercials: a yuppie talking candidly and pre-sumably impromptu about his stockbroker or the merits of his long-distance service. The technique is useful in all sorts of situations.

One of the pitfalls of a side light position is that if the actor turns her head away from the source, the face goes completely into shadow. The addition of a back/side kicker on the nonkey side can help define the features in such a case (Figure 5.8). Alternatively, you could let the face go dark, and define the profile by silhouetting it against a lighter background.

An eye-level side light also tends to cast the shadow of one actor onto another. This problem can be remedied by raising the light higher, throwing the shadow down-ward.

In dance performances, floor-level side lights are used because they accentuate the form and musculature of the dancers. The low position allows the light to be cut off the stage surface, which increases the apparent height and duration of dancers' leaps and enhances the illusion of effortless flight.

Far-Side Key

The previous discussion concerns lighting an actor who is more or less facing the camera. Consider now what happens when an actor is facing three-quarters to the camera (Figure 5.9).

From the camera's perspective, the key light, which is lighting one whole side of the actor's face, is a deeply set side light. The effect is to give the far side of the actor's face an illuminated edge and to place a patch of light on the near-side cheek, while leaving the rest of the near-side portion of the face in shadow. By adding a very limited amount of fill light, the far-side key conveys darkness in the room.

Front Light

When a key light is brought to the front, the scene becomes flatter. Using a direct frontal soft light as the key light is a technique of glamour still photography, where the goal is less to reveal the form as to hide the blemishes. Actors who have undesirable wrinkles are often given stronger doses of super-soft front light.

Hard front light was a convention of glamour cinematography of the black-and-white era. By placing the light so that it shoots dead onto the face, the nose and chin shadows are minimized to a small underline. The eyes appear very bright, and the sides of the face, the temples, and jaw fall off in brightness.

To prevent the front light from flattening out the entire scene, it is often desirable to angle the light down such that it can be cut off the background with toppers and siders (Figure 5.10). It is also helpful to have some distance between the actor and the background; otherwise, a hard shadow becomes unavoidable.

Bottom Light

When you think of bottom light, you automatically imagine an eerie, unnatural visage with lighting under the eyebrows, nose, and chin casting shadows upward

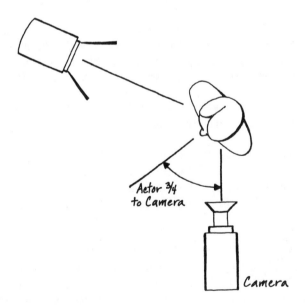

Figure 5.9 Far-side key.

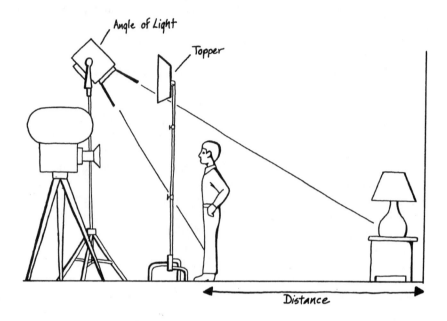

Figure 5.10 On the nose key. This usually requires a topper to prevent the front light from flattening out the background.

from the eyebrows. However, a low light source does not necessarily have that effect. Light that is bounced up from a light-colored floor or table surface can lend the face a soft radiance. Again, lighting angles do not necessarily have any particular meaning.

Naturally, a low position may be used when a light source is at ground level — a camp fire, for example — or when the actor is elevated. Any time you place a light in a low position, you have to be prepared to deal with, or learn to love, the shadows cast upward on the background and ceiling.

High in Front or High to the Side

A high position can give a dramatic effect by putting the eye sockets in deep shadow and underlining the nose, lips, and chin in shadow. In "The Godfather," Gordon Willis used soft, high frontal sources to give Marlon Brando a low-key, intimidating presence.

Eye Light

An eye light is usually placed as close to the camera lens as possible. Eye light makes the eyes twinkle or brings them out of darkness by creating a reflection in the eyeball. The bigger the dimensions of the source, the bigger the reflected dots. Eye light does not have to be very intense, however, because the eyeball is very reflective. An eye light need not flatten out the overall composition.

An *obie light* is a light positioned directly over the camera lens, mounted to the matte box. It has the advantage of panning, tilting, and dollying with the camera. The obie light maintains a minimal level of frontal fill on actors as they pass in and out of other lights while the camera moves with them through a set. Obie lights have dimming shutters, so brightness can be adjusted without affecting color temperature.

Backlights, Kickers, and Hair Lights

Backlight highlights the edges of the face, hair, and shoulders of an actor. It strengthens the lines that delineate the figure from the background. The various back-light positions can also emphasize features of the face and hair. Scenes that occur in relative darkness are often backlit in order to give delineation to the figures and set dressing without lighting them. Backlight is also the best angle to make rain, snow, and smoke visible to the camera.

Three-Quarter Backlight Kicker

A *kicker* is normally relatively low, from a three-quarter backlight position. A light glancing off the side of the face and hair gives form to the jaw, cheek, and hair, and separates that side of the figure from the background. Because of its low, back position, it does not cause problems by spilling onto walls and can easily be kept off the ground. As with all backlights, the problem is always keeping it out of frame and preventing flare on the lens. It is nice to be able to hide the light behind a set piece or furniture.

High Side Backlight

High side backlights, one on either side of the subject, soak the performer in backlight; the effect is powerful and dramatic. You see this technique used in rock concerts and dance performances. It works equally well for an effect in motion pictures. When blended with the frontal lights and applied with more subtlety, a pair of high side backlights rims the head and shoulders evenly and highlights the hair. News reporters and talk show hosts seem to have one or two backlights with them wherever they go. High backlights tend to light up the ground, table tops, and other horizontals.

Rim

A *rim* light, high direct backlight rims the head and shoulders, pulling the actor out from the background. A rim light is a thin highlight. Again, the light will spill onto the floor and must be shaded off the lens.

Hair Light

Positioned somewhere between a rim and a top light, a *hair light* creates a flattering halo effect. Applied with subtlety, it brings out the color and texture of the hair.

Top Light

A *top light* (directly overhead) primarily lights the actor's hair and shoulders. It does not light the face at all, other than the forehead and the bridge of the nose. Although it can be used for dramatic effect, this is not a great position from which to light a person, unless the person is reclining. It can be effective to create a sense of faceless anonymous figures in a room, lighting table tops and horizontal surfaces, without illuminating faces. Sometimes a DP will bounce a top light off of a table to illuminate an actor's face.

Fill

The next important consideration is *fill*. The object of fill light is to bring up the light level in the dark shadow areas of the face created by the key light. To do this soft light must come from a more frontal position than the key light, usually from near the camera. When low light levels are being used, the ambient light level may be sufficient to fill the shadows, or often the fill can be accomplished with a white board placed to bounce light into the shadow areas of the face. When a fixture is used, it must be a large, soft source that will not create additional shadows — a light bounced into a 4 × 4 piece of foam core, or put through heavy diffusion such as 216, or a large source such as a soft light, chimera, or homemade soft box.

The amount of fill light determines the contrast ratio and has a great deal to do with the apparent lightness or darkness and, to some extent, the mood of the scene. If the fill light is strong, bringing the contrast ratio up to 2:1, the scene appears very bright and flat, a look that is termed *high key*. Reducing the amount of fill light brings out the directionality of the key lights, separates the elements of the frame, and makes the colors appear more saturated. Reducing the fill even more allows deep shadows to appear. A high key:fill ratio gives the sense of night or darkness in the room, especially if the scene is lit with edge and side light. This kind of look is termed *low key*.

Most DPs fill by eye, rather than by using a meter. Judging fill light takes some experience and familiarity with the characteristics of the film stock. It may be helpful to turn the fill light off and on to judge its effect.

Set Light

It is sometimes the case that the key lights illuminate the set, and there is need for very little further treatment of it. It may be lit with practicals, which give it pools of light and dark, or the gaffer may place bulbs behind items of set dressing to add interest. When light needs to be added to bring out the background, it is best to be selective with it. Light tends to build up on backgrounds and can start to flatten everything out. Look for ways to break it up or create variation, gradation, or specific highlights.

Backdrops

On a sound stage, the exterior scene outside the windows of the set is very often created using a *translight* or *scenic backing*. A translight is a gigantic photograph which is back-lit (usually with sky pans). Day and night translights are created depicting a back yard, the view from a high-rise office building, and so forth.

Specials

If some object in the set requires a separate treatment, for example, a crystal ball, that object is given a *special*. In the case of the crystal ball, a special might shoot up into the ball through a hole in the table.

Lighting the Scene

The discussion thus far has dealt with lighting a single, stationary actor. Very few movies, however, are about a single individual who never moves. The following light plots show how two different sets might be lit for a scene.

Living Room Scene

Figure 5.11 shows a living room set built on a sound stage.

The scene at hand is set on a cold, overcast winter day. A fire is burning in the fireplace. The actor starts the scene at the window, looking out at the falling snow, then he moves to the armchair and sits down in front of the fire.

The motivating sources for the scene are the lights from the window, the table lamp next to the armchair, the fire, and the chandelier in the front hall. Before we can plan how these sources will function, we first need to know where the camera will be placed. For the shot at hand, the camera will be placed on the right side of the fireplace, taking a profile angle of the actor at the window, panning with him as he moves to the chair, and taking a three-quarter frontal angle of him as he sits down.

The key light at the window naturally comes from outside. The light should be soft, diffuse, and slightly blue in contrast to the warm interior. We use a 4k HMI Fresnel shining into a 6 × 6 ft. frame of light grid cloth. A half CTO orange gel is

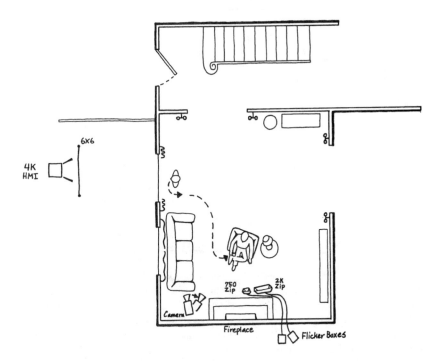

Figure 5.11 Living room scene and key light positions. The 4k HMI through light grid cloth gives a soft cool light through the window, while the two small soft lights on the flicker boxes create the illusion of firelight.

applied to the light to correct the blue HMI source halfway to tungsten. We adjust the light's intensity so that we read the target f-stop on the subject's face when he stands by the window. The intensity falls off as he moves away from the window. The window frame cuts the light, reducing the spill on the back wall and preventing it from spilling onto the armchair.

As the actor approaches the chair, the key shifts from the window to the fireplace. A firelight rig is placed on the floor just out of the frame. The firelight is exposed a half-stop under the target f-stop, colored slightly orange, and made to flicker randomly. (Some techniques for creating this effect are explained in Chapter 6.) The shadows in the room should shift slightly with the dancing movement of the make-believe flames. Because the light from the fire is close to the subject, intensity rapidly falls off behind him. Shadows are cast on the chair but do not reach the back wall.

Backlights and Kickers Now that the two key lights are set, we can consider what other lights we would like (Figure 5.12).

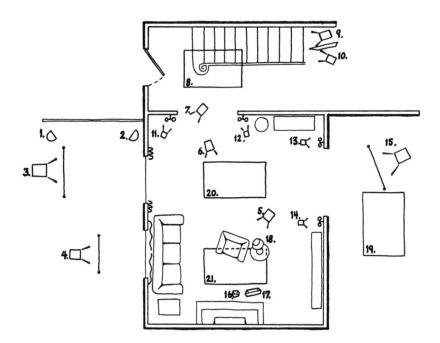

Figure 5.12 Living room scene with back and fill lights added: (1, 2) scoops lighting the painted flat, (3) key at the window, (4) light giving glow around edges of closed curtains, (5) rim light motivated by table lamp, (6) backlight at chair motivated by hallway light, (7) backlight at window, (8) soft box to fill hallway with top light, (9) light on stairs and banister poles, (10) slash on the back wall, (11–14) small Fresnels producing light around wall sconces, (15) light spilling into living room from dining room, (16) 750W soft firelight, (17) 2k zip firelight, (18) table lamp, (19) dining room soft box to light visible walls of next room, (20, 21) soft top fill, put low on dimmers for ambient warm fill.

The position of the table lamp motivates a nice kicker for the seated position. A 650W Fresnel is placed on a stand just out of the frame to the right, aimed around the back of the table lamp. The combined light reading of the practical and the kicker is to be one stop over the target f-stop.

We could also introduce two backlights coming in from the hallway: one to rim the actor's back at the window and one for his shoulders when in the chair. The back-light at the window should be cut so that it does not throw light on the wall and curtains next to him.

Fill   Finally, we will need some fill light. We want to keep contrast in the scene, so we will only need enough fill to give a little detail on the shadowy part of his clothes at the window and as he moves to the chair. A soft source next to the camera would have to be carefully positioned so as not to light up the camera-left wall and to avoid causing a glare in the paneling on the far wall. The scene might also be filled by hanging soft boxes overhead.

Background   Additionally, we must consider treatment of the back walls, hallway, stairs, dining room, and scenery outside the windows, which will all be in the background of the various shots filmed in this room. As the scene continues, we are likely to have actors coming into the hallway, the dining room, the stairway, and so on. We must consider each area that may be used or seen.

In the firelight scene described earlier, it may be enough to bring out the back walls with the glow from the sconces on either side of the hallway entrance. We may want to reinforce the sconces with small Fresnels positioned overhead, throwing soft blobs of light on the walls around the sconces. A light shining down from the top of the stairway would provide an edge light to an actor standing in the hall or on the stairs, and would create a diagonal slash on the far back wall. The hallway might also be lit with a skirted overhead soft box. The scenery flat outside is lit with several blue-gelled scoops or sky pans.

Exterior Night Scene

Typically, when shooting moody, dark scenes or night scenes, the key lights move around to side and back positions. The back cross is a common technique used to light two or more people from the back.

Figure 5.13 shows a setup for a face-to-face conversation at night.

The camera position for the master shot has both actors in profile. Actor A is keyed from the back right, actor B from the back left. From the camera's point of view, these two lights are far-side keys; they put very little light on the visible side of either actor's face, giving a sense of overall darkness. Note that actor B's key light acts as a kicker, or backlight, for actor A, and actor A's key light does the same for actor B. A small amount of fill light is required to keep the side of the faces visible to the camera from going totally black; however, the fill light's intensity must be very carefully controlled to get detail in the faces without overfilling.

Once the master shot is completed, individual, over-the-shoulder (OTS) close-ups will be shot. Figure 5.14 shows the camera placements.

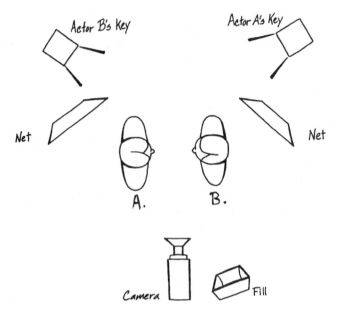

Figure 5.13 Back cross master shot.

Notice that our key lights are already in good positions to light the faces. We will now bring in backlights to keep a rim on the nonkey sides of the faces. The fill light moves with the camera, placed on the nonkey side, and is cheated back and forth for each close-up.

Moving into position for the first close-up, we will want to check the intensity at which actor B's key hits actor A's back. Because A is closer to the light, it may be too hot or bright. Placing a net to bring down the level of B's key will solve this problem. Similarly, when we move the camera for the second close-up, we reduce the level of A's key hitting B.

When shooting the first close-up, we turn off actor A's backlight because it draws attention away from actor B. Likewise, when shooting the second close-up, we turn off actor B's backlight so as not to detract from actor A.

The background consists of storefronts across the street. The DP wants the background shadowy and underexposed two to three stops. Starting with total darkness, we need to bring the light level on the street and storefronts up to a low base level. Our aim is to create an ambient light: moonlight or streetlight. The whole background must be covered completely. If the camera sees the edge of a light's field, where true darkness begins, the ambient effect will be destroyed. To accomplish a widespread and even field, we need to put a fairly big fixture high up and a long way off, typically a 12k HMI on a condor crane 50 to 80 ft. in the air and perhaps 150 ft. away. The size of the light, its height, and its distance depend on the size of the area

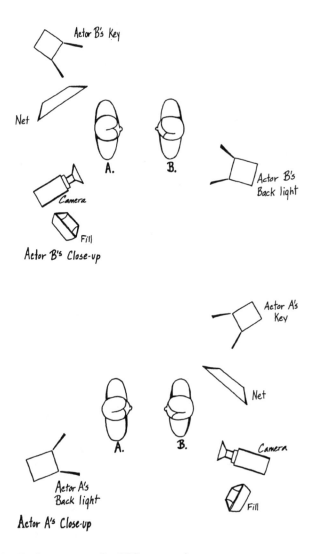

Figure 5.14 Back cross setup for OTS reverse close-up.

to be lit. Notice in Figure 5.14 that for each shot a new background will be seen, and quite a bit of real estate may have to be covered.

To accentuate the darkness of the background, it would be nice in this situation to have a few self-luminous sources in the picture: neon signs, car headlights, or perhaps some steam (backlit) rising out of a manhole. Cinematographers often like to wet down the pavement during night scenes so they can pick up reflections from the shiny surface.

CHAPTER 6

Manipulating Light:

Tools, Techniques, and the Behavior of Light

I can't stand a naked light bulb any more than I can a rude remark or vulgar action.

Tennessee Williams, *A Streetcar Named Desire*

Light has five properties: color, brightness, form, shape/pattern, and movement. The set electrician uses the techniques discussed in this chapter to manipulate and control these five properties.

Color

The lighting crew has two goals when it comes to color. The first is the technical process of matching the color temperature of the light sources to each other and to the rated color balance of the film stock. The second is aesthetic: introducing color into the light to simulate realistic sources, such as firelight, neon light, or blue moonlight. The DP may use tints to enhance the colors of the actors' faces, their clothes, and their surroundings, and give the scene mood — warmth, eeriness, bleakness.

Color Correction

Light is a narrow band of the electromagnetic spectrum as show in Figure 6.1. Wavelengths from 380 to 760 nanometers (nm) are detectable to the human eye as visible light.

The color of a light source is determined by the intensity of the various wavelengths that make up the light. When the full range of wavelengths is combined, the result is said to be white light. Nonetheless, all light has color; every light source has its own balance of wavelengths. Because the human eye adapts to its surroundings, shifts in balance are not always apparent to the human eye unless one light source is next to another in direct contrast.

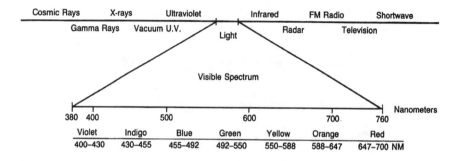

Figure 6.1 The color spectrum is a narrow band within the electromagnetic spectrum. Individual colors of light within the visible spectrum combine to make "white light."

An incandescent light produces light that is orange compared to an HMI, which is stronger on the blue end. Standard fluorescent tubes produce light that has strong spikes at several places in the spectrum, which give it a strong green hue.

Unlike the human eye, film stock cannot adjust to these variations. Color rendition is always relative to the color balance of the film stock: either tungsten (3200K) or daylight (5600K). To appear white on film, the color balance of the light must match that of the film. This is accomplished by applying color correction gels to unmatched sources. The gels redistribute the spectrum by reducing the intensity of selected wavelengths in a given source. CTO (color temperature orange) must be applied to daylight sources to match with tungsten film. CTB (color temperature blue) must be applied to incandescent sources to match to daylight film. A magenta gel must be applied to fluorescent lights to remove the green appearance.

A gel having a secondary color diminishes the amount of the opposite primary color in the light (see Figure 6.4 later in this chapter). Conversely, a gel having a primary color diminishes the strength of the opposite secondary color in the light. For example, amber gel diminishes blue light, and blue gel diminishes amber light. Magenta gel diminishes green light, and green gel diminishes magenta light.

Kelvin Color-Temperature Scale

The color makeup of any source that has a continuous spectrum, such as an incandescent light, can be measured on the color-temperature scale and quantified in degrees Kelvin. Figure 6.2 shows how the distributions of wavelengths differ for sources of different color temperatures.

The Kelvin scale is based on the idea that light is emitted when a substance is heated, in our case, an incandescent filament.[1] How much it is heated determines the color makeup of the light. When heated a little, it glows red. Heated more, it becomes yellow, then white, then pale blue, and finally brilliant blue. The higher the Kelvin reading, the bluer the light.

---

[1] Scientifically speaking, the Kelvin scale is based on a comparison of the color of a source to the color of a perfect black body radiator when it is heated.

Table 6.1 shows the color temperature of various sources. You can see that household bulbs are in fact quite yellow (2800K to 2900K). Tungsten bulbs are much less so (3200K), but still look orange compared to daylight (5600K).

The color makeup of sources that do not have a continuous spectrum — HMIs and fluorescents — can also be given a Kelvin rating termed the *correlated color temperature* (CCT).

Using MIRED Units to Calculate Color Shifts

Tables F.1 through F.3 (Appendix F) tell you what gel to use to get from any color temperature to any other color temperature. Although the Kelvin scale is useful for defining the color temperature of a source, it is an awkward scale to use when quantifying the effect of a color correction gel or filter. You can't simply state that a particular gel creates a 200K shift. The Kelvin shift of a given correction filter depends on the color temperature of the *light source*. A blue gel that alters a tungsten source 200K (from 3200K to 3400K) alters a daylight source 650K (from 5600K to 6250K).

When gel manufacturers quantify the effect of color correction gel, they use micro reciprocal degrees (*MIRED* units), rather than degrees Kelvin. MIREDs provide a linear scale on which to calculate the shift of a given gel on any source.

The MIRED value is equal to 1 million divided by the Kelvin color temperature:

$$\frac{1,000,000}{K} = \text{MIRED value}$$

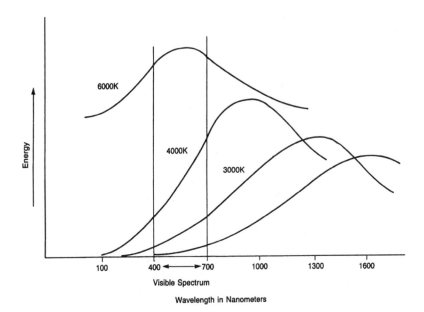

Figure 6.2 Distribution of energy for various color temperatures across the visible spectrum.

Table 6.1 Color Temperatures of Various Sources

Source	Kelvin	Mireds
Match or candle flame	1900	526
Dawn or dusk	2000–2500	500
Household bulb	2800–2900	357–345
Tungsten halogen bulbs	3200	312
Photo flood bulbs	3400	294
1 hour after sunrise	3500	286
Late afternoon sunlight	4500	233
Blue glass photoflood bulb	4800	208
3200K lamps with dichroic filter	4800–5000	208–200
FAY lamps	5000	200
Summer sunlight	5500–5700	182
White flame carbon arc light with Y-1 filter	5700	175
HMI light	5600 or 6000	179 or 167
Sunlight with blue/white sky	6500	154
Summer shade	7000	141
Overcast sky	7000	141
Color television	9300	108
Skylight	10,000–20,000	100

Table F.4 lists the MIRED value for any Kelvin number from 2000K to 9900K. Tables F.5 through F.7 list the color shift in MIREDs of color correction gels of various manufacturers.

The MIRED shift of a particular gel needed to get from any Kelvin temperature (K_1) to any other Kelvin temperature (K_2) is as follows:

$$\text{MIRED shift} = \frac{1,000,000}{K_1} - \frac{1,000,000}{K_2}$$

Note that tungsten color temperature is 312 MIREDs, and daylight is about 179 MIREDs. To correct a daylight source to tungsten, a shift of +133 MIREDs is required. To correct a tungsten source to daylight, a shift of -133 MIREDs is required.

Color-Temperature Meter

A color-temperature meter gives a Kelvin reading of the light hitting the cell of the meter. It is important to realize that although a cinematographer's color meter, such as the Minolta Color Meter II (Figure 6.3), is calibrated at the factory, the readings of two identical meters will often differ.

This type of color meter is accurate for comparing the color temperatures of several light sources, but no Kelvin reading should be taken as an absolute value. When more than one meter is being used to take readings on the set, the meters should be checked side by side under the same light to determine the variation between them.

Light-Balancing Scale — Orange/Blue Shifts

The Minolta color meter automatically calculates the MIRED shift from the Kelvin reading. Minolta calls this shift the *light-balancing* (LB) index number. This number indicates the amount of amber or blue correction gel needed to match the source to the color temperature of the film stock (refer to Tables F.2 through F.4 to determine the closest correction gel to use). To use the LB scale, the color balance of the film stock must be preset on the meter. A three-position selection switch offers the standard film color temperatures: film type B 3200K, film type A 3400K (which is used for some still film stocks), or film type D (daylight) 5500K. The meter also has a manual mode that allows you to input any target Kelvin temperature. Manual mode comes in handy when the cinematographer needs to have all the lights balanced to a nonstandard Kelvin rating. A chart on the back of the color meter also gives the Kodak filter number and the amount of exposure change corresponding to the LB reading (Table F.8). Kodak filters are used in the camera in situations where an overall color correction is needed. For example, when filming a scene in which the practical lamps are unavoidably yellow, the DP can add 1/4 CTO to his lights to match them to the practicals, then cancel out the yellow cast with a blue filter on the lens.

Figure 6.3   Minolta Color Meter II. (Photo courtesy of Minolta Corp., Cypress, CA.)

Color-Compensation Scale — Green/Magenta Shifts

The color temperature meter also gives a *color-compensation* (CC) reading that indicates the amount of green or magenta gel needed to correct a source to appear white on film. Such a correction is typically required by fluorescent lights. A CC reading of 30M (+13 on Color Meter II) is typical for a cool white bulb, for example. This excess green can be filtered out with a full minus-green (magenta) gel. Table F.9 lists green/magenta correction gels and the corresponding color meter readings.

Color-Correction Gels

All correction gels come in densities of full, half, quarter, and eighth correction. Correction gel typically comes in rolls 48 or 54 in. wide and 22 or 25 ft. in length. When gel is cut from the roll, the cut pieces should be labeled (F, H, Q, or E) and organized by size and color.

Converting Daylight Sources to Tungsten

CTO gels are orange, and they warm up daylight-balanced sources. 85 gel corrects sunlight and HMI sources to 3200K. Full CTO or extra CTO correct skylight to tungsten, or 5500K sources to a warm yellow 2800K.

Gelling Windows

When the outside of the window is accessible, gel can be stapled or taped over the outside window frame, which hides the gel more easily. When stapling gel, apply a square of gaffer's tape to the gel and staple through the tape to prevent the gel from ripping. The key to gelling windows is to keep the gel tight and free of wrinkles.

CTO correction is also available in 4 × 8 ft. acrylic sheets. Using acrylic sheets avoids the problems of wrinkles, movement, and noise that gel makes.

With a very light dusting of spray adhesive (Spray 77) you can stick gel directly onto a window or acrylic sheet. Press bubbles and wrinkles out to the edges with a duvatyne-covered block of wood. If gelling windows promises to become an everyday process on a particular location, an elegant system is to cut acrylic inserts to fit the windows, then add ND and CTO gel (using the spray adhesive technique) as needed to suit the light conditions and time of day. Move the inserts around from shot to shot depending on the camera angle.

You can also use snot tape (3M transfer tape) or secure it by carefully taping around the edge of the gel with tape that matches the color of the window frame. Another fast method is to spray water on the windows and apply the gel with a squeegee. This method will not last all day, but it saves so much time that it doesn't matter if it must be redone.

Neutral-Density and Combination Neutral-Density/CTO Correction Gels

Neutral-density (ND) gel is gray; it decreases the intensity of a light source without altering color. ND .3 reduces the intensity one stop, ND .6 two stops, ND .9 three stops, and ND 1.2 four stops. Combination CTO/ND gel and acrylic sheets are commonly used to reduce the brightness of windows.

Converting Tungsten to Daylight

CTB correction gels change the color temperature of a tungsten source toward that of daylight. Typically quarter or half CTB is used when the DP desires a cool blue look to a particular light source.

When the DP is using a daylight-balanced film, tungsten sources are typically avoided. HMI fixtures provide daylight-balanced light that is cleaner, brighter, cooler, and a more efficient use of power. Tungsten lights are very weak on the blue end of the spectrum. Full CTB reduces light transmission by 85%, or about two stops. (The gel is having to absorb 85% of the energy from the light and consequently the hot-burning lights also burn out blue gel very quickly.)

Dichroic Filters

The most common type of dichroic filter (dike) is a glass filter that fits onto the front of some open-face lights to make a tungsten to daylight conversion (3200K to 5600K). The filter reduces light output by two stops. The filter is easily identified by its strange red/blue reflective appearance — like gasoline in a water puddle.

A dichroic filter works by optically canceling out certain wavelengths of light. It does not involve dyes or pigment, but rather reflects selected wavelengths of light by the thickness of a chemical coating on the glass. The thickness of the coating is 1/4 of the wavelength of the selected color's chromatic opposite. Manufacturers can custom make dichroic glass filters in practically any color. Their advantage over gel is that they never fade. They are ideal for long-term installations, where the cost and trouble of replacing faded gel every week outweighs the initial expense of buying glass filters. The one trick to them is that light has to pass through the filter exactly perpendicular to the plane of the glass or the color will start to vary. For some lights a curved glass filter is necessary. Manufacturers include Rosco (Permacolor Glass Filters) and Automated Entertainment Manufacturing (HD Dichroic).

Before the dichroic filter came along, the *MacBeth* filter was used. It is simply a blue glass filter.

Green/Magenta Color Correction

Green and magenta color correction gels were developed primarily to allow color matching between fluorescent lights and other sources. A comprehensive table of fluorescent lamp types and the correction they require is given in the *American Cinematographer Manual — Color Balancing for Existing Fluorescent Lighting*. This table represents the result of comprehensive testing and is by far the best reference. For copyright reasons it cannot be reproduced here.

However, there are still many variables that no table can account for, so testing with a color meter remains the best approach. Table F.9 lists green and magenta correction gels and Kodak filter numbers and corresponding color meter readings that may be useful in this process.

There are three general approaches to matching the color temperatures of fluorescent lights, tungsten lights, HMIs, and daylight: (1) Match all the sources to daylight (5600K), (2) match all the sources to tungsten (3200K), or (3) match all the sources to fluorescent daylight (5600K plus green). Table 6.2 details each approach.

Table 6.2 Strategies for Matching Mixed Color Sources

Strategy	Ceiling Fluorescents	Tungsten Fixtures	HMI Fixtures	Windows	Fluorescent Floor Fixtures	Film Stock and Camera Filters
Match to Tungsten						
Used when the daylight sources are small and manageable (e.g., a night scene, or a room with small windows).	Replace with Optima 32 tubes. Gel warm whites with full minus green. Gel cool whites with fluoro filter.	**Primary fixture** As is.	Apply full CTO gel.	Apply Sun 85 or full CTO gel.	Kino Flo. **Primary fixture** (with KF-32 tubes). Other types use Optima 32; may require 1/8 or 1/4 minus green.	Tungsten-balanced film, no filter.
Match to Daylight						
Good approach in room with many large windows.	Replace with Vitalite tubes. Add 1/4 or 1/8 minus green as necessary. Gel cool whites with full minus green.	Apply full CTB gel (very inefficient).	**Primary fixture** As is.	As is, or with ND as needed.	Kino Flo. **Primary fixture** (with KF 55 tubes). Other types use Vitalite; may require 1/8 or 1/4 minus green.	Tungsten-balanced film with 85 filter. Daylight-balanced film, no filter.
Match to Fluorescent Daylight						
Resort to this if the ceiling lights must remain on and (1) there are too many fluorescent lights to gel or replace them all, (2) the lights are not accessible, or (3) there is absolutely no other alternative.	Existing cool white tubes.	Apply plus green 50 or full CTB and full plus green gel.	Apply full plus green gel.	Gel with window green.	Kino Flo with KF 55 tubes and full plus green. Other types use same type of bulb as in ceiling fixtures. **Primary fixture**	Tungsten-balanced film with 85 and FLB filter, or correct green in lab printing. Daylight-balanced film with FLB or take out green in lab printing.

Gelling Fluoros

When gelling fixtures that have frosted plastic panels, you can cut sheets to lay inside each fixture. If you have to gel tubes individually, place tabs of snot tape along the tube and roll the tube up in gel. Carefully cut away excess gel.

Rosco makes tubular sleeves of color correction gel that can make gelling tubes easier. You can also get clear plastic sleeves that are meant for protection in case of lamp breakage; cut and roll the gel inside them.

Fluorescent Tubes—Color Rendering

Manufacturers provide two ratings to indicate the type and quality of the color rendered by their fluorescent tubes: the *correlated color temperature* (CCT) and the *color rendering index* (CRI). The CCT and CRI are printed on the packaging of the tubes and sometimes also on the tubes themselves. While CCT and CRI ratings give the gaffer valuable information about the general performance characteristics of a given tube, they can be misleading in terms of the color rendering of fluorescent light on film. CCT and CRI are based on the color perception of the human eye, not the peculiarities of film emulsions. Specific color information must be gathered with color-temperature meter.

Correlated Color Temperature　The CCT gives the effective color temperature of the tube to the human eye when the spikes in the color curve are combined together. Fluorescent lights come in various color temperatures. Daylight tubes are designed to light spaces that have supplementary daylight, such as offices with large windows. The light is color balanced toward the blue end of the spectrum (5000K to 6500K) to blend with the window light. Warm lights, which have a color temperature closer to that of household bulbs (3000K), are for use in enclosed spaces where supplementary light comes from table lamps and wall sconces.

Color Rendering Index　The CRI is a rating, from 1 to 100, of the accuracy of a light's rendering of color when compared with a perfect reference source (daylight is a perfect 100). A rating above 90 is considered accurate color rendition for photography. With a CRI above 80 the eye can still make accurate color judgments and the color rendering is termed *acceptable*. Between 60 and 80 color rendering is *moderate*. Below 60 color rendering is poor or distorted.

On location you will run into *standard* fluorescents and *full-spectrum (high-CRI)* fluorescents. Table E.2 (Appendix E) lists specifications for various types of fluorescent tubes. A high CRI tells you that the tube has a nearly complete spectrum of light frequencies and is therefore capable of rendering colors well; however, they often have a strong green spike and require color correction, which typically involves a combination of magenta and CTO gels. The amount of magenta filtering varies and does not necessarily correspond to CRI rating. For example, the Optima 32 (CRI 82) has excellent color rendering on film and requires little or no color correction. A Chroma 50 (CRI 92) shows a strong green spike on film that must be removed with half minus-green gel.

A low CRI rating indicates the tube emits a very limited spectrum of light and is incapable of rendering all colors. These fluorescents are designed to maximize lumen output and raise energy efficiency. They produce two to four times the light output per watt of an incandescent bulb, and they last five to fifteen times longer. Thus, for economic reasons standard fluorescent tubes are widely used in office buildings, warehouses, factories, and commercial buildings. However, they generally have low CRI ratings, 50 to 70, and should be replaced with better tubes.

Coloring Light

Color Chips and Gray Scale

When the film laboratory makes a print or video transfer from a developed negative, the timer or colorist adjusts the exposure and colors of the print to make them look natural. When a DP introduces colors into the lighting, she must take steps to prevent the timer from removing the color in the lab. To give the lab a reference at the beginning of each film roll, the AC films about ten seconds of color chips or gray scale under white, properly color-balanced light. The *chip chart*, or color chart, has a set of standard colors or a scale of gray tones from white to black from which the timer can work. The chip chart must be filmed under light that is exactly the proper color temperature. A light that has been checked beforehand with a color temperature meter should be standing by for chip chart shots. When filming the chip chart, no other light should fall on the chart. You may need to turn off or block lights momentarily to prevent extraneous light from discoloring the chip chart. It is also helpful to the colorist to see skin tone with the chip chart, and even to see the scene in the background with all its "nonstandard" color.

When working with television cameras, the engineer puts up a chip chart in front of each camera before beginning shooting and electronically adjusts the signal from each camera for proper color rendition.

Color Correction Gels for Tints

Color correction gels are used for tints largely because they are readily available and because they warm or cool the light in a way that occurs naturally in real life and is familiar, in the Kelvin scale. They shift the color along a single dimension between orange and blue.

Eighth, quarter, and half CTO and CTB gels are often used to warm up or cool down a source or even an entire scene. A fire light might use half, full, or even double CTO. A sunset or dawn scene might be filmed with a full CTO on the lights to simulate the golden light of the low sun. An exterior winter scene shot on a sound stage might use soft overhead lights gelled with a half CTB to cool the scene to 4100K. "Clean" ungelled directional sources would be added to make sunlight.

When using HMI lights in a tungsten-balanced scene, the amount of blue tint in the light is controlled by the amount of CTO correction applied to the light. When a slightly cool light is desired, a half-CTO is applied, bringing the 5600K source down to about 3800K. This accomplishes the same thing as applying a half CTB to a tungsten source.

Theatrical Gels for Tints

For a more complete palette of tints, theatrical gels offer a vast array of alternative possibilities (Table F.10). Theatrical gels, also called *effects gels* or *party gels*, come in more than 400 shades (in sheets 21 × 24 in. or 20 × 24 in. or in 4 × 25 ft. rolls). Instead of using a quarter CTO, the DP can choose from dozens of warming shades, such as gold, amber, straw, fire, salmon, pink, rose, apricot, and so on. For bringing color to face tones, there are various *cosmetic gels*: cosmetic peach, burgundy, rose, rouge, etc. (also listed in Table F.10). Colors such as salmon, pink, and even chocolate are also used to enhance skin tones. Straw and bastard amber often simulate a low afternoon sun or a flame.

Film emulsions vary in their sensitivity to different colors. A tint may not look quite the same on film as it does to the eye. It must also be remembered that tints must be compatible with the pigments of the wardrobe and set. The color of the light mixes subtractively with these colors. The cinematographer may even conduct screen tests to see on film exactly what effect a given tint will have on a particular face or costume. A test is also the best way to compare the effects of several possible tints side by side.

Saturated Colors

A deeply colored gel effectively narrows the range of wavelengths to those of a specific color. For example, a red gel transmits only the wavelengths around 650 nm. All other wavelengths are absorbed by the gel. The more deeply saturated the gel, the more heat it retains and the more susceptible it is to losing its color and melting. Pairing tungsten lights with red, orange, and yellow gels and HMI or arc lights with blue and purple gels uses the fixture's light spectrum more efficiently and puts less stress on the gels. Protect saturated gels by affixing them away from the heat of the lens, on the barn doors, or on a grip frame. Narrow-beam punchy sources such as PARs will play havoc on saturated gels. Heat-shield is a clear heat-resistance film used to protect colored gels from fading or melting under heat stress. Leave a couple inches of space between the Heat-shield and the gel. Rosco's Therma-shield is a beefier (and more expensive) version that will hold up better than standard heat shield films. Par lights and 2k open-face units often require heat shield, especially with dense colors.

Heat-shield will retard the fading of a gel but is ineffective when a light is simply burning through a gel. In that case, the gel must be placed further from the source, spreading the light over a greater area of gel. Sheets of gel may have to be seamed together with clear J-lar tape to cover the larger beam.

Additive Mixing of Colors

When differently colored lights overlap, they mix to make new colors. This is sometimes desirable, sometimes undesirable. Either way, it is important to know how colored lights mix.

The primary colors of light are red, blue, and green. By mixing these three colors of light, all other colors can be made. Theoretically, if three lights that are gelled primary red, blue, and green are aimed at a white surface with their beams

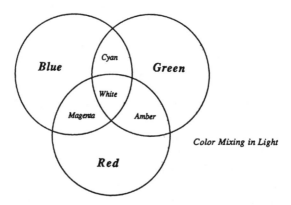

Figure 6.4 Additive mixing of colored light. The overlapping of all three primary colors creates white light. The combination of two primary colors creates the secondary color (amber, cyan, and magenta). (Reprinted with permission from Carter Paul. *Backstage Handbook*. New York: Broadway Press, 1988.)

overlapping, as in Figure 6.4, the area of intersection of all three lights is white. The intersection of two primaries makes the secondary colors (cyan, magenta and amber).

Subtractive Mixing of Colors

When two gels are combined in one light or when colored light is directed at a colored surface, the colors combine subtractively: Only the colors common to both are seen. Having a feeling for subtractive mixing is important for anticipating how the set, wardrobe, and actor's skin tone will appear in tinted or colored light. A red light directed at a blue-green dress, for example, will turn the dress black.

Brightness

Methods of Control

There are many ways to adjust a lamp's intensity. On the set you quickly learn to consider not only which method is the quickest and easiest, but also which method best accomplishes the effect needed.

Scrims Dropping a scrim in the light is the fastest and easiest way to reduce intensity without affecting anything else.

Distance It is often surprising how little you need to move a light to make a big difference in the brightness. This is because the intensity of a light decreases in proportion to the *square* of its distance from the subject. This is known as the *law of squares*. By examining Figure 6.5 you'll observe that if a fixture produces 120 FC at 10 ft., at twice the distance (20 ft.) the intensity will be *one-quarter*, or 30 FC. At three times the distance (30 ft.), the intensity will be *one-ninth*, or about 13 FC.

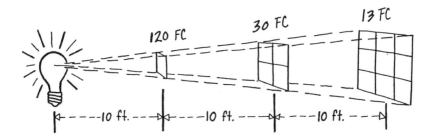

Figure 6.5 Law of Squares: If a square surface of 1 × 1 ft. is illuminated to 120 FC 10 ft. from the light source, at 20 ft. the same amount of light is now spread over a 4 × 4 ft. area. The amount of light on a 1 × 1 ft. area is a quarter of what it was at 10 ft. (120 ÷ 4 = 30 FC). At 30 ft., the intensity is one-ninth of what it was at 10 ft. (13 FC).

Flood or spot Flooding dims the light and increases its coverage; spotting brightens the light and narrows its coverage. With PAR lights, you can change to a wider or narrower lens.

Dimmers Dimmers provide a variable control of intensity but also affect color temperature. See Dimmers below.

Nets Nets are especially useful to control a selected portion of the beam. They are framed on three sides and open on one side. The open side makes it possible to hide the shadow line of the net. Also called *grip single* or *grip double*.

Fingers and dots Fingers are used to reduce the intensity of a sliver of the beam. Dots are used to reduce the intensity of a very small circular area and can be used to even out hot spots in the center of beam field. Both come as single nets, double nets, silks, and solids.

Bobinette Black net fabric that comes in bolts. It is handy because it can be cut to any shape and size, and draped or taped in place. It would be a quick way to dim down a too-bright neon or fluorescent practical, for example.

Neutral-density gel Neutral-density gel is useful for controlling the brightness of an otherwise unmodifiable fixture such as a xenon follow spot.

Diffusion Diffusion media dim and soften the light. The many kinds of diffusion media affect brightness and softness to varying degrees.

Wattage You can replace the fixture with a bigger or smaller unit, or in some instances you can replace the globe with a higher or lower wattage (bulb substitutions are listed in Table E.3).

Shutters Shutters can smoothly reduce the amount of light getting to the subject. They are handy when the light level needs to change during a shot.

Dimmers

A dimmer reduces light intensity by reducing either the voltage or the current to the light. Unfortunately, this in turn reduces the color temperature of the light, turning it gradually more yellow and orange as it is dimmed, as shown in Table 6.3. As a rule of thumb, the light changes 10K per volt. Ten volts over or under line volt-

Table 6.3 Color Temperature and Output at Various Voltages

Voltage	Color Temperature		Light output
	Kelvin	MIREDS	
120 volts	3200K	313 mireds	100%
110 volts	3100K	322 mireds	75%
100 volts	3000K	333 mireds	55%
90 volts	2900K	345 mireds	38%

age increases or decreases the Kelvin temperature by 100K. Dimmers are useful, therefore, only to the extent that the color change is not noticeable or when it is acceptable to the DP.

Several kinds of dimmers are used in film production: household, variac, plate dimmers, and electronic dimmers. Specifications for many commonly used types are listed in Table H.3.

Household Dimmers

Small 600W and 1000W household AC resistance dimmers, called *squeezers*, are often used to control practical lamps and small fixtures. Prepare each dimmer with a plug and socket so that it can be plugged into the line when needed. (Use grounded connectors and 14/3 wire for 1000W dimmers.)

Socket Dimmers

A 150W socket dimmer screws into the bulb socket. They are handy for controlling low-wattage practical lamps.

Variac Dimmers

The variac dimmer, an AC dimmer, is a type of variable transformer called an *autotransformer*. It can boost the power up to 140V or decrease it to zero. They come in 1k, 2k, and 5k sizes (Figure 6.6). Typically they are fitted with an on/off switch as well as a large rotary knob. Some have a three-way 120V/OFF/140V switch.

There is an important difference between a household resistance dimmer and a variac dimmer. A variable resistor, or rheostat, works by interposing a resistance on one wire of the circuit, in series with the light. The resistance opposes the flow of current to the light, which causes the light to dim. A variac does not use resistance; instead, it uses coils to induce a current (like a transformer), the voltage of which can be varied. For dimming filament lamps, the effect of either dimmer is the same; however, for controlling fluorescent ballasts or fan motors (inductive loads), a rheostat will not work. A variac must be used.

Plate Dimmers

Plate dimmers are large variable-resistance dimmers that can be used with either AC or DC circuits running incandescent lights (Figure 6.7).

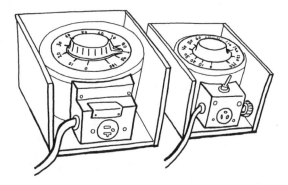

Figure 6.6 Variac dimmers in 2k and 1k sizes. The 1k dimmer knob is marked in volts, from 0V to 140V. The scale on the larger variacs are from 0 to 100, which does not refer to volts. When set at 85, the dimmer will deliver line voltage (120V). At 100% the variac boosts voltage to 140V. (Equipment courtesy of Hollywood Rental, Sun Valley, CA.)

Figure 6.7 Mole-Richardson 2k plate dimmer. (Equipment courtesy of Hollywood Rental, Sun Valley, CA.)

Because better dimmers are available for AC circuits, plate dimmers see most of their action dimming DC in the older studio sound stages. Unlike other types of dimmers, a plate dimmer can provide blackout dimming only when a minimum wattage is pulled through it; if the fixture connected to it is too small, the dimmer will not dim all the way down to blackness. To provide sufficient wattage, it may be necessary to run a *ghost load*, an additional light that does not light the set but provides the added wattage to make the dimmer operate.

Plate dimmers come in various sizes: 1k (775W minimum), 2k (1655W minimum), 3k (2705W minimum), and 5k (500W minimum, a huge 88-lb. unit). Each is equipped with an ON/OFF switch. DC sound stages use large consoles housing twelve or so plate dimmers. The console typically has a number of 1k circuits, some 2k circuits, and a couple 5k circuits.

Electronic Dimmers

The 2.4kW, 6kW, 12kW, and 20kW stand-alone electronic dimmers usually have a slider fader on the dimmer unit as well as a DMX port to control the dimmer from a console.

When a large number of incandescent lights are to be controlled, dimmer packs, or modular dimmer racks, are commonly used. Electronic dimmer packs come in standard sizes: 1.2kW (10A per dimmer), 2.4kW (20A per), 6.0kW (50A per), and 12.0kW (100A per). Electronic dimmers are also available for use in DC-powered installations. A complete list is given in Table H.4. A portable unit like the 12-channel pack shown in Figure 6.8 is compact and relatively lightweight, ideal for location work. Electronic dimmers are covered in more detail in chapter 9.

Separate dimmer circuits are controlled remotely from a *control console*, commonly called a *dimmer board*. A simple console provides sliding faders to set output levels for each channel. Two or more packs may be daisy-chained together and controlled by a single control console when larger numbers of channels are needed. Mul-

Figure 6.8 Strand CD80 dimmer pack. The 12-channel pack shown here has 12 dimmer circuits, each protected by a 20A circuit breaker. The dimmer pack's brains (the controller card) is attached to the face plate (below the breakers), which contains the control cable inputs/outputs, diagnostic indicators, and set-up switches. (Photo courtesy of Strand Lighting, Inc., Ranch Dominguez, CA.)

tiple packs are typically mounted on a rack. To eliminate dimmer hum from the sound stage, dimmer racks must be placed in a separate dimmer room or housed in a sound-proof, air-conditioned cabinet.

Shape, Pattern, and Form

In the following sections we look at how light can be manipulated as it travels from the light source to the subject. We begin by discussing the manipulation of hard light, then move on to ways of creating and manipulating soft light. This discussion encompasses the properties of form, shape, and pattern.

Once a light is placed and turned on the gaffer will want to cut it off areas where it is not wanted (be it with barn doors or flags). He will often want a key light cut off a background wall, or net off an actor who stands closer to the light source. The gaffer will want to break up the background with a pattern, a streak, or a line of shadow. Side-spill leaks should automatically be cleaned up with a flag or blackwrap. To accomplish any of these important goals, there are a few basic laws of physics to be aware of, as well as a number tricks you can use.

Making Cuts and Patterns

A *topper* is a flag or net used to cut the top of a light. Toppers are often used to keep light off background scenery, which also helps the boom operator avoid casting shadows on the walls. Similarly, *siders* and *bottomers* trim light from the side or bottom. A *lenser* cuts light off the camera lens to prevent flair in the filters and lens. A *courtesy flag* is one set up to shade glaring light off the director, DP, or others.

Flags and nets come in various standard sizes shown in Figure 6.9.

A few simple, but very important, rules apply when using any flag, net, pattern, or set piece (such as a window) in front of a light:

To make a soft cut (fuzzy shadow line), place the flag closer to the light. To make a hard cut (cleanly defined shadow line) place the flag closer to the surface onto which the shadow falls. For example, if you put a slash of light on a background wall, and want to light gradually taper off toward the top, you would use a soft-cut topper (a barn door works fine). If you want a hard, defined shadow line, on the other hand, you would want to place the flag well out in front of the light. For the sharpest definition, back the light up and place the flag as close to the wall as possible (without it encroaching into the frame). A larger flag may be necessary to cover the whole beam.

When setting a lenser, a hard cut is preferable. If the camera is on a long lens, the flag can be placed close to the camera. However, when a wide lens is being used, you will run into trouble with the flag encroaching into the frame and it must be worked closer to the light. Halfway between the camera and the light is usually a good, effective placement when practicable.

In order to avoid the encroachment problem, always place the stand on the off-stage side of the flag. First prepare the flag on the stand, then slide it in from the off-stage side until the shadow covers the lens and filters. A lenser must block light from the entire inner face of the matte box. If light hits the filters in the matte box,

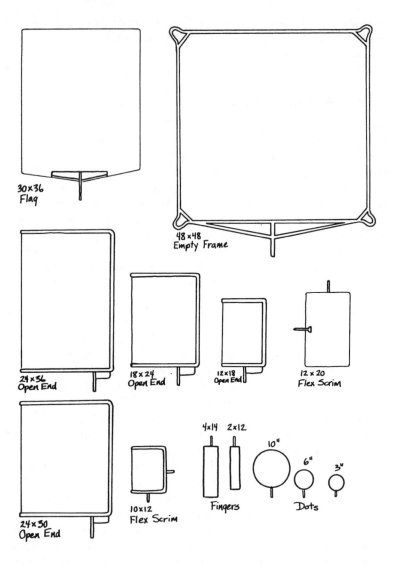

Figure 6.9 Common sizes of flags, nets, frames, and silks, including finger dots and postage stamps.

the image may flare. Try to overhear or observe what lens is being used, and learn to guesstimate the frame line accurately.

With Fresnel lights in flood position, the beam width is roughly equal to the distance from the light. If the flag is placed 3 ft. in front of the light, a 2 × 3 ft. flag will be sufficient. If a harder shadow is needed, you'll have to use a longer cutter (24 × 72 in.) placed further from the light.

Use of the Net

A net can reduce the intensity in a specific area with much greater accuracy than a half-scrim in the light. You can help hide the shadow line of a net by making a soft cut. If a double net is making an obvious shadow line, you can use two single nets clipped together and staggered, so the thickness builds up gradually. You can fine-tune intensity with a net by angling the net slightly. The more oblique the angle, the thicker it gets.

Break-Up Patterns

A break-up pattern is very often used to give texture to the background of a shot. Breaking up the light with a tree branch, gobo pattern, venetian blind, window pattern, or just random streaks of shadow gives the image greater contrast and tonal variation, and helps set off the foreground subject. The gaffer may want to exploit whatever shadow-projection possibilities are offered by the set and set dressing: foliage moving in the wind, a slow-turning fan, water running down glass, lace curtains, a banister.

Again, in order for the pattern to be cleanly defined, the pattern-maker must be as close to the surface as possible.

You will get a cleaner shadow:

- from a point source than from a larger one
- from a stronger light placed further away
- from a Fresnel fixture than from an open-face reflector fixture
- at full flood than when spotted in
- from the edge of the beam than from the center
- by removing the lens from the fixture altogether (though you also lose intensity and flood/spot control)
- by using a donut to remove the edges of the beam with ellipsoidal and xenon lights

The distance also affects the size of the projected shadows. When the pattern is close to the subject and far from the light, the pattern will be of only slightly larger dimensions than the pattern-maker itself. When the pattern-maker is very close to the light, however, the pattern will be projected over a large area, extremely enlarged and distorted in shape — more expressionistic. Thus the size of lamp used, the size of the pattern-maker needed to cover the beam, and the distance of the light and the pattern from the subject must all be taken into account before placing the light. In fact, these considerations may have to be taken into account when designing and placing the sets. For example, if a light is to shine through a window and needs to be placed a considerable distance from the window, ample space must be provided for lights around the set.

Cucaloris

A *cucaloris*, also called a *cookie* or *cuke*, is a plywood flag with odd-shaped holes cut in it. It is used to break up the light into random foliage-like splotches. A *celo cuke* is made with painted wire mesh and creates a more subtle effect because the mesh reduces the light rather than blocking it completely. A cookie does not look convincing if it moves during a take. For realistic moving foliage, use a branchaloris.

Branchaloris

A *branchaloris* is nothing more than a leafy branch found on the ground or broken off a bush and placed in front of a light on a C-stand. It breaks up the light, projects the shadows of branch and leaves onto the scene, and can be made to move naturally as if in the wind.

Tape on an Empty Frame

To make lines through the light — to simulate the frame of a window, for example — take an empty frame (18 × 24 in., 2 × 3 ft., or 4 × 4 ft., depending on the size of the source and the frame's distance from it) and run strips of black tape across it. It is easiest to build the pattern with the fixture in place and turned on, so you can see the effect it is creating.

Soft Light

Soft light results when light is bounced or diffused over a relatively large surface by one of several means: light shining through a large frame of diffusion, light bouncing off of a large white surface such as a foamcore bounce board, a white griffolyn, or a piece of show card; light bouncing from the large face of a softlight; or using a soft box.

With soft light we are no longer dealing with parallel (slightly diverging) rays of light from a single point source, but with rays that are bounced or diffused so they are diffracted at all angles — moving in all directions. Light from a soft source comes to the subject from all points of a diffuse luminous surface, resulting in three qualities that are often very desirable:

1. It creates soft shadows. No clean, sharply discernible line is projected. The shadow lines are broad and fuzzy. Shadows appear as gradations of tone so that the entire image is imbued with a softness that is natural and also very beautiful. The fuzzy quality of soft shadows also makes them easier to hide in situations where multiple shadows would be distracting.
2. Soft light wraps around the features of the subject. Whereas a face lit from one side by hard light is like a half moon — bright on one side and black on the other, lit by a large soft source it shows a gradual drop off of light from one side to the other. Soft light tends to fill in blemishes in the skin. The overall picture has a full tonal range, light to dark, with no harsh shadow lines and with lower overall contrast than when lit with harder light.
3. When lighting shiny or glossy subjects such as an automobile, the reflection of a soft light source in the contours of the metal forms interesting patterns that emphasize shape and curves. Hard light, on the other hand, is reflected as a bright, glaring hot spot.

A soft source can be used to create a soft highlight in dark wood, bringing out dark furniture or paneling by catching a reflection of the light source. The gaffer places the light where it is reflected directly into the camera. Especially in cases where you don't want to throw a lot of light onto the walls, this approach yields a subtle and more natural effect.

Along the same lines, a soft source makes a nice eye light. It reflects in the shiny part of the eye, giving the eyes a special brightness. A large, soft source reflected in this way need not actually shine a lot of light onto the subject; it need only be bright enough to create a visible highlight by reflection.

Softness of Light

Three factors affect the softness of light: the *size* of the face of the source, its *distance* from the subject, and the *diffuseness* of the light. The larger the source, the softer the shadows and the greater the wrapping effect, because the larger source yields more light rays that can come from angles that encircle the features of the subject. This is why it is important when focusing a light fixture onto a diffusion frame or bounce board to completely fill it with light. The surface of the diffusion frame or bounce board becomes the source of light for the scene; the larger the source, the softer the effect.

The smaller the subject, in relation to the face of the source, the more the light engulfs the subject. If the subject is too small it becomes overwhelmed and the image starts to appear flat.

Obviously, the size of the source in relation to the subject also depends on the distance between them. The further away the source, the smaller its effective size. (The Sun, for example, is a very large source but as it is 93 million miles away, its rays are completely parallel, so direct sunlight is about as sharp a light as you'll find.)

Bringing a soft light in as close to a subject as possible maximizes its softening effect. This also has the effect of localizing the light, creating a soft pool around the actor, which then falls off very quickly into darkness. This happens because light level falls off with distance at a geometric rate, so the closer the source is to the actor, the more dramatic the fall off. Conversely, move the source out if you want the light to carry across more space; the further the source is from the actor, the less the fall off around him (relative to the light level at his position).

Controlling Soft Light

Soft light is more difficult than hard light to cut and control, and the softer the light (the heavier the diffusion), the more difficult it becomes. The larger the source, the larger the flags required to block the light. Boxing-in a 4 × 4 frame of heavy diffusion typically requires 4 × 4 or 4 × 8 flags. Flags and nets used close to a large source are ineffectual; the light engulfs the flag. To be useful, the flag must be far enough from the source that it blocks a direction the light is traveling, rather than merely blocking a portion of the face of the source. Large cutters, 2 × 6 ft., are necessary as toppers, placed well out in front of the source. An even larger *teaser* may need to be fashioned from a length of duvatyne attached to a length of 1 × 3 batten.

With soft light you might use a solid where normally you would use a net. Because the shadow is so nebulous, the flag serves to create an area of lesser brightness, rather than a cut. The flag can be angled to increase or decrease its effective size.

Diffusion

Diffusion Materials

There are five basic types of diffusion, each with its own character: spun, frost, white diffusion, silks (and other fabrics), and silent diffusion. Each type is manufactured in several densities (Table F.11). Spun, or spun glass, gives the beam a mild soft edge, but with minimal beam spread, so that the shape of the beam and the effectiveness of barn doors are maintained. Frost, such as Opal or Hampshire Frost, yields slightly more beam spread and softening, but still maintains a discernible beam center. The original direction of the beam is still dominant.

A medium weight diffusion such as 250 diffracts much more of the light. As a result, the beam spreads as it passes through the diffusion. As the diffusion surface itself becomes the source of rays of light equally with the light fixture, the effective size of the source is enlarged to the size of the diffusion frame. Shadows are softened. The light starts to wrap around the edges of objects.

A dense diffusion, such as a heavy frost, 216, or grid cloth, causes wide beam spread. The original direction of the beam becomes secondary to the diffuse multidirectional rays emitted from the diffusion. The light rays are deflected in all directions over the entire area of the diffusion frame. This creates the ideal source for shadowless, wrapping light because the greatest number of light rays are diverted at angles that can accomplish these ends, and because the dominant direction of the light from the fixture is completely removed. It creates a shadowless, even field of light, with no discernible beam center or edge.

Fabrics such as silk, muslin, and grid cloth are dense diffusions often used on large frames. Many gaffers like the diffusing effect of muslin. You can bounce light off it or use it as a diffuser, directing light through it. The fabric is inexpensive and durable, and can be made in any size up to huge 40-ft. squares and larger. Unbleached muslin has a yellow tint, which warms the light without the need for gels. Bleached muslin has less of a tint but retains the warming effect.

Silk is commonly used on an 12' or 20' overhead frame. Silk has a relatively low transmission; it reduces light intensity by about 2-2/3 stops, but despite its density, silk has only a moderate diffusing effect. A light passing through silk still casts a hard shadow, but the silk helps to fill. China silk or 1/4 silk is much lighter, reducing transmission by only 1/2 stop.

Silent diffusions, such as Soft Frost and Hilite, are made of a rubbery material that does not rattle and crinkle when caught by wind, as other diffusions do. These materials are not as heat resistant as normal diffusion, however, and should not be used directly on a light fixture.

As with colored gel, label each piece of diffusion when it is cut from the roll. Mark the type on the corner of the piece with an indelible marker.

Diffusion on the Fixture

Attaching diffusion material to the barn doors of a Fresnel or open-face light takes the hard edge off the beam. It diffuses the light, evens out the intensity across the field, and reduces or removes the central hot spot.

To create as large a source as possible, open the barn doors wide and attach the diffusion to the outside. When using dense diffusion medium, the flood/spot mechanism works in reverse. To maximize the light output, flood the light to fill the diffusion with light. Maximum output is often found just shy of full flood.

Diffusion attached inside the barn doors does allow the barn doors still to have some effect and creates fewer problems with spill and reflections off the back of the diffusion; however, it does not increase the size of the source and therefore does little more than take the curse off the hard light.

Other Ways of Making Soft Light

Croney Cone

The Croney cone, which is named for its inventor, Jorden Crownenweth, ASC (Blade Runner), is a cone that fits in place of the barn doors on the front of the light. A frame fitted with grid cloth or some other diffusion slides into slots on the front of the cone, turning the Fresnel into a soft source with a larger face (Figure 6.10). The diffusion frame can be exchanged easily when a different type of diffusion is desired.

Chimera

Chimera Photographic Lighting makes a variety of collapsible, heat-resistant, fabric soft boxes (Figure 6.11) that incorporate a great many refinements on the basic Croney cone design.

Chimeras are made of heat-resistant fabric stretched and held in shape by flexible, interior, stainless-steel poles. The interior fabric is soft silver reflective material, which increases light output and further diffuses the light. Their design includes two

Figure 6.10   A Croney cone. (Equipment Courtesy of Hollywood Rental, Sun Valley, CA.)

Figure 6.11 Chimera soft boxes. (Photo courtesy of Chimera Photographic Lighting, Boulder, CO.)

effective ways to reduce side spill, 60° and 90° honeycomb grids, and louvers. A second interior diffusion baffle can be added to double-diffuse the light. This ensures that even an intense and punchy light source will be fully diffused.

Chimeras can be fitted to almost any Fresnel, PAR, and open-face fixture in place of barn doors. A "speed ring" is needed to adapt the Chimera to each light (see tables in Appendix H). The Chimera light banks are available in four models. Video Pro and Quartz banks are standard depth and are best used with open-face fixtures. Daylite and Daylite Junior banks are deeper; they are useful for narrower beam fixtures such as Fresnels.

The flaps that close the chimera around the face of the light will get burned by most lights. The flaps are fitted with Velcro, so they can be folded back away from the face of the light. *Always* fold the flaps and open the ventilation holes.

Homemade Diffusion Box

You can build an inexpensive softbox, with many of the same advantages as the chimera. This type of soft box diffuses light from a fixture while also containing the light (Figure 6.12A). It has two separated layers of diffusion. Light becomes diffused as it passes through the layers and also bounces between the layers, further scattering the rays and softening the light. The hood, made of black show card, adjusts the spread of light. A nail-on plate is screwed on for mounting the unit on a C-stand.

A box like this can be made any size or shape, but if you make it just slightly larger than the size of standard frames (24 × 36 in or 18 × 24 in), you can make a slot in the side of the box so that diffusion and color can be easily changed by sliding in a new frame.

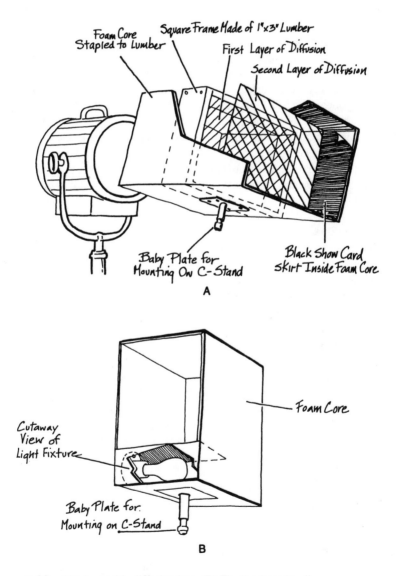

Figure 6.12 (A) A portable diffusion box. (B) The "garbage box."

Homemade Soft Box

Another approach to take is to construct a soft box with light bulbs installed inside the soft box itself. The advantage is that it is self-contained and very light-weight. You can position such a box without having to contend with a heavy light fixture (a short C-stand easily supports it).

Soft boxes can be made quite simply out of light lumber, foamcore, staples, screws, and diffusion. Remember that these materials are flammable, and light bulbs get very hot. Be sure to cut ventilation flaps or holes in the bottom and the top of the box to create a ventilation flow. Leave plenty of space on all sides around the bulbs. Do not put power cords or tape on the inside of the box, where they could come loose, fall near a bulb, and catch on fire. Use #14 or #12 "red/black" wire, not zip cord. Build these homemade devices with large doses of common sense and caution.

Construct the box with black foamcore on the outside, white inside. Use porcelain medium screw base sockets for regular bulbs, photofloods, and mushroom floods, or bayonet mount FEV sockets for small tungsten bulbs. Use several bulbs, and wire each socket separately so that you can vary the brightness by switching bulbs on or off. Cut flaps so that you can reach inside to change bulbs when needed. Place the mounting plate at the center of gravity so that the box balances on the plate and does not create excessive torque on the C-stand. (If you build a snoot for the box, you may need to determine a second center of gravity with the snoot in place and add a second nail-on plate.)

Garbage Box

This type of soft box got its name when an inventive gaffer (now DP, Greg Gardener) hurriedly pulled a cardboard box from the garbage and transformed it into a soft light (Figure 6.12B). The box is lined with foamcore. A ledge shields direct light from the bulb. A white wrap foil lining around the bulb should be used to protect the foamcore from heat. This type of light is used close in to a subject.

Chicken Coop

A chicken coop hangs overhead on rope. This kind of light might be used, for example, over a large dinner table. It is usually rigged so that it can be raised and lowered to increase or decrease the intensity of the light. The one shown in Figure 6.13A is fitted with six photoflood bulbs. A small, single-bulb version is shown in Figure 6.13B. The coop has a duvetyn skirt that can be lowered or raised independently on all four sides to control the amount of light falling on the walls of the room.

Nook Light Coop

Figure 6.14 shows nook lights mounted in a chicken coop frame and pointing upward into the foamcore to create an even, less direct soft light.

China Lanterns

Paper Chinese lanterns are an inexpensive, lightweight soft light or ambient light source. They come in various sizes — 12, 24, and 30 in. spheres — as well as rectangular boxes. Rig the lantern to a C-stand, with a photoflood bulb in a porcelain

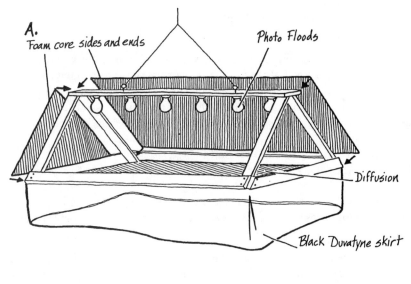

A.
Foam core sides and ends

Photo Floods

Diffusion

Black Duvatyne skirt

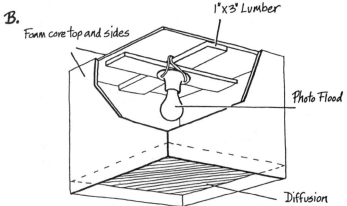

B.
Foam core top and sides

1"x3" Lumber

Photo Flood

Diffusion

Figure 6.13 (A) A homemade skirted six-light chicken coop. (B) A single photoflood soft box.

socket (do not use the 60W plastic sockets that are sometimes sold with the lanterns; the photoflood bulbs will melt them). I always use them on a variac. Hidden in the set, or positioned just off screen and used in close, the lanterns are nice soft "glow lights" and give a localized warm glow. A large ball hung above the set achieves a nice low ambient light level. The ball can be skirted, if desired, to keep spill off walls. The popularity of lanterns inspired manufacturers to come up with more durable fixtures of this type. K 5600 Lighting makes a 200W HMI lantern in 20" or 30" diameter. Chimera has 22" and 30" lanterns which fit video pro ring sizes, or can be fitted with a tungsten halogen socket.

Bounce Light

Soft light can be created by simply bouncing a specular source off a white surface. Following are some examples.

Bead Board and Foamcore   In many situations, a piece of white board can be used to bounce existing light onto the shadow areas of the face to reduce contrast. This is especially common when shooting outside in direct sunlight, where the contrast is very high. A 2-ft. or 4-ft. square of foamcore, taped to and reinforced by a piece of bead board, is standard equipment for fill light. Similarly, a piece of show card placed in the lap of the driver of a car helps fill in shadows.

To fill a fairly large room with soft light, a strong light, such as a 2500 HMI PAR, can be aimed at a 4 × 4 ft. or 4 × 8 ft. piece of bead board or foamcore (Figure 6.15).

Remember that the angle of incidence equals the angle of reflection. If you put the bounce board up high and angle it downward, you can place the lights below and in front of the board, pointing up into it.

Show Card, Cove Light   In a small room where it is difficult to hide lamps, you can tape a piece of white show card into an off-screen corner (Figure 6.16).

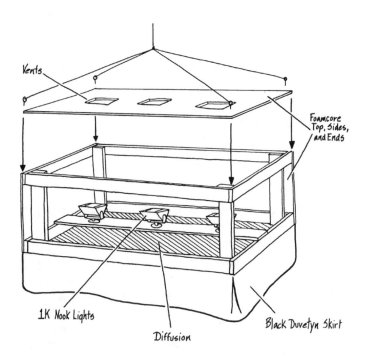

Figure 6.14   A homemade skirted nook light bounce box.

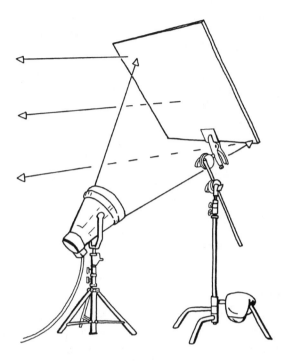

Figure 6.15 A strong, large, soft source produced by bouncing a 2500 W HMI PAR off a 4 × 4 bead board.

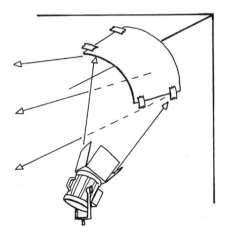

Figure 6.16 Show card taped into a corner creates a soft source without rigging a fixture in that corner.

The reflected light can be better controlled if the show card is curved into a parabola. The fixture is hidden under or above, pointing at the show card, creating a soft light from that direction. You can also use a silver or gold show card.

Ceiling A fast and easy way to fill a room with soft, even illumination is simply to bounce a strong light off a white ceiling. If the ceiling is not white, you can rig a sheet of foamcore to the ceiling.

Griff To create a very big, soft source that might simulate skylight when shooting inside a studio or when a large area needs to be covered with soft light, the gaffer may bounce light into a 12- or 20-ft. square of griffolyn. A couple of large HMIs, one on each side, will do the trick. For exterior scenes, a griff works the same way, bouncing sunlight.

Negative Fill To some extent the shine in a person's face reflects the color and lightness of surfaces around them. Placing a 4 × 4 floppy near an actor removes these reflections, as well as shading off any wayward light.

Movement

The final property of light that can be manipulated is motion: the jumping glow of a television screen, the dancing flames of a fire, the passing of car headlights at night, disco and concert lights, the movement of a handheld lantern or flashlight, a swinging bulb hanging from the ceiling, the projection of rain running down a windshield, the slow, smooth motion of sunlight through an airplane's windows as it banks and turns. Movement contributes to a scene's naturalism, mood, and visual interest.

Flicker Effects: Television Screen, Flame, and Fire

Sit in a dark room with only the television on but don't look at it. Watch the way the light shifts on the walls and faces in the room. You will notice that the blue television light quickly changes in intensity and color when there is a cut on screen and gradually shifts in intensity as the camera pans or as characters move around.

The pace of the shifts depends on what you are watching. MTV creates a constantly changing image. Old movies, on the other hand, tend to play scenes in wide master shots or to intercut reverse close-ups, leaving at least several seconds and even 20 or 30 seconds between cuts. When you are creating an off-screen television effect, you must find a way to mimic the pace of the shifts with the intensity of the light.

There are many different ways to do this, and any method that works is as good as another. A common way is to make a soft box out of foam core and light lumber, and to place several small lights inside it. Use blue gel and diffusion on the front of some or all the lights, as desired. To make the lights flicker, some sort of controller must be used.

Flicker Boxes

Television screen and flame effects are often created using a flicker box such as that shown in Figure 6.17.

Figure 6.17 Magic Gadgets flicker box supplies three 20A circuits, each of which can be set to flicker up to a set peak and down to a set base level. The three circuits can be programmed to create a variety of chase effects, fire effects, and television effects. The box can also serve as three 2k dimmers. (Photo courtesy of Magic Gadgets, Inc., Seattle, WA.)

There are a variety of such boxes on the market. Specifications are listed in Table H.4, Appendix H. A flicker box typically creates increase and decrease in intensity at random intervals. The rate of flicker, as well as the brightness of the light at its peak and lowest intensities, can be set with controls. Some flicker boxes also make blinking light effects and lightning flashes. Flicker boxes having three circuits can produce coordinated flicker effects and chase effects.

Some gaffers use a circular disk of mercury switches to flicker the lights. The switches contain liquid mercury, which completes the circuit when tilted such that the mercury sloshes over the contacts. By artfully tipping and rotating the disk, different lights turn on and off in a controllable yet unregimented way that is very convincing. Operating this type of controller requires a practiced hand.

Another gaffer uses two short fluorescent tubes and has an electrician move his arms in front of the light — simple, but effective.

Fire Effect

Flicker boxes are also commonly used to create a fire effect. When a flame moves, the shadows from the firelight move up and down and from side to side. To get a convincing effect, it is necessary to use at least two lights to simulate a flame.

The best way to get a fire effect is to use fire. If practical considerations (such as the location, the need for fire marshals, and so on) allow it, a fire bar (a gas-fueled pipe with holes along it) can be supplied by the effects department and used as a portable lighting source. If the intensity of the flame is insufficient, supplemental light can be imbued with the look of flame by shining a fixture through the flame of the fire bar.

Moving Lights

Lights are often mounted to a crane or dolly, or handheld by an electrician to make the light move. Reflecting a PAR 64 into a shiny silver tray of water creates lively water striations. Sequences of dimmer cues can be set up to create breathtaking shifts in angle and color. Various special effects lights can be used to create moving projections (*scene machine*), or dynamic concert lighting effects (automated fixtures). There are many exciting ways to move light. The possibilities are limited only by your imagination.

CHAPTER 7

Electrician's Set Protocol

Staging Area

Upon arrival at each new shooting location, one of the first jobs is to establish a staging area where electrical equipment is kept, ready to go onto the set when needed. The best boy will have scoped out a spot that is convenient to the set, but not so close as to block access. Stake out the spot early before all the good ones are taken. The entrance to the staging area must be clear of obstructions. You don't want a line of producers and stars sitting in chairs in front of the area. You need to be able to carry equipment in and out fast.

While the director and DP are deciding on their shots, the electricians can "head-up" a selection of lights on stands in the staging area, ready to be brought into the set when called for. Line up the lights on stands. Organize them in rows — row of midgets, row of tweenies, row of babies, row of juniors, and so on — so that each type of light is readily accessible. Skinny up the legs of the stands so they can be packed together closely. To be totally proper about it, the lights should be arranged with the stand fully lowered, T-handles lined up in a straight line down the back of the stand, power cord hanging on hanger, gels and scrims hanging on the stand (not in the light), and doors closed.

The staging area should be arranged in an orderly fashion for easy access to all the equipment to include: crates of 25-ft. and 50-ft. stingers, gel crate, gel rolls, boxes of practical bulbs and associated electrical parts (zip cord, quick-ons, plugs, porcelain sockets, etc.), variac dimmers, black wrap, tape rolls, closepins, and similar electrical expendables. It is often convenient to keep a selection of essentials (tape, black wrap, closepins, and gel) even closer at hand, in a set box — a crate that is kept on or immediately outside the set.

When a light, stinger, or cable is no longer needed on the set, it goes back to the staging area where it will not create clutter. The light should be "head wrapped" — the stand is fully lowered, the cord coiled, the barn doors closed, and the scrims removed and hung on the stand. If a particular gel or diffusion is being used on all the lights, store it in the scrim box.

Lighting the Set

Grips and electricians have to be alert and always have one eye on the gaffer. You tune into the sound of his voice, and learn to pick it out from the general rumble of noise. An experienced electrician has a sense of the ebb and flow of activity on the set, and knows when he needs to work fast and when there is time to spare. When lighting begins on each new setup all the electricians should automatically come to the set. There is a great deal of activity as the broad strokes of the lighting are put in.

The director's monitor and the camera dolly should be given a hot stinger immediately. The director often needs the monitor to set up the new shot.

A period of tweaking and adjusting follows the broad strokes; a few small lights may be added. Finally the DP declares that the lighting is ready, and the AD calls the actors into the set. Each time the first AD announces a new shot, the electricians working the set should quietly get close to the lights that may need to move and watch the gaffer and DP for orders. Even when lighting activity is at a minimum, there should always be one electrician on the set (unless the AD clears the set for a particular performance). Before you leave the set to grab a soda, conduct business, or go to the rest room, be sure that another electrician is on the set and knows that you are stepping out. If the gaffer needs to step out, he will assign the best boy or a set electrician to cover him, and that person must remain next to the DP until the gaffer returns.

Setting Lights

What's Needed

The gaffer gives an instruction: "Put a baby over in that corner to key these two actors. Give it opal and quarter CTO." You will need a baby stand, a baby with scrim set and barn doors, gels, and diffusion. You will probably also need a 25-ft. stinger to run power to the light. A grip will usually be right behind you with a C-stand and flags, and he should provide a sandbag. You may want to bring a couple of additional gels and diffusion along so that if the gaffer changes her mind, you don't have to go back for them later.

A complete set of appropriate-size scrims and a set of barn doors should be brought to the set with every light. Hang the scrim box on the stand. When the gaffer wants a little less from a light, you should be able to drop in the scrim in seconds. It is very bad form to have to search for scrims. They should always be with the light.

It is also worth repeating that each raised stand should be bagged. The more time you spend on sets, the more you see just how easily stands are toppled. It becomes second nature to check that stands are properly bagged. Similarly, when working in a wind, around Ritter fans, or around helicopters, the grips may need to tie guy lines (not less than three) to the top of the light stand and secure them to bull stakes driven well into the ground. Prop-wash from a helicopter will blow over a Dino on a supercrank like it was a piece of paper, even with 130 lb. of sand on it.

Teamwork

It is important for each electrician to watch for a chance to back up another electrician and jump into the game. When a light is called for, one electrician sets the light, while another runs the power. When an HMI is called for, one person connects the head, the other connects the ballast. If a light is called for at the last minute, all the electricians work in a team: one person carries the head, another grabs a stand, and two more carry the ballast together, throwing the head cables over their shoulders. By the time the head is on the stand, the ballast cable is attached to the ballast, and someone has run power to the ballast. The whole drill takes only a minute.

The trick to teamwork is communication and jumping in to help without getting in another person's way. Communicate. If you're running someone's power for them, or fetching gel for their light, be sure to tell them so. There are some things that are better accomplished by one person alone. If three or four people all jump to set one light, the set becomes like a grade-school soccer game, with everybody playing out of position, chasing after the ball in one roving mass. The director of photography is continually in a race against time. The grip/electric crew can win or lose that race for him. When things gel between crew members, setups come together like a well-practiced play on the sports field, allowing the director of photography time for finesse. In this way a sharp crew can vastly improve the look of the photography, not to mention keeping the days a reasonable length.

Warnings

When carrying large, heavy, or hot equipment through the set, call out warnings such as, "Coming through — watch your back" or "Hot points — coming through." You don't want to singe the director's arm with a hot light. I once heard a grip carrying dolly track use the warning, "Duck or bleed!" This cleared the way quite effectively.

When turning a light on, call out, "Light coming on" before you hit the switch. This is a courtesy to the actors, stand-ins, and crew who are in front of your light. It is meant to warn them not to look at the light. Unfortunately, when novices hear the warning, they often do just the opposite and momentarily blind themselves, but after that they quickly learn. It is a good idea to tilt the light up away from the set or to put a gloved hand in front of the light as you turn it on. That way the light doesn't come on suddenly, and you give the actors or stand-ins a second to adjust to it before you pull your hand away. This kind of courtesy is not just a matter of politeness, but also one of professionalism. Saying "Light coming on" also alerts the gaffer and DP that your light is in place, powered, and ready to be focused.

Similarly, avoid blinding people in general. If a working light needs to be moved, don't let it swing around and blast into people's faces.

If you are about to plug in a light and you can't tell if the switch is on or off, you can give the warning, "Possible hot stab." This is especially important if the light is aimed at someone or if the light coming on is likely to be an annoyance to the DP or gaffer. An accidental hot stab can be forgiven if you give a warning. It is important to make a habit of turning lights off at the switch before unplugging them to avoid hot stabs.

Whenever a flash camera is used on the set, the photographer should call out, "Flashing" before snapping the shot. This is mainly a courtesy to people in front of the camera, but it also alerts the electricians that a camera is about to flash. This way, the flash is not mistaken for an electrical arc or a bulb exploding or burning out.

Safeties

When a light is hung above the set (suspended from the ceiling, set walls, or overhead pipes), a safety line should be tied around the yoke and around a permanent structural support capable of holding the weight of the light if it should come off its stud. The best type of safety line is aircraft cable, sometimes called a *dog collar* because it has a loop in one end and a carabiner or dog leash clip at the other. In the absence of aircraft cable, sash cord or safety chain can be used. Be sure to leave enough slack in the safety line for the light to be panned and tilted.

Barn doors should also come with safety chain connecting them to the light to prevent them from falling. If a light does not have a barn door safety, use bailing wire or safety chain to attach the doors before hanging the light.

Focusing Lights

Once the light is in place, notify the gaffer that you are ready to focus it. When you turn the light on, the grunt work stops, and the real craft begins — manipulating the light so that it accomplishes the desired effect. While the electrician handles the light, the gaffer either stands on the set with the light meter or views the scene from the appropriate camera angle. Very often the gaffer will start with the light at full spot to aim the beam. A gaffer will hold out a fist where he wants the beam spotted. The electrician spots the light onto his hand, then returns the light to full flood. Another way gaffers sometimes focus the light is to view the light fixture through a contrast glass. The gaffer then directs the lamp operator with hand signals. The following are common instructions:

Pan lamp-left or **lamp-right**   Lamp-left is your left when you are facing the direction that the light is facing. Lamp-right is your right.

Camera-left or **camera-right**   Camera-left is your left when you are facing the direction that the camera is facing. Camera-right is your right.

Tilt up   Tilt the light up.

Tilt down   Tilt the light down.

Flood it out   Turn the flood/spot knob slowly toward flood until told to stop. Say "Flooding."

Full flood   Go directly to full flood.

Spot it in   Turn the flood/spot knob slowly toward spot until told to stop. Say "Spotting."

Full spot   Go directly to full spot.

Stem up   Raise the stand.

Stem down   Lower the stand.

Walk it back   Move the stand and light back.

Walk it in   Move the stand and light closer to the action.

Lock it down   The light is aimed correctly; tighten the T-handles to lock that position.

Walk away   It's perfect. Make sure that everything is secure, and you're done with that one. "That's a purchase" is a similar phrase.

A scosh   Technical term for an increment slightly less than a smidge or a tad, as in "Flood it out a scosh."

Door it off the back wall   Lower the top barn door.

Drop in a double   Put in a double scrim. Say "Double in" when finished. You also hear expressions like "Slow it down" or "Bring it down to a dull roar."

Home run   Two doubles in a light.

Grand slam   Two doubles and a single in a light.

Pull the wire   Pull out all scrims. Say "Wire out" or "It's clean" when no scrims are in.

Bottom half-double   Put in a half-double scrim oriented to cut the bottom. Say "Bottom half-double in."

Waste some of that   Pan or tilt the light so the hot spot isn't directly on the action.

Do off/on or **A-B**   Switch the light off and on so that the gaffer can observe what the light is accomplishing. Announce "On" as you turn it on and "Off" as you turn it off.

Shake up that shiny board   As the sun moves, shiny boards have to be readjusted. Move the board to check that it is properly aimed. The phrase can refer to lights in the same way.

Flag the light   Pass your hand back and forth in front of the lens to show where the beam is hitting.

Give me a slash here   Bring the barn doors together to create a line where indicated.

Rotate the beam   PAR lights have an elliptical beam, rather than a round one. You can turn the lamp housing to orient the beam horizontal, vertical, or at any angle.

Dress the cable   Neaten up the cable or run it out of sight or out of the way.

Dress the light   Something is hanging off the light (that is, a safety chain or diffusion is hanging into the shot). Clean it up.

Change that out for a deuce   Replace the light with a 2k fixture.

Count to ten   Hold off on what you are doing; things are changing and it may not be needed after all.

Cancel the baby   Yup, sure enough we don't need that light.

Fire it up   Turn it on.

Cool the light   Turn it off. You also often hear "Save the lights."

Strike the light   When referring to an HMI, strike means turn it on, as in "Strike it up."

Strike the set   Take down all the lights and return them to the staging area.

It is customary for the electrician to respond to the gaffer's directions by repeating each direction back as he performs it. This assures the gaffer that she has been heard and someone is following her instructions. When she says,"Flood it out," the electrician responds,"Flooding" as he does so. When delay is involved, he lets the gaffer know he has heard her before proceeding; if she asks for a light, the electrician responds,"Flying in" as he goes to fetch it.

Walkie-Talkies and Radio Headsets

The clamor of the crew calling out these sorts of instructions to one another can be a distraction for the director, actors, and DP when they are trying to communicate on set. Walkie-talkies or radio headsets are an invaluable tool for the grip/electric crew. They cut down on the noise on the set and save the electricians a lot of running. If you need something from the staging area, for example, and someone has just gone over there, you can quietly ask that person to bring you what you need on the way back without yelling or running.

When using headsets or walkie-talkies, be sure to use proper mike technique: Press the button fully, allow a second for the transmitter to engage *before* you start speaking, and don't let up on it until *after* you have finished your last word. Otherwise your first and last words will be cut short. When speaking, keep the mike about an inch from your mouth for a clear, strong signal.

Typically a walkie-talkie has many channels, which may be assigned to various departments. Usually the assistant directors are on channel one, while the electric, grip, and transportation departments claim their own channels.

The gaffer initiates a conversation by asking for someone by name: "David, come back," or simply a general call for aid: "Electric." Respond with your name: "Go for David." Always acknowledge a transmission by saying "copy" or some similar response. If the gaffer's transmission is interrupted by another transmission, say "You were stepped on, say again." If the signal breaks up during transmission, say "You broke up, come again," or repeat back what you think he said and ask for confirmation. A broken signal is often an indication that the battery on the transmitting walkie is low and should be exchanged for a fresh one. Common usage has evolved to include various CB radio codes, such as

Q: "What's your 20?" = Where are you?
A: "I'm ten one-hundred" = I'm in the john.

Use concise phrases. Brevity is the soul of wit, as Shakespeare said; try not to clutter up the frequency with rambling. If a lengthy explanation is unavoidable, you may want to change to an unused channel so as not to monopolize the frequency. Say "Go to three." Then change to channel three and wait for a response. When the conversation is finished, say "Back to five" or whatever the original channel was.

Last but not least, turn down the volume on your walkie to zero during takes, and remember to turn it back up again when the take is finished. There are few blunders more embarrassing and less forgivable than ruining a take by allowing your radio to blurt out, "Hey Hank, when's lunch?" in the middle of a tense performance.

Hand Signals

Before radios came into common use, electricians used hand signals. Even when working on a show with radios, you will still find times when hand signals are needed. They are shown in Figure 7.1.

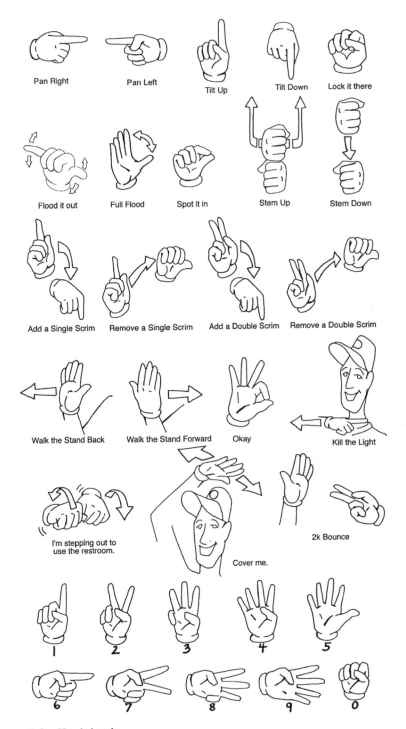

Figure 7.1 Hand signals.

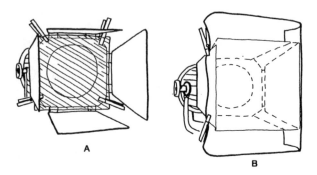

Figure 7.2 Gel and diffusion can be attached either inside the barn doors (A) or outside the doors (B).

Applying Gel to the Fixture

The most common way of attaching gel or diffusion to a Fresnel or open-face light is to clip it on with closepins (Figure 7.2B). Look out for light reflecting off the back of the gel and bouncing onto the walls of the set. Encircle the gaps in the barn doors with black wrap to block gel-reflection spill.

Don't be stingy with gel; cut a square of gel big enough so that light does not leak around the side of the gel causing white spill. Placing the gel on the inside of the barn doors (Figure 7.2A) also prevents spill but will put more heat stress on the gel. Generally this works well with Fresnel fixtures when they are flooded out. When using a dense gel, a particularly hot fixture (PAR or open face), or when the lamp is spotted, the gel will lose color.

Gel frames can be used in some circumstances with some types of fixtures but generally the scrim slot is too hot a place for gel. Never put a scrim next to a gel frame. The hot scrim will melt the gel.

Stingers and Cabling

A set can quickly become a rat's nest of tangled cables if care is not taken when running cables and stingers. Here are some guidelines.

Circuit Balance and Capacity

The best boy electric is responsible for distributing the loads on the cables and the power source so that circuit loads are balanced and cables are operating within their capacities. Each electrician must know the cable layout, know where you can find outlets, and keep tabs on the amperage on circuits that are operating near capacity. When balance (between phases) or circuit capacity are critical, keep the best boy abreast of new lights being added. With large lights (5k or larger), consult with him as to which circuit should be used before plugging in.

Exceeding the amperage capacity of a wire or plug causes it to heat up and eventually to melt the insulation. A bad connection inside a socket or plug also overheats the insulation. When lights are left on for more than 20 minutes, it is good practice to touch the cables and plugs from time to time to check for overheating. It is normal for cables to run warm, but if they become hot to the touch replace cables as necessary and notify the best boy electric.

If a fuse blows repeatedly, there is something wrong: The circuit is overloaded or there is a short in the light, the plug, or the outlet. Redistribute the plugs, add more circuits, repair the short. Do not replace the fuse with an oversized fuse or copper slug — it'll eventually cause a meltdown. It is helpful to tag the plug of 2k lights so that you can identify them among the many cords at the outlet box, and keep them on separate 20A circuits.

Cables Crossing the Set

Keep cables out of the shot and out from underfoot. An electrician rarely runs a cable in a direct line from power to light. Before running the cable, consider the best way to run it. Avoid crossing doorways, especially if there is a chance that the door will work in the scene. Run stingers around the edge of the set. Gaffers often say you can tell a good electrician by the cable you can't see. The most convenient setup is to have the distribution cables run above the set with power drops in strategic locations. This eliminates a lot of cable running around the set.

Cables Crossing Work Areas

When cable has to cross an area where there is foot traffic — a hallway or doorway — use cable crossovers (Figure 7.3), or put a rubber mat over the cable and tape it securely to the floor with wide gaffer's tape.

If there is a danger of people tripping on the bulge of the mat, put diagonal stripes of yellow tape across it so that it will be noticed. When cables cross an area where vehicles or carts will be moving, the cables should be protected with cable crossovers. HMI cables especially should never be left vulnerable.

Figure 7.3 Cable crossover. (Photo courtesy of Peterson Systems International, Duarte, CA.)

Appropriate Length

Use appropriate length stinger to reach the light. A clothesline cable, one that is taut and off the floor, is an accident waiting to happen — someone is sure to trip on it. Stingers normally come in lengths of 25 and 50 ft. Use the appropriate length. A rule of thumb for fast identification is as follows: A 25-ft. stinger has about seven coils, and a 50-ft. stinger has 14. When a light is on a stand, the power cord should fall straight to the ground at the base and have some slack coiled or in a figure-eight at the base. Keep excess cable coiled neatly. Place the coil such that if the stand is moved, the cable will pay out from the top of the coil, not from the bottom.

When lights are hung from pipe, be sure to leave two loops of slack cable hanging at the light. If the light later needs to slide down, or pan around 180°, you'll need slack to play with. Run the power cable down the pipe to the service, or to the end of the pipe. Tie it to the pipe at intervals with mason line or sash cord.

Preventing "Kick-Outs"

When connecting two cables, use a stress knot or the cables' tie-rope to hold the connection together (Figure 7.4).

This helps prevent a "kick-out" (accidental unplugging). In the event of a kick-out or "gap in the line," the electrician must quickly track down the culprit connection. As with everything else on the set, remaining aware of what is happening around you will help you spot kick-outs immediately.

Repatching

You will sometimes need to unplug a light that is in use in order to replace a cable, run power from a different direction, or readjust the loads of various circuits. Before you unplug the light, inform the gaffer of the need for a repatch, and as you disconnect it, call out "Repatch." This assures everyone that the light has not gone

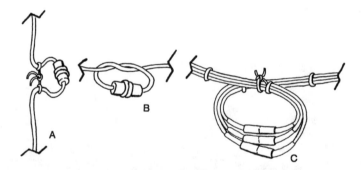

Figure 7.4 When there is danger of an accidental kick-out, use a strain relief. (A) A dangling connection held with the tie-ropes. (B) A simple strain relief for a stinger running along the ground. (C) Banded cable connection point.

out accidentally. Frequent repatches can be irritating for the gaffer and DP. In many situations it may be best to find another way to solve the problem.

Standby Stingers at Outlet Boxes

To streamline the process of powering lights as they are added, have at least two stingers standing by at each power drop or gang box, coiled and ready to be used.

Labeling Stingers and Power Cords

Labeling cables helps immensely in identifying problems and recabling lights when needed. When a cable runs out of the set through a rat hole, over the top of the set, or up into the pipes or greens above the set, both ends of the cable or stinger should be labeled with tape. Indicate the lights it is powering, for example, "2k window light" or "stair sconces." Similarly, when using a dimmer board the gang box or female receptacle of the power cord is marked with the channel number. See Rules for Cabling in Chapter 9 for notes on labeling and laying out distribution equipment.

When lights are hung from a grid it is helpful to be able to identify each light by number. Label each light so the number is visible to the gaffer on the ground below. Write the numbers large and legible on 2-in. tape on the underside of each unit. Mark the tails (the plugs) with the same numbers. With the lamps numbered, it is easy for the gaffer to communicate what he wants: "Plug lamps 10, 14, and 18 into the same dimmer and work them on a cue."

Labeling Dimmer Settings

When setting a dimmer level, start with the dimmer at line voltage. Say "line voltage." The gaffer may then specify a setting to try, "set it at 90%," or he may just say "lower...lower...lower, good." Keep telling him the level, "that's 80...70...60." Once it is set, make a mark on tape to indicate the setting. If several settings are used, number them. After the shot is completed, leave these markings on the dimmer — they may be needed again.

Dimmers hum. At close range they will create problems for the sound recordist. The electrician can anticipate this and position dimmers accordingly.

Coiling Stingers and Cable

All cables and stingers are coiled clockwise. Each loop puts a twist in the cable. When uncoiled it must be allowed to untwist, or it will start to twist onto itself.

The stranded copper wire inside a cable has a natural twist; coiling counterclockwise works against the grain. When a cable is consistently coiled in the same manner each time it is used, the cable becomes "trained" to coil that way. A trained cable will coil easily. If a cable is coiled different ways with each use, it becomes confused and unmanageable.

The over–under method shown in Figure 7.5 is used for coaxial cable, dimmer control cables, and audio cable.

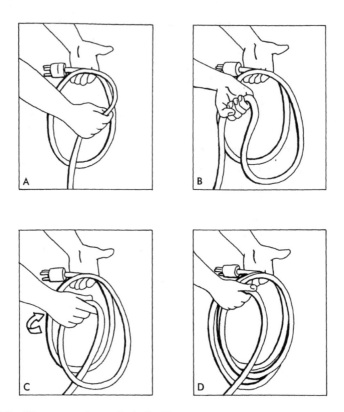

Figure 7.5   The over–under method of coiling control cables. (A) Start with a normal loop. (B, C) Give the second loop a twist to the inside. (D) Make the next loop normal. Alternate back and forth between a normal loop and a twisted loop.

Every other loop counteracts the twist so the cable can be unraveled without twists. Using the occasional underhand loop sometimes makes a cord more coopera-tive.

Small Bulbs, Practicals, Wiring, and Switches

Types of Bulbs

Photoflood Bulbs and PH Bulbs   Photoflood bulbs are color-balanced for use in photography (3200K, 3400K, and 4800K) and come in various wattages, as shown in Appendix E. The 211 (75W) and 212 (150W) are often used in table lamps and suspended China-hat practicals. Higher wattage photofloods are often used in soft boxes, Japanese lanterns, and scoop lights such as Smith Victor lights. Most pho-toflood bulbs burn very hot and have a short life, in order to provide the high color temperature.

Household Bulbs A selection of low-wattage household bulbs — 15W, 25W, 40W, 60W — is handy for making practicals glow without being overly bright. A household bulb's color temperature falls between 2600K and 2900K, which appears yellow on film. If the color shift is objectionable, it can be removed with CTB gel. Alternatively, the DP may add 1/4 CTO to the artificial lights to match the warmth of the practicals. The color shift can be removed in the lab or with the use of a blue filter on the lens (Kodak 82 series, see Table G.8). In many instances a warm color shift is appropriate for the scene; for example, lamps naturally appear slightly warm, and the DP leaves it.

Candella Base Bulbs Some candelabra wall sconces and chandeliers take candela-base bulbs; this is something to check during location scouts. The bulbs, usually low wattage, are very warm. Round makeup table bulbs (40W and 60W) are small, soft, very warm (2600–2700K) bulbs that can be grouped to make an inexpensive, soft glow-light.

Mushroom Floods — R-40 and others Flood and spot lights of the mushroom-shaped variety incorporate a silver reflector inside the bulb for better output and throw. Common wattages are 75W, 150W, 300W, and 500W (EAL). Tungsten 3200K bulbs are available in 200W, 300W, 375W, and 500W wattage (see Table E.1). The rest fall between 2800K and 2900K. The R-40 size is the most commonly used. A Lowel K-5 kit includes sockets, mounting bracket, and barn doors that snug onto the front of an R-40 bulb. There are a wide variety of other reflector bulbs. The size is indicated by the number; for example, in R-40/FL, R stands for reflector and 40 is the size in eighths of an inch (40/8 = 5 in.). FL indicates flood. Smaller R-30 and R-20 bulbs are great for track lighting, lighting wall art at close range.

MR-16 MR-16 bulbs are tungsten halogen projector bulbs with a 2-in. parabolic reflector. They are 3200K and very bright. They are now commonly used in track-lighting fixtures. They come in a variety of wattages, voltages, and reflector types. The track-lighting type is 12V, uses a transformer, and has a GX-5.3 base, shown in Figure E.1, Appendix E. Fortunately, 120V versions of MR-16s are also available with a standard medium screw base in 75W and 150W. The VNSP MR-16, which has a mirror-like parabolic reflector, makes an amazingly bright narrow column of light. The tiny size, brightness, and color temperature of MR-16s make them a very useful bulb for making small pools of light.

Linestra Tubes These are incandescent tube-shaped bulbs 12, 20, or 40 in. long 3/4 in. diameter. Their color temperature is 2800K. They are very lightweight, and can be attached with tape or bailing wire. They are used in sets, lighting shelving, for example.

Fluorescent Bulbs The most common type of practical fluorescent bulb you will encounter is T-12 base (bi-pin) in 4 ft., 3 ft., and 2 ft. sizes. In industrial spaces you will often run into 8-ft. slimline-base tubes (Appendix E). These bulbs can be easily replaced with High CRI bulbs (Durotest Optima 32 or Vitalite). Older desk lamps sometimes take small T-5 tubes.

Controlling Practicals

It is standard practice to put practical lamps on dimmers so that their intensity can be easily adjusted. However, there are other ways to dim a bulb that do not alter the color temperature. Spraying the bulb with a light speckle of black streaks and tips is a fast way to reduce the bulb's intensity. (Don't spray a hot bulb, it will burst.) Sometimes you will only want to reduce brightness in one direction. This can be done by spraying one side and not the other. Holding a lighter close to the bulb and letting the carbon build up on the bulb is another good way to dim it. The carbon wipes off more easily than streaks and tips. Placing diffusion on the inside of the lamp shade and installing ND gel around the bulb are also ways to dim a practical.

Light Cues

Hand Cue

If an actor turns a wall switch on or off during a scene, the wall switch can be wired to a deuce board switch that controls the lights. On location, however, it is often necessary for an electrician to perform the lighting cue with a dimmer or switch when the actor reaches for the light switch. The electrician must position himself somewhere out of the way and out of the shot, but where he can see the action to hit the cue. Experienced actors help sell the cue by covering the switch with their hand so that the camera does not see the exact moment that the switch flips.

Switchover

In a night scene, when an actor turns off a bedroom light and the room goes dark, the lighting must switch from practical sources to moonlight or exterior sources. Darkness is commonly simulated by underexposed, blue, directionless lighting. The transition may require a switchover in which some lights are turned off and others are turned on in the instant that the actor turns off the lights. The problem is that the time required for one group of filaments to dim and the other group to heat up prevents the switchover from being instantaneous, and the audience can see the new lights coming on. Some special techniques can be helpful to sell the switchover.

One solution is to have the night group on the whole time. Unfortunately, this can look phony because the moonlight appears to be as bright as the light in the room, and the blue color of the night group discolors the lamplight. However, if the change happens before any of this becomes too noticeable, this can be a workable solution. If the scene ends with the lights turning off, the blue group can be kept very low so as not to distract for the bulk of the scene.

If the scene carries on in darkness after the lights go off and the actors must be visible in the dark, then a special transition is needed. Here is a clever way to handle this transition: Keep the night group on throughout the scene, but at levels that are one and a half to two stops below the lamplight. This will look natural. When the interior light is turned off, begin to open the camera aperture on a slow five-second change. The effect is similar to that of the human eye adjusting to the dark. Additionally, the audience's eyes will be adjusting to the new light level, which hides the aperture change.

Wiring Small Fixtures

Practical Lamps

On any interior set, the art department will provide practical sources: table lamps, wall sconces, floor lamps, desk lamps, china hats, or a chandelier, for example. Each time you begin shooting on a new set, one of the first things to take care of is the wiring and testing of practicals, and changing the bulbs as desired by the gaffer.

Lamps and sconces typically come from the prop house with bare wires and will need to be fitted with plugs. If a lamp or sconce is metal and it is not UL listed, a grounding wire is required and zip cord (18/2) may not be used. UL listed lamps do not require a ground wire. When necessary, use wire nuts to insulate wire splices, as shown in Figure 7.6.

Quick-on plugs stab the zip cord with copper spikes, eliminating the need for screw terminals. Quick-on plugs and sockets are designed to be used with 18/2 zip cord only. Note that in-line taps don't have polarized sockets, so a polarized plug won't fit. You may have to clip the flare off the male plug with wire snips, or use a

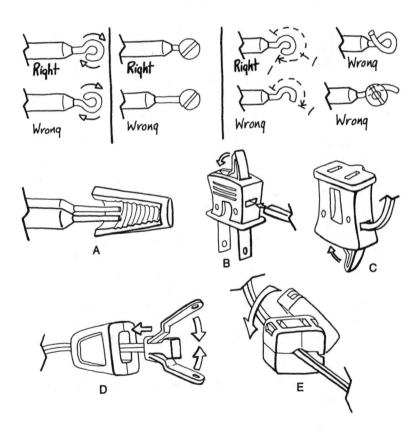

Figure 7.6 (Top) Tips on connecting wires to terminals. (A) Wire nuts on wire splices. (B) Male quick-on. (C) Female quick-on. (D) Male quick-on. (E) In-line tap.

cube tap as an adapter. It is best to use a female quick-on for the terminal end of zip cord; if an in-line tap is used, fold the wire back once it is through the tap and *wrap it with electrical tape*. Do not leave an exposed end — someone is bound to get bit.

Some notes about zip cord: 18 AWG (American Wire Gauge) zip cord is often used to wire practicals. It may not be used with any fixture having a ground wire. It is rated for 10A maximum, and it will not withstand overamping. It can be dangerous to make long zip cord runs because the resistance in the cord is so high that a dead short at the end of a long run of cord will not trip the circuit breaker. The cord will burn up before it will trip the circuit protection. Keep zip cord runs short (6 ft. or less), and use stingers for longer runs.

Practical Outlets

A well-made set will have practical wall outlets. These are very convenient for plugging in practical, set dressing appliances (a toaster, for example), and small lights. On the outside wall the outlet box usually has a short tale with an Edison plug, which should be connected to a dedicated 20A circuit.

Wiring Plugs, Sockets, Switches, and Connectors

When wiring or repairing electrical devices, be sure to *make as solid a connection as possible*, bringing together as much surface area of copper at each terminal, and making each terminal tight and secure. Plugs, sockets, connectors, and switches are the weak spots in a circuit. They create resistance that can eventually heat up the wires, which further degrades the conductors and their insulation, further increases resistance and heat, and eventually poses a shock and/or fire hazard (or simply causes a nuisance by burning out).

Second, also for safety reasons, any time you install or replace a switch or connector, *pay attention to the proper polarity*. On plugs and sockets the gold terminal is for the HOT (black) wire, and the silver terminal is for the neutral (white) wire. The green terminal is for the green grounding wire. (On zip cord the hot wire has a rib on the insulating jacket, while the neutral wire does not.)

If an electrical device is connected with reverse polarity (i.e., the neutral and hot wires are reversed), a potential safety hazard exists. The switch controlling the fixture, which normally interrupts the hot wire, now interrupts the circuit on the *return* wire (neutral). Although the fixture still functions, it has a hot lead running to the lamp when turned OFF — a hot lead looking for a place to ground. So, even though the fixture is OFF, it is still HOT. If, for example, someone attempted to change the bulb, thinking that because the switch is off the light is safe, they could be in for a jolting surprise. This is precisely why one should always unplug a fixture before putting a hand inside it, even if the switch is off.

For the same reason, when installing a switch, *a single-pole switch must be connected on the black wire*, not the white.

Double-Pole Switches

For 220V circuits and lights 2k or more, it is necessary to have a switch that interrupts both wires at once. This is known as a *double-pole* switch (Figure 7.7).

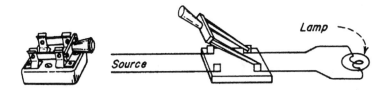

Figure 7.7 Both wires are disconnected when the fixture is turned off with a double-pole switch. Most fixtures of 2k and larger use a double-pole switch. (From H. Richter and W. Schwan. *Practical Electrical Wiring*, 15th ed. New York: McGraw-Hill, 1990. Reproduced with permission of McGraw-Hill.)

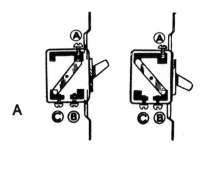

Figure 7.8 (A) A *double-throw*, or *three-way*, switch has three terminals. It switches current flow from A-C to A-B. (B) When connected as shown, three-way switches allow the circuit to be switched from two places. The circuit can be made live or dead at either switch, regardless of the position of the other switch. (From H. Richter and W. Schwan. *Practical Electrical Wiring*, 15th ed. New York: McGraw-Hill, 1990. Reproduced with permission of McGraw-Hill.)

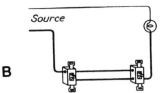

Three-Way and Four-Way Switches

It is sometimes handy to have two or more switches in different locations to control a circuit. To do this, wire two *three-way* switches as shown in Figure 7.8.

When more than two switches are needed, a three-way switch is connected at the beginning and end of the chain of switches, and any number of *four-way* switches can be connected between them (Figure 7.9).

In either case, any of the switches will close and open the circuit, regardless of the position of the other switches.

Safety

You don't have to work on sets long before you see that in a rush people can forget their common sense. This is how people get hurt and equipment gets broken. Make safe work practices habitual, and you will avoid needless injuries, especially when working under pressure. Work swiftly but never run.

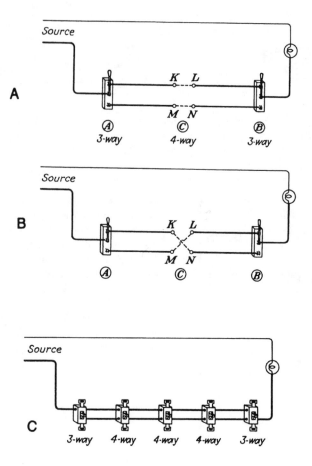

Figure 7.9 A *four-way* switch is used when controlling lights from three or more places. (A) and (B) show how a four-way switch works. (C) Any number of four-way switches can be connected between two three-way switches. (From H. Richter and W. Schwan. *Practical Electrical Wiring*, 15th ed. New York: McGraw-Hill, 1990. Reproduced with permission of McGraw-Hill.)

Ladders

When working with suspended lights, you must often work from a ladder. If the ladder seems at all shaky, have someone hold it and spot you at the bottom of the ladder. Use the appropriate size of ladder. Don't use the top step. Don't stretch to reach a light that is too far from the ladder; instead, get a taller ladder, or climb down and move the ladder you have.

Two people often need to work from two sides of the same ladder when rigging two lights very close together. When you step onto someone's ladder, say "On your ladder," and when you step off again, say "Off your ladder."

Parallels

Parallels are quite frequently used as a lighting platform. They are quick and easy to assemble and, if used with proper caution, can be safe. However, caution is the watchword. Almost any veteran electrician can tell you a story about an accident involving parallels.

Parallels must be set on level ground or be leveled with leveling jacks. On uneven ground it can be hard to tell what is level; a plumb line or bubble level should be used. A leaning parallel is an accident waiting to happen. Be sure that weight is distributed evenly on the platform, especially when people are climbing or lifting equipment up to the platform. Use bodies as counterweight when necessary. Never mount lights outside the perimeter of the railing.

Large light stands should be strapped down to the platform. Ratchet straps and nylon webbing are ideal, although chain or rope can do the trick if properly used. Remember to take account of the force of the wind blowing on 4-by frames. Tie guy lines to the bail or stand when needed. Tie the power cable to a vertical post on the platform, leaving plenty of slack to maneuver the light.

Working Aloft

Anytime you work at a height — on a ladder, greens, catwalk, parallels, or truss — remove your tool belt. Tie any tools you need to your belt. If you do drop something, yell a warning, such as "Heads up," "Headache," or just "Look out below!" Dropping a tool from the catwalks can get you kicked off a studio lot.

Remember to bring a tag-line so you can hoist equipment up as you need it. The tag-line should be tied off at the top end so that it cannot fall. Call "Line out" before you toss down the line. When you toss an item up to a worker, call "Airmail" to alert the people around you; then if the catcher misses, no one gets cracked on the head.

Protecting Floors

Protecting the floor becomes a concern when shooting in a private home or in a set where the floors might be scratched by metal stands. A number of precautions can be taken. One is to put crutch tips on the feet of each stand. Tape the rubber tips in place with gaffer's tape. A stock of crutch tips should be ordered in advance after the location is initially scouted.

Layout board (1/4 in. hard cardboard that comes in 4 × 8 ft. sheets) can provide a protective covering over the floor. It is usually laid out over the entire area and taken up wherever it will be seen in the camera's frame. A more temporary substitute is a furniture pad placed under the stand.

Sprinkler Systems

With the fire marshal's permission, make a practice of putting Styrofoam cups over sprinkler heads to insulate them from the heat of the lights. In the category of big blunders, few are more conspicuous than activating the emergency sprinkler system and dousing the actors and sets in water. Placing a hot light too close to a sprinkler head can easily melt the soft alloy valve that normally holds back the flood. There is no way to stop an activated head from flowing once it has started, and the water in the pipes will continue to drain through for hours even if the sprinkler system is immediately turned off at the source.

Smoke, Fire, and Other Bad Smells

Lights get very hot and can easily start a fire. Common sense and proper care are essential to the prevention of accidents. In the event of a small fire, a quick electrician may be able to smother the flames with gloved hands or with a furniture pad. Know where the fire extinguishers are.

An electrician with a good nose and good eyes can detect a potential fire before it becomes serious. If you smell smoke, don't cause a panic, but let the other electricians and grips know so they can help look for the source. The smell of burning wood may be caused by a toasting clothespin or a light placed too close to a wooden set piece. The smell of burning plastic or rubber may be traced to smoldering insulation on a cable connection or in-line switch. An overheated stinger is a common offender. Check the lights for burning gel or diffusion, or smoking flags or nets. Check the set walls and ceiling for bubbling or smoldering paint. On DC stages, keep your nose open for the sharp, metallic-burning smell of an arcing paddle connector. When a paddle comes partially unplugged it will arc, which eventually burns up the contacts on the plugging box. Keep looking until you find the source of the smell. The problem may be something obscure, such as burning bakelite plastic in a defective deuce board.

A smoking light is usually the result of some foreign matter getting into the light and burning up. Dusty lights will often smoke for a short time when they are first turned on. Moths are relentless kamikazes. They will keep an open-face fixture smoking all night as they bake themselves one after another. Outside in a ventilated area this does not pose a danger to anyone but the moths. Inside, though, it may be necessary to turn off a smoking light and clean it out. Sometimes the only way to clean the light is just to let the substance burn off. For example, after a light is repainted, it should be taken outside and turned on for 10 or 15 minutes until it stops smoking.

Lamp Repair

When a lamp fails, be sure to label the light so that it doesn't get brought back onto the set by mistake. Put an X across the lens with 1-in. tape, and write "NG" (no good) or "BO" (burnt out) on it. If you know what is wrong with the light, write that on it also (for example, blown bulb, bad switch, bad plug).

Common repairs include changing the globe, replacing the power switch or plug, reconnecting the power cord to the head, repairing the flood-spot mechanism, and cleaning corroded contacts with contact cleaner. Most lights are not too complicated and can easily be repaired if replacement parts can be obtained. Before starting any type of repair, double-check that the fixture is disconnected from the power. If time allows, the best boy simply has new equipment delivered in exchange for the broken equipment.

The Wrap

When filming is completed at a given location, all the equipment has to be packed back into the truck. It may take two or three hours when a lot of equipment is in use. Especially after a long day, it is everyone's dearest wish to get the truck packed as quickly as possible and get home. It is one of the best boy's responsibilities to begin the wrap early and have as much of it done as possible before the actual wrap is called. Early in the day, the best boy organizes the removal of superfluous equipment from the set, and the coiling of cable that will no longer be needed. Once the last setup is lit, any equipment not in use should be stowed and ready to drive away.

When wrap is called, lights are switched off and the equipment starts coming back to the truck. I find it works best if the best boy remains at the truck and packs the equipment as it is brought to the lift gate by the electricians. This avoids equipment getting piled up at the gate.

Wrapped lights should look like the one shown in Figure 7.10.

The bail is swiveled up over the top of the light. The power cord is coiled, tied, and hung over the bail. The barn doors are shut. Scrims, diffusion, and gel have been removed and returned to the scrim and gel boxes. Spreader lenses are removed from PAR lights. The globes should be removed from larger lights (12k and 18k HMIs) before travel.

Coiling Feeder Cable

The fastest way to coil feeder cable (banded, 2/0, or 4/0) is to stand with your legs apart and coil in a clockwise circle on the ground. With a little practice you can get into a rhythm, pulling the cable toward you with one hand, then the other, guiding

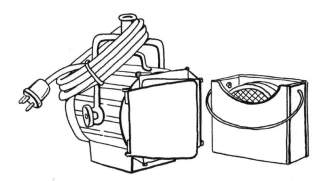

Figure 7.10   A properly wrapped light. Some electricians prefer to tuck the cable inside the bail to prevent it from getting caught on other equipment.

it into a coil. If you are fighting the natural twist of the cable, the coil will not want to lie flat, and the unnatural twist will age the cable. The ideal size for a coil is tight enough not to be floppy and unmanageable, but not so tight and tall that it becomes impossible to stack. Use the tie strings to secure both ends firmly. Loose ends tend to swing around and hit people and generally get in the way. Lift with your knees, not with your back. Never jump down (off the gate for example) with heavy cable on your shoulder. You will know as soon as you do it that it was a mistake. Your knees and ankles may never forgive you.

Inventory

The best boy conducts an equipment inventory as he loads. If each shelf has been labeled with the type and quantity of lights it holds, this process is quite straightforward. Bungy off each shelf as soon as it is complete; this helps you keep track of what is still missing, and once all the shelves are filled the truck is ready to go without further delay. Putting each light in its proper place is not just a matter of organization, it can be crucial to fitting everything on the truck. Before leaving any location, someone should make an idiot check of the set, looking in each area where lights were placed during filming.

CHAPTER 8

Electricity

Units of Measure

Four basic units of electrical measure are as follows:

amperes (current)
volts (electromotive force)
watts (power)
ohms (resistance)

To understand these units and how they relate, it is helpful to use the analogy of the flow of water from a water tank through a hose. Before we begin to explore this analogy, we must first introduce one more unit of electricity — the *coulomb*. The coulomb can be thought of as a specific quantity of electrical power, the same way that a gallon is a specific quantity of liquid. Don't try to imagine how much a coulomb is; just remember that it is a quantity of electricity.

Rate of Flow — Amperage

When water flows through a hose running from a tank of water, the size of the hose determines how much water will flow in a given amount of time (Figure 8.1).

We measure this rate of flow in gallons per minute. In an electrical circuit, the rate of flow of electricity from a battery or generator is measured in coulombs per second, commonly known as *amperes*, or *amps* (A) for short. One coulomb per second equals one ampere. The volume of electricity per second is the *amperage*, also called the *current*. In practical terms, amps represent the amount of power being drawn by the load (lights) connected to the service.

Pressure of Flow — Voltage

When water flows out of a drinking fountain, it is under a small amount of pressure and rises in a small arc. If the same amount of water is delivered under high pressure, because of a clogged fountain spigot, for example, it shoots high into the

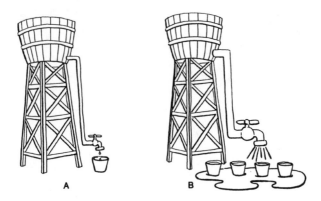

Figure 8.1   Amperage is analogous to the rate of flow.

Figure 8.2   Voltage is analogous to the pressure of flow.

air, goes up your nose, and hits you in the eye. In the water tank example, the height of the tank above the ground determines the water pressure in the hose (Figure 8.2).

A water tank raised 100 ft. in the air provides ten times the pressure (in pounds per square inch) as that same tank when it is 10 ft. off the ground.

The pressure under which electricity is delivered is called the *voltage* (V). A flashlight operates on 1.5V, a car battery at 12V, and a wall socket at 120V. Voltage is the force with which current is pushed through a resistance.

Another way to think of voltage is as the difference in potential energy between two points in a circuit. The potential energy of the water in the tank is proportional to its height above the spigot at the end of the hose — the difference in their heights. When we measure voltage with a voltmeter, we read the difference in voltage potential between the hot wire and the neutral wire.

Work — Wattage

Returning to the water tank analogy, the amount of water flowing from the tank at any one moment is the product of flow rate and pressure. The size of the pipe and the height of the tank together determine the total amount of water that will flow from the tank.

The total amount of electrical power being delivered at any one moment is measured in watts. The wattage is the product of the amperage (flow rate) and the voltage (pressure). Wattage is the measure of the amount of work being done in any one instant. It is the same idea as horsepower; in fact, 746W = 1 horsepower. Wattage can be thought of as total power output; in the case of lighting fixtures, wattage is light output.

For the purpose of billing, the power company's meter counts the electricity consumed in kilowatt-hours (abbreviated kwh). (As we have already established, one kilowatt is 1000W, abbreviated 1kW or simply 1k.) The wattage being used at any given time is reflected in the speed at which the disk in the meter is turning. Kilowatt-hours measure the total amount of electrical power consumed over a given amount of time — the rate at which power is consumed in a given moment, measured in kilowatts, multiplied by the hours that power is consumed at that rate.

The Power Equation

Watts are mathematically related to volts and amps as follows:

$$\text{watts} = \text{volts} \times \text{amps}.$$

Electricians use this important equation frequently when making load calculations. An easy way to remember it is to think of West Virginia (W = VA).

There are other ways to state the same relationship:

$$\text{volts} = \frac{\text{watts}}{\text{amps}}$$

$$\text{amps} = \frac{\text{watts}}{\text{volts}}$$

To give an example of how both amperage and voltage contribute to the wattage, consider two 60W bulbs: a household bulb and a car headlight. The household bulb runs on 120V and pulls a current of 0.5A. The car headlight uses a 12V battery but pulls electricity at a rate of 5A. The total power consumed and the total amount of light emitted are the same for the 60W household bulb and the 60W car headlight:

$$\text{Household bulb: } 120V \times 0.5A = 60W$$

$$\text{Car headlight: } 12V \times 5A = 60W$$

In formulas, voltage, wattage, amperage, and resistance are represented by the symbols E, W, I, and R, respectively.[1] The relationship between these four forces can be stated numerous ways. All the possible permutations are shown in the formulas wheel (Figure 8.3).

The magic circles illustrated in Figure 8.4 provide an easy way to use these two equations.

Calculating the Amperage of Lights

Actual Amps

To calculate the amperage pulled by a given light fixture, divide the lamp's wattage by the line voltage. For example, for a 1k light operating at 120V, we make the following calculation:

$$\frac{\text{watts}}{\text{volts}} = \text{amps}$$

$$\frac{1000W}{120V} = 8.3A$$

Paper Amps

A quick and easy method for calculating amperage is to divide the wattage by 100 — an easy calculation to do in your head. Dividing by 100 will overestimate the amperage, which introduces a safety margin of several amps per light. This is known as the *paper method* of calculating amperage (Table 8.1)

To calculate the total current being pulled through a cable, simply add up the amps pulled by each light. For example, if two 1k babies are connected to one circuit, the calculation is as follows:

$$\frac{1000}{100} + \frac{1000}{100} = 10 + 10 = 20A.$$

Using a 20A circuit allows a built-in safety margin of 3.4A (the actual amperage at 120V is 8.3 + 8.3 = 16.6A). By the same token, the amperage capacity of cable can be expressed in paper amps. A 2 AWG cable rated for 190A (real) has a maximum paper amperage of 228A (single-conductor, 90°C, entertainment cable). Knowing

---

[1] P is also commonly used as an abbreviation for power. W (watts) will be used in this book.

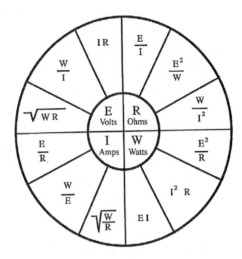

Figure 8.3 The formulas wheel gives every permutation of the relationships between voltage, amperage, wattage, and resistance. (Reprinted with permission from Paul Carter. *Backstage Handbook.* New York: Broadway Press, 1988.)

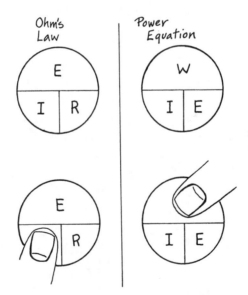

Figure 8.4 A simple way to remember the most common of the equations in Figure 8.3 is to use "magic circles." On either of the circles shown, cover the symbol you want to find with your finger. The relationship that remains is the formula. For example, to determine amperage (I) from a known resistance (R) and voltage (E), put your finger on the I, and read E divided by R. To determine wattage (W) from amperage and voltage, put your finger over the W, and read I times E.

Table 8.1   Amperage of Lights, Calculated by Paper Method and Exact Calculation for All the Common Wattages

Watts	Paper Amps	Real Amps
100	1	.8
200	2	1.7
250	2.5	2.1
300	3	2.5
420	4.2	3.5
500	5	4.2
600	6	5
650	6.5	5.4
750	7.5	6.25
1000	10	8.3
1500	15	12.5
2000	20	16.7
4000	40	33.3
5000	50	41.7
8000	80	66.7
9000	90	75.0
10,000	100	83.3

this, it is an easy matter to determine if a cable is being overamped. In the example below, note how much easier it is to add the paper column than the real column.

Wattage	Paper	Real
300	3	2.5
500	5	4.2
1000	10	8.3
2000	20	16.7
4000	40	33.3
5000	50	41.7
10,000	100	83.3
	228	190 (rounded to the nearest amp)

Paper quantities are 1.2 times the real amperage.

Resistance and Ohm's Law

So far we have a mental picture of a lamp operating at the standard 120V, drawing current (amps) in order to generate a particular wattage output. However, this is an incomplete picture of the forces acting on a circuit. What prevents an ambitious 60W light bulb from drawing more current and becoming a 600W light bulb? The force we are missing is *resistance.* Understanding resistance and how it relates to power and current gives a much clearer picture of the forces at work in a circuit.

Resistance is the opposition to the flow of current created by the load put on the circuit by the fixtures plugged into it, and by the resistance of the wires themselves. Resistance is measured in ohms, which is abbreviated as the Greek letter omega (Ω).

The resistance of a particular conductor or lamp filament can be considered constant,[2] determined by its physical properties and construction. The resistance of the filament limits the amperage that can be pushed through it by a particular voltage, and therefore determines its ultimate output in Watts.

Ohm's Law

Ohm's law can be stated three ways:

$$I = \frac{E}{R} \qquad\qquad amps = \frac{volts}{resistance}$$

$$R = \frac{E}{I} \qquad\qquad resistance = \frac{volts}{amps}$$

$$or\ E = I \times R \qquad\qquad volts = amps \times resistance$$

$I = E/R$ calculates the amperage drawn by a particular load, knowing the line voltage and the load's resistance. To see how this equation works, we'll use it to illustrate the dramatic effect of line loss. All conductors, such as cable, have resistance. In a long length of cable, the resistance causes a perceptible drop in voltage from source to load because resistance turns some power into heat in the cables. This is known as *line loss.* Looking at $I = E/R$, we can see that if voltage decreases (due to line loss), the amperage will also decrease. We can calculate that if the voltage is reduced to 108V, a 2000W bulb (normally 16.6A, 7.36Ω), will only draw 14.7A:

$$I = \frac{E}{R} \qquad\qquad \frac{108V}{7.36\Omega} = 14.7A.$$

The total power output of the 2000W lamp is sliced down to 1584W:

---

[2] The resistance of a piece of wire is constant at a given temperature. Any metal has less resistance at a lower temperature; as temperature increases, so does resistance. With tungsten this effect is very pronounced — when cold it has very little resistance, but when heated it has very high resistance. As a result, tungsten lights have high inrush current with a cold start. Once at operating temperature, however, resistance is constant. In contrast, the resistance of copper changes little with temperature.

$$W = I \times E \qquad\qquad 108V \times 14.7A = 1584W.$$

The problem is compounded by the fact that a light only operates at full efficiency at its rated voltage. Operating at 108V (90% of its rated power) the 2k will in fact only produce about 68% of its normal light output. That's one wimpy 2k — a 32% loss of output caused by a 10% loss of voltage. Light output decreases geometrically with line loss.

Resistance of a Light

Ohm's Law stated as $R = E/I$ can be used to calculate the resistance of a load (a light fixture). The resistance of a particular load can be calculated by dividing its rated voltage by the amperage. For example, a 5k bulb (rated 5000W at 120V) pulls 41.67A. The resistance of the lamp can be calculated as follows:

$$\frac{120V}{41.67A} = 2.88\Omega.$$

Resistance of Cable

The resistance of a particular length of cable is equal to the voltage drop in the cable divided by the amperage running through it. If there is a 4V drop in a length of cable carrying a 40A load, the resistance of that length of cable is

$$\text{ohms} = \frac{\text{volts}}{\text{amps}} \qquad\qquad (R = \frac{E}{I})$$

$$\frac{4V}{40A} = 0.1\Omega.$$

Line Loss

As a rule of thumb, electricians assume that 4/0 and 2/0 cable have a 1V drop per 100 ft. when the cable is moderately loaded (at 50% capacity 4/0 has 1.2V drop per 100 ft., 2/0 has 0.9V drop per 100 ft.). The drop increases to around 4V per 100 ft. when running at the full ampacity of the cable. You can anticipate there will be significant line loss any time there is a fairly long run of cable and the cable is being loaded near its maximum ampacity rating. Table C.1 gives exact voltage drop per 100-ft. for various cables.

The three variables that affect the amount of line loss are length, wire thickness, and amperage load. Remember these three principles:

1. The resistance of a conductor increases directly with its length. The longer the run, the greater the line loss.
2. The resistance of a conductor decreases in proportion to its cross-sectional area. The larger the conductor, the less the line loss.
3. Voltage drop varies directly with the load. The larger the amperage load, the larger the line loss.

To overcome the line loss, the generator operator will often simply increase the voltage at the generator so that the voltage at the set is correct (115–120V). However, if you increase the voltage at the generator to overcome line loss, keep two things in mind. First, if equipment is being powered at the upstream end of the cable run (such as the producer's trailer at base camp), the upstream equipment will be over voltage (the producer's computer is toast). Secondly, voltage drop is proportional to amperage load. When the amperage load is reduced significantly, voltage must be turned down at the generator to prevent any remaining lights from being over voltage. If a lot of big lights are suddenly turned off, the voltage will jump up and the remaining load is over voltage (the sound cart is toast).

To avoid these problems, it is necessary to minimize line loss by increasing the wire gauge.

Effects of Line Loss and Low Voltage

If line loss results in low voltage at the set, it causes a number of serious problems for the operation of lights. As we have already discussed, light output falls off geometrically as the voltage decreases. The dramatic loss of output was shown in our earlier example.

Additionally, as the light intensity decreases, so does the Kelvin color temperature of the emitted light. As the intensity decreases, the color goes from white to yellow to orange.

One final reason why it is important to keep line loss within reasonable tolerances is that a loss of voltage also translates into a loss of power. From the equation $W = I^2R$, we see that the power loss in a given cable increases as the square of the amperage. If you double the ampere load on the cable, the voltage drop will also double, but the power loss will increase fourfold. The power source has to work harder, burning more fuel, or more kilovolt-amperes, because it is using power in heating up the cables in addition to running the lights. The performance of the generator — its maximum effective load — is reduced.

Other Causes of Line Loss

Line loss also occurs when a connection is weak or loose, when a cable is frayed, when a connector is only partially inserted, and when a connector or conductor is loaded beyond its capacity. Each of these situations creates a hot spot in the cable and connector, which further degrades the insulation. Circular coils in a single-conductor, current-carrying cable create impedance, resulting in line loss and increased heating. Good set practices — such as checking for good contact between connectors, taping connectors, avoiding circular coils, and replacing overheating parts — help rid you of the annoyance of inexplicable line loss and melted connectors.

Line Loss Calculations

The figures in Table C.1, Appendix C, were calculated using Ohm's Law: $E = IR$. Using Ohm's Law, we can calculate the thickness of cable needed to limit the voltage drop to a selected percentage, the distance a particular cable can carry a known amperage, or the exact voltage drop for a particular cable.

Calculating Voltage Drop

Single Phase Circuits We can calculate the theoretical line loss in any cable by inserting the resistance of the cable into Ohm's Law:

$$\text{voltage drop} = \text{amperes} \times \text{ohms}$$

The resistance of copper cable in ohms per 100 ft. is given in Table C.2, Appendix C.

Say, for example, that we have a 400-ft. run of #2 AWG banded cable powering 7500W of lights (62.5A, or about 31A per leg). We want to find out what the voltage drop will be. To do this, we multiply the amperage per leg by the resistance of 2 AWG cable (0.0162Ω per 100 ft.) and by the length of cable. Note that the length of cable is multiplied by 2 to give the total distance from source to load and return.

$$\text{voltage drop} = \frac{\text{wire resistance}}{100 \text{ ft}} \times 2 \times \text{one-way distance} \times \text{amperage}$$

$$\text{voltage drop} = \frac{0.0162}{100} \times 2 \times 400 \times 31 = 4\text{V}$$

A voltage drop of 4V gives a line voltage of 116V, which is acceptable. You would multiply this result by 0.866 for three-phase circuits.

Simple Equation for Single-Phase Circuits

$$\frac{\text{amperes} \times \text{one-way distance in feet}}{\text{cmils}} \times 21.6 = \text{voltage drop},$$

where amperes is current per leg, and cmils is the cross-sectional area of the cable in circular mils, as listed in Table C.2, Appendix C.

This equation uses 10.8Ω per mil foot (at 25°C) for copper (times 2 because the two-way distance is needed). This figure is an average. Actual resistance depends on wire gauge and temperature.

Three-Phase Circuits With three-phase power, use the following equation to calculate voltage drop:

$$\frac{\text{amperes} \times \text{one-way distance}}{\text{cmils}} \times 18.7 = \text{voltage drop}$$

18.7 is 21.6 times the square root of 3, divided by 2 (i.e., 0.866).

Three-Wire 120/208 Derived from Four-Wire, Three-Phase System

When you create a three-wire, 120/208V feeder cable from a four-wire, three-phase system, use the following equation to calculate line loss on that feeder:

$$\frac{\text{amperes} \times \text{one–way distance}}{\text{cmils}} \times 18.7 \times 1.5 = \text{voltage drop}$$

Wire Size

To calculate the wire size needed to limit the line loss to a particular number of volts, use the following formulas.

For single-phase circuits:

$$\text{cmils} = \frac{\text{one–way distance} \times \text{amperes} \times 21.6}{\text{voltage drop desired}}$$

For three-phase circuits:

$$\text{cmils} = \frac{\text{one–way distance} \times \text{amperes} \times 21.6 \times 0.866}{\text{voltage drop desired}}$$

Distance

To calculate the maximum length of a particular cable for a given line loss, use the following formulas:

For single-phase circuits:

$$\text{one-way distance in feet} = \frac{\text{voltage drop} \times \text{cmil of cable}}{\text{amperes} \times 21.6}$$

For three-phase circuits:

$$\text{one-way distance in feet} = \frac{\text{voltage drop} \times \text{cmil of cable}}{\text{amperes} \times 18.7}$$

Overcurrent Protection

From Ohm's Law ($R = E/I$), you can see that the higher the amperage flowing through a fixture, the lower the resistance in the circuit, and conversely, the lower the resistance of a fixture, the more amperage is allowed to flow. But what happens if there is no resistance? If you create a dead short by touching the two wires together, the uninhibited current flow rapidly increases to the maximum available from the power source, which may be thousands of amps. The amperage in the circuit becomes extremely high, far beyond the amperage capacity of the cables. The wires heat up, burn, and melt (quite possibly setting the building on fire), or if the amperage is high enough, will vaporize the cables in a matter of seconds. Overcurrent protection is needed for this reason.

An *overcurrent device* (a fuse or circuit breaker) cuts off power to the circuit if the current exceeds a specified limit. The amperage capacity of cables used downstream of the overcurrent device is matched to the amperage capacity of the overcurrent device. Thus, circuit protection is designed to prevent the possibility of thermal meltdown from an overloaded or shorted circuit.

Current-Carrying Capacity of Cable

The amperage capacity, or *ampacity*, of cable is assigned to each type of cable based on the wire gauge, the maximum operating temperature of the insulation, and the conditions under which it will be used. Let's look at these factors individually.

Wire Gauge

Wire sizes are numbered using the American Wire Gauge sizes shown in Figure 8.5.

For wire sizes from 18 AWG to 1 AWG, the smaller the number, the bigger the wire. Cables larger than 1 AWG are numbered 0, 00, 000, and 0000 (pronounced "one ought," "two ought," "three ought," and "four-ought"). These sizes are usually written 1/0, 2/0, 3/0, and 4/0.

Cables bigger than 4/0 are referred to by their cross-sectional area, measured in circular mils (cmil), and are rarely used as portable power cable in film production.

Multiconductor cable is labeled with the gauge and the number of conductors denoted as follows: 12/3, where 12 is the gauge of the cable, and 3 is the number of conductors.

Maximum Operating Temperature

Testing laboratories test each type of cable insulation and assign it a maximum temperature rating. The more current run through the cable, the warmer it becomes. The rating reflects the temperature that the wire can safely reach without damaging the insulation. When insulation becomes overheated, it may become brittle, crack apart, or melt. The temperature rating provides a margin of safety between the maximum operating temperature of the cable and its breakdown point.

Tables B.1 and B.2 list the ampacity of various sizes and temperature ratings of cable. Note that the ampacity of a cable rated at 60 or 75°C is substantially lower than that of cable rated at 90°C. Be sure you assign the proper amperage to the cable you are using.

If a cable rated at 90°C is connected to a fuse rated at only 75°C, the cable may transfer heat and may overheat the fuse. In this case, a larger jumper cable must be used to prevent heat transfer. The jumper cable must be sized to carry the needed amperage at the lower temperature rating.

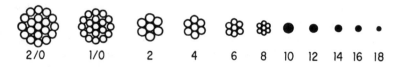

Figure 8.5 Actual diameters of common sizes of copper wires without insulation. (From H. Richter and W. Schwan, *Practical Electrical Wiring*, 15th ed. New York: McGraw-Hill, 1990. Reproduced with permission of McGraw-Hill.)

Types of Feeder Cable

Type W Cable

Type W cable is a portable, extra–hard-usage power cable manufactured to meet the requirements of NEC Article 400 (portable cords and cables) and is acceptable for temporary wiring according to Articles 520 (Theaters and Similar Locations) and 530 (Motion Picture and Television Studios and Similar Locations). It is flexible and abrasion resistant. It may be oil, solvent, and sunlight resistant, and flame tested. Carol Super Vu-tron cable is also flexible down to –50°C.

Entertainment Industry and Stage-Lighting Cable EISL (Types SC, SCE, and SCT)

Entertainment cable is a portable, extra–hard-usage cable with the same insulation characteristics as type W cable, but is 20% smaller and lighter than type W due to the improved materials used in the insulating jacket. You will often see 105°C cable used, but it is not listed in the ampacity tables because the temperature rating must also match the temperature rating of the circuit protection, which is usually not more than 90°C. Use the 90°C column of the ampacity table for 105°C cable.

Welding Cable

For many years welding cable was commonly used for feeder because it was more flexible and lighter than other types of cable available at the time. However, welding cable has never been approved for this purpose. The misapplication of welding cable became an issue during the 1984 Olympic Games in Los Angeles, after which there was a general conversion to type W and entertainment cable on the West Coast. Although some small rental houses may still rent it, the NEC prohibits the use of welding cable in motion picture distribution systems, except as a grounding wire.

Decoding Feeder Cable Labels

Electricians learn to identify wire gauge by appearance. Occasionally, however, you have to check the gauge by reading it off the insulation. For example, 2/0 type W cable is almost as large as type SC 4/0 cable.

Single-conductor feeder cables are imprinted something like this:

Royal Entertainment Industry & Stage-Lighting Cable 2/0 AWG 90°C 600V
    (UL) NEC 520 & 530 Outdoor

Royal is the manufacturer.
Entertainment…Cable is the type of cable.
2/0 AWG is the size of the cable according to the American Wire Gauge standard.
90°C is the maximum operating temperature of the insulation.
600V is the maximum voltage of the cable.
UL indicates that the cable is listed with Underwriters Laboratories.
NEC 520 & 530 indicate that the cable meets the requirements of National
    Electrical Code Articles 520 and 530, which apply to the entertainment
    industry.
Outdoor indicates that the cable is approved for outdoor use.

Table 8.2 Insulation Designations

S	Portable cord designed to withstand wear and tear, consisting of two or more stranded conductors with a serving of cotton between the copper and the insulation to prevent the fine strands from sticking to the insulation. Fillers are twisted together with the conductors to make a round assembly that is held together by a fabric overbraid. The outer jacket is rubber-like thermosetting material.
SJ	Junior service. The same as S, but with a thinner jacket. Junior service cord may not be used in areas governed by NEC Section 520-53(h), 520-62(b) (live audience situations). It may be used in other situations as long as it is not subject to abuse (continually stepped on or rolled over).
SV	Junior service. The same as S, but with an even thinner jacket.
SO	S cord with an oil-resistant neoprene jacket. Designated for extra hard usage.
SOW	S cord with oil- and water-resistant jacket.
SPT	Standard two-conductor "zip cord" or household lamp card. Cord with thermoplastic insulation. Warning: In long lengths, 18 AWG or 16 AWG zip cord will burn up before it will trip the circuit breaker. Even with a dead short, 100′ of #18 zip has so much resistance that 20A will start a fire and not trip the breaker.

Decoding Multiconductor Cable Labels

Multiconductor cable, used for stingers and power cords, is marked as follows:

12/3 Type SJOW-A 90°C P-123-MSHA—Type SJO 90°C

12/3 indicates the gauge (12) and the number of conductors in the cable (3).

Type SJOW-A is a code for the type of insulation (S cord with a light oil- and water-resistant jacket).

90°C is the maximum operating temperature of the cable.

P-123-MSHA indicates that the cable is approved by the Mine Safety and Health Administration (MSHA).

Type SJO 90°C is an alternative designation given to this particular cable.

Table 8.2 gives the meaning of some common insulation designations.

Other Factors that Affect Ampacity

Ampacity is not printed on cable because outside factors influence the operating temperature of the cable, which may lower its effective maximum amperage. The ambient temperature around a cable, the number of cables and the distance between them, whether the cables are in a raceway or conduit or standing in free air, and whether the circuit is run continuously or intermittently (periodically allowed to cool) all affect the operating temperature of the cable and therefore the allowed ampacity. The NEC specifies how much a cable must be derated in each of these circumstances. Keep this in mind when cabling. When cable runs are in well-ventilated areas and the room temperature is normal or cool, no derating is necessary. When cables are tightly bundled or stacked one on another, placed in narrow raceways, or subject to hotter than normal ambient temperatures, the insulation may be overheated if the cable is loaded to full ampacity. Keep this in mind when selecting cable gauge under such circumstances.

Ampacity of Overcurrent Devices

Because electrical conductors heat up over time, when circuits are to be loaded continuously for more than three hours NEC 220.10(b) requires that the overcurrent devices (such as circuit breakers) are derated to 80% of their maximum rated ampacity, unless the circuit breaker is a special type, which is designed to operate at 100% continuously. Many modern distro boxes use continuous rated breakers (see Table 9.2) For example, a circuit protected by a 100A breaker may not be loaded beyond 80A continuously for more than three hours. If the circuit is loaded continuously beyond 80%, a cool-down period lasting at least half as long as the on time is required. When a feeder supplies a circuit having a combination of continuous and noncontinuous loads, the rating of the overcurrent device may not be less than the noncontinuous load plus 125% of the continuous load. (A *continuous load* is defined by the code as a load that is expected to continue for three hours or more.)

Ampacity of Connectors

Like cable, connectors have a maximum amperage rating. Obviously, you must not run more power through a cable than the connector is rated for, regardless of the rating of the cable. Connectors tend to be the weakest part of the system. Bates and Edison connectors will overheat and melt if they are overamped or (most commonly) if there is poor electrical contact between connectors. If left too long the connector melts and is destroyed. The amperage ratings of connectors are discussed in Chapter 9.

Parallel and Series Circuits

Several lamps can be connected in a single circuit in one of two ways: in parallel or in series (Figure 8.6). Lighting equipment is almost always connected in parallel.

In a *parallel* circuit, the *voltage* is the same at every point of the circuit. The amperage of the whole circuit is equal to the sum of the amperages drawn by the separate fixtures.

In a *series* circuit, *amperage* is constant throughout the circuit. The sum of the voltages of the lights is equal to the voltage of the circuit. For example, to use 28V ACL PAR lights (aircraft landing light) with a 120V source, four 28V lights are connected in series ($28 + 28 + 28 + 28 = 112V$). The total resistance in the circuit is equal to the sum of the resistances of the fixtures. In a series circuit, if there is a break in the circuit at any point (if a filament blows, for example), the entire circuit is interrupted and none of the lights receive power.

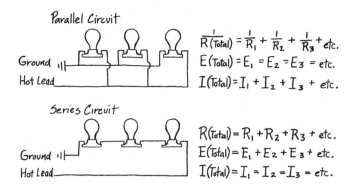

Figure 8.6 In a parallel circuit, voltage is constant everywhere in the circuit, and the sum of the amperages of the fixtures equals the total amperage of the circuit. In a series circuit, amperage is constant everywhere in the circuit, and the sum of the voltages of each figure equals the voltage of the circuit.

Types of Distribution Circuits

There are three basic types of distribution circuits: three-wire DC (240/120V), three-wire single-phase AC (240/120V), and four-wire three-phase AC (208Y/120 or 240Δ/120). To start with, the most basic distinction between these circuits is the difference between AC and DC current.

Direct Current and Alternating Current

A *direct current* power source — a battery or DC generator — has a positive terminal and a negative terminal. Electrons flow from the negative terminal through the circuit to the positive terminal. The *polarity* (direction of flow) never changes, and the current maintains a constant voltage.

Alternating current, which is supplied by the power company or by an AC generator, has a hot lead and a neutral lead.[3] The polarity of the circuit alternates from positive to negative and back to positive again. In the United States, alternating current operates at 60 cycles per second, or 60 hertz (Hz) (Figure 8.7).

Europe and other parts of the world use a 50 Hz, 240V system or another system. Appendix I gives the kind of power used in cities throughout the world.

During each cycle, the voltage of a 60 Hz 120V system goes from 0 to +170V, back to 0, reverses polarity, goes down to –170V, and back to 0 again. It does this 60 times every second. Because the cycles occur rapidly, there is no time for the filament

---

[3] The *neutral* wire is also called the *common*, the *grounded lead*, or the *white* wire. As neutral is the most familiar term to most electricians, I have adopted it for this edition of this book. Officially, however, this is considered incorrect usage; the common wire is not actually "neutral" unless the hot legs are equally loaded. The term *grounded lead* is officially correct, but is too easily confused with *grounding wires*. They serve two completely different functions in a circuit. See Grounding later in this chapter.

of a bulb to dim during the short time when the voltage passes 0, which is the reason the bulb provides a constant glow. The effective, or RMS (root mean square), voltage of a circuit is 120V ($\sqrt{2}$ × peak voltage, or 0.707 × 170 = 120V). A voltmeter reading will give you the effective voltage. A lamp connected to the circuit will operate at the effective voltage of 120V.

Alternating Current and Direct Current on the Set

Both AC and DC power are used on sound stages and on location. Many of the large Hollywood studios still use DC house power in some or all of their stages, including Warner Brothers, Paramount, Universal, Sony, Twentieth Century Fox, Walt Disney Studios, CBS Studio Center, and Culver Studios. Most new studio facilities use AC, and AC is used for most location filming as well.

Either AC or DC can be used to power tungsten lights. A 120V DC circuit will light the bulb to the same brilliancy as a 120V AC circuit. DC current cannot be used with AC HMIs, variac dimmers, or other equipment that has an AC transformer. Plate dimmers or electronic DC dimmers must be used to dim DC circuits. Carbon arc lights run on DC. To covert AC power to DC a *rectifier* must be used. To convert DC to AC an *invertor* must be used.

Safety Considerations

DC is often used when filming near water because it is considered to be safer. You are less likely to get a shock from a DC system. With an AC system, you can complete a circuit by touching a hot wire and standing on the ground, but with a DC circuit, you can only complete the circuit by touching the positive and the negative wire simultaneously. The ground beneath your feet does not complete the circuit unless the DC system is grounded, and few are.

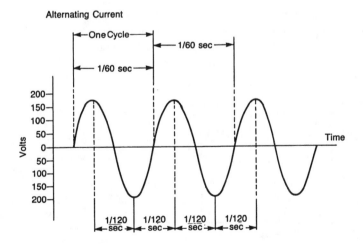

Figure 8.7 Sixty-hertz alternating current makes one full cycle in 1/60 second and hits peak voltage every 1/120 second. The effective, or RMS, voltage is 120V.

Also, the shock from a DC circuit and the shock from an AC circuit are different. (See "Electrical Shocks" later in this chapter.)

Switches and Breakers

There are some important differences between AC and DC switches and circuit breakers. It is a property of DC current that when there is a narrow gap between contacts, the current will arc and begin to burn the contacts (a carbon arc light operates on this principle). Every time a switch is opened or closed, a short gap exists for an instant. If the current is allowed to arc each time the switch is opened or closed, it will burn away the contacts of the switch very quickly. To prevent the arc, DC switches and circuit breakers are spring-loaded so that the contacts snap together quickly.

The most common household switches, AC-only switches, do not require this feature and operate quietly, without a snap. Do not use AC-only switches or breakers with DC circuits. The letters AC appear after the rating on the switch.

AC-DC switches can be used with either AC or DC power. If AC does not appear on the rating of the switch, it is an AC-DC type. If an AC-DC switch is to be used to control an incandescent light, it must have a "T" (tungsten) rating (a slightly beefier switch is needed to handle the high initial inrush current drawn by a cold tungsten filament).

DC Three-Wire System

Most DC stages are actually powered by two generators connected in series to provide a three-wire system with two hot legs (red and blue) and one common leg (white) (Figure 8.8).

Connecting the load between either one of the hot legs and the common leg gives 120V. Connecting the load between the negative blue leg and the positive red leg gives 240V.

Location generators usually provide only two-wire DC. However, it is theoretically possible to get 240V DC service by connecting two two-wire DC generators in series to create a three-wire 120/240V DC system. In practice, dual generators are typically bonded to the same tractor. If either positive or negative DC legs are

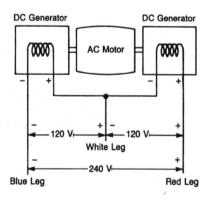

Figure 8.8   A three-wire 120/240V DC generator configuration for DC sound stages. An AC motor drives two DC generators connected in series. The blue leg is usually the negative leg, and the red leg is the positive. The voltage potential between them is 240V. The white leg gives a voltage potential of 120V when connected to a circuit with either hot leg.

grounded to the chassis, which they probably are, connecting them in series will cause a dead short. To run two generators in series, either the ground must be lifted or two generators must be on separate mounts.

Polarity

Polarity is the direction of flow of electricity in a circuit. In DC circuits, electricity flows from the negative terminal of the power source, through the circuit, to the positive terminal. DC polarity is important when powering carbon arc lights. This equipment will not operate properly if the polarity is reversed. *In a three-wire DC circuit, the blue leg is always negative and the red leg is always positive* (see Figure 8.8). If you were connecting a carbon arc light to the blue leg, you would connect the positive lead to the white wire. If you were connecting it to the red leg, you would connect the negative lead to the white wire. The white wire is negative with respect to the red leg and positive with respect to the blue leg.

You can check the polarity of a DC circuit by using a DC voltmeter; or a magnetic compass, which will point in the direction of flow when held next to a current-carrying wire.

Alternating Current: Single-Phase, Three-Wire Circuits

While most incandescent lights run on 120V, larger HMIs and 20ks run on 208V or 240V. A single-phase, three-wire AC system, which provides both 120V and 240V power from three wires, is commonly used in film distribution systems as well as in most homes and commercial buildings (Figure 8.9).

Like the three-wire DC system, this system consists of two hot 120V legs and a neutral. By connecting the load between one hot leg and the neutral, you get 120V. By connecting the load between the two hot legs, you get 240V. The neutral wire is

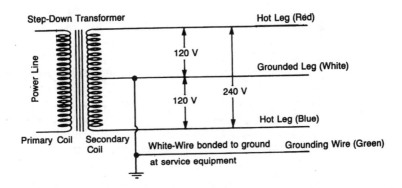

Figure 8.9 A three-wire, 120/240V AC configuration used in all types of AC buildings. The coils represent the primary and secondary coils of the transformer that steps down the voltage from the power lines. The neutral, or white, wire taps into the midpoint of the secondary coil and is a grounded wire. The voltage potential is 240V between red and blue, and 120V between white and red or between white and blue.

always white. The two hot legs will be two other colors (blue, red, or black), but never white or green.

Note that although this type of circuit is known as a three-wire circuit, it actually uses four wires. The fourth wire is a green-coded grounding wire used for grounding non–current-carrying parts of the lights and electrical hardware (see Grounding later in this chapter).

You might wonder whether using the neutral wire to serve two circuits doubles the load on the neutral wire. Would the neutral wire have to be twice as thick as in a single circuit to carry twice the amperage? The answer is no. The current flowing through one leg always flows in the direction opposite that of the current in the second leg. When the loads are the same on both legs, the current in the white wire is effectively zero. When the load on one leg is greater than that on the second, the neutral wire carries the difference in amperage of the two legs.

For example, assume that the red leg and the blue leg are carrying 50A each. The loads are even, so the two loads traveling through the neutral wire cancel each other out. If we remove 10A from the red leg and put it on the blue leg, making the red leg 40A and the blue leg 60A, the neutral wire will carry the difference (20A).

Cautions

There are a couple of disastrous mistakes to avoid when cabling. You must be careful not to connect the wires incorrectly. If you do, the lights on one circuit will receive 240V, which will blow out 120V lamps as soon as you try to turn them on. When a plugging box is intentionally plugged to serve a 220/240V light, it must be clearly marked. If in any doubt, check the voltage with a voltmeter before plugging in any lights.

Secondly, be sure that the white wire is never inadvertently disconnected once the lights are on. If the white wire is taken out of the circuit, the voltage applied to

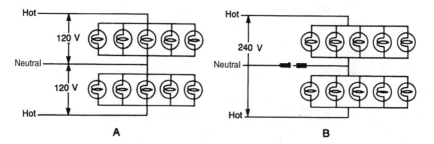

Figure 8.10　(A) A typical three-wire 120/240V system with five lamps connected to each leg. The red and blue legs are separate circuits sharing the neutral lead. (B) When the white wire is pulled, the red and blue legs become connected in series with 240V total voltage. If both sets of lamps have exactly the same resistance, the voltage is divided evenly in two, at 120V each. However, if one leg has more resistance, it receives more voltage and the other leg receives less. (They always add up to 240V.)

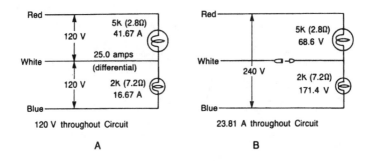

Figure 8.11   (A) A three-wire system with 5k on one leg and 2k on the other. (B) With the white wire pulled, two legs are connected in series with 240V applied to the circuit. The 2k will be blown by the 171V power.

the circuit becomes 240V, and the two sides of the circuit become connected in series (Figure 8.10).

Theoretically, if the amperage load on both legs were exactly the same, the voltage on each side would still be 120V (240 divided by 2). However, chances are that one leg is pulling more amperage than the other. The difference in resistance creates an imbalance in the voltage. The voltage on one side of the series circuit drops, while the other side shoots up, and will start to blow out bulbs on that side of the circuit in a matter of seconds.

Consider a simple example of a three-wire system with a 5k fixture on the red leg and a 2k fixture on the blue leg (Figure 8.11)

With the neutral connected, each light receives 120V. The 5k pulls 41.67A and has a resistance of 2.88Ω. The 2k pulls 16.67A and has a resistance of 7.2Ω. If the neutral wire were disconnected, the two lights become connected in series in a 240V circuit. Unlike a parallel circuit, the amperage in a series circuit is the same in every part of the circuit, and the total resistance of the circuit equals the sum of the resistances of all the lights.

We can calculate the amperage for the circuit as follows:

$$I \text{ (amperage)} = \frac{E \text{ (voltage of circuit)}}{R \text{ (sum of the resistances)}} = \frac{240}{(2.88 + 7.2)} = 23.81A$$

Knowing the amperage of the whole circuit, we can now calculate the voltage ($E = I \times R$) being applied to each light:

$$\text{Voltage of the 5k: } 23.81A \times 2.88\Omega = 68.6V$$

$$\text{Voltage of the 2k: } 23.81A \times 7.2\Omega = 171.4V$$

From this we can see that the fixture with the greater resistance, the 2k, will receive a higher voltage, which will blow the lamp. Notice that the sum of the voltages of the lights is equal to the voltage of the whole circuit (68.6 + 171.4. = 240).

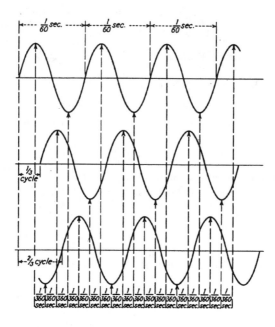

Figure 8.12 Three-phase current. (From H. Richter and W. Schwan. *Practical Electrical Wiring*, 15th ed. New York: McGraw-Hill, 1990. Reproduced with permission of McGraw-Hill.)

Three-Phase, Four-Wire Systems

Most commercial buildings, including sound stages, have three-phase power. Location generators also put out three-phase power. You will sometimes see the word phase abbreviated with the Greek letter phi (ϕ).

A three-phase, four-wire system consists of three 120V hot legs (referred to as phase A, B, and C, coded black, blue, and red) and a neutral leg (white). The three phases each operate at 60 cycles per second. Each phase, however, operates a third of a cycle out of sync with the next (Figure 8.12).

If you think of one cycle as a 360° circle, each phase begins the cycle 120° after the last.

208Y/120V System

The circuit shown in Figure 8.13 is a wye-connected three-phase system. It is called a *wye* or *star* because of its shape. When a load is connected to any one of the hot wires and the neutral wire, the voltage is 120V.

When a load is placed between any two hot wires, because the two phases are 120° apart the voltage is 208V.

Note that a three-phase, four-wire system actually uses five wires. The fifth is a green-coded grounding wire used for grounding non–current-carrying parts of the

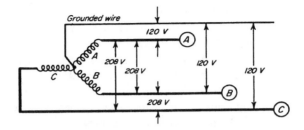

Figure 8.13 A 208Y/120V three-phase system. The three coils shown represent the secondary coils of the transformers that stepdown the voltage from the power line. A 208/120V system can supply 120V single-phase circuits and 208V three-phase circuits at the same time. (From H. Richter and W. Schwan, *Practical Electrical Wiring*, 15th ed. New York: McGraw-Hill, 1990. Reproduced with permission of McGraw-Hill.)

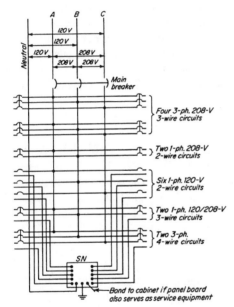

Figure 8.14 Five types of circuits can be derived from a 208Y/120 (four-wire, three-phase) system. (From H. Richter and W. Schwan, *Practical Electrical Wiring*, 15th ed. New York: McGraw-Hill, 1990. Reproduced with permission of McGraw-Hill.)

lights and electrical hardware (not shown in Figure 8.13; see Grounding later in this chapter).

Circuits Derived from the 208Y/120V System

The five types of circuits that can be derived from a wye-connected, four-wire, three-phase system are as follows (Figure 8.14):

120V, two-wire circuit, single-phase Three separate circuits can be made by tapping any one of the hot legs and the neutral leg. When loading the three legs, it is important to keep them evenly balanced.[4]

208V, two-wire circuit, single-phase This circuit is made by tapping any two of the three hot legs. The larger HMI ballasts run on 208V, 230V, or 240V. When running three-phase (208Y/120) power, select 208V input power on the ballast. Again, as much as possible, keep the load evenly balanced between the phases by tapping A and B, B and C, and C and A evenly.

120/208V, three-wire circuit, single-phase By tapping two of the three hot legs and the neutral leg, you have the option of providing 120V or 208V power. Doing this you can use distribution boxes made for three-wire systems. Be sure to label each box (RED/BLUE, BLUE/BLACK, or BLACK/RED) so you remember what's plugged into what. Keep the load evenly balanced by tapping evenly: A and B, B and C, and C and A.

208V, three-wire circuit, three-phase This type of circuit uses all three hot wires and has no neutral. Service wired this way is usually a designated branch circuit for machinery, such as a large air-conditioning unit or three-phase motor. Such circuits are not suitable for tie-ins. It is unsafe and forbidden by the NEC to use a ground wire tapped from another circuit to get 120V single-phase circuits from the legs of a three-wire, three-phase system.

208Y/120, four-wire circuit, three-phase Branch circuits with this configuration provide all the possibilities mentioned above.

480Y/277V System

Large fluorescent lighting installations operate more efficiently on 277V power, so some industrial buildings use a 480Y/277V system. The system works the same as the 208Y/120V system, but at a higher voltage. The cables are usually coded Brown, Orange, and Yellow. This system has no direct applications for film lighting and would require a stepdown transformer to be a usable power source. (Mole-Richardson is one manufacturer offering stepdown transformers of this type.)

Delta-Connected Systems

Delta-Connected Four-Wire, Three-Phase System In factories and large industrial buildings, you will sometimes come across a four-wire, three-phase delta-connected system. Its name comes from the circuit's resemblance to the Greek letter delta (Δ). The voltage across each of the secondary coils of the transformer is 240V (Figure 8.15).

To supply 120/240V service, one coil is tapped in the center. The tap is grounded and becomes the neutral lead for a three-wire, single-phase 120/240V circuit. Single-phase 120V power can be gained by connecting to A and N, or B and N. The tapped coil is usually larger than the other two, so it can handle the extra load.

---

[4] Note that the neutral white wire is a current-carrying wire in the circuit, not actually "neutral." When it functions this way it is officially termed the *grounded wire*. Technically, the grounded wire is a "neutral" wire only when it is connected with all four wires in the same circuit. However, *neutral* is the term most familiar to electricians, and I'm going to use it anyway.

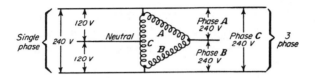

Figure 8.15   A 240V three-phase delta-connected system delivers single-phase 240/120V current and three-phase 240V current. (From H. Richter and W. Schwan, *Practical Electrical Wiring*, 15th ed. New York: McGraw-Hill, 1990. Reproduced with permission of McGraw-Hill.)

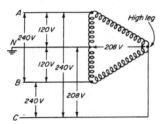

Figure 8.16   In a delta-connected system the voltage from the neutral to the high leg is 208V power, not 120V power, as you would expect from a wye-connected system. (From H. Richter and W. Schwan, *Practical Electrical Wiring*, 15th ed. New York: McGraw-Hill, 1990. Reproduced with permission of McGraw-Hill.)

Connecting to C and N produces 208V, single-phase power (Figure 8.16). This is called the *high leg*, and it has caught many an electrician by surprise. If you are used to a wye configuration, you would expect any of the three ungrounded leads to give 120V when connected with the neutral. The high leg on a delta-connected system gives 208V because it has the added voltage of an extra half-coil. Because the extra half coil is 120° out of phase, it adds 88V to the 120V of the full coil (88 + 120 = 208). Obviously, the high leg would burn out any 120V light connected to it.

240V and 480V Three-Phase, Three-Wire Delta   There are a couple of variations on the delta-connected system. Three-wire systems may be either 240V or 480V across each coil. In an alternative delta configuration, one corner of the delta is sometimes grounded.

Grounding

There are two kinds of grounding: (1) system grounding — the grounding of one of the current-carrying wires of the installation, and (2) equipment grounding — grounding the non–current-carrying parts, such as lamp housings and ballast casings.

System Grounding

As noted in the preceding discussion, the white, or neutral, wire is always a current-carrying *grounded* lead. The white wire is grounded to the service equipment (the main power box in the building), which in turn is grounded to the transformer delivering the electricity from the power line. The service equipment is grounded to earth by some means (e.g., a metal pipe of an underground water system, a ground rod, sunken building steel, or a made electrode, which is a large electrode placed in the ground during construction).

Equipment Grounding

Grounded neutral wires are not to be confused with *grounding* wires. The U-shaped prong on an Edison plug is for the grounding wire. Grounding wires are not meant to carry current under normal circumstances. They carry current only when there is a fault inside a piece of equipment and the housing becomes hot. If no grounding wire were connected (Figure 8.17A), anyone who touched the fixture would complete the circuit to ground through his or her body and would receive a shock. With a grounding wire connected to the housing (Figure 8.17B), electricity seeks the path of least resistance, and the bulk of the electricity completes the path to ground through the grounding wire instead of through a human body. The faulty fixture remains safe to touch.

The grounding wire is bonded to the service box, as is the neutral wire of the circuit. When a fault occurs, current coming back on the grounding wire will make a

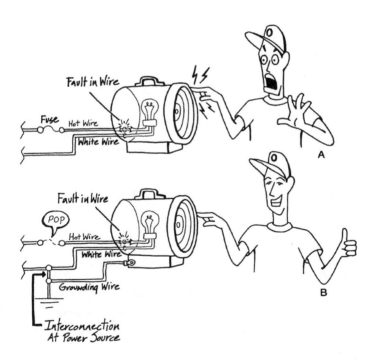

Figure 8.17 (A) A fault in a metal fixture makes the entire housing hot. Anyone who touches the hot fixture may complete a circuit to ground and get a shock. (B) A grounding wire carries the fault current safely to ground and pops the fuse or circuit breaker.

dead short with the bonded neutral. If enough current flows through the grounding wire, it will blow the fuse or trip the circuit breaker protecting the circuit. However, if the fault only makes loose contact (high resistance), it will create a lot of heat but may not pop the fuse.

Proper equipment grounding is essential to safety. It is one of the things that the fire marshal and electrical inspector will look for on the set.

The grounding wire can be smaller than the current-carrying wires; however, it must not be so small that the resistance in the wire prevents it from tripping the breaker in case of a fault. The NEC provides a table indicating the minimum sizes for grounding wires (see Table B.3).

Ground-Fault Circuit Interrupter (GFCI)

A ground-fault circuit-interrupter is an additional protective device (either incorporated into a specially designed circuit breaker or into a 120V outlet) that detects fault currents much smaller than that which would trip a normal circuit breaker or fuse. It is designed to protect people against shock current in the event of a fault. In household wiring GFCIs are required to be installed in bathroom outlets, outlets near sinks, outdoor circuits, and on any electrical equipment operated in proximity to a swimming pool, hot tub, or the like. Similarly, when filming in a bathroom or near a pool, a GFCI should be incorporated into the circuits powering the lights near the water. The danger of wet environments is that water underfoot greatly increases the conductivity of one's body to ground. Should leakage current occur, the GFCI will trip so fast that the shock current is less than that required to cause any serious injury.

A GFCI works by continuously comparing the current of the hot wire to that of the neutral wire. Normally the current flowing to a load on the hot wire is identical to the current returning on the neutral wire. However, if there is a defect in the wiring or the fixture, some current will leak to ground, causing a differential between the two wires. If there is a differential of .005A or more, the GFCI will disconnect the circuit in less than 1/60 of a second.

Some rental houses can provide special Edison outlet boxes with GFCI circuit breakers or outlets for use near water. It is quite simple to build a GFCI-protected outlet box. You can buy all the parts at an electrical supply store, or even a hardware store. Note: Unlike normal circuit breakers, a GFCI breaker has a neutral terminal as well as a hot, to which the load wires are connected. A GFCI breaker has a white pigtail, which connects to the neutral grounded bus of the panel box. All GFCI circuits are equipped with a test button (which, when pressed, should cause the circuit to shut off) and a reset switch. GFCIs are also called *ground fault interrupters* (GFIs), *residual current devices* (RCDs) in England, and *earth leakage detectors* (ELDs) in Australia.

Power Factor

When we calculate cable loads and generator loads we use the equation: watts/volts = amps. However, with some AC equipment this statement is not true: *It underestimates the actual current*. When a piece of equipment has inductive properties (magnetic ballasts) or capacitive properties (electronic ballasts and electronic dimmers), *power factor* must be considered in order to make proper load calculations. (Power factor is sometimes denoted as pf or cos θ.)

A load such as an incandescent light or heating element has no inductive or capacitive properties. It merely creates resistance in a circuit. A purely resistive circuit is said to have a power factor of 1.0 or 100%, and the equation watts/volts = amps is correct. *Unity* power factor is another term for this. When the load involves coils such as those in a transformer, motor, or magnetic ballast, *inductive reactance* comes into play, and the power factor is less than 100%. Inductance opposes the flow of current, causing current to *lag* behind voltage. The increase and decrease of current (which normally corresponds with the increase and decrease of voltage, 60 times a second) lags behind the voltage. With voltage and current out of phase, more current is required to accomplish the same amount of work. If you measure the amperage and the voltage, then multiply the two together, you get what's called the *apparent wattage* (expressed in volt-amperes). When power factor is low, apparent wattage will be higher than the *true power* (the watts of power actually used by the equipment). As one electrician put it, if apparent wattage is a glass of beer, power factor is the foam that prevents you from filling it up all the way. The size of the feeder cables, and the rating of the power source, must be sufficient to supply the *apparent wattage* (beer plus foam), even though only the beer counts as far as how much actual drinking is being accomplished. Load calculations must therefore include power factor.

Similarly, if the circuit has a capacitive component, such as with some electronic ballasts, *capacitive reactance* produces a power factor of less than 100%. Capacitive reactance causes current to *lead* voltage, which once again results in reduced efficiency. A few HMI ballasts have power factor correction circuits, which help restore the efficiency of a ballast.

Power Factor Calculations

Power factor is the percentage ratio of watts to volt-amperes:

$$pf = \text{rated wattage/volt-amperes}$$

$$\text{watts} = \text{volt-amperes} \times pf$$

For single-phase circuits, volt-amperes = volts × amps. For three-phase circuits, volt-amperes = 1.732 × volts × amps (1.732 is the square root of 3).

The power factor of a ballast or motor is sometimes, but not always, written on the equipment. To calculate the actual amperage needed to power equipment when the power factor is known, use the following equation:

$$\frac{\text{rated wattage}}{120 \times pf} = \text{required amperage}$$

To illustrate, suppose you are powering four 6k HMIs. If we made the mistake of discounting the power factor, we would incorrectly calculate the amperage as follows:

$$\frac{4 \times 6000}{120} = 200\text{A}$$

If the units have a power factor of 80%, the actual amperage required will be

$$\frac{4 \times 6000}{120 \times .80} = 250\text{A}$$

From this we see the importance of taking power factor into account. The amperage is significantly higher than thought — 50A higher.

Harmonic Currents on the Neutral Wire

With incandescent lights, if we draw equal current from two hot legs (assume a single-phase, three-wire, 120/240V system), there will be no return current on the neutral; the current cancels out between legs. In some situations this would allow the neutral wire of the feeder cables to be smaller than the hot wires.

When using magnetic ballasts, it is normal to have as much as 20 to 25% of the total amperage return on the neutral when the legs are evenly loaded. The current returning does not completely cancel between legs because inductance causes current to lag behind voltage. For this reason, when using many magnetic ballasts, it is wise to provide a neutral that is at least as large as the hot wires.

With electronic ballasts that do not have power factor correction, current leads voltage, and with this equipment about 80% of the current does not cancel out between legs. When operating many electronic ballasts, the neutral wire of the feeder cable must be substantial enough to carry the sum of the currents of the hot legs, times 80%.

It is common practice to double or triple the neutral wire when powering large numbers of electronic dimmers or electronic ballasts. By the same token, you can overload the neutral wire of the transformer or generator if it is not sized to handle return current, especially with 208Y/120 circuits.

Meters for Measuring Electricity

Set electricians should carry some kind of voltage tester with them at all times (Figure 8.18).

An inexpensive voltmeter (Figure 8.18C) is quite adequate because with constant use meters run the risk of being damaged. Meters and testers come in many shapes and sizes. A simple voltage tester (Figure 8.18H), when connected across a circuit, indicates with a LED display whether a circuit is 110V or 220V. An inexpensive, needle-type AC/DC voltmeter reads voltage from 0 to 500V with adequate accuracy. This type of meter can usually also measure resistance in ohms.

Most electricians invest in a small digital multimeter (8.18I), such as the Beckman DM73 or equivalent, which measures AC and DC voltage, detects continuity, and measures resistance. More expensive digital multipurpose meters, such as those manufactured by Fluke (8.18E), incorporate hertz and amp features in addition to voltage, resistance, and continuity. The best boy electric must be able to make meas-

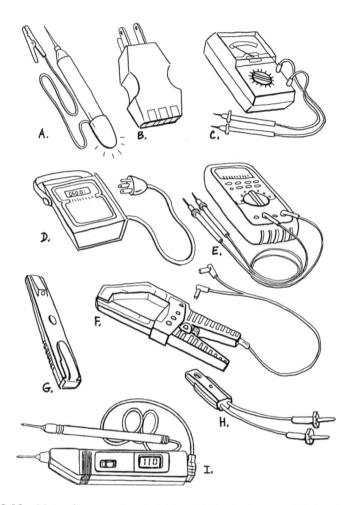

Figure 8.18 Meters for measuring electricity. (A) Continuity tester. (B) Circuit tester. (C) Voltmeter. (D) Line frequency tester. (E) Digital multimeter. (F) Amp probe attachment for multimeter. (G) Voltage sensor. (H) Voltage tester. (I) Digital multimeter.

urements of this kind. Voltmeters, ammeters, hertz testers, and continuity testers are also manufactured as separate meters.

Measuring Voltage

A voltmeter has two probes. Touch the probes to the terminals of the circuit to be measured. When probing exposed terminals, be careful as you position the probes not to put your fingers on or close to the terminals. When measuring a DC circuit, if the needle deflects to the left, off the bottom of the scale, the polarity is reversed. Check that your probes are properly connected; reverse them to get a measurement.

Measuring Frequency (Hertz Rate)

A frequency meter is used to measure the frequency of an AC circuit in cycles per second (Hz). There are several types of frequency meters. The most popular frequency meters simply plug into an Edison outlet (Figure 8.18D). In addition, some clamp-on ammeters have a hertz-reading function.

Another type of frequency meter, the Cinecheck meter, does not take the reading from the power lines at all, but instead from the light emitted by an HMI fixture (magnetic ballast only). Simply hold the meter up to the light and read the frequency.

Measuring Amperage

An amp probe (Figure 8.18F) is used to determine the amperage traveling through a single conductor. Amp probes are generally AC only; however, some more sophisticated meters can measure DC amperage as well. The amp probe has two curved fingers that close around an insulated single conductor cable. The probe measures the strength of the magnetic field created around the cable by the current running through it. The strength of the field is proportional to the amperage running through the wire. The amp probe gives a reading in amperes.

Testing Continuity

Unlike all the other testing equipment discussed in this section, a continuity tester (Figure 8.18A and I) is only used when power is not connected to the circuit. The tester is used to check for a break in the line. If the line is continuous, the tester will beep or light up.

A continuity tester is handy to check if a bulb or fuse has blown. If the filament of the bulb is intact, the tester will show continuity across the terminals of the bulb.

Testing Circuits

A circuit tester (Figure 8.18B) is used to test Edison outlets. It tells (1) if the circuit is hot, (2) if the polarity is correct, and (3) if the grounding wire is present.

A voltage sensor (Figure 8.18G) is a handy device that senses the magnetic field of electricity. Although it gives no quantitative reading of amperage, the sensor is extremely useful for checking if a wire is hot. Put the sensor near the wire, and press the button. If it beeps or lights up, then the wire is hot.

Electrical Shocks and Muscle Freeze

In the event that an electrician comes into contact with a hot wire and completes a circuit, the biggest danger is that his muscles will be frozen by the current and he will not be able to pull away from it. If this happens, the most important thing is to get him away from the current as quickly as possible. The length of time a person is shocked will determine the severity of injury and the likelihood of cardiac arrest and death. Do not touch someone who is being electrocuted. Unless you can move faster than 186,000 miles per second (the speed of light), you will become part of the circuit.

Pushing the victim with a wooden plank or an apple box is a safe way to disengage him from the circuit. A running, jumping body block can work as long as you are in the air when you hit the victim and do not complete a circuit to ground.

Once the victim is away from the circuit, check for pulse and breathing. Begin CPR immediately if there is no pulse. Call for professional medical assistance.

In addition to the duration of contact, the severity of damage from a shock is proportional to the number of vital organs transversed, and especially the heart. The most lethal path electricity can take is into one arm and out of the other. As electricity travels across the chest and through the heart, it can very easily cause ventricular fibrillation or stop the heart entirely. For this reason, when making a tie-in or dealing with hot, exposed wires, many electricians handle the wire with one hand and put the other hand in their pocket or behind their back if possible.

It is a common misconception that voltage is what kills a shock victim. In truth, high voltage can be dangerous because it has a tendency to arc, but it is the amperage that damages the muscles and heart.

The amperage of a shock is a combination of the current in the circuit and the resistance present (Table 8.3). The resistance of dry skin, for example, is about 100,000Ω. This resistance is enough that brief contact with a 100V circuit will allow about 1 milliampere (mA), or 0.001A, to flow through the body, which is enough to bite you, but not enough to cause damage (Table 8.4). In contrast, the resistance of wet skin is about 1000Ω, which allows about 100mA to flow through the body. This is enough to cause ventricular fibrillation, impede breathing, and cause unconsciousness and possibly death. Wearing thick rubber electricians gloves is recommended any time you are exposed to live lugs and cables.

AC current can be more deadly than DC current for several reasons. Although both types of current have the effects listed in Table 8.4, AC can freeze a body to a conductor with one fifth as much current as DC. Alternating current can more easily cause fibrillation and cardiac arrest because the 60-Hz polarity cycle is a harmonic of the rhythm of the heart and because AC current has a peak voltage of 170V, while DC is a constant 120V. However, this is not to say that DC power cannot hurt and kill a person.

Every electrician must have a healthy respect for electricity if he or she aims to have a long and successful career. People are killed every year by accidental electro-

Table 8.3   Effect of Resistance on Amperage of Shock

Condition	Resistance	Amps
Dry skin @ 100V	100,000	1mA
Wet skin @ 100V	1,000	100mA
Open cut @ 100V	500	200mA
Dry skin @ 10,000V	100,000	100mA

Table 8.4 Effect of Ampacity on Shock Victims

Current	Effect on Body
1mA or less	No sensation (not felt)
More than 5mA	Painful shock
More than 10mA	Muscle contractions; could cause a "freezing" to the electrical circuit for some people
More than 15mA	Muscle contractions; can cause most people to become frozen to the electrical circuit
More than 30mA	Breathing difficult; could cause unconsciousness
50–100mA	Ventricular fibrillation of the heart possible
100–200mA	Ventricular fibrillation of the heart certain; death is possible
Over 200mA	Severe burns and muscular contractions; the heart is more apt to stop beating than to fibrillate; death is likely
1A or more	Permanent damage to body tissues; cardiac arrest, severe burns, and probable death

cution — the majority by faulty equipment that has been poorly maintained, but some by their own ignorance or foolishness. Pressure from the powers that be, long hours, and physical exhaustion can cloud good judgment and clear thinking. Be aware of your physical and mental state. As a professional, your judgment of a situation has weight; don't discount it. No matter how frantic things get, when it comes to dealing with exposed live conductors, remember to slow down, think about what you are doing, and don't let anyone distract you. No situation in filmmaking is worth the risk to your life and health.

Electrical, Building, and Fire Codes

The National Electrical Code

The National Electrical Code is a book of regulations and requirements that have been developed in the interest of protecting life and property. The code is sponsored and published by the National Fire Protection Association (NFPA). The code itself is purely advisory as far as the NFPA is concerned. However, individual states can adopt the code as law. When a state adopts the code, the state, or any city or municipality in it, may add to the rules of the code, but none may relax its requirements.

You can buy a copy of the code at any technical bookstore; be warned, however, that the code is written in NEC-speak. It can be frustratingly confusing to read if you do not understand the unexplained context behind each directive. This section attempts to explain and clarify the rules of the code that are important to film lighting technicians.

The code covers every conceivable use of electricity, from basic wiring methods and materials to pipe organs and "hydromassage bathtubs." The two sections of the code that deal directly with film and television production are Article 520, "Theaters and Similar Locations," and Article 530, "Motion Picture and Television Studios and Similar Locations." However, many other sections of the code also apply: grounding (Article 250), cable types (Article 400), and overcurrent protection (Article 240).

Article 520 covers live theaters, concert halls, movie theaters, and motion picture and television studios that incorporate assembly areas such as those used for game shows, situation comedies, variety shows, concerts, and so on. This article covers only those areas of an auditorium that are occupied by or are within 10 ft. of a live audience. Article 530 covers all the areas of stages that do not have audiences. Code books 1996 and later include a separate section, Article 525, to cover carnivals, circuses, fairs, and similar events.

Outdoor Use

The 1996 code provides definitions for various equipment used in motion picture and television production (530-2). Our equipment is defined by the code as portable equipment. Article 530-6 allows that portable lighting and distribution equipment "shall be permitted for temporary use outdoors provided the equipment is supervised by qualified personnel while energized, and barriered from the general public."

Cords and Cables

For areas covered by Article 520 (audience areas), cords must be designated for "extra hard usage." The following types are permitted: S, SO, SEO, SOO, ST, STO, STOO, G, EISL, and W (NEC 400-4, note 5, and Table 400-4). No junior service (e.g., SJO) cable may be used, except in break-out assemblies such as from a Socapex dimmer line (1996 NEC 520-68 Exception No. 4).

In areas covered by Article 530, cords may not be fastened by uninsulated staples or nails. For circuits protected by a 20A breaker or smaller, splices and taps may be made in the cord as long as "approved devices," such as wire nuts, are used (NEC 530-12).

Switches

Each lighting fixture or other electrical device must have an externally operable ON/OFF switch within 6 ft. of the fixture. This is in addition to any remote switches that may be connected (NEC 530-13).

UL Listing

Underwriters Laboratories and other similar agencies test electrical parts such as plugs, sockets, switches, and wire, as well as lights, appliances, and other electrical equipment. If a product is approved, it is said to be listed and is marked UL. Common plugs and sockets that are unlisted are usually of poor quality and should be avoided. The specialized equipment used in filmmaking may be unlisted simply because the manufacturer must pay to put the product up for testing.

All electrical equipment and hardware used on a set must be either listed or specially approved by the local authority that has jurisdiction. Los Angeles has the luxury of having its own testing laboratory to get city approval for unlisted products.

Guarding Live Parts

It can be stated generally that all live parts must be enclosed or guarded to prevent people and conductive material from making accidental contact. This is true for all types of equipment, connectors, cables, bull switches, panelboards, splicing boxes, dimmers, rheostats, lights, and so on (NEC 530-15). The NEC defines guarded as "covered, shielded, fenced, enclosed, or otherwise protected by means of suitable covers, castings, barriers, rails, screens, mats or platforms to remove the likelihood of approach or accidental contact by persons or objects to a point of danger" (NEC 100). The intent of this rule is to protect unsuspecting laypeople.

Overcurrent Protection

Fuses and breakers interrupt only the hot legs. The neutral grounded lead should not be interrupted by circuit protection.

Location Automatic overcurrent protection (circuit breakers or fuses) must be provided within 25 ft. of every reduction of wire size (NEC 240-21 exception no. 3). For example, when splitting from 2/0 cable to 100A whips, there must be breakers in the junction box or along the wires within 25 ft. of the split. To meet this requirement, soft-Y connectors (e.g., 100A Bates to two 60A Bates) are supposed to have in-line fuses.

The 400% Rule: Oversizing DC Circuit Protection Circuit protection may be up to 400% of the amperage rating of the cable (NEC 530-18). For example, this allows you to make a 4/0 run from a 1600A DC service panel and run up to the cable's rated capacity (400A/leg), without the need for further circuit protection. You can run a 5k directly off a deuce board (which has a 200A fuse; NEC 530-18c). Note: This allows you to oversize the circuit protection. It does not allow you to load the cables for more than their rating.

"Plugging Boxes" and Distro Boxes

Plugging boxes (e.g., four-hole boxes) are not permitted to be used for AC power. Any wire smaller than no. 8 AWG connected to a paddle/stage box must have appropriate fuses in the connector.

An AC power distribution box (AC Plugging Box, Scatter Box) is an AC distribution center containing grounded, polarized receptacles and may contain overcurrent protection.

Feeder Cables

You may not load cables beyond their rated capacity. Amperage capacity tables appear in Articles 310 and 400 of the code; these tables are reprinted in Appendix B. All neutral and ground cables must be identified by color coding — by either the color of the single conductor connector or by being wrapped with 6 in. of colored tape or sheath. White and neutral gray are reserved for grounded neutral leads only. Green is for grounding leads (sometimes green with yellow stripes). In addition, if more than one electrical system is being used in the same area, the hot wires must also be color coded at each end (e.g., a 480V air conditioner in use at the same time as a 120V system). Yellow is not a great color to use around sodium lights because it looks the same as white.

Connectors

Single-conductor cables must be attached to the connectors with solder, by crimping, or with a set screw.

Grounding connections are not allowed to depend solely on a solder contact because if a fault exists, the heated solder will melt. Solder connections are allowed with other legs because if the connection breaks, the worst that will happen is loss of power. However, if the grounding connection breaks, electrocution and fire are possible.

Branch Circuit Connectors   The code defines a branch circuit as the conductors between the last overcurrent protection device and the load. In other words, a branch circuit is the portion of the circuit between the last set of breakers or fuses and the lights. The code requires that multipole connectors used in AC branch circuits be polarized and that the grounding wire makes contact first and disconnects last. A standard U-ground plug or Bates connector is an example of such a connector. The amperage rating of plugs and receptacles shall not be less than that of the overcurrent protection. Plugs and receptacles, such as Edison twist-lock and Bates, can be used interchangeably for either AC or DC as long as they are listed for AC/DC use, and are marked to identify the system to which they are connected (530-21[b]).

Feeder Connectors   When connecting single-pole cables to a hot system, the order must be as follows: (1) ground (where used), (2) neutral, and (3) hot conductors. Disconnect from a hot system in the reverse order.

The code lists three permissible ways to ensure that ground is made first and broken last:

1. The connection makes it impossible to connect or disconnect wires when the source is hot.
2. A mechanical device makes it possible to connect the wires in only the proper order. The same device ensures that disconnection is made in the reverse order. Abbott panels are an example of a connector that works this way.
3. A caution notice provided adjacent to the line connectors indicates the order in which the connection should be made.

The 1996 code requires that single-pole connectors be listed (UL) or approved by local authority. It also requires that when used with AC, the male and female connectors lock together with a mechanical locking devices (530-22). At this writing the 1996 code has not yet been adopted in LA. Old nonlocking connectors are being grandfathered in. Tape will serve as a locking device until the transitional period is over.

Grounding

NEC Article 250 covers grounding in depth. The important points for set lighting applications follow.

All equipment supplied with AC must be grounded back to the source of power (the can or generator) by means of a continuously connected equipment-grounding conductor. When using house power, you must use the grounding bus of the particular can from which the power is being drawn; you may not ground to a different can.

The grounding wire may be smaller than the current-carrying wires in accordance with Table 250-95 of the code, which is reprinted in Table B.3 of this book.

Alternating Current Generators When using an AC generator, the non–current-carrying metal parts of the lighting equipment and grounding receptacles shall be bonded to the generator frame (via the grounding wires), and the neutral must be bonded to the generator frame (NEC 250-6[c]). If the generator is mounted on a vehicle, the frame of the generator must be bonded to the frame of the vehicle. (Vehicle-mounted generators are bonded together upon installation; this is not something the electrician has to do.)

Direct Current Equipment DC equipment operating at not more than 150V does not have to be grounded, although grounding is not prohibited.

A DC HMI ballast provides AC to the head. Therefore, the head must be grounded to the ballast so that if there is a fault in the head, it will trip the breaker in the ballast. A DC ballast need not be grounded to the power source. When using several DC ballasts within 10 ft. of one another, the grounds should be connected together.

Connections for the purpose of grounding must use an approved ground fitting or ground rod clamp. Tie-in clips or spring clamps are not permitted.

Fire and Building Codes

Fire codes provide that there must be fire lanes leading to exits. There must be a space of 4 ft. between the walls of the sound stage and sets or equipment. These fire lanes must be kept completely clear of equipment. Outside doors surrounding the area of filming must be unlocked and unobstructed.

Fire codes are different in every city, and they change regularly. It is up to the best boy electric to keep up to date on the code having jurisdiction over the city in which filming is taking place. The best boy electric checks in with the fire marshal on the first day of filming to establish rapport, to inform the fire marshal of his plan, and to see if any plans will raise problems or require special action.

OSHA and the Industry Wide Labor–Management Safety Committee

The Industry Wide Labor–Management Safety Committee is sponsored by the Contract Services Department of the Association of Motion Picture and Television Producers. It is an advisory body made up of Studio Safety Professionals, Labor Union business managers, and producers in order to publish safety bulletins in response to accidents and common safety complaints. There are safety bulletins on the full range of topics, from firearms to helicopters to sky diving. The ones that apply to set lighting directly are Bulletin #22, "Guidelines for the Use of Elevating Work Platforms...," and Bulletin #23, "Guidelines for Working with Lighting Systems and Other Electrical Equipment." Most rules are based on electrical code or common sense safety, and the concepts they address are expressed throughout this book.

CHAPTER 9

Electrical Distribution

Many systems of cable connectors, junction boxes, and distribution boxes are in use in the motion picture industry today (Figure 9.1).

You can often find two or more different systems working on a set servicing different pieces of equipment.

The component parts of a distribution system are as follows:

Power source   The power may come from one or more of a number of sources: (1) a mobile generator; (2) designated studio circuits, which are powered by a municipal transformer or turbine generators; (3) a tie-in to the service panel on location; (4) a location power drop; (5) a battery or battery pack; or (6) available wall circuits. Power sources are covered in Chapter 10.

Main disconnect   The main disconnect, a bull switch with current-limiting fuses or circuit breakers, provides a main switch to shut down all power at the end of the day or in an emergency. It also provides main circuit protection for the power source. In the case of a generator, the main breaker switch or fuse is part of the generator.

Main feeder cable   This cable, usually 4/0 or 2/0 copper cable, carries power from the power source to the set. The four most common types of feeder cable connectors are lug, mole-pin, Cam-Lok, and Abbott connectors.

Spider box   The spider box, or junction box, functions as a cable splicing point and provides a means of dividing the power into several runs of main feeder cable.

Distribution boxes or **portable remote switchboards**   Feeder cables terminate into distribution boxes, which provide a point to subdivide current into a number of smaller gauge subfeeder cables. Any time you reduce cable size, the NEC requires that there be proper overcurrent protection within 25 ft. of the change (NEC 240-21). Distribution boxes provide circuit protection and multiple outlets (usually 100A each) for subfeeders and lights. A portable remote switchboard provides one or more main switches, usually 200A per leg.

Dimmers   Dimmer packs are powered from the main feeder, and are used to control some or all of the lights.

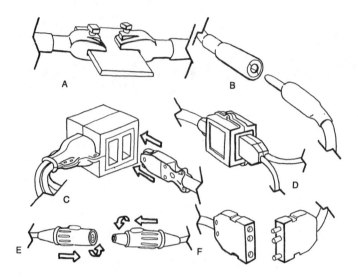

Figure 9.1   Common feeder and fixture connectors. (A) Lugs attached to bus bar or spider. (B) ½ in. mole-pins. (C) Four-hole stage box and paddle. (D) One-hole stage box with two half-paddles plugged into it. (E) Cam-Lok connectors. (F) Bates three-pin connectors.

Subfeeders   Smaller gauge feeder cable delivers power from the distribution box to outlet boxes or to subsequent distribution boxes. Banded 2 AWG cable is typical. (Banded cable is simply four or five single-conductor cables held together in a single bundle by bands of tape at regular intervals.)

Extensions   Extension cables with 100A or 60A *Bates* connectors, 100A or 60A *Metric* connectors, or 100A *stage extensions* (paddle connectors) run from the distribution boxes to the larger lights.

Gang box, quad box, or **"lunch box"**   Provide 20A outlets for plugging in the smaller lights. Typically location equipment uses Edison outlets. On stages you sometimes run into lamps and outlet boxes fitted with 20A twist-lock or 20A Bates outlets. Outlet boxes plug into the distribution boxes or extension cables.

Distro Systems

Feeder Cable

The first thing to determine in planning a cable run is the size of the main feeder. Estimate what the maximum total amperage requirement will be (including headroom for HMI startup). Factor in-line loss based on the length of the main run.

A small setup, 380A or less, can run on three-wire, single-phase banded cable. A medium-size setup, using more than two large guns (12ks, 10ks, maxibutes), will typically require 2/0 cable (300A per leg max, 600A single-phase, 900A three-phase max). A large setup (or especially long run) will require 4/0 cable (400A per leg, 800A single-phase, 1200A three-phase max). On a large studio sound stage, or for a night scene that takes in a lot of acreage, multiple cable runs may be required involving multiple power sources.

Starting at the power source and moving toward the load, the first type of connector encountered attaches the distribution system to the power supply. Generators are commonly fitted with bus bars for lug cable, and/or Cam-Lok receptacles, and/or mole-pin receptacles.

Sister Lugs

Lugs are heavy-duty copper or bronze-cast clamps that screw onto the copper bus bars of the power supply and spider boxes.

Lug cable — heavy, single-conductor, usually 4/0 or 2/0 cable with lugs at both ends — is used for primary feeders, running from the bus bar to the spider box and from spider box to spider box.

When connecting lugs to the power supply buses, use a crescent wrench or speed wrench (ratcheted) to ensure a tight connection. (By coincidence, the gap of the jaw of the lug is the same size as the square head of the lug bolts, so in a pinch you can use one lug to tighten the bolt of another lug.) Lugs are either soldered to the ends of the cables, clamped on with a socket set screw, or crimped around the wire with a 15-ton hydraulic crimper.

Spider Boxes

A spider box is an intermediate cable splicing point used to join lengths of lug cable, or to divide power in several directions. A spider box houses several 1/4 in. thick copper bars held in a transparent Plexiglas insulated frame. Spider boxes provide a bar for each wire of the distribution cable; each bar can accommodate between four and eight lugs. Spider boxes may have two, three, four, or five bars, depending on the number of wires in the circuit. Holes in the Plexiglas frame provide access to the lug bolts, which are tightened to the bars using a T-handle 3/16 in. Allen wrench (Figure 9.2).

Warning: Never use a green bus bar as a current-carrying bus; it is a grounding bar only. The green bus bar is connected directly to the external metal straps, which will create a serious short and shock hazard if the bus bar is connected to a hot lead.

The ampacity per cable and per bar of a spider box is determined by the number of lugs per bar. See amperage data in Table 9.1.

Mole-Pin Feeder Cable

Mole-pin connectors are single-conductor, 1/2 in. diameter, slip-pin connectors. Mole-pins are used on feeder cables and on the head cables of some larger lights. A lug-to-mole-pin adaptor, or jumper (Figure 9.3A), connects mole-pin feeders to the spider box or deuce board.

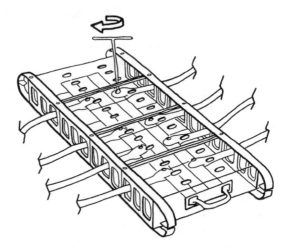

Figure 9.2 The four-bar spider box shown here allows up to six lugs per bar. Lug nuts are tightened with a T-handle Allen wrench through the holes in the Plexiglas frame.

Table 9.1 Ampacity of Spider Boxes

| Cable slots per bar | Continuous | | Intermittent | | | |
	Amps per cable	Amps per bar	Amps per cable	Amps per bar	Minutes on	Minutes off
4	300	600	325	650	20	6
6	280	840	325	975	20	10
8	270	1080	325	1300	20	14

The amperage data in Table 9.1 apply to all spider boxes based on the number of lugs per bar. This table gives Mole Richardson's recommended maximum loading.

Mole-pin feeder cables are widely used for 2/0 cable and on banded #2 AWG cable. On banded cable, the legs are color-coded with rubber sheaths at the base of the connectors. Mole-pins are made that can fit cable sizes from 4/0 to as small as 10 AWG.

The pins of a mole-pin connector have a thin slit cut down the center, which allows the pin to flex and put friction on the inside of the female receptacle. With use, the pins can become bent together so that the pin no longer creates the friction that makes a good connection. If this happens, wedge the blades of a wire snipper or knife into the gap to pry the two halves apart. Similarly, the female connector can get spread and loose, especially those of three-fers. Weed out and replace ill-fitting connectors.

At this writing, it is standard practice to wrap pin connections with gaffer's tape to prevent the connection from pulling apart. (Tab the tape so it is easy to pull off.) The 1996 NEC (where adopted) requires that feeder cable connectors on AC circuits have a mechanical locking mechanism to hold them together.

Reversed Ground System

With all types of pin connectors, the male and female are oriented with "pins to power," meaning that the male pins point toward the power plant and the female end goes towards the lights. This is true of all cable, except when a reverse ground is used; the pin on the grounding wire is pointed downstream.

Some rental houses and studios make their banded cable with the grounding pin reversed; the female end points toward the power source. Many best boys also run their single conductor cable with the grounding wire connectors in reverse. The idea is to make it impossible to plug a hot wire into the grounding wire by mistake.

Three-Fers

Three-fers are used to branch three feeder cables off of one (Figure 9.3B). A standard three-fer interconnects one male pin with three female receptacles. One three-fer is used on each leg. They are color-coded.

Grounding Stars and Grounding Clusters

A grounding three-fer, or grounding star used with a reverse ground system, interconnects three male pins with one female receptacle. A grounding cluster or "squid" is a soft-wired set of connectors that serves the same purpose.

Suicide Pins

A suicide pin is a male-to-male mole-pin adaptor (Figure 9.3D). It gets its name from the fact that when the adaptor is plugged in, it exposes a hot pin. Obviously, you should never leave a bare suicide pin plugged into a live wire. Suicide pins are used to reverse the direction of the connectors on the grounding wire or to make a feeder loop (see Rigging later in this chapter).

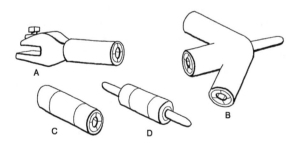

Figure 9.3 Adaptors. (A) Lug-to-mole-pin adaptor. (B) Mole-pin three-fer. (C) Female-to-female mole-pin adaptor. (D) Suicide pin male-to-male mole-pin adaptor.

.515 Pins

It is a little known fact that there are two sizes of half-inch pin connectors: mole-pins, which are 0.500 in. in diameter, and .515 pins, which are identical to mole-pins but with 0.515 in. diameter. Mole-pins and .515 pins are not really compatible, although a strong person can force a male .515 into a female mole-pin, which bends both connectors. You will sometimes encounter equipment having both kinds of pins and will have a struggle to make the connections properly.

Cam-Lok Cable

Cam-Lok connectors are single-conductor connectors used on 4/0 and 2/0 feeder cable, alternative to lugs and spider boxes. Cam-Lok is also the most common input connector for dimmer packs.

The male and female connectors twist-lock together with a cam mechanism which ensures full contact yet is easy to connect and disconnect. However, to ensure a good connection, the connectors must be twisted until tight, not simply inserted. The connectors are shielded with rubber so that bare metal cannot be left exposed, and the connection is protected from water. The rubber is color-coded red, blue, black, white, or green appropriately.

Cam-Lok connectors should not be connected or disconnected "hot" (when powering a load). This is true for all connectors, but especially with Cam-Loks, because if the pin within the Cam-Lok connector gets pitted and warped from arcing, it can eventually seize up and the connectors will be permanently stuck together.

A Cam-Lok "T" allows two Cam-Lok connectors to be plugged into one. A soft two-fer, which does the same thing, is simply two female Cam-Lok connectors wired to one male Cam-Lok connector.

Remote Switchboards

Switchboards (commonly called *location boards* or *deuce boards*) work with any three-wire system: AC or DC. On DC sound stages switchboards are commonly used to provide circuit protection at a workable amperage — 200A/leg. (In most cases, the circuit protection for DC cans is located in the powerhouse, not in the sound stage, and is set at 1200A per leg.) Once the feeder cables have reached the vicinity of the set, they are usually connected to a switchboard. These switches control power to various areas of a large set or to several separate sets within one stage. An ace board has a single switch (400A total). A deuce board divides power between two switches (800A input total) (Figure 9.4).

A four-way board divides power between four switches (1600A input total). The input feeder lugs connect to bus bars on the switchboard. Sets of output bus bars are provided on the front of the unit. Each output circuit has individual circuit protection and separate toggle switches that control internal high-amperage contactors. The contactors can be controlled by toggle switches on the switchboard or from a remote toggle switch box or a practical switch wired into the set. A main switch is provided in both locations to switch all contactors at once. Control cables run down to stage level, from which all the switches throughout the stage can be controlled.

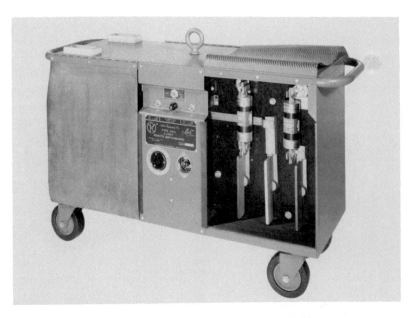

Figure 9.4   A deuce board with two high-amperage, remote-control, fused switches in a stackable casing. The deuce board shown is designed for a three-wire 800A AC or DC input and two three-wire 400A outputs (200A per leg). (Photo courtesy of Mole-Richardson Co., Hollywood, CA.)

Switchboards are designed to be stacked. An eyelet is provided on the top of each unit for hoisting it into catwalks.

On DC sound stages, *stage boxes* (paddle connectors) and *stage extensions* run from the deuce boards to the lights and floor drops. (More about the DC paddle system will be discussed later.) On AC systems banded cable runs from the deuce boards to 400A distro boxes around the set. AC deuce boards are also available with 100A Bates outlets and circuit breakers.

AC Power Distribution Boxes

Whatever the feeder cable — lug, mole-pin, Cam-Lok, or what have you — the feeder cable terminates into a distribution box (also known as an *AC plugging box*). The distro box provides a fused stepdown point for the subsequent smaller circuits that service the lights. Circuit protection (breakers or fuses) are required within 25 ft. of any reduction in cable size (NEC 240-21). 100A Bates outputs are widely used on distro boxes. Some boxes also offer 240V 100A Bates, 60A Bates, or Edison outlets.

Figure 9.5 shows the line of Mole-Richardson distribution boxes. Figure 9.6 illustrates a box (made by Union Connector) in use on set.

Table 9.2 lists specifications of a sample of commonly used distro boxes. Some questions to consider when ordering boxes: Single-phase or three-phase? Input con-

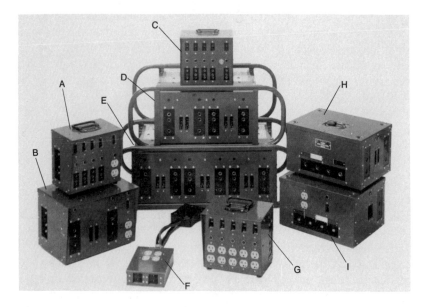

Figure 9.5 Mole-Richardson distribution/spider boxes. (A) Bates/Edison outlet box: 100A Bates in, four 20A Bates out, one 20A duplex Edison out, 100A Bates feed-through. (B) Bates step-down box: 100A Bates in, two 60A Bates out, 100A Bates feed-through. (C) Bates outlet box: 100A Bates in, five 20A Bates out, 100A Bates feed-through. (D) Single-phase spider/distribution box: lugs in (red, blue, white, and green), four 100A Bates out. (E) Three-phase spider/distribution box: lugs in (red, blue, black, white, and green), six 100A Bates out, two 208V 100A Bates out. (F) Gang box: 100A Bates in, four 20A Edison out. (G) Edison outlet box: 100A Bates in, five 20A Edison out. (H) Banded pin box: mole-pins in, single phase; four 100A Bates out; pin feedthrough; courtesy duplex Edison receptacle. (I) 240V banded pin box: mole-pins in, single phase; two 240V 100A Bates out; pin feedthrough, courtesy duplex Edison receptacle. (Photo courtesy of Mole-Richardson Co., Hollywood, CA.)

nector type? AC/DC or AC only? Do you need 240V 100A outlets for 12ks and 20ks? Do you want some boxes that feed through? Features I find very useful are indicator lights (help with trouble shooting) and courtesy outlets (in a dark stage it's good to have a small work light at each box).

Bates Three-Pin Connectors

Bates connectors come in several sizes: 20A, 30A, 60A, 100A, and 240V 100A (Figure 9.7). They are three-pin connectors: hot wire, neutral, and ground (except the 240V 100A connector, which is a ground and two hot wires, no neutral). 100A and 60A extensions (100 ft., 50 ft., or 25 ft.) run from the distro boxes to the lights and gang boxes. 100A Bates connectors are used on lights of more than 7.2k: 10ks, 9k maxibrutes, 8k softlights. 60A Bates are used on lights 2k to 7.2k: 5ks, 9-lite FAYS (5850W), 4ks, 2500s, 4k softlights, 5k skypans, etc. A 100A-to-60A adaptor/splitter

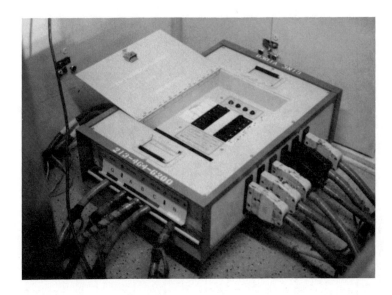

Figure 9.6 The Union Connector Polybox. The box pictured has three-phase lug inputs and six 100A Bates and six 60A Bates outlets. (Photo by author.)

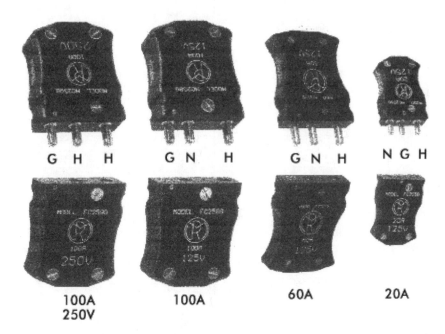

Figure 9.7 Pin configurations for Bates connectors of various sizes, Ground (G), Neutral (N), and Hot (H). The 100A, 240V connector is similar to the 100A connector but the neutral pin is instead a hot pin and is positioned closer to the center of the plug.

Table 9.2 Distribution Boxes

Input Connector	Total Amps	Mod. #	Description	Phase	Output Connectors	Features
Mole Richardson Cam-Lok	900A AC	4801	120/208V, three-phase	Three	6 100A, 120V 3 100A, 208V 1 20A Duplex	Circuit breakers, circuit lights
	600A AC	4671 4681	Face-mounted input Pigtail input	Three	6 100A, 120V 1 20A Duplex	Circuit breakers, circuit lights
	300A AC	4621 4631	Face-mounted input Feed thru	Three	6 100A, 120V 1 20A Duplex	Circuit breakers, circuit lights
	400A AC	4881	120V, feed-thru, single phase	Single	4 100A, 120V 1 20A Duplex	Circuit breakers, circuit lights
	200A AC	4661	240V, feed-thru, single phase	Single	2 1100A, 240V 1 20A Duplex	Circuit breakers, circuit lights
Remote Switchboards (lugs)	800A	3801	AC or DC deuce board	Single AC/DC	4 200A Fuses (lugs)	2 remote switches Dimmable casters, stackable
	1600A		AC or DC four-way board	Single AC/DC	8 200A Fuses	4 remote switches, Dimmable casters, stackable
Spider/Distro Boxes (lugs)	800A AC	3951	208/120V, three-phase	Three	6 100A, 120V 2 100A, 208V 1 20A Duplex	Circuit breakers, circuit lights
	600A AC	4891	208V/120V, three-phase	Three	4 100A, 208V 2 100A, 120V	Circuit breakers, circuit lights
	400A AC	4901	120V, single phase	Single	4 100A, 120V 1 20A Duplex	Circuit breakers, circuit lights

Table 9.2 Distribution Boxes

Input Connector	Total Amps	Mod. #	Description	Phase	Output Connectors		Features
Mole Pin	400A AC	4851	Pin-thru banded box	Single	4	100A, 120V	Circuit breakers, circuit lights
					1	20A Duplex	
	300A AC	4911	120/240V Pin-thru banded box	Single	2	100A, 120V	Circuit breakers, circuit lights
					1	100A, 240V	
	200A AC	4861	240V, Feed-thru, single phase	Single	2	100A, 240V	Circuit breakers, circuit lights
					1	20A Duplex	
100A Bates	100A AC	3961 4961	Lunchbox 5-duplex outs Feed-thru version	Single	5	20A Duplex	Circuit breakers, circuit lights
	100A AC	3941 4841	Lunchbox 5-20A Bates outs Feed-thru version	Single	5	20A Bates	Circuit breakers, circuit lights
	100A AC	3991	60A Bates	Single	2	60A Bates	Circuit breakers, circuit lights
					1	20A Duplex	
	100A AC	3971	30A Bates/Duplex	Single	2	30A Bates	
					2	20A Duplex	
	100A AC	4651	30A Bates	Single	3	30A Bates	
	100A AC	4641	60A Bates, 240V	Single	2	60A Bates 240V	
	100A AC	5001432	100A gang	Single	4	20A Edison	Circuit breakers
60A Bates	60A AC	5001545	60A gang, 3-circuit	Single	3	20A Duplex	Circuit breakers
	60A AC	5001467	60A gang, 2 circuit	Single	2	20A Duplex	

Table 9.2 Distribution Boxes

Input Connector	Total Amps	Mod. #	Description	Phase	Output Connectors	Features
Matthews Cam-Lok (or with pin adaptors)	1200A	387639	Feed-thru, "spider," bullswitch	Three	2 Sets of Cam-Lok	Circuit lights, 400A fuses
	600A	387627	"TDB 60,000W AC" 3-phase, 120V	Three	6 100A Bates	Continuous-rated cicuit breakers, circuit lights
	600A	387638	Bull Switch, 200A fuses	Three	1 Set of Cam-Lok	Circuit lights, 200A fuses
	600A	387637	Feed-thru, 120V	Three	6 100A Bates	Continuous-rated circuit breakers, circuit lights
	400A	387601	"TDB 40,000W AC" 400A box, single phase, 120V	Single	2 100A Bates 4 60A Bates	Continuous-rated circuit breakers, circuit lights
	400A	387636	Feed-thru, 120/220V	Single	2 100A 120V 2 100A 220V	Continuous-rated circuit breakers, circuit lights
100A Bates	100A	387643	100A thru-box	Single	5 20A Duplex	Circuit breakers, circuit lights
	100A	387630	"Hollywood Box," 5 fuses	Single	5 20A Edison	5 fuses
60A Bates	60A	387623	"Hollywood Box," 20A Bates	Single	3 20A Bates	3 fuses
	60A	387606	"Hollywood Box," 3 fuses	Single	3 20A Duplex	3 fuses
	40A	387602	"Hollywood Box," 2 fuses	Single	2 20A Duplex	2 fuses

This list is meant to give a representative sample of the configurations commonly available. By no means does this table represent a complete list of manufacturers or types.

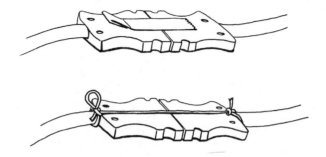

Figure 9.8 Bates connectors often need to be held together with tape or string.

must typically be used to connect these lights to the 100A outlet on the distro box. 30A Bates are used in theater and are not found in film work. 20A Bates plugs are found only on theatrical lamps (ellipsoidals and PAR cans) and in television studios in which all the lighting equipment is used in-house only. Such facilities are installed with permanent numbered circuits around the walls of the stage, in the floor, and mounted to overhead pipes. This permanent feeder system is hard-wired to a patch panel and dimmer board. 20A Bates extensions are used instead of Edison stingers. Distro boxes with 20A Bates outlets can be ordered if a large number of Bates-fitted lamps will be used, but ordinarily in location work Edison outlets are used for lamps 2k or less. Lamps with 20 Bates plugs require an adaptor pigtail (Edison male/Bates female).

Bates connector pins are sized and positioned asymmetrically so they make ground first, break ground last, and they are polarized — they cannot be plugged in incorrectly. Bates connectors will melt if they become overheated; keep them strictly within their designed amperage limits. Where one Bates cable plugs into another, tape the connection so they don't pull apart (Figure 9.8).

Ironically, Bates no longer manufactures connectors. They are made by many equipment companies, including Mole-Richardson, Paladin, Union Connector Co., and Group 5 Engineering, but they continue to be referred to as Bates. They are also sometimes called Union connectors: Union Connector Co. makes several designs including some with mechanical hooks that lock one connector to another. Bates connectors are also commonly called *pin connectors*, which is not to be confused with single-conductor, mole-pin connectors, which are also referred to simply as pin connectors.

Edison Boxes

Gang Boxes with Breakers

Edison gang boxes are fitted with either a 100A or a 60A male Bates. A "lunch box" (Figure 9.5G) provides five 20A duplex circuits (10 Edison outlets) with 20A circuit breakers and indicator lights on each circuit. Some also provide a 100A female outlet, so you can feed through to subsequent boxes.

Figure 9.9 A Union Connector outlet box. This box is fitted with 20 Amp Bates outlets. Edison pigtail adaptors are required.

Alternately, boxes may be fitted with 20A Bates (Figure 9.9) or 20A twist-lock outlets instead of duplex. The advantages of breakers are that a tripped breaker is easy to find, and breakers can be used to switch a circuit on and off (makes it a lot easier to switch off a light that is hung out of reach). The disadvantages are that circuit breakers are more expensive and more delicate than fuses and can only be tripped a finite number of times before they need to be replaced, which drives up the maintenance costs for the rental house.

Fused Gang Boxes

A 60A fused gang provides two or three 20A fused duplex outlets. A 100A fused gang has four or five 20A Edison outlets. Each circuit has a separate 20A fuse. Spring holders for spare fuses are mounted next to the fuses. These fuses do blow from time to time. It is worthwhile to keep a couple of spares with you so you can replace a bad one immediately and return the circuit to service.

Adaptors

There are as many kinds of adaptors as there are different combinations of connectors: lugs to mole-pin, lugs to Cam-Lok, full stage to 60A Bates, 20A Bates to Edison, 20A twist-lock to 20A Bates, and so on. Figure 9.10 shows a number of PBU (parallel blade U-ground) and twist-lock plug types. Adaptors often come in the form of a pig tail, or soft-wired adaptor, which is nothing more than a foot or so of cable with a different connector on each end. When ordering equipment, the best boy must take care to order the adaptor needed to connect each piece of equipment. When referring to an adaptor, designate the male end first.

15 Amp 125 Volt Grounding
2 Pole 3 Wire
Standard for residential / commercial.
5-15 R (receptacle); 5-15 P (plug)

15 Amp 250 Volt Grounding
2 Pole 3 Wire
Room air-conditioners, heavy-duty tools.
6-15 R (receptacle); 6-15 P (plug)

15 Amp 277 Volt Grounding
2 Pole 3 Wire
7-15 R (receptacle); 7-15 P (plug)

20 Amp 125 Volt Grounding
2 Pole 3 Wire
Room air-conditioners, heavy-duty tools.
5-20 R (receptacle); 5-20 P (plug)

20 Amp 250 Volt Grounding
2 Pole 3 Wire
Room air-conditioners, heavy-duty tools.
6-20 R (receptacle); 6-20 P (plug)

20 Amp 277 Volt Grounding
2 Pole 3 Wire
7-20 R (receptacle); 7-20 P (plug)

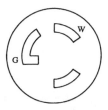

15 Amp 125 Volt Grounding
2 Pole 3 Wire
Common in older stages.
L5-15 R (receptacle); L5-15 P (plug)

20 Amp 125 Volt Grounding
2 Pole 3 Wire
Standard for stage use.
L5-20 R (receptacle); L5-20 P (plug)

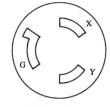

15 Amp 250 Volt   Grounding
2 Pole 3 Wire
For special stage applications.
L6-15 R (receptacle); L6-15 P (plug)

20 Amp 250 Volt Grounding
2 Pole 3 Wire
For high voltage stage use:
heaters, fog barrels, etc.
L6-20 R (receptacle); L6-20 P (plug)

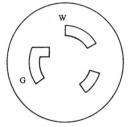

30 Amp 125 Volt Grounding
2 Pole 3 Wire
Not standard for stage use.
L5-30 R (receptacle); L5-30 P (plug)

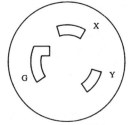

30 Amp 250 Volt Grounding
2 Pole 3 Wire
Not standard for stage use.
L6-30 R (receptacle); L6-30 P (plug)

Figure 9.10   Types of connectors. (Reprinted with permission from Paul Carter, *The Backstage Handbook.* New York: Broadway Press, 1988.)

100A to 2 100A splitters   The idea of this splitter is to give you more outlets for 60A splitters, 100A gangs, and lights. Note: Under no circumstances should this splitter be used to pull more than 100A total.

100A to 2 60A splitters   Order as many of these as you have lights and gangs with 60A tails. Note some adaptors are fitted with in-line 60A fuses. Be sure to stock spares and be on the lookout for burn-outs.

240V 100A Bates snake bites (mole-pin to Bates adaptors)   If you get caught without a 240V Bates outlet for a 20k, this solves the problem. Note: Although very handy, there is no circuit protection here either.

3-wire 100A Bates snake bites (3-wire mole-pin to 2 100A Bates)   In the absence of a distro box, a snake-bite patches directly into three-fers. Note: Although very handy, there is no circuit protection here either.

Edison to 20A Bates pigtails   You will need adaptors with any theatrical lights you order.

100A Bates to mole-pin adaptors   Be sure to ask the type of connector for any large lights you order. If the light has mole-pins, you may need to adapt to 100A Bates.

Cam-Lok jumpers (lug to Cam-Lok)   Jumpers are typically used to lug dimmer packs into a spider box.

Lug jumpers   10-ft. lug jumpers are handy to connect deuce-boards to a near-by spider box.

Banded jumpers   Handy to wire a 400A distro box into a spider box.

DC Paddle/Stage Box System

The paddle/stage box system is a two-pole, nonpolarized, ungrounded system of plugs and receptacles that has been in use longer than any other system. It is still used today for DC rigging on sound stages. It was originally designed as a DC system and, strictly speaking, was never approved for use with AC power. However, as AC power became more common on sets, the system came to be used for both AC and DC. Many rental houses retrofitted their stage boxes with grounding leads to meet NEC grounding requirements for AC power. In 1992 authorities began to enforce the 1987 NEC ban on the use of stage boxes and paddle plugs with AC current.

In some cities, local authorities may grant local approval or simply overlook the use of stage boxes with AC power. In such cases, the production company must weigh the liability of using the unapproved system. In the event of an accident in which there is injury or damage to equipment, the insurance company may deny claims. In addition, under Occupational Safety and Health Administration (OSHA) legislation, criminal claims can be leveled at supervisory crew members for condoning the use of unapproved equipment.

Stage Boxes

At the destination, *stage boxes* (or *plugging boxes* as they are referred to in the NEC) plug into the mole-pin feeder cable, or they use lugs to connect directly to a spider box or deuce board. Stage boxes are referred to by the number of holes they have: one-hole, two-hole, four-hole, or six-hole box. Lights with *stage*, or *paddle*, connectors plug directly into the stage box. A gang box plugs into the stage box with a paddle connector (Figure 9.11).

A normal full stage plug (1 in. thick) can carry a maximum of 85A. A half stage plug (1/2 in. thick) can carry 20A and can fit two to a hole in a stage box (Table 9.3).

Stage boxes come in both two-wire (single-circuit) and three-wire (120/240) versions. The color-coded sheath at the base of the mole-pins or lugs identifies the legs. When you connect the box normally — blue to blue, red to red, and white to white — you get two 120V circuits (Figure 9.12A).

Three-wire boxes are painted red on one side and blue on the other to show the leg into which the paddle is plugged.

Connecting a Stage Box for 240/120V Power

To get 240V current from a stage box, connect the feeder to the box as follows: red to white, white to red, and blue to blue (Figure 9.12B). This connects the two hot legs to the blue side of the stage box, making it 240V. The red side still runs 120V on the red leg. Whenever you "240" a stage box, be sure to mark it boldly with a big piece of tape.

Stage Extensions

A stage extension has a stage plug on one end and a one-hole or two-hole box on the other. It is used as an extension for the bigger lights that have paddle connectors, or for Edison gang boxes.

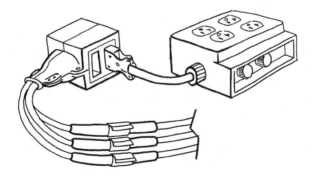

Figure 9.11   A fused gang box plugged into a stage box.

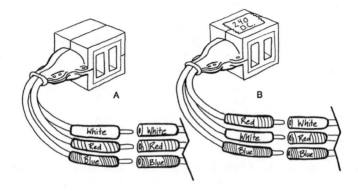

Figure 9.12 (A) A four-hole stage box connected normally provides four 120V outlets, two on the red leg and two on the blue leg. (B) A four-hole box connected red to white and white to red provides 240V power on the blue side and 120V power on the red side.

Table 9.3 Ampacity of Stage Boxes

Stage Box	Circuit Type	Amps per Hole	Amps per Side	Amps Total
One-hole	Two-wire	50	—	50
Two-hole	Two-wire	45	—	90
Four-hole	Two-wire	85	—	170
Four-hole	Three-wire	85	110	220
Six-hole	Two-wire	85	170	265
Six-hole	Three-wire	85	170	340

Precautions with the Stage Box System

1. The holes of stage boxes are large enough to put your fingers into, which presents a hazard. Tape over holes that are not in use, especially when children or animals will be present.
2. Be very careful not to misplug a three-wire system to the stage box and run 240V accidentally. Always label 240V circuits.
3. There is little to prevent moisture from getting into the connections when water is present. When shooting around moisture (e.g., on dewy grass, near a sprinkler system, in the rain, in a bathroom, near a pool), raise pin and stage box connections up on apple boxes. Wrap the connections in visqueen or plastic garbage bags.

4. When plugging in cables and lights using DC current, make sure that the fixtures are turned off. Making a hot stab — plugging in a light when it is turned on — with DC is a dangerous business because the contacts will arc and start to weld before they can become fully connected. Gases can build up and cause an explosion. If you have to make a hot stab, insert the connector with one well-aimed, straight, firm motion — so it goes in all the way at once. Avoid hot stabs whenever possible.

Meltric/Abbott System

The Meltric/Abbott system (Figure 9.13) is used on a limited number of stages around Hollywood.

The system uses 400A or 200A Abbott connectors on the feeder cable and Meltric 225A, 100A, and 60A connectors for the subfeeders. The entire system is equipped with five wires for three-phase AC power, but it can be used for single-phase AC if not all of the wires are used. Wheeled distribution boxes provide step-down points with circuit protection. There are several kinds of distribution boxes: the main disconnect, the feeder splicing block, the feedthrough feeder distribution box, and the subfeeder distribution boxes. Meltric 100A banded cable extensions are used for subfeeder. Meltric 100A-to-100A "octopus" three-fers and Meltric 100A-to-60A "squid" three-fers divide the three-phase power into single-phase 120V circuits. Fused 90A and 50A gang boxes provide Edison or twist-lock outlets for the smaller fixtures.

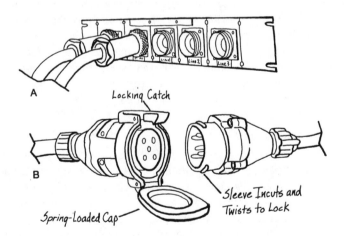

Figure 9.13   (A) An Abbot sequentially locking panel. (B) Meltric connectors.

Meltric Connectors

Meltric connectors feature a positive mechanical lock, spring-loaded connector caps, and a five-wire polarized "make first, break last" pin configuration that prevents wires from being plugged incorrectly. The connectors are spring-loaded so they spring apart when released and must be pushed together with force to connect them. Because of their rugged design and many features, the connectors are larger and heavier than other distribution connectors.

Abbott Connectors and Sequentially Locking Panels

The sequential safety-lock panel is designed to make it impossible to connect and disconnect the feeder cables in the wrong order. A locking mechanism prevents any connectors from being connected before the ground. Once the ground is connected, the neutral must be connected next, and only then can the hot wires be connected.

Other brands of connectors have similar sequentially locking panels. Posi-loc is a system for Cam-Lok connectors, and VEAM B-lok is a similar panel for VEAM single-conductor connectors. Sequentially locking panels are not required by code, and while some feel that they make the distribution system idiot-proof, the use of panels on every female connection is generally an unnecessary encumbrance.

Rigging

On large sets, a rigging crew prerigs the cabling and hangs whatever lights are to be used prior to shooting. The rigging crew is supervised by the *rigging gaffer*, who plans the cabling for the sets. She sees to it that the lights on the floor and above the set are supplied with adequate power. She strategically places power drops so that plugging boxes are readily available at any place on or above the set to allow additional lights. The rigging gaffer plans the placement and cabling of switchboards and dimmer racks as required by the situation or as requested by the DP and the gaffer. She oversees the rigging and testing of the power system from beginning to end.

On smaller productions, the best boy may serve as the rigging gaffer and go out with a couple of extra electricians to prerig locations.

Distribution Strategy

Planning the cabling and distribution for a set or location requires planning, forethought, and calculation. During filming, an electrician working the set should only need to glance around his immediate area to find power for his light, and yet the cable must remain neat and invisible to the camera at all times. An electrician should rarely require a 50 ft. stinger on a set that is properly cabled, nor should a stinger have to cross a room if the distribution is effectively laid out. You should never find yourself having to run four or five stingers out a door and around a corner; one properly placed 100A box can eliminate a lot of work, mess, and task-time. No matter how far away the gaffer wants a light, getting power should not create a crisis; cable should be standing by, ready to be run out to it.

Set Power — The "Ring of Fire"

Here are some rules of thumb for laying out set power on location and on sound stage alike. Provide a "ring of fire" — surround the set with power on all sides. Rigging is not only a matter of having sufficient amperage available, but of having outlets placed so that one is always close at hand. No matter where the camera is placed, you should have a 100A gang box ready to pull in behind camera. In each room where action is to take place, have 100A whips (with gang boxes) coiled outside each door ready to come in when needed. In a room with only one door, provide 100A whips on the opposite side of the room (through a window, through a rat hole in the set, over the top of the set wall, or dropped from the grid), ready to come in should the door have to close. Provide at least 100A to each side of a room. In a large room provide 100A whips every 50 ft. (hidden outside windows, in side rooms, through rat holes, or ready to drop from the grid). In a house with a staircase, you will need power at the top of the stairs. Hide cables that cross doorways by routing the cable up and over the top of the door.

Substantial amounts of power are often required outside windows to power large units pointing into the room, as well as units lighting up an exterior (at night). When shooting on a stage, a *translight* or *scenic painting* will often be hung outside windows to provide an exterior backdrop (a cityscape, suburban street, mountain woodland, or what have you). Translights are typically backlit with a row of skypans. When shooting in a room with a lot of windows, you can expect that the gaffer will want to put some large units outside. Have the necessary distribution box positioned accordingly. Provide 120V *and* 220V service.

The DP may want to place lights inside buildings across the street, or create a streetlight effect on background buildings. To provide for this eventuality, you may need to have several hundred feet of banded cable run out, hidden from the camera.

Planning the Rig

Let's start with a quick overview of the process of planning a rig.

1. Walk the set, and decide where you will need service: floor drops and high boxes. Add up the amperage demand.
2. Add to that the amperage demand of the prerigged lights.
3. The total will be the amperage carried by the main feeder run. On a large studio stage, several separate circuits supply cans are installed throughout the stage; for each area, power is drawn from the nearest can. In this case, add up the amperage demand for each circuit, which gives the amperage of the cable run from each can. Note that stages are often wired with more than one can per circuit. On a feature stage, for example, there may be eight cans that

serve four circuits — two cans per circuit. If the amperage of each circuit is 3200A, you must run the loads so that the two cans that serve that circuit do not carry more than 3200A between them. Each studio keeps a rigging bible, which charts the hook-up and capacity of the cans on each of the studio's stages. If you are unfamiliar with the stage, check the rigging bible.

4. Calculate the number of switchboard circuits and dimmer circuits that will be needed. Decide where this equipment can be most strategically placed so as to minimize the length of cable needed.

5. Estimate the amount of cable and distribution equipment needed to run from the switchboards or dimmer circuits to the lights and plugging boxes.

You now know all the equipment that will be needed for the rig: feeder cable, switchboards, dimmers, distro boxes, subfeeder cable, extensions, and plugging boxes. The best boy can place the equipment order with the rental house or studio lighting department.

Power Drops and High Boxes

A good rule of thumb for placing drop points is to put at least one drop outside each entrance to the set, next to each doorway. If there is an expanse between entrances, you might also place a drop at the midpoint of the wall. Most set walls can fly out when the drop must be used. On location, you might run a drop in through a window or around through another room to provide power in the center of the set.

When working from green beds, the drops can come straight down from the green beds. It is best to keep the rigging above the stage whenever possible to minimize the amount of cable on the floor. In a typical studio stage, the cable is run in the catwalks above the rafters, and from there drops are made to the green beds or directly to the stage floor.

High boxes are typically 25-ft. plugging boxes that are coiled and tied to the hand rail of the green bed, ready to be dropped or used aloft when needed.

Calculating Amperage Demand

Let's assume that we are powering the following lighting units:

Quantity	Unit	Actual Amps	Paper Amps	Actual Total	Paper Total
8	10k	83.3	100	666.6	800
10	8k soft	66.6	80	666.6	800
10	4k soft	33.3	40	333.3	400
20	5k Senior	41.67	50	833.3	1000
48	2k Junior	16.6	20	796.8	960
48	1k Baby	8.3	10	398.4	480
Totals				3695	4440

In addition to these lights, assume that we will need to provide six 200A drop points and two 200A high boxes.

Quantity	Unit	*Actual Amps*	*Paper Amps*	*Actual Total*	*Paper Total*
Total Lights				3695	4440
6	Drops	200	240	1200	1440
2	High	200	240	400	480
Grand Total				5295	6360

The easiest way to make load calculations is to use the paper method. Our total paper load is 6360A. The actual amperage will be 5295A.

Calculating Cable Runs

Direct Current Cable Runs   4/0 cable has a maximum amperage rating of approximately 400 A. A normal three-wire circuit using 4/0 cable delivers 400A per leg and 800A total. If more amperage is required, the cable can be doubled (back in the heyday of DC rigging this was known as a half-million run), tripled (a 750 run), or quadrupled (a million run). Table 9.4 shows the maximum amperage that can be drawn by various configurations, and Figure 9.14 shows the configuration of wires for each run.

When running fewer neutral wires than hot leg wires, it is crucial that you maintain a balanced load. The neutral wires will not be overloaded as long as the two hot legs remain evenly balanced. Remember that the neutral only carries the difference in amperage between the two hot legs. During operation, the best boy must never let the two legs become unevenly loaded by more than the amperage capacity of the neutral wires.

Returning to the preceding example, we have a total amperage demand of 6360A (paper). Assume that we are using a DC sound stage that has four 3200A circuits serving eight cans. We will draw 1600A from four of the cans (each on a differ-

Table 9.4   DC Cable Runs

Type of Run	Number of 4/0 Pcs	Amps per leg	Amps Total	Configuration Hot	Ntrl	Hot
4-2-4 (Million Run)	10	1600	3200	4	2	4
3-2-3 (750 Run)	8	1200	2400	3	2	3
2-1-2 (1/2 Million Run)	5	800	1600	2	1	2
1-1-1 (1/4 Million Run)	3	400	800	1	1	1
2-wire	2	400	400	1	1	0

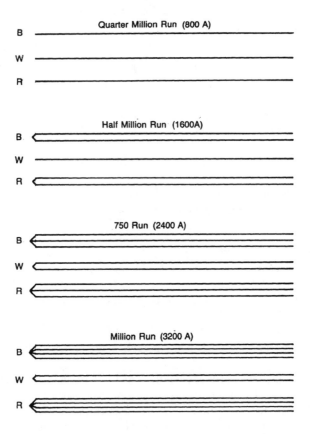

Figure 9.14 Wire configurations.

ent circuit). Each 1600A run can be cabled with a 2-1-2 run (a half million run), delivering 800A per leg, or 1600A total. Four 1600A runs gives a total of 6400A potential, enough to cover our 6360A demand.

Alternating Current Cable Runs A 4/0 run of three-phase AC can deliver up to 1200A, at 400A per leg. A 4/0 run of single-phase three-wire AC delivers 800A, at 400A per leg. If more amperage is required, it is best simply to make a second run (all wires) from the power source.

Assume that all the power drops and high boxes in the preceding example are to be AC. (Dimmer racks and HMI lights require AC.) The demand was a total of 1600A (1200A for drops, and 400A for high boxes). If the AC service is single phase, we could meet this demand by making two 4/0 runs of single-phase, three-wire AC. At 800A each, the total is 1600 A. If the AC service is three-phase, we would make two runs: one run of 4/0 (1200A) and one run of 2/0 (about 900 A), for a total of 2100A.

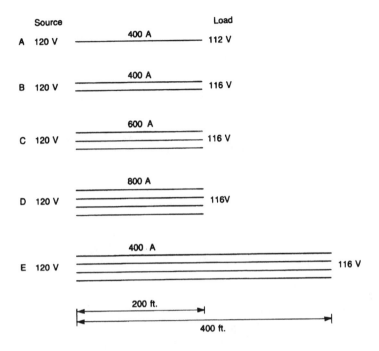

Figure 9.15   Double, triple, and quadruple cable effect on line loss.

Line Loss   Figure 9.15 shows the effect on line loss of increasing the cable. You might think that doubling the cable also allows you to pull more amperage; however, increasing the amperage increases the line loss. The doubled cable allows you to have a longer run without problems from line loss, but you cannot then add amperage without the problem of line loss returning. Appendix C gives the line loss per 100-ft. for various types of cable and load circuits.

Making a Cable Loop

A trick used to double the effective amperage of the cable or to cut line loss by half is to form a complete circle of cable around a set, running cable around either side of the set and joining the legs at the back of the set at a spider box or with suicide pins. Joining the cables does not change the total maximum amperage, but it doubles the maximum amperage you can have on either cable run. For example, if the cable were #2 AWG (rated at 152A), the maximum amperage you could have without joining the cables would be 152A per leg on each run. With the cables joined, you can run up to 304A per leg anywhere in the circle (Figure 9.16).

Switchboards

The next step is to calculate how many switchboards you will need. Each switch is fused at 200A per leg. To determine the number of switches, you must calculate how many of each type of light can run on a single switch.

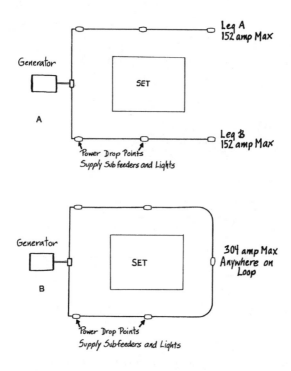

Figure 9.16 (A) Two runs of 2 AWG banded cable allows 152A per leg on each run. (B) By connecting the cables at the ends, up to 304A can be run anywhere in the loop.

For example, we have eight 10k lights, pulling 100A each (paper). We can put two 10k lights on each 200A leg, allowing four 10k lights per switch. To serve all eight lights, we will require two switches (a deuce board). Table 9.5 gives the number of lights per switch for each of the lights. Using Table 9.5, we can calculate the switch requirement as shown below:

Quantity	Unit	Lights per Switch	Switches Required
8	10k	4	2
10	8k soft	6	2
10	4k soft	6	2
20	Senior	8	3
48	Junior	24	2
48	Baby	48	1
6	200-A Drops	2	3
2	200-A High Boxes	2	1
Total Switches Required			16

Table 9.5   Lights per Switch

Fixture	Number of Units per 200 amp switch
10k	4
8k softlite	6
5k senior	8
2k junior	24
1k baby	48

Note that this table does not necessarily reflect the way that the lights will be connected; it simply offers an efficient way to calculate the switch requirement for these lights. The actual hookup will depend on the layout of the lights on the set.

We require 16 switches to serve the lights in this example. We could use 16 single switches, eight deuce boards, or four four-way boards, depending on the layout of the switches on the set. For this example, we'll use four four-way boards positioned in the catwalks above the four corners of the set. We run our 4/0 cable lines from the closest can up to each four-way board.

Rigging the Set

During rigging, the distribution system remains disconnected from the power source and from the lights and electrical appliances. Only after the whole distribution system has been laid out and the system has been tested for shorts and discontinuity is the system connected to the power source and the main switch turned on. The best boy checks the line voltage before any lights are plugged in to make sure that the power plant has been adjusted and is running properly and that cabling is properly connected.

Rules for Cabling

When laying cable, the crew typically starts at the power source and works toward the set, first laying out the feeder cable, then placing and connecting the switchboards, then running power to the greens and stage floor, and finally hanging the lights.

Keep the cables neat, as out of the way as possible, and well organized. Keep the cables on the sides of the catwalks to provide room to walk. In catwalks, cables may also be strung along overhead hooks called *deer antlers*.

Make First, Break Last   When cabling is added to or removed from a system that is hot, the ground connection must be made first and broken last. This is called the make first, break last rule. Many electricians make it a habit to make connections in the proper order, regardless of whether the system is hot. The idea is that if you get in the habit of doing it the right way every time, you'll never do it the wrong way when it matters.

Excess Cable   Any excess cable should be left at the load end of the cable, where it will be available if it is needed later. In green beds and catwalks, excess cable should be run out in a straight line and then turned back on itself and run to its end point (Figure 9.17).

Avoid sharp bends in cable. They will cause hot points in the cable. Never leave a live cable in a circular coil because this can cause serious line loss and can heat up and ruin the cable.

Root Out Bad Contacts   Each time you attach two pieces of cable, check the pins and be sure each connector is making solid contact. Use a pin-splitter tool to bend smooshed pins apart. Nightmarish flicker problems are caused by bad, bent contacts in Bates cable or pin cable. Having to track down a bad cable because lights start flickering during filming is a horrible experience. The expression on the DP's face as he watches banks of lights go dark one after another while his crew scrambles around behind the sets yelling "repatch" is enough to ruin a gaffer's whole day. Any questionable cable should be put aside, tagged boldly with tape.

Identifying Cable, Switchboards, and Spider Boxes   When laying out single conductor cable, it is extremely important to identify each cable properly. Each end of each cable can be identified with knots in the tie ropes (Figure 9.18A) or with colored tape. Tie the appropriate knots at both ends of each cable before uncoiling it.

Many different runs of cable are often placed in a single catwalk. It is useful to be able to identify quickly the cables of a single run. To do this, lace the wires of each run together, as shown in Figure 9.18B. Lacing the cables also helps keep the runs neat.

At each junction point between cables, the switch number, circuit number, or dimmer number should be labeled with 2-in. white tape on the spider box, deuce board, or distribution box. Switchboards should be labeled with the switch number and circuit number. It is also helpful to identify the intended function of the circuit, such as drop-in, high box, top lights, and so forth. A set lighting technician who is unfamiliar with the layout must be able to understand the circuitry by reading the labels on the cables and equipment.

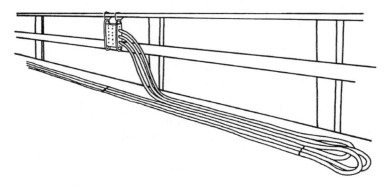

Figure 9.17   Cable laced back on itself.

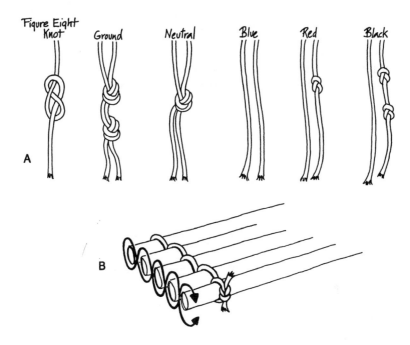

Figure 9.18 (A) On single conductor cable, use knots in the tie ropes to identify the wires. Figure-eight knots are easy to untie after use. Knots have the advantage of being readable in the dark. (B) By lacing a five-wire cable run with sash, you can separate the cables of one run from those of other runs.

When AC and DC are being used on the same set, be sure to mark all outlet boxes either AC or DC. Write DC labels in black pen and AC labels in red pen so that the type of power is immediately obvious.

On spider boxes and distro boxes, identify the color of the hot legs with colored electrical tape or simply by writing Red, Blue, or Black on a piece of tape. During filming an electrician can immediately see what leg he is plugging into and tell the best boy if need be.

Dimmer Circuits Each dimmer circuit serves a single light or a group of lights that always acts as a single unit. Each circuit has a number that corresponds to a fader number on the control console. Every cable between the dimmers and the lights is labeled with the circuit number. When rigging lots of dimmer circuits, affix white tape to both ends of all the cable before you run it. That way it is an easy matter to mark the cable as you run it and you don't have to carry tape around with you. Tab spare cable also so that it can be easily labeled when it is added.

Knots

Every electrician should know the following knots.

Bowline When lifting equipment onto a catwalk, use a bowline (Figure 9.19A) to tie the rope to the equipment.

Clove Hitch A cable tension relief is made using a clove hitch on the cable (Figure 9.19C). A clove hitch uses the weight of the cable to grip the cable tightly. The two loose ends of rope are looped around a support and tied with a square knot

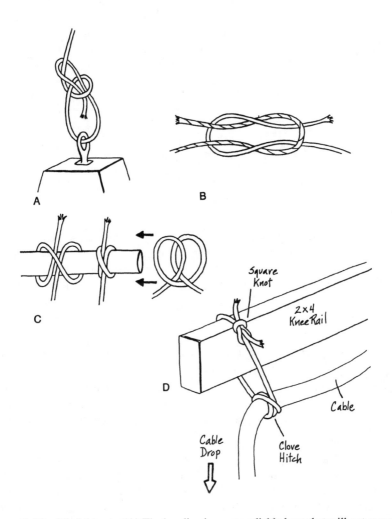

Figure 9.19 Useful knots. (A) The bowline is a very reliable knot that will not come loose when stressed. It is often used for tying ropes to equipment for lifting aloft. A real ace can tie this knot with one hand — a useful trick. (B) The square knot is used to tie one rope to another. (C) The clove hitch is used to hold tight to a dead weight, such as a vertical cable drop. (D) The clove hitch and square knot are used as tension relief on a cable drop.

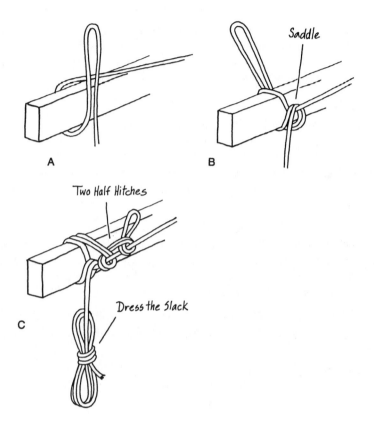

Figure 9.20 The high safety knot is used to tie off a taut line.

(Figure 9.19B). When tying off a cable drop from a catwalk or green bed, tie the cable to the knee rail or standing post (Figure 9.19D). Do not tie off to wood smaller than a 2 × 4.

High Safety Knot   A high safety knot (Figure 9.20) is used to tie off a line that has tension on it, such as that from a dead weight or block and tackle. The *saddle* cinches the line so that it will not slip while you tie the two half-hitches to secure it.

Trucker's Hitch   The trucker's hitch (Figure 9.21) is used to tighten a rope, as when tying something down or securing a rope around equipment to hold it during travel. A fancy trucker's hitch is shown in Figure 9.22.

Rigging Lights

When lights are mounted to pipe, all cable should run to one end of the pipe and from there up to a tie-off point. The bundle of cable is sashed to the pipe at regular intervals. Leave two loops of slack at each head so it can be panned and tilted.

In some situations lights must be suspended (Figure 9.23) by rope using a block and tackle to hoist them into position. A one-to-one block and tackle can be used for smaller lights. For larger and heavier lights, a two-to-one or three-to-one block and tackle is necessary (Figure 9.24).

Testing

Once the entire distribution system is in place, it must be thoroughly wrung out, that is, each circuit from beginning to end must be tested for short circuits, continuity, correct voltage (120, 208, or 240), and line loss. In the process of testing you may find blown fuses, tripped circuit breakers, blown bulbs, bad connections, burnt-out cable, and so on. By the time you are finished, you have a pristine rig ready for the shooting crew.

Check for Shorts   Before connecting the feeders to the power source, check all lines for short circuits. You can do this quite simply by taking a 120V test bulb that is plugged into a hot outlet and touching the two contacts to two of the feeder wires at a time. If the test bulb lights, there is a short between those wires. Check each wire in combination with each of the other wires.

Check the Voltage   Next, turn the power on, and check the voltage at each outlet box. Be sure that none of the boxes accidentally has the wrong voltage (120 or 240).

Check the Lights   At this point, you can plug in all the lights and begin to turn them on. Check that each light is working.

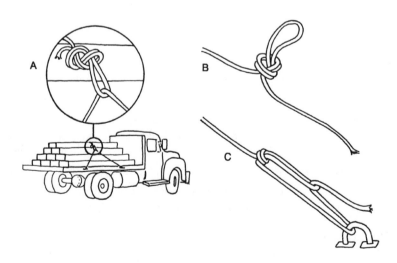

Figure 9.21   The trucker's hitch is used to tighten a rope around equipment to secure it in place. (A) A trucker's hitch using two ropes. (B, C) A trucker's hitch using a single rope.

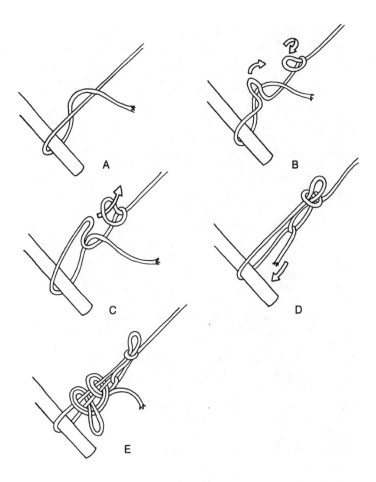

Figure 9.22 This hitch allows you to tighten the rope as you would a trucker's hitch; however, it is more easily adjustable, and the knot can be removed quickly by simply removing the half hitches and tugging on the loose end. Unlike the standard trucker's hitch, no knots are left in the rope.

Check for Line Loss With all the lights on, use a precise voltmeter to check for line loss. First check the voltage at the power source; then check it at the end of each run. Be sure that you are checking at the farthest point from the power source on each run. If the line voltage is abnormally low, check for bad connections and bad cable on that run.

Check the Hertz Rate If magnetic HMI ballasts are to be used, check the line frequency. It should be constant at 60 Hz.

Figure 9.23 A row of eight-banger soft lights shining down through the ceiling of the set, rigged to the rafters with blocks and tackle. This rig creates soft top light for a three-level set built for "Star Trek: Deep Space Nine" on Stage 17 at Paramount Studios. Note that the blocks and tackle are tied off to the hand rail with high safety knots. In addition, each light is tied off with guy wires and secured with chain. (Rig by Frank Valdez. Photo by author.)

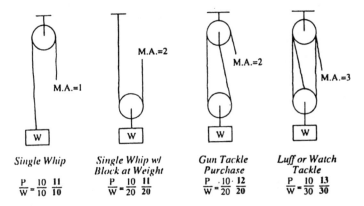

Single Whip	*Single Whip w/ Block at Weight*	*Gun Tackle Purchase*	*Luff or Watch Tackle*
$\frac{P}{W} = \frac{10}{10} \frac{11}{10}$	$\frac{P}{W} = \frac{10}{20} \frac{11}{20}$	$\frac{P}{W} = \frac{10}{20} \frac{12}{20}$	$\frac{P}{W} = \frac{10}{30} \frac{13}{30}$

Figure 9.24 Block and tackle mechanical advantage configurations. The moving part of the block and pulley is called the *sheave*. Heavy lights, like the eight-bangers shown in Figure 9.23, are rigged with the luff tackle, which gives a three-to-one mechanical advantage. Smaller lights could have a single whip with no mechanical advantage. (Reprinted with permission from Paul Carter, *Backstage Handbook*. New York: Broadway Press, 1988.)

Electronic Dimmer Systems

An electronic dimmer system consists of a control console (which controls and displays the dimmer status of the dimmers) and the dimmer packs (the actual dimmers, Figure 6.8).

How an SCR Dimmer Works

An electronic dimmer is a *silicon-controlled rectifier* (SCR). Rather than increasing or decreasing voltage (the amplitude of the AC sine wave), as with a variable transformer, an SCR dimmer increases and decreases power by chopping up the sine wave (Figure 9.25).

At 100% power the sine wave looks normal. At 50% power the dimmer switches off the circuit during the rise in the sine wave, then switches on at the peak of the wave. The level to which the dimmer is set determines the point in the sine wave at which the dimmer activates. The dimmer deactivates each time the wave passes through zero. *Note: Because the sine wave is chopped up, SCR dimmers cannot be used on line with fluorescents, HMI fixtures, or electric motors (such as motorized stands and fans). Using electronic dimmers with such loads can cause damage to both the dimmer and the load.*

Control Signals

The console communicates with the dimmers using a small signal cable. Older consoles use an analog system with individual 10V DC control signal circuits running to each dimmer requiring a multiwire cable (one wire per dimmer plus a common).

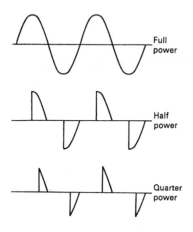

Figure 9.25 The AC wave form of a SCR dimmer circuit. At half-power the sine wave is actually clipped off halfway through its cycle.

The dimmer matches its power output proportionally to the voltage of the control signal from 0 to 10V. Modern systems communicate using a multiplexed analog signal (AMX192) or digital protocol (DMX512). Dimmer levels are encoded by the control console and connected using an AMX four-wire or DMX five-wire control cable. A controller card in the dimmer pack decodes the multiplexed or digital signal. An AMX192 signal can control as many as 192 channels with a single control cable. DMX 512 protocol can control up to 512 channels. The control cable from the console is daisy-chained from one dimmer pack to the next, looping the signal through as many packs as needed.

Control Consoles

There are three levels of sophistication to control consoles: *manual* boards, *memory* boards, and fully *automated* computer boards. The manual board has a set of sliding faders that directly correspond to the channel numbers. A typical 2-preset board has a duplicate row of faders used to preset the fader positions for the next lighting cue. The two sets of faders are typically referred to as scenes X and Y. A crossfade fader is provided to make a smooth transition from dimmer settings for scene X to those of scene Y. Most modern boards provide a single-handle or split-handle proportional dipless crossfade, which crossfades smoothly between presets without an intensity dip during the fade. Each set of fader levels is called a *scene preset*. In the days when manual boards were in common use, the board operator had to write down all the fader settings as the lighting designer created them during the prelight or tech rehearsals. During the performance, the board operator was constantly busy setting faders for the next lighting cue on the inactive scene preset. When prompted, he executed the crossfade to the new scene, and then began to reset all the faders for the next cue. Because cues sometimes needed to follow each other in rapid succession, boards with three, four, or more scene presets (hundreds of faders) were common.

Fortunately, the memory board was invented. A memory board is an enhanced manual board that memorizes and replays channel settings, freeing some or all of the faders to be reset to a new state. In this way, a limited number of presets can be set up, memorized, and replayed without having to reset fader levels.

Other common features are separate nondim (switch) circuits, timed crossfades, a grand master blackout switch, and on some boards, chase effects circuits. Momentary switches, which allow the board operator to flash the lights with a touch of his fingers, are a common feature on rock-and-roll boards.

Most dimmer boards provide *submaster faders*, which allow you to group faders and control each group with a separate submaster fader. When a submaster is created, the board records the levels of all the dimmers and assigns those levels a given submaster fader. When the board operator brings the submaster fader up to full, all the dimmers come up to their assigned levels. A board may have anywhere from four to several dozen submasters, and each submaster can be "piled on" to the others. In other words, if the board operator creates a submaster for the key lights, and another submaster for the gobo pattern lights, and a third submaster for back lights, each group of lights can be added to the others. When a dimmer is assigned different levels in two or more active submasters, the dimmer takes the level of the higher submaster setting.

Sophisticated computer boards provide automatic, timed, crossfade memory so that the cues crossfade automatically at the preprogrammed speed. All the board operator has to do during the performance is hit the cue button when prompted; the board automatically executes the crossfade. A crossfade may be programmed to happen instantaneously, to dim smoothly over a couple of seconds, or even to fade almost imperceptibly over a matter of minutes. Computer boards can handle hundreds of complex timed level manipulations and even overlap multiple cues with ease.

Definitions

As you can already tell, when you start talking nuts and bolts about dimmer systems, you quickly run into a whole new language. It is important to understand the standardized meanings of terms like patch, circuit, channel, preset, cue, etc. These terms are very often misused or used interchangeably. Understanding the following list of definitions also helps clarify the way this equipment works in general. Most of what follows is taken almost directly out of the Strand CD80 operators manual.

Circuit Everything downstream of the dimmer, from the dimmer's output (Bates connector) to the lighting fixtures themselves.

Dimmer The device controlling power to a circuit and lighting fixtures. Two lights on one dimmer circuit cannot be separately controlled.

Channel Device controlling a dimmer or group of dimmers. In a simple system there is a slider for each channel. On most current control systems, channels are numbers, accessed by numeric keypad. Multiple dimmers may be controlled by a single channel to which they are *patched*.

Patch Historically, the process of physically connecting circuits to dimmers. Now usually refers to electronic assignment of dimmers to channels. "Patch" does not refer to the assignment of channels to cues or submasters.

Preset   A predefined set of intensities for a set of channels, stored in memory for later replay.

Memory   Storage location for preset information.

Cue   Process of recalling a preset from its memory location and putting the result on stage.

Submaster   A controller (usually a linear slider) that allows manual control of groups, effects, cues, or channels.

Fade   A gradual change in stage levels from one set of intensities ("look") to another.

Up-fade   The portion of a fade that involves only channels that are increasing in level.

Down-fade   The portion of a fade that involves only channels that are decreasing in level.

Crossfade   A fade that contains both an up-fade and down-fade. Also may refer to any fade where the levels of one cue are replaced by the levels of another cue.

Bump   An instantaneous change in stage levels from one set of intensities ("look") to another.

Strand CD 80 Pack

The Strand CD 80 Digital Pack is among the most commonly used portable dimmer packs in motion picture work. What follows are some crib notes on operation and trouble-shooting.

CD80 packs are configured in one of the following ways (see Table G.3, Appendix G for additional specifications):

24	1.2kW dimmers, 15A circuits
12	2.4kW dimmers, 20A circuits
24	2.4kW dimmers, 20A circuits
6	6kW dimmers, 50A circuits
6	12kW dimmers, 100A circuits

For larger dimming jobs, a rolling rack combines multiple packs into a single compact rolling welded aluminum cabinet.

48	2.4kW dimmers, 20A circuits
24	6kW dimmers, 50A circuits
24	12kW dimmers, 100A circuits

Input power feeder connectors are typically Cam-Loc. Output connectors are Bates (20A, 60A, or 100A according to circuit size). Some 1.2k and 2.5k dimmer packs are fitted with *Socapex* outputs. A single Socapex cable carries six separate 20A circuits. When lights are being individually controlled on 20A circuits, Socapex cable makes cabling much less cumbersome. It comes in long lengths: 200, 150, 100 , 50, and 25 ft. At the lamp end of the cable, a breakout adaptor connects to the Socapex cable, providing six numbered 20A Bates receptacles.

Installation and Setup

CD80 packs must receive adequate ventilation and be kept within reasonable temperature and humidity levels with no condensation. The packs are not designed to be used outdoors. As many as eight packs may be stacked vertically. Do not place more than two units side by side unless there is at least 24 in. between packs. Otherwise, the exhaust heat from one pack is blown directly into the intake vent of the next pack. Keep vents clear from obstruction, dirt, fibers, paint particles, and so forth.

Ideally, the rack is mounted in a special air-conditioned, soundproof cabinet, which eliminates both the problems of cooling and noise.

Digital Pack Controller "Card"

The brains of the CD80 pack is the Digital Pack Controller, commonly known as the *card*. The digital controller is made of a face plate mounted on a control card. The control card slides into slots in the front panel of the dimmer pack. Two thumb screws secure it in place. In case of failure, the entire card can be replaced in the field. The Digital Pack Controller can be removed and installed without disconnecting any wiring. With the input power turned OFF, loosen the thumb screws and pull on the thumb screws to slide the controller out of the pack.

To install the controller (again power OFF at source), line the controller up with guides on each side of slot and slide the module in carefully until it touches the connector in the pack. Firmly set the controller by pressing on both ends of the module. Tighten in place with thumb screws.

The face plate contains the connectors, buttons, and indicator lights that affect everything the dimmer pack does (Figure 9.26).

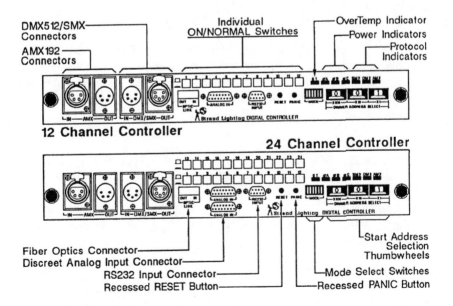

Figure 9.26 CD80 dimmer pack controller card face plate.

- Input and output connectors for AMX control cable (4-pin XLR).
- Input and output connectors for DMX/SMX control cables (5-pin XLR).
- Input connectors for 12 or 24 discrete analog control signals.
- Input connectors for fiberoptic cable (obsolete).
- RS232 connector for connection with computer (obsolete).
- Three power indicator lights (green) that show each input power phase present (øA, øB, øC). Use these to check the input power lines.
- Three protocol indicator lights (yellow), which show the protocol currently being decoded (AMX, DMX, or analog).
- Six MODE select DIP switches used to set various important parameters of operation. Table 9.6 outlines the function of each of these six DIP switches. Be especially sure switches 2 and 6 are set properly or the dimmer pack may not work properly. If you change dip switch settings during operation, press the RESET button to enter changes.
- Overtemperature indicator light (red) — the dimmer pack will shut down automatically and this light will come on if the heat sink temperature exceeds 85°C. This would happen if the vents were blocked, if ventilation were inadequate, or if the fan motor failed.
- Three numbered thumbwheels used to assign the first dimmer number for the pack. For example, when several 12-channel packs are daisy-chained together, the first pack would be assigned channels 1 to 12 by setting its thumbwheel to 1. The second pack's thumbwheel would be set to 13 (assigned channels 13 to 24).
- Recessed "panic" button. When pressed this button turns all dimmers ON. Push it again to return dimmers to normal operation. Use a bent paper clip or other small probe to get to the recessed button.
- Recessed RESET button. When pressed this button tells the card's processor to restart.
- 12 or 24 two-position push-buttons. When set to the IN position, each button turns ON the associated dimmer to full and overrides the control signal, or operates the dimmer in the absence of a control signal. When the button is in the OUT position, the dimmer operates normally and the backlit button shows the approximate level of the associated dimmer.

Phase Fuses

Three small (.250A fast blow) phase fuses are located on the controller card. If phase B or C fuse blows, the controller will not work the dimmers connected to that phase. If the phase A fuse blows, the controller will be completely disabled. Replacing the fuses requires no special tools or procedures. With input power turned OFF, remove the controller card from the pack, replace the faulty fuse, and carefully reinsert the controller module.

Dimmer Law Selection

Dimmer law refers to the response of the dimmer to the control signal over the range of fader settings. A direct one to one relationship between control signal and

Table 9.6   MODE Select DIP Switch Settings

Position 1	<u>OFF</u>	no effect
	ON	no effect
Position 2	<u>OFF</u>	Three-phase operation
	ON	Single-phase operation
Position 3	When using analog and multiplexed protocol simultaneously, this switch determines if the output signal to the dimmer is the *sum* of the two signals (up to 100%) or the *highest* of the two signals (pile-on).	
	<u>OFF</u>	Highest takes precedence (pile-on).
	ON	Dimmer level is analog + protocol.
Position 4	OFF	0–15 VDC input level for analog input
	<u>ON</u>	0–10 VDC input level for analog input
Position 5	<u>OFF</u>	In the event of loss of control signal, the dimmers will retain current levels for 30 minutes.
	ON	In the event of loss of control signal, the dimmers will black out.
Position 6	OFF	Uses every *other* control signal starting with the thumbwheel number (use with 6kw and 12kw dimmers when using Strand lighting systems AMX192 where 6kw/12kw dimmer assignment is being made in the control console).
	<u>ON</u>	Uses sequential control signals starting with the thumbwheel number.

Notes: I have underlined the setting that you typically want.

Press the RESET button to enter changes during operation. The control board reads these settings only during startup. Changing them while in operation does nothing in most cases, until you press RESET.

dimmer output gives a fairly abrupt rise in light level as the fader is increased, whereas a modified square law gives smoother control over the lower end of the dimming curve. Dimmer law selection is made using the jumper on the control board as shown in Figure 9.27.

To match the law with an analogue control signal, disable the jumper. To use the modified square law, install the jumper as shown.

Single/Three-Phase Selection

In addition to MODE switch 2 (setting for single or three-phase), 1.2kw, 2.4kw, and 6kw packs have an interior single/three-phase selection plug on the power terminal block. The factory default setting is three phase. To check the setting, remove the top cover of the pack and check the position of the phase selection plug shown in Figure 9.28.

Close up the pack and connect the input leads. Check the green power indicator lights to confirm that proper phases are powered.

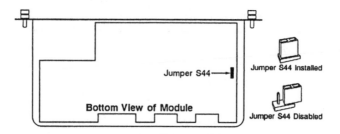

Figure 9.27 Dimmer law curve jumper location on controller card.

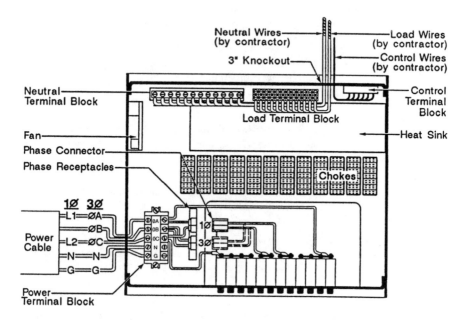

Figure 9.28 The CD80 internal phase selector plug (1.2kw, 2.4kw, and 6kw packs only) factory default setting is three phase.

Thumbwheel Setting

Set the thumbwheels to the first dimmer number to which this dimmer pack is to respond. The digital controller will start looking at dimmer signals starting at the signal number set on the thumbwheel.

For example, if you had three 12-channel packs that are to be controlled by a 36-channel console, you would set pack one thumbwheel to 1, pack two thumbwheel to 13, and pack three thumbwheel to 25. This assigns channels 1 to 12 to the first pack, channels 13 to 24 to the second pack, and channels 25 to 36 to the third pack.

Each pack is independent of the others. You can set two packs to the same set of signal numbers if you require more than one physical dimmer for each dimmer number.

The start numbers do not have to be a multiple of 6 or 12. You can start one dimmer pack at 1 (dimmers 1 to 12) and the second pack at 9 (dimmers 9 to 20). This will give you two dimmers each on dimmers 9 to 12.

Troubleshooting

Problems affecting the entire pack

No phase LED lit.
- No power to the dimmer pack. Check distribution and cable connectors.
- Controller may not be seated correctly. Remove and reinstall the controller.
- Fuse F1 (phase A) may be open (blown). Replace with a 0.250A fast blow fuse if required (see Phase Fuses).
- If the fuses are okay and you can turn the dimmers ON with their individual push-buttons, the controller module is defective. Replace it with a spare and return it to owner or Stand Lighting for repair.

Phase B or C LED not lit.
- Fuse F2 or F3 is probably open. Replace the fuse. (See Phase Fuses.)

All phase LED lit but no protocol indication.
- Control console is unplugged or control cable is disconnected.
- Incoming control wiring may be miswired, or one or more conductors broken. Replace control cable or check its continuity and wiring.

No control of dimmers (dimmers are always OFF).
- If the OverTemp light is ON, the pack has shut down from overheating. Make sure that the air intake and exhaust are not blocked and wait for the thermostat to reset.
- The thumbwheel settings may be set to an incorrect address. Double-check your settings.

No control of dimmers (dimmers are always ON).
- The "panic" button may be ON, or the individual dimmer push-buttons may be ON.

Line noise   The chopped wave form of an electronic dimmer can cause electromagnetic interference, current harmonics commonly called *line noise*. As described in Chapter 8, this can cause residual current to be carried on the neutral wire. In some situations and with some equipment, the neutral wire of the feeder cable may need to be doubled and even tripled when powering large numbers of dimmers. Symptoms of this problem are visible flicker in the lights and unusually large return current on the neutral wire.

Problems confined to one phase   Problems that are confined to one phase are usually related to controller problems or to the dimmer pack being incorrectly set up for the type of power in use.

Consecutively numbered dimmers will not go ON.
- One phase of the power feeding the pack is off or not connected.
- The controller module may be incorrectly inserted. Remove it and carefully reinsert it into the dimmer pack.
- One or more output control circuits (in the controller) have failed. Swap the controller card with a known good spare. If the problem goes away, return the defective controller for repair.

One or more dimmers on the same phase do not come up to full or do not track correctly.
- MODE switch 2 may be incorrectly set. Make sure the pack is set up for the type of power being used.
- The phase fuse may be open.
- One or more output control circuits (or the controller) may be defective. Replace the controller with a spare, and return the defective card for repair.

Problem with individual dimmers   Check the following:
- Dimmer circuit breaker ON.
- Load wiring and lamp operating properly (not burnt out). Check the load wiring and lamp by turning ON the push-button switch for that dimmer circuit. If nothing comes on, the problem is in the wiring or the lamp itself.

If you still have a problem it is either a defective controller, defective discrete analog control wiring, or a defective SSR, circuit breaker, or choke. Each of these parts is designed to be easily replaced in the field.

- Check the controller module by replacing it with a known good spare. Make sure the MODE switches are set the same way on the replacement controller. If the problem goes away with the new controller, return the defective controller for repair.
- Check for defective SSR, choke, or circuit breaker by checking the voltage at the circuit breaker output, choke output, and SSR output with the dimmer ON (see Figure 9.28). The component with an input but no output is defective (most commonly the SSR). Replace the defective component.
- If the dimmer works from the console (protocol input), but not from the discrete analog input, there is a problem in the discrete analog circuitry, external to the pack.

Dimmers flicker when at 50%
- Control card is defective. Replace.

CHAPTER 10

Power Sources

Putt-Putts (Portable Honda Generators)

For small amounts of remote power, a portable Honda-style "putt-putt" generator is a very handy unit to carry on any show. In rough terrain it enables lighting in places a heavy diesel plant cannot reach. At night a putt-putt can save running hundreds of feet of cable to power one 2500 PAR to light the deep background. A Honda can power work lights during wrap, allowing the main plant to be shut down and the cable wrapped. One Hollywood insert company (which shoots mostly MOS establishing shots and pick-ups for movies and television shows) lights all their night exteriors quite nicely with little more than three putt-putts and a dozen Par 64s.

A typical 45-A (5500 watt) Honda generator that you get from a film equipment supplier will have been retrofitted with precision speed control and appropriate output connectors — 60A Bates, Twist-lock or Edison. (There is also a 6500 watt model, which is significantly noisier.) Fuel capacity is generally 4.5 to 5 gallons, which will last 6 to 8 hours. The arrangement of the electrical circuits is also commonly modified for our use. From the factory, the alternator has two windings, wired in series, which provide two 20A 120V circuits and one 45A 240V circuit. In this configuration you cannot pull more than 20A per side, and it works best if you keep the two circuits evenly loaded. In this configuration, for example, you could not run a 5k or 4k PAR HMI (unless you used a European 240V lamp or ballast). In order to make use of all 45 amps available, on one 120V circuit, a special retrofit must be made to the alternator. When Crawford or Young retrofit a generator, they split the windings so that you can switch between parallel windings (one 45A 120V circuit) or series (two 20A 120V, one 45A 240V circuit). When using the 60A Bates outlet, be sure that the unit is switched to 120V mode. You will also encounter generators that are hard-wired with the coils in parallel, with no 240V outlets, that you can run to full capacity on one 45A circuit.

Troubleshooting

With such a small engine, the governor can be touchy and is easily upset by variations in the load or in the fuel flow. The resulting variations in the Hz rate can cause HMI "flicker." It is a wise precaution to monitor Hertz rate with an in-line meter, and many gaffers use flicker-free ballasts when powering HMIs from a putt-putt to allow greater tolerance for variation in Hz rate. The governor tends to be less stable with light loads. You will get more consistent performance if you load the unit to near full capacity and do not change the load during the shot (with flicker devices or sudden light cues).

Hiccups in the power line are commonly caused by inconstant fuel flow. The generator must be on level ground. The fuel tank is mounted only slightly above the carburetor; on a slope, with the fuel tank on the low side, fuel can get too low to flow properly, which disrupts the power. When powering lights on a moving vehicle or vessel, rocking or jerking can interrupt fuel flow, which causes hiccups in the power line. This can be helped by keeping the tank topped off, but the best solution is to use a unit which has been retrofitted with a fuel pump.

A common breakdown on the Honda is the circuits that recharge the battery. If they fail, the battery will go flat; as it does, the governor will have difficulty maintaining consistent RPM. First the hertz rate becomes unstable, starts oscillating, and then slowly drifts lower and lower. If this happens you can fix the problem temporarily (and get the shot) by jumping the battery with a car battery.

Another common trouble with these units is difficulty in starting due to flooding. In order to avoid flooding the carburetor during transport the fuel valve must be shut off. The carburetor has a very low head and will flood and dribble fuel all over the place if the valve is left open.

The performance of a small engine is greatly affected by air density. At high elevations (above 3000 feet) power output decreases 3 percent per 1000 feet. In the mountains the mixture will need to be leaned out or the fuel/air mixture will be too rich, causing the engine to run rough and possibly foul the spark plugs.

Young Generators, Inc. extensively retrofit their Hondas to remedy the weaknesses mentioned. A fuel pump reduces fuel flow problems. The circuitry is completely reworked, with a split solenoid (50A 120V, or 120/240V AC), beefier regulator, better battery charging system, and numerous other refinements. A fuel solenoid automatically shuts off fuel upon shutdown to eliminate dribbling and flooding. The generator is mounted on four large pneumatic tires and encased in a protective metal roll-cage. It weighs about 440 pounds.

Full-Size Generators

Movie generators are baffled to minimize noise for sound recording. They are very precisely electronically governed at $60 + 0.2$ Hz to be reliable when used with HMI lights, and are equipped with a hertz readout, and hertz adjustment on the main control panel. Similarly, voltage is precisely maintained electronically and can be adjusted. Dual plants of 750A to 1200A are commonly mounted on the tractor of the production van (see Figure 2.2). Trailer-mounted "tow plants" are also common, ranging from small 200A up to 2400A. The smaller sizes (200A, 350A, 450A, and 500A) commonly use gasoline engines. Larger plants (500A, 750A, 900A, 1000A, 1200A, 1500A, 1800A, 2400A, 2500A, or 3000A) require diesel engines. (Rating

Figure 10.1 Trailer-mounted 1000A generator. The vents on the top open automatically when the engine is turned on. The side doors provide access to the engine. On the back of the unit, the bottom doors cover the bus bars and power distribution outlets, and above that the digital control panel.

generator capacity in amps is actually an anomalous and confusing invention of our business. In all other applications, generators are rated in kilowatts. A 60kW generator is said to have a 500A capacity at 120V; a 144kW generator has a 1200A capacity, and so on.) A 1000A AC/DC generator, like the one shown in Figure 10.1, is the typical workhorse for motion picture work.

Most generators used today are relatively simple to operate, fully automated, and self-diagnostic. The Young generator shown in Figure 10.1 is typical. It has a selection switch (either on the control panel or inside one of the rear doors) that allows you to choose between single-phase 240/120, three-phase 208Y/120, or two-wire DC with up to 200A single-phase AC delivered concurrently. Some models can also offer the option of 480Y/277 three-phase power. Circuit breakers or electronic overcurrent protection protect the generator from short circuits. Most generators on the West Coast provide copper bus bars for the connection of lug feeder cable. Generators are also commonly fitted with Cam-Lok and/or Mole-pin receptacles (Figure 10.2). The Young generator shown has dual voltage regulators, dual electronic governor controllers, and dual fuel pumps to provide redundancy in case a part fails. Young generators will automatically shut down when they are about to run out of fuel. (This is not true of all generators. You can have significant downtime when a diesel motor has run out of fuel because you have to bleed the fuel lines to get the air out.)

Figure 10.2 The distribution panel provides bus bars and mole-pin and Cam-Lok connectors for each wire. On the left are the DC bus bars. On the bottom right are the AC bus bars. Above right are 120/240V bus bars for AC when run concurrently with DC. There is also a 12A Edison outlet for courtesy light. At the far right bottom is the grounding bus.

Smaller trailer-mounted generators typically have a fuel capacity of 80 to 150 gallons. A 500A diesel generator under full load burns fuel at a rate of about 3.8 gallons per hour. The larger plants typically hold 200 gallons. A 750A plant burns between 3 and 8 gallons per hour depending on the load. A 1200A plant burns 15 gallons per hour at full load, 8 at half load. A 500A gasoline generator consumes about 6 gallons per hour at any load.

Generator Placement

The sound department has a vested interest in where the generator is placed. Despite baffles that deaden engine noise, generators can still be a nuisance for the sound department. Place the generator around the corner of a building or behind a big vehicle, far from the set. Point the noisiest parts (the exhaust ports) away from the set. Electricians must sometimes run very long lengths of feeder cable to get the generator far enough from the set; once placed it can be a lot of trouble to move it, so it is worth getting it well placed initially.

The quieter the location, the harder it is to hide the generator. For example, one crew was shooting in the desert where it is very quiet and very hard to find large structures to hide things. The crew had already run every piece of cable they had, and the generator was sitting miles away but was still ruining the sound takes. Finally, out of desperation, the best boy had a hole dug 14 ft. deep and backed the generator into the hole. There is a theory among best boys that if the sound mixer can't see it, he won't hear it. Unfortunately, in this case the sound mixer could still hear the interred generator. This just goes to show that you can't always please the sound mixer, no matter how hard you try, but you have to exhaust every possibility before you can give up. (Another tactic I've tried on a remote western shoot was to build a thick haystack around the plant on three sides (allowing plenty of clearance so as not to create a fire hazard).

The generator operator or transportation personnel must make sure the plant is secured and stationary. The emergency brake must be engaged, if equipped, or chocks placed under the wheels to prevent movement (fire code regulations). It is a common misconception that the generator must be perfectly level to operate. Although a good policy when possible, this is not generally true. The main consideration is for the fuel in the fuel tank, but if the fuel intake is properly installed (in the *center, curb-side* at the *bottom* of the tank), being out of level will not adversely affect fuel intake. If conditions dictate that you must run the generator out of level, make sure the fuel filler and vents are high and the fuel pick-up point is low.

Finally, the fire marshal will have several concerns related to generators. The generator must not be parked under anything that is likely to catch on fire, such as dry foliage. (Remember exhaust ports point up.) It must not block fire hydrants or exits. A multipurpose fire extinguisher (20-BC) or equivalent must be available. If the generator requires refueling, it must be shut down before refueling begins, and a "static line" attached between the fueler and the genie. There must be no smoking near the generator.

Generator Operation

Walk-Around Inspection

Before starting the generator each day, the operator makes a walk-around inspection of the plant to include the following:

1. Open manual air vents if necessary. Most large generators' vents open automatically when the engine is started (they use oil pressure to hold them open). This is a great convenience, but it also serves to help you forget to open them when they must be opened manually. The engine will overheat very quickly without proper cooling. In rain or snow, the top air intake must be closed to prevent water getting in the air supply. The secondary air intake door must be opened instead. A valve, usually found near the back doors, may have to be closed to cut off oil pressure from the top door.
2. Check the oil at the beginning of every day. Add oil when needed. Inspect the engine compartment for leaky hoses or oil-soaked insulation.
3. Check the water level once or twice a week, and add water if necessary.
4. Remove the fuel cap and check the fuel level. The tank should be topped off each night to prevent water condensation inside the fuel tank overnight. (With gasoline engines, do not switch a flashlight on at the mouth of an open fuel tank. The spark in the switch can ignite the gas fumes.)

5. Check the Racor fuel filter for water and crud, which may have collected on the bottom of the clear bowl. Drain if necessary (see Draining the Racor Filter).

6. Check fan and alternator belts.

Starting the Generator

Run the distribution cables. Be sure no lights or other loads are connected to the distribution system. Connect the feeder cables to the generator. Place the generator's master power switch in the OFF position.

1. Check that the generator is set for single-phase AC 240/120, three-phase AC 208Y/120, or DC operation as desired. Some generators use a large selection switch (located inside, back, right) to switch large contactors from one configuration to another. Be aggressive when turning this switch. A solid connection is needed. Make sure the switch is fully locked in position. If the switch fails to make full contact or is left between settings, the results can be catastrophic.

2. Flip the STOP/RUN switch to RUN (Figure 10.3), press the ignition switch or turn the ignition key. Leave the IDLE/RUN switch in IDLE while the generator is not feeding the distribution system. Most generators have automatic starters and start easily. Allow the generator to warm up in IDLE for a few minutes before switching it to RUN. Look up as soon as the engine starts; watch that the cooling doors are open and watch the exhaust color (more on exhaust shortly).

Figure 10.3 The digital control panel. Top row, from left to right: voltmeter selector switch, which selects which leg the voltmeter reads; AC voltmeter; three ammeters, one for each leg; and frequency meter. The lights below the frequency meter show engine diagnostics; the lights above the frequency meter indicate which type of power is being used. To the right of the frequency meter are the hertz adjustment knob, DC voltage meter, DC ammeter, four engine instruments, and ignition switch/power switch.

3. When the best boy is ready to turn on the power, alert the gaffer and electricians that "the lines are going HOT." You do not want to shock someone down the line who may still be connecting the lugs to a spider box.
4. When you are ready for power, flip the IDLE/RUN switch to RUN, and turn the main power switch ON.
5. Check the voltage output meter and set the voltage using the adjustment knob. Be sure to recheck voltage after changing from single-phase to three-phase or vice versa. Voltage will need adjustment. You can use this knob to offset voltage drop in the cables. The voltage reading should be taken from the farthest outlet from the generator.
6. Check the hertz reading. It should be hovering right around $60 \pm .2$ Hz, and it should be stable, never jumping more than .1 Hz at a time. If a small adjustment is necessary, adjust the frequency with the adjustment knob or screw.
7. If you are in a public area, cover the live panel with rubber matting and mark it "Danger Live Wires."
8. During operation periodically monitor the ammeters. It is best to keep the load evenly distributed between legs — no more than 50A between legs as a rule of thumb.
9. Periodically check the engine instruments: oil pressure, battery charge, water temperature, and fuel pressure (if installed). These gauges can warn you of impending problems such as a fuel filter clogging or a battery losing its charge — problems that could very soon shut down the generator (and the production). More on this in Troubleshooting.

Shutting Down the Generator

1. Turn off all the lights and other loads.
2. Turn off the generator's main breaker or power switch.
3. Switch the generator to IDLE and allow several minutes for cool down.
4. After 3 to 5 minutes turn the ignition switch OFF.
5. Close manual air vents if necessary.

Grounding Generators

At this writing, according to the latest L.A. City regulations, a generator that is fully insulated from the ground by rubber tires or other means need not be grounded with a ground stake. However, if the generator cannot be insulated from the ground, then the grounding bus must be connected to a grounding electrode. The grounding electrode may be either an 8-ft. copper or steel stake driven fully into the ground (NEC Section 250-6[c]) or a building's grounding electrode. The connection to the electrode must be made with an approved bolted clamp; spring clamps are not allowed. Do not use a water pipe or lawn sprinkler system pipe for ground. The pipe may not be metal underground, and it is not an approved ground in any case.

When a generator is being used in addition to a tie-in to building power, the generator should be grounded with a stake, *and* the ground must also be bonded to the ground of the building. This puts both circuits at the same voltage potential. By neutralizing any difference in potential, you eliminate the chance of getting a shock from touching a light powered by the genie while touching the building ground, for example, through a metal handrail, radiator, or plumbing pipe. However, if the generator is only powering equipment on the outside of the building and equipment powered by the two sources are never used in proximity to each other, the generator need not be bonded to the building ground.

When a generator is fully insulated from the ground, it operates as a closed system. All the lighting fixtures are grounded to the generator. If there is a ground short, the generator's circuit breakers will trip to protect the circuit.

For these safety features to work, the generator must be set up such that the neutral wire is bonded to the generator frame and the generator frame is bonded to the truck frame. On some older AC/DC generators, the neutral was lifted (not bonded to the frame). In the event of a ground short, the current coming through the ground wire could not make a dead short and trip the main breaker, leaving the entire frame of the generator truck hot. You can double-check that the neutral is bonded to the frame using a wiggy (a type of voltage tester) or a test lamp, and connecting the test leads to the neutral and to the ground on the truck's frame. (Note: an electronic voltage meter will give erroneous readings in this application.)

Selecting a Generator

The size of generator selected for a job should be based on the power requirements for that job. While one naturally might want a larger generator "just in case," overkill can be bad for the plant. A generator should not be run continuously at less than 20% of its maximum load. Over time, running under very light loads causes all sorts of problems, including glazing the cylinders, which can destroy the engine. Nothing is better for a rough-running engine than to be run at full capacity for a couple hours. You'll see a lot of soot and smoke in the exhaust at first until the engine has cleaned itself out. Generator rental companies use *load banks* (big resistance banks) for this very purpose as part of regular maintenance schedule.

Tractor-mounted plants Flexibility in load capacity is one reason it is advantageous to have two tractor-mounted plants. In addition to having backup in case one plant fails, you have the ability to run a lot of power or very little as necessary. Tractors provide increased fuel capacity, up to 300 gallons — enough to keep a plant running for as long as three or four days.

Tow plants The advantage of a tow plant is that it is generally quieter than a tractor-mounted plant — the large flat fuel tank effectively blocks sound so it does not reverberate out from under the plant as it does with a tractor-mounted plant. When filming a period western in a peaceful, remote stretch of New Mexico, you can hear a car three miles away, let alone a 200hp diesel engine 500 ft. up the mesa. You need a quiet plant or you'll be running cable up hill and down dale.

Generator vans Young Generator Inc. has also built custom cargo vans with 250A, 500A, and even 750A capacity generators installed inconspicuously inside. The van makes relocating the generator fast and easy, and allows it to be hidden in the shot if necessary.

Gas versus diesel   Either a gasoline engine or a diesel engine drives the alternator. There are pros and cons to each. The advantages of a gasoline engine are that it runs very quietly, has low NOx emission (nitrogen oxide), and is not as heavy as a diesel engine. A basic carburetor can digest inferior fuels without serious effects on the engine's operation better than a fuel injection system used by diesel engines can. The disadvantages of gasoline engines are that gas engines have limited power output — up to 60kW (500A), they have higher fuel consumption (gas engines have static fuel consumption under any load, even under no load), and they use flammable gasoline, which is not permitted in harbors and other fire critical areas.

The primary advantages of a diesel engine are high reliability, low maintenance, and high fuel efficiency. It has more power and can turn larger alternators. Also, diesel fuel is "combustible" rather than "flammable," so it is safer. On the down side, diesel engines are hard cold-starters; diesel engines are more sensitive to fuel contamination and more critical of lubricants and coolants. As a result of the higher combustion pressures, diesel engines must be made of heavy materials. A 1200A tow plant can weigh upward of 10,000 lb. High combustion pressure also means more noise (you can always tell the distinctive diesel knock), higher emissions [NOx and particulate matter (PM) — soot], but much lower hydrocarbon and ROG emissions.

Electrical Configurations

A generator alternator has three sets of coils, each 120° offset from the last, creating three-phase AC current. In order to provide 120V DC, or single-phase AC (or both), additional circuitry is required. To allow flexibility, alternator coils are tapped at various strategic places (Figures 10.4 and 10.5).

Each phase (marked L1, L2, and L3) is tapped in four places. The tap points are marked 1 through 12. From this many configurations are possible (Figure 10.5).

Basic Troubleshooting

A fully equipped, modern generator will automatically shut down if it senses a mechanical problem, such as low oil pressure, low coolant pressure, high water temperature, overspeeding, or overcranking. Any of these problems is easily diagnosed by inspecting the engine warning lights and instruments followed by poking around inside the generator housing, and looking for the problem. If a generator shuts down, check the indicator lights *before* turning the start switch off.

If you have a familiarity with engines, you may be able to make a reasonable guess at the cause of the shutdown. Overheating could be caused be a rupture in the cooling system (low coolant pressure and high temperature) or a blocked or burnt-out thermostat (high water temp). Most likely is a plugged radiator (pollen, insulation fluff, etc.) or broken fan belt.

Low oil pressure indicates a ruptured oil line, leaking oil, or low oil.

A "charge" light indicates the battery has not been charging, pointing to a problem with the alternator, a broken belt, a break in the wiring between the alternator and

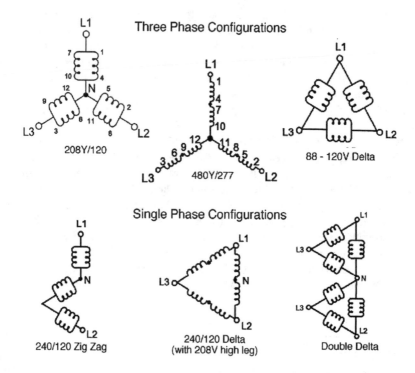

Figure 10.4 Alternator coils are tapped in 12 places to allow versatility in possible electrical configurations. A multipole, heavy-duty, rotary switch configures the coils. 208Y/120 three-phase is the standard configuration. 88V-120V Delta three-phase is used to create AC and DC concurrently (see Figure 10.5). The zigzag configuration uses all six coils to create 240/120 single-phase (The gap between N and L2 is the "open leg" of a delta, giving 120V.) Note that in each configuration all six coils are tapped evenly regardless of the ultimate output. (Courtesy of Young Generators, Inc., Arroyo Grande, CA.)

the battery (some generators have a fuse or circuit breaker in this line), or a bad battery. An important note here is that the electronic governor that controls the engine speed relies on battery power to operate. Unlike a car motor, which requires little battery power to run, the electronic governor requires a much larger amount of battery power. A failed charging system typically shows itself in a slow loss of AC hertz rate and an inability to pick up a load.

Troubleshooting — Mechanical

Fuel System

The fuel system is vital to the proper running of a diesel engine and the biggest area of potential problems. Bubbles of air in the fuel lines can make it impossible to maintain consistent hertz rate. Contaminants in the fuel can clog fuel lines over time.

Fuel is drawn into the pickup at the bottom of the fuel tank. If you have problems after the plant has been moved and there is a lot of crud coming into the fuel filter, it may be because the fuel intake is raised off the bottom of the tank and crud on the bottom of the tank has gotten stirred up. Or the tank may now be on a slight incline, causing water at the bottom of the tank to reach the intake. The water and crud on the bottom of the tank will gradually build up until it reaches the (raised) fuel intake, at which time the engine will not run because it is drinking pure water and crud.

Fuel is pumped through the Racor filter, which separates out any water and contaminants. The clear bowl on the bottom of the filter shows any water or crud that has accumulated. It can be drained out using the valve on the bottom of the bowl. In wet, humid climates (northwest and eastern United States) the Racor will fill up much faster than in dry climates.

To drain water, hold a container under the drain, open the valve at the bottom of the filter bowl, and then activate the electric fuel pump to force the water from the bottom of the filter assembly. If your generator does not have a fuel pump upstream of the RACOR, you may have to loosen the T-handle and remove the top cover before draining fuel from the valve. Refill the filter with clean fuel before closing the cover.

Fuel is pumped to the primary and secondary fuel filter canisters, which are usually close to the main fuel pump. This pump raises fuel pressure to 20 to 50 psi and pumps fuel to the fuel injector. A fuel pressure gauge is sometimes installed at this point in the system. The fuel pressure gauge is helpful to forewarn the operator if a clog is developing somewhere in the fuel system. Make note of the normal fuel pressure. A downward trend in fuel pressure usually indicates a clogging fuel filter. If pressure is unstable and the gauge is all over the map, it indicates that the system is sucking air.

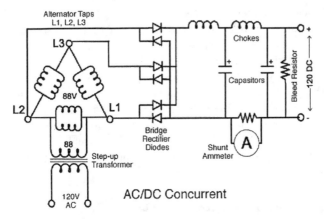

Figure 10.5 AC and DC are derived concurrently from an 88V Delta three-phase AC configuration. A step-up transformer creates 120V AC by tapping between L1 and L2 (a second transformer between L2 and L3 would be used to create 120/240V AC). The three 88V AC legs are converted to 120V DC using rectifier diodes, chokes, and capacitors. (Courtesy of Young Generators, Inc., Arroyo Grande, CA.)

Bleeding the Lines If a diesel engine is allowed to run out of fuel, the fuel lines get air in them, and must be bled before the generator will restart. Use the following procedure:

1. Fill the fuel tank.
2. Activate the electric fuel pump. On some plants this is accomplished by pressing the engine ON/OFF button. Others have a switch installed next to the pump inside the engine housing. If the fuel pump stops clicking, repeat this step.
3. Bleed the Racor filter. Unscrew the top of the filter and let the fuel pump fill the filter to the top. Then screw the top back down.
4. Operate the small hand pump on the side of the injector pump for 60 seconds.
5. Start the generator.
6. If it doesn't start, open the injector #1 with a 19 mm or 11/16 in wrench until fuel spurts out.
7. Repeat steps 5 and 6 with injectors 2, 3, and 4.

Bad Fuel If you get bad fuel in the system, you must clean out the entire system. Start by adding a dewatering additive and/or biocide to the fuel (see Fuel Care and Additives). Switch to the backup fuel system (if equipped). Next clean the fuel filters and fill them with clean fuel. There are *four* of them: one in the electric fuel pump, the Racor filter, and two canister filters near the injectors.

Fuel Care and Additives Condensation on the insides of the fuel tank will cause water in the fuel. Avoid this by filling the tank before leaving it overnight. Daily use of a dewatering additive is a great insurance policy, as they remove their weight in water, eliminating the most common cause of generator failure, dirty fuel. Additives such as Fuel Power combine a water dispersant and antigumming agent; they clean the injectors and reduce smoke.

Cold Weather: There are two types of diesel fuel. In warm states such as California, you only ever see one type —diesel 2; however, diesel 2 turns to a gel and becomes gooey and waxy about 15° to 32°F. In cold climates diesel 1, which is thinner, becomes necessary. Diesel 2 is normally preferable because it contains more BTUs (more energy). Use local fuel when in cold climates. "Pour point depressants" such as Polar Power prevent diesel fuel from waxing up at freezing temperatures. Use it before the fuel has a chance to gel. If you get caught in the sudden freeze with diesel 2 in the tank, use Melt Down additive to unclog gooey fuel lines. (Kerosene is sometimes used but is illegal because of EPA requirements.) Warming the fuel tank with a heater also helps.

Troubleshooting — Electrical Problems

The two control systems of the electrical component of a generator are the voltage regulator and the electronic governor. The *voltage regulator* increases or decreases the magnetic field strength inside the alternator to control output voltage. It then compares output voltage to a preset (adjustable) target value and automatically adjusts field strength to match it.

The *electronic governor* controls engine RPM, which is directly proportional to hertz rate, so delicate control of the throttle (gas engine) or fuel injector (diesel) is required. The governor receives a signal from a sensor, which tells it how fast the engine is turning. (The sensor is a magnetic pickup that actually counts teeth on the flywheel as it turns.) The governor compares this speed to the desired speed (which results in 60 Hz) and increases or decreases the gas accordingly.

Snags in either the voltage regulator system or the governor system can cause electrical problems; however, more often than not, problems that show up in fluctuations in voltage or hertz rate are caused by other factors.

Visible flicker in the lights Visible flicker is rarely caused by faulty frequency regulation, as is often erroneously assumed. Do not confuse "HMI flicker" (a pulsing visible only on film) with visible flicker. Most often visible flicker is caused by poor connections in the distribution cables. I have tracked down many a flicker and found a bad Bates connector or pin connector was at fault. Especially if flicker is limited to particular lights, or a single leg of power, the problem is unlikely to be with the generator.

Lights flicker on all phases. Voltage periodically jumps and dips Peaks and dips in voltage are sometimes caused by buildup of corrosion on the voltage adjustment knob on the control panel. Several swift twists back and forth (load disconnected) will usually clean it out and should get rid of the problem. This knob is one of the weakest links in the system. Subjected to the elements, the rheostat can get a buildup of dirt and corrosion. Faulty contact in the rheostat can make it very hard for the voltage regulator to work effectively.

A second possibility: Flicker and voltage fluctuations occurring on all three phases are often caused by a bad neutral connection. Feel the cable connections for hot spots. This will lead you to the problem cable or connector.

A final possibility is fluctuations coming from the voltage regulator itself. This usually occurs as a "bouncing" instability, about 2 pulses per second. Very occasionally you'll have had to switch to the backup voltage regulator, which can be selected with a switch inside the generator housing. Be sure to shut down the generator before changing from 1 to 2. *Never switch between regulators with the engine running.*

Generator does not produce any power The voltage regulator power input or field output has become disconnected, or the regulator may have failed.

Voltage goes through the roof High voltage indicates that the voltage regulator's sensing input is disconnected. If the sensing input is disconnected, the voltage regulator will sense that the voltage is too low (it senses zero voltage). It will increase voltage in the field output more and more to try to compensate, and the generator output voltage will go through the roof.

Unpredictable, irregular changes in frequency Look for air bubbles rising up through the RACOR fuel filter. Air bubbles may be caused by low fuel in the tank or by a pinhole leak in a fuel line. A restriction in the fuel line has a similar effect.

Unstable frequency, governor lever is "hunting," overshooting, then undershooting Check that there is no play in the throttle/governor linkage, and that the linkage moves freely without stickiness. Clean it and spray it with lubricant if necessary. In the case of a carburated engine, may be caused by a sticky throttle due to (1) high venturi pressure hampering the throttle valve (wiping some oil on the bearings will often free up a stiff butterfly and allow the governor to control the hertz rate properly) or (2) carburetor ice. Placing a load on the generator will lower the vacuum and usually eliminate the problem; otherwise, shut down and allow the ice to melt.

Unstable frequency, governor lever oscillates and does not stabilize Governor control may need calibration. An adjustment is made with the "I", "A," and gain controls on the little electronic governor box.

Engine overspeeds The "I" pot on the governor controller adjusts overshoot. The engine will overspeed briefly when load level changes if it is set too high. Alternately, hertz may be set too high or be faulty, or governor is faulty.

Slow frequency drift (typically downwards) Battery going flat (failed engine alternator), moisture in electronic governor controller (dry it with a hair dryer or work light), or a bad electronic governor controller.

Wet Cell Battery Packs

In situations in which no other power source is practical — such as when shooting in a moving car, a boat, a remote cave, or some equally inaccessible place — battery packs can provide the needed power. By connecting ten 12V wet cell (lead-acid) batteries in series, a DC voltage of 120V can be obtained. Commercially available battery packs are specially made with nonspill caps on the cells, typically housing five 12V cells to a case. Each case weighs about 130 lb. Batteries are made in various capacities, ranging up to 100 ampere-hour (AH) and more; however, a 45-AH rating is typical. As an example, when fully charged and operated continuously at 80°F, the Molepower battery pack, manufactured by Mole-Richardson, provides power as follows:

4000W for 20 minutes
3000W for 40 minutes
2000W for 1 hour
1000W for 2 hours and 40 minutes

As you can see, a battery's capacity is affected by its rate of discharge: the lower the rate, the greater the total power output. At lower temperatures, wet cell batteries have reduced capacity; the times noted should be reduced by 7% for each 10°F below 80°F. Additionally, if the battery is not run continuously, its total running time will be greater than the times noted. Finally, the performance of wet cells decreases with age. In a given battery pack, there will likely be a mix of newer and older cells, making it hard to predict the battery's performance precisely.

The voltage of a lead-acid battery decreases as it discharges, very slowly at first, and more rapidly as it nears the end of its charge. The state of charge can be found by checking the specific gravity of the electrolyte with a hydrometer. The water level should be checked and topped off with distilled water when necessary.

It takes 6 to 8 hours to charge a wet cell battery pack properly. A trickle charger is often used (input: 120V AC, 15A, 60 Hz; output: 120V DC, 12A). A battery pack can be shock-charged in about 15 minutes, but this is very dangerous — it can cause permanent damage to the batteries, does not fully charge the electrolyte, and is not recommended.

Great care must be taken not to tip a lead-acid battery. Spilled sulfuric acid will cause serious damage to the equipment and people with whom it comes into contact. If a battery spills, the area must be thoroughly doused in water to dilute the sulfuric acid.

There is also a more expensive, lightweight, maintenance-free, lead-acid battery that is fully sealed, in which the electrolyte is in the form of jelly or absorbent felt. The battery can be operated in any orientation except completely upside down without any danger of spill. Fully sealed lead-acid batteries typically have a lower AH capacity than other types: 20 to 30 AH is typical.

Power on Location

When shooting in a location where a generator is impractical, you can use one of the following alternatives to provide power: (1) have the power company make a line drop and install a kilowatt-hour meter at the location or (2) tie into the building's service at a panelboard.

Line Drops

A line drop is sometimes less expensive than renting a generator. If shooting will take place in one location over several weeks and the building cannot supply sufficient power, you can have the power company make a line drop from the power lines and install a kilowatt-hour meter at the location. An electrician can then install a panelboard with main breakers for the system from which the film's distribution system can draw power. The line drop has advantages over a tie-in because it is a designated circuit with sufficient amperage; it has advantages over a generator because it is silent and does not burn fuel.

Tie-Ins

A tie-in taps power directly from a building's service box, drawing power from the building's permanent feeder cables. In many locations, such as homes, hotels, and warehouses, a tie-in to house power may save a tremendous amount of cabling and expense.

Tying in is potentially very dangerous. You can be killed by inadvertently contacting hot wires. Furthermore, a mistake can cause serious damage to the facility and to the film equipment. If you are going to do tie-ins, learn the procedure from an experienced electrician. Do not attempt it yourself until you know the routine thoroughly. Tying in can be relatively simple in some locations and difficult in others. If the tie-in is difficult, do not hesitate to have the production company call a licensed electrician to make the tie-in.

The information that follows is not sufficient for a novice to attempt the procedure. It is included merely to help lighting technicians identify types of house circuits, to know the procedures that are legal and safe, and to understand the safety role of the person assisting the electrician who performs the tie-in.

Obtaining a Permit

In the city of Los Angeles, when there is some likelihood that a tie-in will be needed at a location, the location manager files an application for electrical inspection for that location. In California, temporary electrical work does not require a licensed contractor. The code requires that the tie-in must be made by a "qualified person," usually the gaffer or best boy electric. At this writing, the term *qualified person* is not defined by the NEC and is subject to the interpretation of the jurisdiction that has authority. City inspectors can be expected to visit the location to confirm that the tie-in is properly made. If the inspector finds deficiencies with the work, he or she can shut down a production until the problems are remedied. It is therefore very important that tie-ins be made by the book. Any questions about a given situation should be directed to the local building and safety department.

Rules differ in other cities. Check with the agency that has jurisdiction in the area in which filming is to take place.

Power Demand

Depending on the demands of the situation, a tie-in can work in one of two ways: by adding to the load of an existing service or by replacing the load of an existing service. If the power demand is not very large, for example, when running a few supplemental lights that are hard to reach with generator power, a tie-in may be made that relies on the surplus amperage available on house circuits. An amp probe is used to measure the existing current flow to determine the surplus that may be used and to monitor the loads once the tie-in is made.

On the other hand, if the power demand is large or if there is not enough surplus amperage available from the existing service, then the only way to use house circuits is to shut off or disconnect the circuits to supply the needed amperage to the film's distribution system. In a factory warehouse, for example, there might be some large machinery that won't be operating during filming and that has 100A or 200A breakers in the panelboard. The electrician can remove these breakers, disconnect the wires to the machinery, and install breakers with wires running to the film's distribution system.

Investigating the Existing Service

There are two important factors in deciding if a tie-in is practicable in a given location: You must determine (1) whether the service has the surplus amperage needed and (2) whether and how the distribution cables can be connected to the panel.

If no box has a hinged door that offers access to the power cables, remove the panel-board cover, which is held in place by metal screws.

Warning: Remember that everything is hot. You will receive a serious shock if you allow any part of your body or any metal object you are holding to touch the hot buses or to come between two hot buses, which may catalyze an arc. Stand on an insulating material. Wear insulating rubber electrician's gloves whenever working inside a hot panelboard.

Types of Service

The amperage rating of the service will vary with the size of the installation. A small older house, for example, might be equipped with two 60A fuses (three-wire, single-phase). A commercial building is likely to have three-phase service panels of 600A or more. In addition, this type of installation often has three-wire, single-phase subfeeders of sufficient amperage to be of use.

Commercial buildings may also have high amperage, three-wire, three-phase circuits designated for large air conditioning units or other big machinery. These circuits are inappropriate for tie-ins because they are designated specifically for the machinery they feed, and they do not provide a grounded neutral lead.

Every panelboard has a small metal placard that gives the amperage, voltage, and number of phases of the panel. This information should be confirmed by inspecting the panel carefully and measuring the voltage across the legs with a voltmeter. (See Chapter 8.)

Existing Amperage Load

The next step is to determine how much power the installation is already servicing. Use an amp probe to measure the current running through each hot leg and through the neutral. The surplus amperage available is the amount running through each leg subtracted from the amperage rating on the fuses.

For example, suppose you are working with 200A fuses on a single-phase circuit. The red leg measures 75A, the blue measures 125A, and the neutral measures 50A. (The neutral carries the difference between the two hot legs.) This leaves 125A available on the red leg and 75A available on the blue leg. Subtracting a safety margin of 20A per leg, you have 160A available for the lights as long as the building's load does not change.

If you will rely on the tie-in for most of the power, it is wise before shooting at a location to take several measurements at different times and to determine the peak demand. Take measurements when the building is fully occupied. Watch for variables, such as air conditioning, that cycle on and off.

Before Tying In

Ideally, the power should be turned off at a main switch (Figure 10.6) while the tie-in is performed. If there is a main switch that can be shut off, shut it off. More often than not, power cannot be cut off, and the tie-in must be made to a hot circuit.

An assistant should always be present while the electrician makes the tie-in. The assistant is there to help the electrician should he get into trouble. If there is a

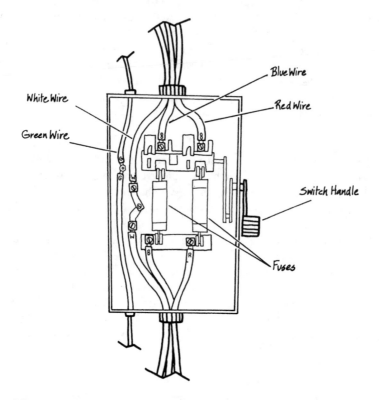

Figure 10.6   A single phase three-wire bull switch.

main switch for turning off the power in an emergency, the assistant should stand with her hand on the switch. (Should an accident occur, the priority becomes saving the electrician from electrocution, and the switch should be used and the consequences dealt with later.) If there is no switch, the assistant should hold a 2 × 4 or an apple box to use to knock the electrician away from the panelboard should he make contact and become frozen to the terminals. The assistant should have a flashlight handy in case the lights go out. She can also help guard against distractions. Make it a policy not to let anyone talk unnecessarily while the electrician is making a tie-in.

The electrician performing the tie-in must be insulated from the ground. He should stand on an apple box or a piece of rubber matting.

Making the Connections

The electrician first suspends the tie-in cables from a structural support above the box with sash cord so that the ends of the cable dangle. This takes the weight off the connections. The tie-in cables are not connected to the rest of the distribution system when making the tie-in. A bull switch should be connected immediately downstream of the tie-in, and it should be switched off.

If it is possible to make the tie-in with one hand, it is good practice for the electrician to put the other hand in his pocket or behind his back to prevent the possibility of completing a circuit through the heart.

The tie-in is made downstream of the main breaker or fuses. It should never be made upstream (on the service side) of the main breakers. If a short circuit is accidentally created upstream of the main breaker, the breaker in the transformer on the pole will be tripped and could shut off electricity for a whole city block.

There are two approved ways of connecting wires to a panelboard. The first is to connect wires to circuit breakers. The second is to insert wires into existing wire holes in lugs on the panelboard.

There is a third way to connect wires to a panelboard — clamp onto the lugs in the panelboard with power clamps. However, at this writing it is in question whether the use of power clamps for tie-ins is allowable. Power clamps do not qualify under NEC 110-14 and 110-14(a) as suitable electrical connectors or as suitable grounding connectors under NEC 250-113. Authorities vary in their policies regarding the use of power clamps.

Connecting to Circuit Breakers

If there are identifiable circuits that are not needed during filming, the easiest way to tie in is to remove one or more of the installation's circuit breakers and replace them with two larger breakers of equivalent total amperage (Figure 10.7)

If the panelboard has 100A or 200A breakers in it already, they can be disconnected from the house load and connected instead to jumper cables that lead to suitable connectors (mole-pins, Cam-Loks, lugs, or what have you). This approach guarantees that the distribution system will not overload the panelboard.

To remove a circuit breaker, first switch the breaker off. Then unplug the breaker from the bus bar by rocking it back away from the bus and then sliding it out of its channel. When tightening down the terminals of the circuit breaker, use a torque screwdriver or wrench, and observe the tightening torque marked on the circuit breakers. The NEC requires proper torquing, which is critical to the proper functioning of the breakers.

Manufacturers have various designs for circuit breakers and panelboards. If you plan to replace several breakers with one or two larger ones, check the make and model of the breakers used at the site. If the panelboard has a placard reading "Caution — series rated system," circuit protection depends on the breakers of branch circuits and the upstream breakers operating together. When tying into such a system, you must provide a current-limiting fused switch box downstream of the tie-in to protect the circuit properly.

Connecting to Lugs

Do not attempt this type of tie-in on an energized system. The power must be switched off at a main switch before any lugs may be loosened. Connecting wires directly to the panelboard lugs requires that you loosen the lugs. If any lug is loosened when the panel is energized, the wire would arc violently and would very likely burn up. You could 220 the building, the same as pulling the neutral on a three-wire circuit.

Figure 10.7   A tie-in to 100A breakers. The tie-in cables are the black cables that run out the bottom of the panel box. The bus on the left is the neutral wire. The smaller bus on the right is the grounding wire.

When tying in directly to the panel lugs, you must provide a fused switch box with current-limiting fuses within 25 ft. of the tie-in point. Be sure that the fuses are the current-limiting type.

The lugs on the panelboard are normally occupied by the wires feeding the house. If the hole in the lug is oval, it is a multiwire lug and is approved for more than one wire. If the hole in the lug is round, it is a single-conductor lug and it is not approved for two wires; nonetheless, it is sometimes possible to get a second wire into a single-conductor lug, depending on the sizes of the wires and the lugs.

After Tying In

To comply with the NEC, once the tie-in is complete the open panelboard must be guarded from accidental contact. Rubber matting attached to the face of the panelboard provides proper protection. You can secure the matting with the screws and screw holes of the panelboard cover. The panelboard can be further guarded by locking the door to the room. Place a sign that says "Danger Live Cables" or "Danger High Voltage" across the face of the panelboard. Place additional signs across the doorway to the room to prevent people from getting near the open panelboard.

When the system is ready to be energized, notify the gaffer and electricians. Everyone must be warned before current starts running through the cables. Once the connection is made and the bull switch is on, make a point of telling the gaffer and other electricians, "We're hot."

Using Available Power

Sometimes you simply don't have the option of using your own distribution system. You are forced to use the existing circuitry at the location. When you use available power, the best boy electric should first find the breaker box and check the amperage of the circuits. They are usually 15A or 20A. Count the number of separate circuits. Number the circuits and label the outlets with the circuit numbers. If hair-curling irons or blow dryers are going to be plugged in, determine which circuit they are on. Run stingers from different sections of the house so that as many circuits as possible are available to you.

The electrical code specifies that in new houses there must be two designated 20A circuits around the counter of the kitchen. These circuits are handy because they are not wired to any other outlets. Other designated circuits are those for the laundry and the water heater, which may be 208V or 240V. Wall outlets, including the fused 20A bathroom outlet, usually share circuit breakers with other outlets and overhead fixtures. Small houses may have only one circuit per floor. Larger houses may have two or three circuits per floor.

Small apartments often have as few as one or two circuit breakers per apartment. Each apartment has separate circuits, however, so if it is possible to run power from other apartments, you can power more lights.

CHAPTER 11

Special Circumstances and Equipment

Theater and Concert Lighting Fixtures

Each lighting venue has its own set of demands. The fixtures designed and developed for lighting the stage have been perfected for that task. The *ellipsoidal reflector spotlight* (ERS) gives the stage lighting designer the strong throw, versatility, and control needed to light a stage from some distance. The *PAR* can gives the concert designer a highly durable, reliable fixture that has the raw strength to pump light through saturated gels onto the concert stage. Each type of fixture is an answer to a particular lighting need.

Naturally, these fixtures are employed when filming stage performances, but their special qualities are also very handy in other situations. A Leko can make a hard cut where there is no room to make a hard cut with a flag. For example, a woman answers her front door; she is lit by light bounced off a piece of show card taped to the inside wall beside the door. An ellipsoidal can make the hard cut necessary to prevent direct light from hitting anything but the card.

Theater and concert lights usually come ready to be hung in a theater, with a pipe clamp bolted to the bail, and a short tail power cord with 20A Bates connector. When ordering theatrical lights be sure to order *bail blocks* and Bates to Edison *pigtail adaptors* to adapt the fixtures for your use (on stands with an Edison outlet box). A bail block bolts to the bail in place of the pipe clamp and typically fits both baby and junior stands.

Ellipsoidal Reflector Spotlights

The ERS (known as an *ellipsoidal* or *Leko*[1] in the United States and as a *profile spotlight* in Europe) is the workhorse of theater lighting (Figure 11.1). Ellipsoidal spotlights are listed in Table A.12.

---

[1] Leko is a trademark of Strand Lighting, but is widely used to refer generally to ellipsoidal spotlights.

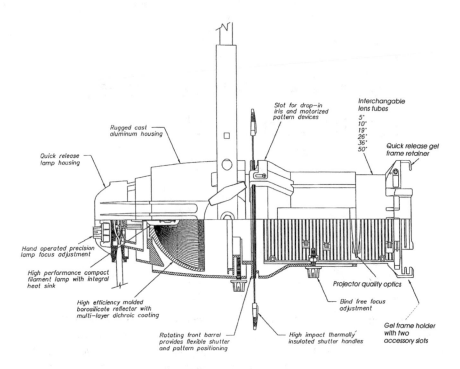

Figure 11.1 Innovative advances in the design of the bulb, reflector, and lens assembly allow this 575W light to outperform standard 1k ellipsoidals while providing exceptionally sharp shutter cuts without halation, even distribution of light throughout the field, extended pattern life, and eliminating shutter jams due to heat warping. You can put two Source Fours on a 1.2kW dimmer circuit, doubling the dimmer capacity. (Courtesy of ETC— Electronic Theater Control, Inc., Middleton, WI.)

The fixture is designed to give a long controllable throw in order to light a stage from fairly distant positions. The fixture is able to project a beam that can be shaped by shutters, by an iris, or by a gobo pattern. The shape of the beam is determined by the shape or pattern in the gate aperture. Light collected from a highly efficient ellipsoidal reflector passes through the gate; the shape or pattern in the gate is then brought into focus by a lens assembly in the barrel. The gate can be brought into sharp or soft focus by sliding the barrel forward or backward. The narrower the beam angle of the lens, the greater the throw and intensity.

Four cutting shutters (top, bottom, left, and right) can be pushed into the path of the beam to shape it into a square, rectangle, triangle, or whatever is needed. Immediately in front of the shutters is the gobo slot, into which a metal cutout pattern can be inserted. Hundreds of gobo patterns are available — a wide variety of widow and venetian blind patterns, foliage patterns, clouds, cityscapes, stars, flames, practically anything you can name. Motorized rotating gobo devices are available that create theatrical moving flame and water patterns by projecting two counter-rotating gobo patterns. Many fixtures also have a rotatable front barrel, which provides flexibility in the positioning of shutter cuts and gobo patterns. An iris can be placed in the gobo slot to adjust the aperture of the circular beam, or to use the lamp as a follow spot. Colored gel is placed in a gel frame holder at the front of the light. A *donut* is a metal mask that slides into the gel frame slot. It is used to sharpen gobo patterns and clean up color fringes at the beam edge (at the expense of some light output).

The field of an ellipsoidal is normally very even. If the bulb gets out of alignment in relation to the reflector, the lamp shows a noticeable hot spot. A screw or hand-operated knob in the back of the fixture adjusts the alignment. To change a burnt-out bulb, the back section of the fixture is removed.

Ellipsoidal fixtures are designed with either a fixed beam width or a "zoom" barrel. Some manufacturers refer to individual fixtures by lens diameter and focal length (6 × 9 in. has a 6-in. lens and a 9-in. focal length). Others refer to lamps by field angle (such as 40°, 26°, 20°, 10°, and 5°). Gaffers often have to scratch their heads when they see these figures, not knowing which type will work for which application. You can easily calculate the beam diameter and light intensity of any fixture using data given in Table A.12. The explanation at the beginning of Appendix A tells you how to use the tables. Generally speaking, wide-beam Lekos of 250W and 500W are used above stage in small theaters, 750W and 1000W 6 × 9 and 6 × 12 fixtures are used above stage and in the front of the house in medium-sized theaters, and 6 × 16 or 8 × 16 1k and 2k fixtures are used for long throws from the house.

PAR Cans

PAR cans are the workhorse of rock-and-roll lighting (Figure 11.2). They are popular because they put out a lot of light per watt, more than any other incandescent fixture, and can drive light through even the most saturated gel colors. They are simple, lightweight, maintenance-free, and made for the heavy-duty life of the concert tour. Their design is as simple as they come — a PAR lamp mounted inside a can that provides a gel frame slot at the front of the barrel. PAR cans don't generally come with scrims. The gel frame is typically 10 in. in diameter and any 10 in. scrims (Mighty-Mole) will fit the slot.

PAR cans use 1k PAR-64 bulbs (the same bulbs used in maxibrutes and Mole-PARs, see Tables E.4, E.5, and E.6). Smaller PAR cans using PAR-56 and PAR-36 lamps are also available. The beam pattern is oblong, not round, but it can be turned in the housing to make the best use of its orientation. PAR lamps come with various spreads: wide flood (WFL), medium flood (MFL), narrow spot (NSP), and very nar-

Figure 11.2   PAR can.

row spot (VNSP). For an even narrower, very intense beam, an aircraft landing light (ACL) can be fitted into a standard PAR-64 housing. ACL globes operate on 28V but can be run in series in gangs of four and connected to a 110V circuit.

Follow Spots

Follow spots (or *front lights*), with their powerful long throw, are a staple of music concerts, skating events, circus events, and theatrical performances (Figure 11.3).

Follow spots are designed to follow a performer on a distant stage, necessitating the following controls: an *iris* lever, which controls the size of the circular pool of light; a *douser* lever for "blacking-out"; *shutters,* which "strip out" the top and bottom of a circular pool, creating more of a rectangle; and a *color changer,* which introduces any of several colored gels. The *trombone handle* is used to set the size and intensity of the beam. A *fine focus* knob is used to sharpen or soften the edges of the beam. The setting of this knob varies with the distance of the subject and the trombone setting used. Follow spots are mounted on gimbals, which allow the operator to pan and tilt the light smoothly to follow action on the stage.

The size and light source type vary with application. Small 1k quartz-bulb follow spots, such as the Strong Trouperette, are common for short throws of 30 to 60 ft. (100 FC), such as in a night club or school auditorium. Slightly larger 575W HMI and 700W xenon units have throws of 50 to 160 ft. (100 FC). Large follow spots, such as the Strong Super Trouper with a 1k or 2k xenon globe, are used for lighting performers from the back of very large auditoriums and arenas. The Super Trouper has a throw of 130 to 340 ft. (100 FC). The Gladiator and other similar follow spots using 2500W and 3000W xenon globes have throws of up to 460 ft. (100 FC).

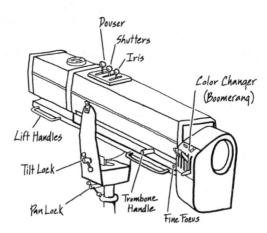

Figure 11.3 The Super Strong Trouper follow spot. (Equipment courtesy of Strong International, Inc., Omaha, NE.)

Operating the Follow Spot

Operating a follow spot smoothly and properly is something of a specialty. There are a few important points to remember. Unless otherwise specified, the trombone and iris should be arranged to light the performer from head to foot. Always keep the performer's face lit, if necessary losing other parts of the body. Panning and tilting must be smooth and in perfect harmony with the movements of the performer, neither leading them nor getting left behind, and keeping small movements fluid and subtle so as not to be distracting. When you receive direction to *iris out* from head-and-shoulders to full-body, tilt the light down as you iris out so that the light stays centered on the body. If you are to come out of black on a performer, get the light aimed before opening the douser. If necessary, you can surreptitiously get accurate aim by closing the iris down to a pinpoint, then quickly open the douser, aim the light, douse it, and open the iris up again. Very often follow spots are used to *Ballyhoo* — the classic sweeping of light over the stage and the audience in big random figure-eights. You can expect to be asked to ballyhoo at some point. When a group of performers are to be covered with a single light, the beam has to widened out so much that the top and bottom of the beam start to create unwanted spill problems. In this case, you may be asked to *strip it out* using the shutter to cut the top and bottom of the beam, again making the beam cover the performers from head to foot.

In film work it is convenient to be able to adjust the intensity of the beam. This can be accomplishes in a couple different ways. The simplest way is to use the trombone. Trombone forward to intensify the light, and trombone back to dim it. The gaffer will meter the light on stage and give you one or more working intensity settings, mark the settings on the barrel, and make sure the trombone does not slide out of adjustment. Once the trombone is set for intensity, the iris is used to size the beam. A second way to dim a spot is to put neutral density gel in one or two gel slots.

The boomerang (color changer) typically has six gel frames, which can be introduced into the beam using one of six levers on the end of the barrel. By common convention, the changer levers are numbered from 1 to 6 from front to back. Most changers are designed so that you can roll through the colors; as each new lever is applied, the previous lever automatically releases. You can release all the levers and go to white light by pressing a button underneath the changer levers.

When the spot is not in use on stage, it may be panned off into the ceiling of the arena or into the sky, or it may be doused. Xenon lights should not be turned off unnecessarily, as this drastically decreases the life of the very expensive xenon bulbs. The douser can be closed for several minutes without causing damage to the light. Do not use the iris or shutter to do this, however, as they will be damaged. Like any xenon light, xenon follow spots use a power supply that converts current to DC. Xenon bulbs are flicker-free at any frame rate and have a daylight color temperature. The bulbs are extremely sensitive to temperature and must be cooled with fans when running. After shutdown the bulb must be allowed to cool with fans running for at least five minutes. *Never shut down the power before the light has been allowed to cool.*

Follow spots are designed to be used with colored gels. Despite their candle-power, they should not burn through gel; the optics are arranged so that the beam is least hot as it passes through the gel stage of the barrel. In addition, large follow spots use cooling fans to cool the gel in use. If the gel burns through quickly in one place, it is a sign that the bulb or reflector may be out of alignment. There are adjustment knobs on the back of the larger lights that are used to align the bulb. If the gel fades quickly, you may want to check that the gel fan is working (on the underside of the boomerang) and that the air intake is not clogged.

Effects Lights

Xenon Lights

Xenon globes have a very short arc length and an extremely bright arc, which makes them easy to collimate into a highly focused beam with very little scatter (Figure 11.4).

The beam is perfectly circular and very narrow. The beam diameter can be controlled with an electronic flood/spot switch on the head and ballast. The intense shaft of daylight-balanced (5600K) light is sometimes used to simulate sunlight or a searchlight. Xenon fixtures are used in concerts and light shows to create spectacular air lighting effects. Their vibration-resistant design also makes them suitable for use in helicopter and armored tank searchlights.

Xenotech, among other manufacturers, has developed a line of high-output xenon lights designed primarily for concert, theatrical, and motion picture use. They are made in various sizes. The smallest is a powerful 75W flashlight that can be powered by a clip-on battery or by 110V mains. In full spot, the flashlight can deliver 600 FC at a distance of 100 ft. The smaller xenon fixtures (150W, 500W, 750W, and 1000W) run on single-phase 120V. The power supplies for larger units (2000W, 4000W, 7000W, and 10,000W) may take either 208-230V single-phase or 208-230V three-phase, depending on the type. The power supplies provide the startup charge and regulate power to the head. On/off and flood/spot functions can be controlled from the ballast and the head. Xenon lights operate on a pulse DC (equivalent to square-wave current), which allows flicker-free filming at any frame rate up to 10,000 fps.

The lights can be ordered with a normal yoke or with a remote-control articulating base and color changer and douser accessories. When operated by a computer-controlled remote, a line of xenon lights can be preprogrammed to perform moving beam effects in unison, or each unit can be controlled separately for different purposes.

Xenon lamps have long lives, greater than 2000 hours. There is no color shift over the life of the globe, and the color temperature is independent of voltage and current fluctuations. Xenon lamps require very careful temperature regulation, and they must use forced air cooling, which makes them somewhat noisy. Forced air cooling should continue for at least five minutes after the light has been turned off.

During the life of the globe, evaporated tungsten is deposited on the upper inner wall of the envelope and slowly reduces light output. The globe should be turned over after half its rated life. These unavoidable deposits are what define the end of a globe's usefulness. Frequent ignition charges accelerate the wear of the electrodes and

Figure 11.4 Xenon lights have a very small arc length, allowing the beam to be focused into an intense, very narrow shaft. (Photo courtesy of Xenotech, Inc., Sun Valley, CA.)

hasten the darkening of the envelope. Xenon light operators should therefore try to avoid unnecessary shutdowns and startups. If the light is temporarily not needed, pan it into the sky rather than shutting it off.

A xenon bulb is always under substantial internal pressure, and the pressure increases when hot. A xenon globe does not break; it explodes. It must always be handled with the utmost care and should never be handled until completely cooled. Bulb manufacturers recommend the use of protective eyewear (or better, a full-face mask), cotton gloves, and even protective bodywear when handling the globes. For safety reasons, globes should not be operated more than 25% past their rated lifetime. Xenon globes must be installed with proper polarity (Figure 11.5).

If operated with improper polarity, the bulb can be rendered useless in a short amount of time.

Automated Lights

Impressive lighting showmanship has always been a tradition in rock-and-roll lighting. State of the art automated luminaires are capable of creating breathtaking effects in the hands of a creative designer and a skilled console operator. Dozens of

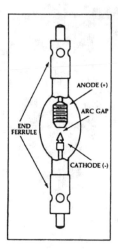

Figure 11.5 A xenon globe.

lights can be programmed — choreographed — to make sweeping pans and flourishes, weaving beams of light into patterns in the air. The lights have dozens of features. The operation of lighting systems such as Vari-lite, Intellabeam, Cyberlight, Roboscan, and others is complex, typically requiring the skills of a specialist. However, without getting into too much detail, we can get a general idea of what is possible by looking at one fixture as an example.

The Cyberlight, designed by Lightwave Research, employs a 1200 SE HMI source (5600K). Light travels through a complex tunnel of mechanisms, including: motorized zoom, variable iris, variable frost (hard or soft edge), optical dimming and blackout, a three-tier color system (infinitely variable dichroic color mixing system, eight-position color wheel, color correction), bidirectional variable speed rotating gobo wheel (four gobos), fixed gobo wheel (eight gobos), and variable-speed strobe shutter. The light can also produce a number of optical effects, such as a multi-image prism, split color, near photo-quality image projection, wave glass, and a mosaic color effect. The light comes out the end of the fixture and hits a moving mirror, which is panned and tilted by a high-resolution, microstepping motor capable of panning the beam smoothly 170° and tilting 110°. All features are remotely controlled using a special LCD lighting controller or a USITT DMX-512 console. The control cable is standard XLR. The fixture is 44 in. long and weighs 91 lbs.

Blacklights

Ultraviolet (UV) light, blacklight, occupies a place in the electromagnetic spectrum just below violet, the shortest visible wavelength of light. It is invisible radiant energy. The UV spectrum is subdivided as follows:

UV-A   350–380 nm blacklight
UV-B   300–340 nm used for suntanning
UV-C   200–280 nm harmful burns can result

Right around 365 nm, in the middle of the UV-A spectrum, you get maximum transmission for exciting luminescent pigments and materials. When acted upon by UV rays, fluorescent and phosphorescent materials are excited to a retroreflective state and emit visible light and vibrant color. Because blacklight works on some materials and not others, you can create interesting images, such as a disembodied pair of white gloves juggling three glowing orange balls.

Blacklight Blue fluorescent lamps (BLB — 4 ft., 40W typically) don't have a lot of punch; however, when used in close they can be quite effective. With a bright reflector and high-output ballast (e.g., Kino Flo), fluorescents offer an even, soft light from a large source.

In order to create radiant energy at about 365 nm, one needs a light with high UV output (Mercury Vapor or Metal Halide) and a carefully designed UV filter that blocks the visible light (400 to 700 nm) and the UV-B and UV-C wavelengths. The-atrical rental houses typically stock Mercury Vapor or Metal Halide floodlights ranging from 250W to 400W. These lamps use a deep-dyed, pot-poured, rolled, or blown glass filter.

For lamps larger than 400W, a UV dichroic coating is necessary to take the extreme heat. Such filters can be used on fixtures up to 18k HMI and on xenon lights. Xenotech and Phoebus both carry dichroic UV lenses for their xenon lights. Auto-mated Entertainment in Burbank has developed UV filters for 12k and 18k HMIs, and 200W, 1200W, 2500W, and 4k SE Pars. Automated also has their own UV and "glow in the dark" pigments and dyes.

Wildfire Inc. is another innovator in this area. They have developed a line of UV lights, including a 400W Fresnel, 400W floodlight, 400W ellipsoidal spotlight, and 250W wide spotlight in a 20°, 50°, or 90° beam diameter. The units operate with ballasts and head feeders like HMIs. Wildfire also offers a wide variety of lumines-cent materials and paints, including nontoxic dyes, hair spray, lipstick, fabrics, plas-tics, adhesive tapes, confetti, PVC flexible tubing, and more.

DN Labs is also active in this market, with a line of small lights and specially formulated, highly efficient luminescent rods and sheets that can be machined and won't break.

Photographing with Blacklight

To determine the exposure with blacklight, take spot meter readings of the lu-minescent materials to be filmed under the UV lights. In order to glow vibrantly on film, they should be overexposed by one stop. The effect is less vibrant at exposure and slightly dull one stop under exposure. A UV filter must be used on the camera lens because the lens cannot focus UV light the same way it can focus the visible spectrum. Without the UV filter, UV produces a hazy softening in the image.

UV light can be combined with conventional light and still create a luminescent effect. The balance depends on how much the effect is to be featured. One could light the scene normally and add UV lights on luminescent materials to give them an extra vibrancy, or a scene could be lit to a lower level with conventional lights so that the luminescent materials stand out. With nothing but blacklight lighting a scene, a woman wearing a luminescent wig and dress, for example, will appear to have no hands or face — only the clothes and hair will show up.

Lighting Automobiles

Directors of photography sometimes specialize in one type of work; photographing automobiles for commercials is one such niche, sometimes referred to as sheet-metal photography. Lighting a car requires special consideration because the metal is glossy and highly reflective. When lighting any shiny object, you are not so much projecting light onto the subject as creating an environment around it that, when reflected, defines its shape, separates it, and creates highlights and shadow. By manipulating the shape of the reflected highlights and shadows, you can actually alter the apparent shape of the subject. Car lighting specialists use this technique to de-emphasize less appealing contours of their subject with the same delicate care that feature DPs often take in lighting the face of a star.

Fisher lights are large rear-lit soft banks specifically designed for this type of work (Fisher Productions, Inc.). They are made in 10 × 40 ft. and 17 × 52 ft. sizes. The bank is suspended from overhead support and can be panned, tilted, and angled remotely. The banks are lit with rows of 1k tungsten lamps, which are individually controlled by a dimmer — 40kW (10 × 40) or 96kW (17 × 52). Dimmers are standard 208Y/120 three-phase AC with Cam-loc tails (adaptors when necessary). When flicker-free daylight-balanced light is needed, the 10 × 40 bank can also be fitted with a 50kW DCI system (twenty 2500W DCI lamps, powered by dimmable electronic ballasts). By manipulating brightness and color across the whole area of the bank, effects such as twilight sky can be created. Fisher supplies their own technicians with the special rig.

Chimera Photographic Equipment also makes large soft banks called F-2 Banks (5 × 10, 10 × 20, 10 × 30, 15 × 30, or 15 × 40 ft.). Lights can be rigged to the center suspension bar or to a grid above.

Fiber Optics

A fiber optic cable is a flexible or semiflexible glass cable that conducts light energy produced by an illuminator light box. There are a number of fiberoptic systems available, with different features and applications.

LTM makes a flicker-free 250V HTI (5600K) illuminator and a system of fiberoptic cables that is commonly used for miniatures, to light car interiors, and for table-top product shots where a conventional bulb would melt the product or cause an electrical hazard — lighting up inside soaps or fluids, or underwater. The light emitted from the end of the fiberoptic cable comes out as a beam and can be fitted with a 2-1/2 in. Fresnel lens and barn doors, a miniature lightbar, or used bare. The system gives a choice of two cable configurations: either the CML-4 (four 8 ft. long, 3/8 in. cables) or CML-100 (100, 2-1/2 ft. long, 3/16 in. diameter fiber bundles). Various lens attachments, extensions, and accessories are available. The cables are extremely small and flexible, can be easily hidden, and can get into some tight little spots. Because of the makeup of the cable, the light can become green in lengths longer than 8 ft., and a magenta correction gel may need to be used.

DN Labs makes a 1200W HMI illuminator (either electronic or magnetic) that illuminates eleven 1-1/2 in. diameter fiberoptic cables very brightly. DN Labs also makes a 250W (3000K) illuminator, and a 75W 12/24V AC/DC illuminator. which is ideal for moving car work. These illuminate a single fiberoptic cable. Clearflux™ fiberoptic cable comes in various sizes and types: OD 1/4 in., 3/8 in., 1/2 in., and 3/4 in. core, in either side lit (entire length glows) or end lit (which transmits light to the end).

Innovision Optics makes a fiberoptic system that uses either 150W or 250W tungsten, or a 150W metal halide illuminator that has a choice of dichroic colored glass filters built into it. Flexible and semiflexible optic cables come in various types and sizes. One type glows along its entire length like a flexible neon rope. It can be heated and bent into semipermanent shapes and letters. Core sizes are 3/16 in., 1/4 in., 3/8 in., and 1/2 in., in up to 70 ft. unspliced lengths. To increase intensity, you can attach an illuminator at both ends.

Neon

When the art department provides neon lights, it is often necessary to dim the neon to make it look good on film. Bobinette or black hose stockings work if the neon is out of focus in the background, but when the neon is seen clearly, it is useful to dim them electronically. Variac or triac dimmers can generally be used for short periods, but when the neon is to be left on, the art department should order special neon dimmers. Other dimmers can overheat and burn out the neon transformer. The way to know if a dimmer is overheating a transformer is to use an ammeter on the power line either going into or coming out of the dimmer. If the dimmer setting is a bad match for the transformer, the amperage flow will jump way above the rated amperage of the transformer. A transformer rated at 2 or 3 amps can start drawing 15 or 20 amps and burn up.

Neon transformers are sized to the particular tube they are lighting. The voltage and milliamp output of the transformer will depend on a number of factors, including the type of gas used and the length of the tube. If you run into trouble with the neon going out when dimmed, using a larger transformer will help. The milliamp output of the transformer drives the neon tubes. A transformer with a higher milliamp output will keep the tube lit when dimmed.

Camera-Synchronous Strobe Lighting

Clairmont Camera and Unilux, Inc. have designed high-speed strobe lighting systems that synchronize the flash of the lighting units with the shutter of the camera. Each frame of film is given a very bright, very short flash of light. When a camera operates at 24 fps, the exposure time is normally 1/48 second. With the Unilux strobe unit, the flash is 1/100,000 second. The effect is to remove all motion blur from an image. Strobe units are often used for shooting slow-motion close-ups of pouring liquids, such as in beer and soft drink commercials. Each drop of beer is sharp because in each frame the moving drops are frozen in a microsecond of flash. The lights can be synchronized with the camera shutter at frame rates from 1 fps up to 650 fps.

Unilux strobes have been used in music videos to capture dance in an ultra-sharp, jerky style. By using a special-effects generator box, the lights can create a strobe effect by not exposing every frame. This appears on film as a series of flashes with performers jumping suddenly from one position to another. Using a sequencer circuit, the lights can also be made to chase so that in each frame light comes from a different head.

Unilux H3000 System

Unilux has been designing and improving strobe systems since the late sixties. The first such system was so large that it required a special studio. With each model, the lights have become smaller, lighter, and simpler to operate. Today's strobes are as portable and as easy to operate as 1200W HMIs

Figure 11.6 The Unilux H3000 system. Pictured here are five heads, two control units, and the shipping case. (Photo courtesy of Unilux, Inc., Hackensack, NJ.)

The H3000 system consists of three heads and a control console to which the three lights are connected. Figure 11.6 shows a system using two control units and five heads.

Control consoles can be daisy-chained together to control as many lights as needed. The H3000 system takes single-phase, 50 or 60 Hz, 220V power at about 10A per head. An older Unilux system uses three-phase 208/120V power and draws about 5A per head.

Unilux heads use a special spiral-shaped quartz xenon bulb (which resembles something out of Dr. Frankenstein's lab). They have a daylight color temperature of 6000K, and they operate relatively cool. The heads can be oriented in any position.

The strobe system synchronizes to the speed of the camera using a sync cable connected to the camera's speed control accessory receptacle. The strobe speed follows the camera shutter speed to give one flash each time the shutter is open and one flash each time it is closed, which is when the camera operator can see through the lens.

Operation

Figure 11.7 shows the front panel of the control console.

When you turn the power switch on, the lights go into preview mode. They flicker at 60 flashes per second at a relatively low light level. This speed is just fast enough that the strobing is not annoying while setting the lights. Once the lights are roughly positioned, you are ready to take some light readings. Before you can take readings, however, you must select the maximum flash rate for each light. The maximum flash rate settings are, in frames per second, as follows: 120, 130, 150, 160, 200, 210, 230, 240, 290, 320, 340, 360, 560, 580, 640, and 650 fps. The maximum flash rate should be set at or above the fastest film frame rate that will be used in the shot. If filming at less than 120 fps, set the flash rate to 120 fps. The brightness that the lights can attain is inversely proportional to the speed of the flashes that you set. When you set the flash rate, you are also setting the intensity of the flash. When the camera rolls, the flashes will be uniform in intensity at any speed up to the maximum

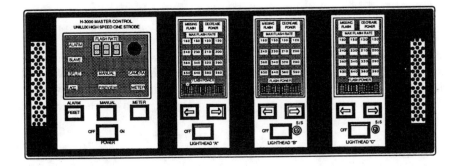

Figure 11.7 The front of the Unilux H3000 control unit. (Illustration courtesy of Unilux, Inc., Hackensack, NJ.)

Figure 11.8   The back of the Unilux H3000 control unit. (Illustration courtesy of Unilux, Inc., Hackensack, NJ.)

speed you've set. Electronics within the control console monitor the operation of the equipment and signal errors such as camera speeds above the maximum flash rate setting or missing flashes.

Note that high-speed cameras sometimes give off a spike pulse when they are coming up to speed. This will trigger an alarm on the console. Press the alarm reset button. If the alarm is not triggered again, you can safely assume that there is no problem once the camera is at speed.

Let's say that we will be filming at 200 fps. We set the maximum flash rate to 200 for each of the light heads. Now we are ready to take light readings. A word of warning: If the main power switch is turned off, the settings will be lost, so it is helpful to circle the setting numbers on the console with a white grease pencil.

Strobe light must be measured with a flash meter. A flash meter is able to sense and capture an exposure measurement from a quick flash of light. Unilux provides Minolta flash meters with their lights. To take a reading, press the meter button on the control console. The lights will come up to the intensities you've set. Note that the lights continue to flash at 60 flashes per second in meter mode. When you're done taking readings, press the meter button again to return to preview mode. The control console will automatically return the lights to preview mode after three minutes.

When you are ready to start filming, the lights will automatically come up to the preset intensity when you turn the camera on. The flash rate is slaved to the camera speed and will increase and decrease speed in tandem with the camera motor. The frame rate at any given moment is shown on the control console. The control console also displays the source of the flash rate signal: camera, meter mode, preview, accessory port (such as the special effects generator), or slave input (used when the console is slaved to another console).

Controlling the Light

A focusing snoot can be used to concentrate the beam into a spot of adjustable size. Unilux lights don't generally come with barn doors, but Mole Studio Junior barn doors and 10-1/8 in. scrims fit the ears.

Mixing Sources

In many instances, cinematographers find that the Unilux image is overly sharp. To make the image look more natural, you can mix Unilux with tungsten or flickerless HMI sources. A good mix is to set Unilux two stops brighter than the supplemental sources.

To calculate the exposure when mixing Unilux with supplemental sources, measure the two sources separately, and then add the two readings. Remember that twice as much light equals one stop more, so if the Unilux reading and the supplemental readings are the same, effectively doubling the light, the exposure is one stop more than the individual readings. If Unilux is one stop brighter, the supplemental lighting is half as bright, and you would add a half-stop to the Unilux reading. If Unilux is two stops brighter, the supplemental light is one quarter as bright. You would add a quarter stop to the Unilux reading.

When Unilux lights are used alone, changing the frame rate does not change the exposure. Because the heads flash the same amount of light on each frame, the exposure time does not change with the frame rate as it does with normal lights. When mixing Unilux with supplemental light, if you double the frame rate, the exposure time of the supplemental light is cut in half. You would need to double the intensity of the supplemental light to keep the same proportion of light from the two sources. In other words, the f-stop you read from the tungsten sources must take the frame rate (shutter speed) into account before it is compared with the Unilux reading for the purpose of setting light levels.

Sync Delay Box

The sync delay box is a separate circuit box that comes with every system. With all cameras except Arriflex, the camera sync cable is connected to the sync delay box, and the box is then connected to the "others" camera input on the back of the control console. The sync delay box serves three potentially helpful functions: shutter sync, cutoff speed, and polarity.

Shutter Sync   With each camera used, the shutter sync should be checked by removing the lens and observing the shutter opening with the Unilux lights running. If the shutter is not completely open each time the light flashes, the sync delay circuit should be used. Turn the circuit on, and set the angle of shutter delay from 1° to 359°.

Cutoff Speed   When set to automatic, the cutoff speed circuit does not let the flash rate go below 60 fps. This is to avoid annoying strobe speeds as the camera slows down at the end of each take (used when filming at frame rates above 60 fps). The switch can also be set to cut off at 10 fps or at 1 fps.

Polarity   With some Panavision cameras, the polarity of the sync pulse is inverted. The polarity switch flips the polarity so that the control console gets a usable signal. If the shutter won't sync up, try changing the polarity.

Split Sync   The split sync configuration allows you to get two stops more light when operating at frame rates above 60 fps with any camera that has a rotating shutter. As noted earlier, each head normally flashes twice for each shutter rotation:

once for an exposure (shutter open) and once for the camera operator (shutter closed). The split-sync configuration eliminates the second flash, which cuts the flash rate in half, provides extra power to the heads, and quadruples their light output.

To provide light for the viewfinder, the viewfinder flash is diverted to one or two separate heads. The viewfinder lights do not affect the exposure because they are off when the shutter is open. When the system is in meter mode, the viewfinder light is off so that it will not affect the exposure readings.

Special Effects Generator

The special effects generator makes strobe and chase effects possible. These are used quite often for music videos. Strobe effects have also been used on such features as *Throw Momma from the Train* and *Jacob's Ladder* to create the flashing light of a train passing in a tunnel.

The special effects generator has eight channels. Each channel can control an individual light or an entire console of three lights. Each channel can be set to skip between one and nine frames between flashes.

A sequencer circuit makes the channels chase — firing each head separately in sequence. Simply select the number of channels, from one to eight.

Notes

Be aware that the strobes can trigger a seizure in people who have photosensitive epilepsy. Make sure that everyone on the set is aware that strobes will be used. People with this very rare reaction generally know to stay away from strobes and will avoid them.

High Platforms for Lighting

There are various hydraulic and motorized lifts and arms that are commonly used as platforms for lights and for rigging lights aloft. Telescoping boom platforms, scissor lifts, and man lifts are invaluable tools, both on the sound stage and on location.

Telescoping Boom Platforms (Condors)

The standard moonlight rig consists of one or two 12k HMIs mounted to the basket of a telescoping boom platform, raised high above the scene. Condor, Snorkelift, JLG, and Simon are the dominant makes, but "Condor" is the common name for boom platforms. An electrician is designated to operate the platform and the lights mounted on it. Productions often need to bring on an extra hand for "Condor duty," so for electricians who are just starting out, knowing how to operate a boom platform is an important skill for getting your foot in the door.

Operation

This type of platform is self-propelled at speeds of 0.7 to 3 miles per hour (mph). Some are designed with an electric motor for indoor use; larger platforms use gasoline or diesel motors. The boom and turret can be controlled from either the basket or a side panel on the chassis. The drive train can only be controlled from the basket. Platforms come in various sizes and have maximum heights of 30, 40, 60, 80, and 120 ft.

The operation of different makes varies little. The Snorkelift TB-A80, which has an 80 ft. boom is shown in Figure 11.9.

The controls are similar for most other types and sizes. The better rental companies include an operator's manual in a weatherproof canister on the equipment, so if you are unfamiliar with a particular model, you can consult the manual. Most operations are self-evident, however, once you understand the basics.

Safety Precautions

Electronics provide ramping in all the controls, including boom operations, which helps smooth out the natural jerkiness of the machinery. You will run into older or less sophisticated models for which the controls act very abruptly. All models, especially these, require considerable care in operation, especially when lights are rigged in the basket.

When driving the platform any significant distance, it is good practice to drive with the boom fully retracted and parallel to the ground. This position gives the operator the best field of view over the top of the chassis. The most natural (and therefore the simplest and safest) configuration for driving is with the steering tires toward the front and the boom slung off the back (see Figure 11.9D). When the boom is raised and extended, the platform automatically drives at a slower speed.

The use of a safety body harness attached to a short rope (not more than 4 ft. free fall) and a large snap hook that hooks to the basket rail is required by OSHA when operating a boom platform. Boom platforms are normally very stable, even when the arm is fully extended. However, physics being what it is, stability is severely compromised if the chassis is not level. Do not operate the machinery on more than a 5° gradient (6 in. rise in 10 ft.). Some lifts have an automatic safety device that precludes operation on uneven ground. The transportation or grip department can help level the vehicle. When a slight gradient is unavoidable, it is best to orient the chassis pointing up and down the hill, and to rotate the boom with the weight on the uphill side or, if necessary, the downhill side, but not out to one side. Chock the wheels. The vehicles can creep if left on an incline.

A chassis can be driven when the boom is extended; however, this is not recommended when the chassis is not on perfectly level ground or when the weight is off-center. At full extension, this can be a dicey business. It is best to avoid making the boom sway with jerky starts and stops, as this will throw the operator around in the basket and can even catapult her out of the basket entirely.

Do not use the boom arm as a crane. Don't sling objects below the basket. When working over pedestrian or automobile traffic, use cones, signs, or flags to mark the area and control traffic around the base of the boom. Do not use reverse or forward as a brake when moving in the opposite direction.

Never operate a boom within 10 ft. of power lines. Ten feet is the absolute minimum clearance recommended, but most experienced operators double that fig-

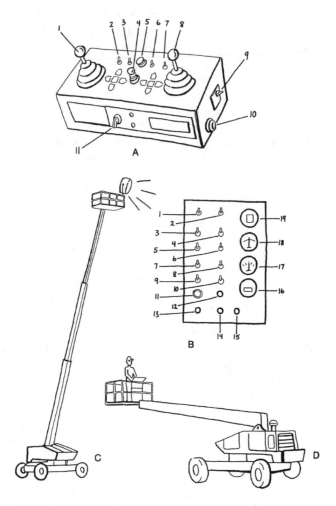

Figure 11.9 Snorkelift operation. (A) Platform basket control panel: (1) boom control lever (up/down, rotate left/right), (2) engine throttle (low/high), (3) drive range (low gear or high gear), (4) boom arm (retract/extend), (5) panic button for emergency stop, (6) platform levels (tilts the basket), (7) emergency power ON/OFF switch (battery power), (8) drive lever (forward/reverse, steering left/right), (9) platform rotate, (10) horn, and (11) ignition switch and circuit breaker. (B) Ground control panel on side of chassis: (1) platform/ground control selector switch, (2) boom/axles selector switch, (3) engine throttle (high/low), (4) emergency power ON/OFF switch, (5) boom arm (extend/retract), (6) boom control lever (up/down), (7) boom control lever (rotate left/right), (8) platform level, (9) platform rotate, (10) ground controls (ON/OFF; works like a dead man pedal: must be held on to operate boom functions), (11) start button, (12) choke, (13) system circuit breaker, (14) throttle circuit breaker, (15) choke run circuit breaker, (16) Hobbs meter, (17) Amp meter, (18) oil pressure, and (19) engine temperature. (C) Boom arm extended. (D) Boom arm retracted in position to drive chassis. Note that the boom is raised so that the driver can see over the top of the chassis. The steering wheels are at the front. (Equipment courtesy of ADCO Equipment Rental, City of Industry, CA, and Snorkelift, St. Joseph, MO.)

ure. Consider the gauge of the power lines and leave liberal clearance. The power lines that run down city alleys carry 2400 to 13,800V. Main power lines carry even more. At these high voltages, current can arc 10 ft. or more if given the chance to ground, especially in moist salt sea air. Similarly, do not operate over live power lines.

Rigging Lights to the Basket

When two lights are to be rigged to the basket, weight becomes a concern. Most platforms have a 500-lb. weight limit. The maximum weight limit is printed next to the panel door on the chassis. The make of the light fixtures and weight of the cables, grip rigging, and the weight of the electrician must be considered. With two 12k fixtures in the basket and a small electrician, you will be operating right at the weight limit. Ballasts should not be put in the basket. See weight data in Table A.5.

Condor Mount

Various manufacturers make hardware for securely mounting large lights to the basket of a boom platform. The grips who rig the mount will need to be given an idea of which way the light will need to face in order to position the mount conveniently. To mount the lights, tilt the basket forward so that it is easy to reach from the ground. Lift the light onto the mount. Then, with someone holding the light, tilt the basket back to level.

Grip equipment, such as a 4-by gel frame, can be secured out in front of the light using ear extensions (Figure 11.10A) or a grip helper (Figure 11.10B).

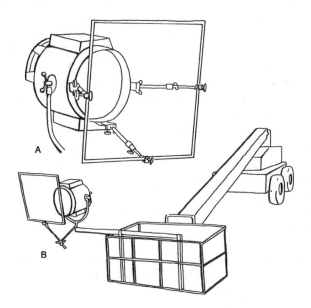

Figure 11.10 Mounting 4-by frames. (A) Ear extensions made by American Studio Equipment. (Equipment courtesy of American Studio Equipment, Sun Valley, CA and Concept Lighting, Sun Valley, CA.) (B) Grip helper and Condor bracket manufactured by Matthews Studio Equipment, Inc., Burbank, CA.

A meat axe is commonly secured to the rail of the basket to provide a means of manipulating nets and flags out in front of the light. A cut is often needed.

Always tie a safety around the bail to the basket. The safety should be 1/2-in. hemp, nylon rope, or, best of all, 1-in. tubular webbing. A 10-ft. length is sufficient to run a loop through the knee rail and over the yoke with plenty of slack for maneuvering the light. Loop the safety around the knee rail so that if the light falls, it will swing under the basket and not smash into it.

Once the lights are rigged on the basket, the operator must use a light touch on the controls and operate the chassis and boom as smoothly as possible. Jerking the lights around with abrupt movements puts a great deal of stress on the mount.

Rigging without a Platform Mount

A fixture can be mounted by securing a steel junior stand to the inside corner of the basket with chain vise grips. This is not a recommended method, however, because the stress can bend or break the stand. If you are going to mount lights in this manner, use only steel hardware (aluminum stands should never be used for 12ks) and do not drive with lights rigged. If the chassis must be moved, remove the heads first.

Cabling

The head cable must be long enough to reach the ground when the boom is at its full height. A head cable extension is usually required to make the run. As always, the head cable should have a strain relief at the head. A second strain relief should be attached to the basket. Leave plenty of slack head cable in the basket so that the fixture can be maneuvered.

When there is more than one cable, run all cables together in a single bundle. It is best to position the cables so they leave from the center of the basket next to the control console, where the boom joins the basket. This minimizes strain on the platform hydraulics (four 12k feeder cables may weigh 120 lb. or more).

It is easiest if the cable can hang straight down to the ground from the basket. In some situations, this is not possible: It may block traffic, get into the shot, or cause other problems. When the cable cannot be hung straight down, it must be tied to the boom arm. The best way to do this is to extend the arm out fully at ground level and tie the cable to the arm at the top of each boom section. Some boom arms have eyelet rings on the arm. Thread motorcycle straps or 1/4 in. hemp through the eyelets and loop them around the cable.

Never place the ballast behind or in front of the chassis. If you need to move the chassis, this causes delay. In the worst case, you could run it over.

Be aware that you can sometimes receive a shock by touching two heads at the same time. This is also true when touching two ballasts or when touching two platforms. This is not normal, but it has been known to happen. You can check for current between units with a voltmeter.

Condor Duty

An evening of Condor duty is made up of a brief period of rigging and positioning the light, occasional radio calls to refocus it, and long hours of sitting at the top of the boom doing nothing. Of paramount importance is to make yourself comfortable and to guard against boredom. Drape sound blankets or duvetyn around the sides of the basket to protect yourself from the wind. Some rental companies offer rubber matting for the floor of the basket, which helps stop the wind. Bring an apple box and a couple of furniture pads to sit on.

You can construct a very comfortable chair with one furniture blanket and seven to nine large grip clips. Use three of the grip clips to clamp one edge of the blanket to the top rail on the narrow side of the basket. This will be the back of the chair. Now clamp the sides of the blanket to the knee rail on either side (next to the control console and next to the gate). The sides of the chair provide a wind block. Before lowering the basket, be sure to remove the blanket so that you have an unobstructed view below you.

Rig a stinger for a reading/work light and an electric heater. A PAR 64 with a spot lens functions well as both a light and a heater. Have a supply of flags and nets tied to the basket in case they are needed once you are aloft. Keep a tag line in the basket so you can pull up any additional equipment. Wear appropriate clothing; bring extra layers to put on later in the evening in case it gets colder. Take some food and drink along to nibble on. Bring a good book (this book, for example).

Man Lifts and Scissor Lifts

A man lift is a small portable lift, usually having a capacity of around 300 lb. and a maximum platform height of 20 to 36 ft. (Figure 11.11A).

It is commonly used on sound stages as a platform from which to work on hanging lights and cables. A man lift has wheels and casters to roll the unit from place to place. Outriggers stabilize the unit for extension. An electric motor powers a cable system that raises and lowers the platform.

A scissor lift is a battery-powered, electrically self-propelled hydraulic lift (Figure 11.11B). A typical scissor lift has a 700- to 1500-lb. capacity and a maximum height of 20 to 40 ft. (depending on the model). Scissor lifts can be used as lighting and camera platforms. Again, only use this equipment on level ground, and always extend the outriggers before elevating the platform.

When fully charged, the batteries should last for many hours of intermittent operation; however, scissor lifts should always be plugged in and charged overnight. If the lift will not operate, check the DC voltage across the batteries (usually 24V powered from four 6V batteries arranged in series). If the batteries are drained, the lift will need to be charged for several minutes before it can be operated, and it should remain on charge until fully charged.

Musco Lights

The Musco Light Company began as a mobile sports lighting service but has found a place in the motion picture industry for lighting very large expanses. A Musco consists of a truck-mounted boom arm with a bank of 6 to 15 high-efficiency 6k open-face HMI fixtures. Because of its high-efficiency reflector, each 6k unit puts out as much light as a standard 12k HMI Fresnel. The smallest Musco truck has a maxi-

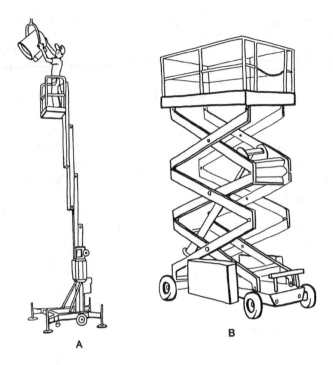

A   B

Figure 11.11 (A) Man lift. (B) Scissor lift.

mum boom height of 80 ft., and the largest goes to 100 ft. (120 ft. with a jib arm). The trucks are completely self-contained and self-sufficient, with their own sound-baffled generators and operators (Figure 11.12).

The lights can be controlled by the gaffer or DP with a handheld remote-control unit or by the Musco operator with levers at the base of the boom. Each light can be panned 359°, tilted 220°, flooded, and spotted remotely. The entire boom arm rotates 180° on its base.

The fixtures have a standard daylight color temperature of 5600K. Some are available with flicker-free electronic ballasts. A 15-head array can flood a 300 sq. ft. area up to half a mile away from the truck at a level of 20 FC. At maximum spot, a 50 sq. ft. area that is 100 ft. from the light can be illuminated to 13,000 FC.

When gel or diffusion is needed, it is placed on a large frame that surrounds the entire bank of lights on three sides. The frames can be gelled ahead of time by Musco's field operators, or they can be gelled by set grips on the day before use. It takes exactly three rolls of 48-in. gel to cover the whole frame of the 15-light array.

Other Moonlight Rigs

When more height is required than a boom platform can provide, a crane truck can be used. The larger crane trucks have boom heights of 225 ft. with caged platforms. These types of cranes usually come with their own driver.

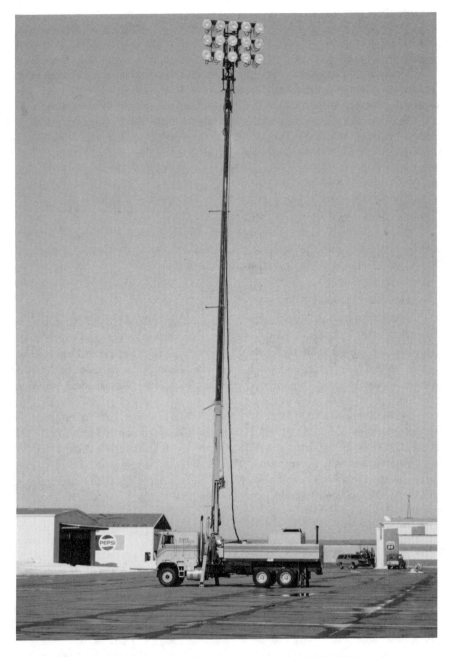

Figure 11.12 A Musco truck. (Photo courtesy of Musco Mobile Lighting, Ltd., Oskaloosa, IA.)

Some gaffers prefer to use a large, soft source for night moonlight ambiance. This has prompted the design of rigs such as a suspended 12 × 12 ft. softbox lit with an array of 2500 PARs or 12ks.

Fisher Productions, Inc. (who make specialized suspended soft banks for car photography) makes a special rig, named appropriately, the "Moonlight." It is a 8 × 17 ft. soft bank lit with ten 2500W DCI lamps (an 18k tungsten version is also available). Flicker-free DCI electronic ballasts allow for about 1-1/2 stops of dimming and color temperature adjustment from about 4500K to 6000K with no gel added. Slide-in filters allow for even greater color correction. The bank is suspended from a 80 ft. telescoping arm. Stabilizing cables run from the light bank to arm so it can be panned and tilted. All lamp adjustments are made remotely from the ground. Power requirements are 208Y/120 three-phase AC (75A per leg) Cam-loc (with adaptors supplied for other connectors).

Because a large source can only create soft shadows if it is relatively close to the subject, rigs of this type are best positioned fairly close overhead. Distant backgrounds can be more easily lit with standard hard sources.

Helium Balloons

Another ingenious contribution to our lighting arsenal is the helium balloon. By placing HMI or tungsten lamps inside a sealed diffusion ball and filling it with helium, you can create soft 360° light without the need for a high platform. The balloon is attached to a tether and winch to set the height of the balloon. Balloons are particularly useful in delicate interior locations, such as an old cathedral, where rigging lights could do damage to the location.

Balloons are available in sizes from a 5.25 ft. diameter, 2000W tungsten unit with an operating height of 10 to 30 ft. (Lunix 160 by Airstar) up to an 18.4 ft. diameter, 12,000W unit with a maximum height of 164 ft. (Solarc 500, Airstar). Helium is an inert gas and is not combustible; in fact, it is a cool gas, which helps ventilate the enclosed lamps. When stabilized with guy lines the largest balloon is safe in winds up to about 22 mph. For manufacturers and distributors, see Appendix H, under Airstar, Leelium, or LTM.

Underwater Lighting

The Old Drop-a-Bulb-in-the-Pool Method

In the days of Esther Williams, it was standard procedure to light water ballet sequences by submerging bare 10k incandescent bulbs in the pool. Power was DC. The feeder cable was soldered to the terminals of the globe, and the connection was potted with a big glob of epoxy or latex rubber to make it watertight. (In the early days, they used tar.) As daring as it may sound, this technique and a similar scheme using a small PAR bulb were the predominant methods of underwater lighting until the early seventies, and they are still used today.

Note that tungsten halogen bulbs cannot be used underwater in this way; they must be surrounded by air. Water cooling would prevent the globe from reaching

250°C, which is required to activate the halogen cycle. Without the halogen cycle, the globe will blacken with tungsten deposits in a matter of hours.

Naturally, there are a number of safety and efficiency concerns with this type of arrangement. For starters, if the bulb burns out, you have to pull up the whole cable to solder on a new globe, which creates a lot of downtime. Second, having a large amperage running though every cable increases the danger posed in the event that a hot wire contacts the water. Third, the bulbs must be submerged before they are turned on because the temperature differential between the hot globe and the cool water can cause the glass of a bulb or PAR lens to crack or explode. Finally, if the bulb breaks under water, the result is a hot wire in contact with water.

In the late sixties, Birns Oceanographic lights, which were underwater lights manufactured for the oil industry, began to be used in underwater cinematography. The Snooper, Snooperette, and 2k Columbia consisted of standard double-ended tungsten bulbs mounted in front of a reflector in a casing with a heavy cover glass. They can be used to depths of 3000 ft. The lights have to be submerged before they are turned on to prevent the cold water from shock-cooling the glass and cracking it. The lights were an improvement over what was available before, but they are heavy and very inefficient.

Modern Underwater Fixtures

For an underwater lighting system to be safe, it must (1) be a completely sealed system, watertight from cable to bulb; (2) provide a sensing device and shutdown mechanism in case an electrical fault occurs; and (3) overcome the problem of thermal stress on the glass that is in contact with water.

James Cameron's epic adventure film, *The Abyss*, revolutionized underwater lighting technology. Forty percent of the live action footage was filmed underwater in a huge tank, 209 ft. in diameter and 55 ft. deep. The project offered two young inventors the opportunity to realize a project they had had in mind for some time. Pete Romano, an underwater cameraman, and Richard Mula, a gaffer and engineer, developed the 1200W HMI SeaPar, an efficient underwater PAR light, to meet the needs of this extremely demanding project. The SeaPar and other underwater fixtures are now supplied by HydroFlex. Additionally, they offer the 1200W HMI HydroPar (an update of the SeaPar), the 1000W Incandescent HydroPar, and a small, handy incandescent 650W SeaPar (Figure 11.13A and 11.13B). SeaPars work equally well out of water, in the rain, or submerged to depths of more than 250 ft. Birns and other manufacturers now also offer similar systems.

The lights find use not only in underwater scenes but in any scene in which water is present. For example, a scene in *Batman II* has the actors wading knee-deep in floods. If a SeaPar head accidentally falls into the water, there is no danger and no harm done, and power cords can be run underwater.

Safety Features

The system is watertight. Ballasts and main distribution cables remain above the surface. The head cables run down into the water. SeaPars use watertight plugs that can be plugged and unplugged underwater with the power off. The connectors

A

B

Figure 11.13 (A) SeaPar lights in use underwater. A 1200W SeaPar HMI lights a rusted wreckage for the cameraman. (B) Diver holds two battery-powered incandescent PAR 46 lights. The underwater weight of the lamps with batteries is about 2 lb. each. (Photos courtesy of Hydro Image, Los Angeles, CA.)

have locking sleeves to prevent kick-outs. A hot female lead can be left unplugged in water because the female plug naturally holds air within the deep contact pockets so that electricity does not come into contact with water. All cables and connectors are watertight. Regular type W and entertainment cable are approved for use in water. The connection point on the head is made so that even if the head cable gets cut, water cannot enter the head.

To provide a fault-sensitive shutdown mechanism, the system operates on AC current with a grounding lead. All metal parts are grounded. The HMI ballasts are fitted with two ground fault interrupter (GFI) circuits that sense the presence of leakage current. If there is more than a 5 mA differential between the hot leg (outgoing current) and the neutral leg (incoming current), indicating that fault current is leaking through to ground, a relay cuts power to the ballast in less than 1/60 second. This is less current than is required to harm an individual, even if the person is in contact with the fault source.

The second GFI serves as a redundant backup. In addition, a fourth lead is used: A ground-return lead connected to a relay circuit constantly monitors the integrity of the grounding lead and will shut down the power if ground is removed or lost. Finally, the outside glass covers on SeaPar fixtures are made of special thermoshock-resistant glass that can withstand sudden extreme temperature changes.

Operational Features

Spreader lenses are held inside the watertight cover glass. On some lights, the spreader lens is factory mounted to the PAR lamp. On the newer ones, the spreader lenses can be exchanged (out of water) by simply unbuckling the cover on the front of the fixture. Spreader lenses have very little effect underwater if they are on the outside of the fixture.

A retaining ring buckles to the front of the fixture. The retaining ring holds scrims, gels, and diffusion, and simultaneously prevents any light leakage to the sides. The retaining ring allows water to circulate around the gel for heat dissipation. Barn doors and snoots can be mounted to the front of the retaining ring.

There are two lock knobs on the bail on either side of the light. One is the tilt lock. The other, the rotation lock, is used to orient the elliptical beam. The fixtures can be used in any orientation.

Lighting Underwater

During the filming of *The Abyss*, director of photography Mikael Salomon used the lights in all the ways you normally do in a dry sound stage. He bounced light off griffolyn, used griffolyn flags to control the light (duvetyn turns brown in water), used color and diffusion on the lights, and so on.

Water acts as a color filter. Within 10 ft. of the surface, 70 to 80% of the red end of the spectrum is absorbed, leaving only blue light. The brilliant colors of sea life appear dull in the blue light that filters down from the surface. Only when you shine a light on them do the magnificent colors come to life. Fill light is therefore used to help bring back good color to subjects at depths greater than about 16 ft., even when existing exposure is sufficient. Fill light may also be called for when shooting a subject from below. Light can be bounced off the bottom of a white pool, off a white board, or shone directly at the subject. At depths greater than 130 ft., supplemental light is necessary to get an adequate exposure, and of course underwater lights come into play anytime you are shooting at night.

Water is usually somewhat cloudy and acts as a diffusion, much like fog. It reduces light transmission and softens the light as it bounces off the particles in the water. However, the beam angle of the light in clear water is the same as in air. It is important to keep the cloudiness consistent. In a pool, a filtering system must be used, and the floor of the pool must be vacuumed to start with a clean pool. Once all the divers are in the water, you can add substances to make it murkier if necessary. When filming *The Abyss*, fuller's earth, diatomite (a swimming pool filter agent), small amounts of milk, and blue detergent were added to the water to make it very blue and hazy. To avoid stirring up particles resting on the bottom, underwater crews often do not use fins. Instead, they wear weights and walk around on the bottom of the pool.

Exposure readings are taken using an underwater reflected light meter. The Sekonic Marine II, for example, has a 10° angle of acceptance. You aim the meter in the direction you wish to shoot and set the aperture accordingly. The water is brighter above the diver and falls off into darkness below the diver, so meter readings should be taken in the appropriate direction. Underwater cinematographers generally have underwater housings for other light meters as well.

An underwater scene lit only from underwater looks dead and flat. Except for the bubbles, you can't even tell that you are underwater. To bring the water to life, you need light coming through the surface, creating dancing striations of light. For a night scene, you might use a heavy backlight from above the surface and a small amount of soft underwater bounce (a 1200W HMI into a 4-by white griffolyn, for example).

Underwater lights are often used to light up swimming pools or fountains, even when the camera will not be submerged. A light placed at the bottom makes the entire pool glow and throws moving highlights on surrounding people, buildings, trees, and so on.

Electricity and Water

The danger of water is that it is a conductor. Salt water (which is essentially what the body is made of) is a better conductor than fresh water. Neither is a very good conductor, but enough of one to pose a threat to life under certain circumstances.

Remember that to get a shock, a diver must become part of a closed circuit. Water is ground, and in water a diver becomes part of the ground. The greatest danger is to reach out of the water and touch a hot wire or a metal housing with a fault in it, directing electricity exclusively straight through the body: in through the arm, through the lungs and heart, and out through the lower half of the body. This scenario could very easily kill a person. That is why it is so critical that the casing of a light and all accessible metal parts be at ground potential and, if there is a ground fault, that the circuit is automatically interrupted by the GFI before an accident can occur.

As a matter of safety, all electrical equipment, including submersibles, submarines, pumps, cables, and lights, should be routinely checked for leakage current before being put in the water.

A bare wire underwater sets up an electrical field around it and seeks the path of least resistance to complete the circuit to ground or to a neutral wire. If the neutral or grounding wire is close by, as in the case of a sheared cable, the field will be very strong between the two wires and will spread around the fault, weakening with distance. The size of the field depends on the amperage available and the impedance imposed by the size of the wires. This is the reason that it is better to use lots of lower amperage cables rather than a few very high amperage ones. For example, if a 10A circuit power cord in fresh water gets cut by a boat propeller, water will set up a field with a diameter of about 5.6 ft. (minimum safe distance). A cable carrying 100A, on the other hand, sets up a field 49 ft. in diameter.

Another reason many small amperage cables are preferable to a few high amperage ones is that GFIs on 20A circuits are very dependable. The higher the amperage, the greater the noise in the system and the less dependable the GFIs become.

A diver can feel it when he is coming close to an electrical field. If you have ever put your tongue on a 9V battery, you know the taste that comes into your mouth, and you can feel a tingle in the fillings in your teeth. Closer to the field, you begin to feel the tingle of electricity in your body. A diver who is inside a strong field may experience the effects of electrical shock: trouble breathing, muscle freeze, cardiac fibrillation, and cardiac arrest.

In an earlier chapter, the effects of AC and DC on the body were discussed. DC current poses a less lethal threat because it requires more amperage to cause muscle freeze and to interfere with other important muscles, such as the heart and lungs. Although HMIs are always AC (even AC/DC ballasts run AC to the head), their increased light output means that they replace an incandescent light of much higher amperage, so they pose no greater threat than the alternative. However, because AC circuits are grounded, the safety features previously discussed diminish any potential threat to a safe level.

Shooting in the Rain

The primary concerns when shooting in the rain, real or artificial, are that all the electrical circuits are safe and that the lights are covered and stay dry.

Cabling and Distribution

The preceding section discussed the electrical safety hazards posed by water. Similar hazards exist any time the ground is thoroughly wet. In fact, water is a better conductor when it is mixed with the minerals of soil. A muddy field is more conductive than a freshwater pool. Guard against bare contacts coming into contact with water and ground by elevating all connection points on apple boxes. Wrap all electrical connections in visqueen or heavy-duty plastic garbage bags to prevent water falling onto connection points. When cable is to be run in wet areas, it should be inspected prior to use. Look for deep nicks in the outer sheath.

Rain poses an additional hazard: Everything and everyone tends to get wet, and wet hands and feet will pose little resistance should you come into contact with a fault. Light fixtures must be grounded. It is a wise precaution to test lighting fixtures for ground fault leaks prior to use in a wet environment.

Rain Tents

Lights must be protected from falling and blowing moisture. If water falls or blows onto the hot lens, the thermal shock can crack or shatter the lens, especially when the bulb is in flood position, and the lens is hottest. If water leaks into the housing and touches the globe, the globe will burn out or explode. With HMIs water causes serious problems with the electronics. Water can also cause corrosion to the metal parts of the fixtures.

Protect the lens with a gel frame of heat-shield gel or a thin color (1/8 CTO or 1/8 CTB). Place rain hats over the lights. Celo screen — a tough, plastic-covered, wire screen — works well to cover fixtures. Bend it over the light and grip clip it to the bail on either side. Alternately, a flag covered with a garbage bag works for small lights. Larger lights require a 4-by flag wrapped in visqueen or a griffolyn. (Check for holes in the griff first.) A 12-by or 20-by griff is handy to cover a number of units at once. Rain hats should be positioned so that rain runs off away from the fixture; don't let rain collect and form a pool in the flag.

Lighting Rain

Falling water is most visible to the camera when lit from the back. Rain shots are typically done by placing rain between the lens and the actors, and the general area before the camera, and supplementing it with rain falling in puddles, on the tops of cars, and in places where it would be noticeably lacking were it not there. A gentle trickle of rain might also be used over the actors to keep them dripping.

Anytime the ground is wet, the camera will pick up reflections and highlights of sources within the frame. The DPs often deliberately place self-luminous dressing in the frame to pick up these highlights.

Lightning Effects

Creating a convincing lightning effect can be difficult. It requires a very bright, very brief flash, several stops brighter than the exposure used for the set lighting. To be convincing, it should flicker slightly and vary from flash to flash. For a small area, shutters are sometimes used in front of a fairly large fixture; however, this is a marginally effective technique when used in a large area.

For many years, the brightest and most convincing lightning effect was accomplished with a scissor arc. A scissor arc consists of a bundle of carbon rods wrapped in wire and attached to a scissor device that brings the carbons into contact with the opposite electrode. When the two are brought together, all hell breaks loose, and an extremely bright sputtering flash lights up everything within a block. The scissor arc is positioned a distance from the action and is placed up high on a scaffold. Should you ever be on a set where a scissor arc is used, stand clear of the fixture, and watch out for fragments of hot carbon falling from the fixture. A hot piece of carbon can melt right through asphalt.

Lightning Strikes

More recently, Optec Inc. has developed *Lightning Strikes*, a programmable lightning machine that can drench the set in light for up to three seconds. The light comes in two sizes, 70,000W and 250,000W, and several heads can be connected to a central control unit and fired simultaneously or separately. The color temperature is 5600K, and the unit is dimmable to about 20% output with no change in color temperature. The units can be very precisely controlled and flash sequences can be programmed, so identical flashes can be repeated in take after take. The 70k head's peak output yields 350 FC at 100 ft. with a 45° beam spread. The units can be ordered with fully sealed waterproof housings for use with rain towers.

There are a variety of different control units. The *undulating controller* comes standard with each light and is used for manual or automatic random lightning flashes. The *precision fader* is a programmable controller with which one can create, repeat, and loop up and down fades. It is great for creating an explosion effect, for example, with a big initial flash and slow decay, spiked with lesser secondary explosions. Each sequence can be up to four seconds, and the unit can hold up to four sequences. The unit comes with four preprogrammed sequences, but you can create custom sequences using a simple joystick to edit the sequence. Each sequence can change level up to 24 times a second. Machine gun fire flashes can also be created with an on, off, on, off pattern.

The *quad controller* controls up to four lights separately or in unison with eight memory banks that record firing sequences for playback. The control unit can also be hooked up to a MIDI music system–video or audio playback unit to cue the flashes using timecode as a timing base.

The lights can also be run using a DMX controller. Brightness level and "mode" are controlled on two adjacent channels; constant, slow undulation; medium undulation; or fast undulation are controlled by the "mode" pot. Multiple lights can be synchronized or operated separately.

Each head operates on 208–250V service (single phase, or two legs of a three-phase service; 220V or more is preferred).

Fixture	70,000W	250,000W
Weight	35 lb.	55 lb.
Dimensions	33 × 14 × 10 in.	42 × 17 × 11 in.
Mount	1-1/8 in. Jr. Pin	1-1/8 in. Jr. Pin
Voltage	208-250V AC 50/60 Hz	208-250V AC 50/60 Hz
Current	300A momentary	1000A momentary
Power Requirements		
Mains or house	63A minimum	200A minimum
	100A optimum	300A optimum
Generator	350A (at 120V)	1200A (at 120V)
	or 45kW or 52kVA	or 145kW or 185kVA

Generator companies recommend that when two 70,000W heads are used, the plant should have at least a 750A capacity; when three 70,000W heads are used, the plant should have at least a 1200A capacity. The 70k unit draws about 300A when fired. Because the time is so short, it can safely be run on 100A house current. (It is treated like an electric motor starting load.) Although this is a fairly substantial intermittent load, the peak power is within 5% of nominal RMS power, meaning that there is no momentary drain much greater than the nominal power, as there is when striking HMI units, for example. A sudden heavy load like this will affect all the lights on a generator. They may blink each time the strike hits. To guard against surge current affecting the set lighting, most gaffers order an additional generator to handle the Lightning Strikes units. If you have to run both on the same generator, use the smaller 70k unit, keep the bursts short, and do not to have more than half the amperage capacity of the generator devoted to lightning units.

Shooting on Moving Vehicles

The standard method of shooting a scene in a moving car is to tow the car and mount the camera to the side door or the hood of the car. The tow vehicle is equipped with a sound-baffled generator and various rails and platforms to which lights can be mounted. Some very specialized vehicles, such as the Shotmaker trucks, support the camera on a crane arm, which makes placing the camera a relatively easy task and provides an opportunity to approach a driving scene with some dynamic camera moves (Figure 11.14A).

Another approach is to put the car on a low-riding flatbed trailer, a *process trailer*, and to tow the trailer (Figure 11.14B). The trailer rides low to the ground so that the height of the car above the pavement looks normal to the camera. Taking the air out of the car's tires once it is on the trailer also helps. The largest trailer for this purpose is two lanes wide, allowing room for the camera, lights, and crew. It usually works out well to tie HMI ballasts to the rigging on the roof of the cab. Run cables along the speed-rail, keeping them neatly tied and out of the way. Be sure nothing is going to slip loose, rattle, drag, or get under the tires when the car gets on the road.

There are many techniques for lighting the interior of a car. The basic problem with daytime car interiors is the contrast between interior and exterior. The light level on the faces has to be brought up so that the exterior scenery is not overexposed. When lighting a car on a sunny day, one approach is to use large HMI sources on the tow vehicle to simulate sunshine on the actor's faces. On an overcast day, the supplemental lights may be shone through diffusion material attached on the windshield (assuming that the camera does not see the windshield).

Shooting at night poses a different set of problems. For a city street scene, an open aperture is needed to make naturally lit storefronts visible. You would therefore shoot at relatively low light levels with small fixtures taped to the dashboard, for example. Some DPs like to have several small lights mounted at various angles to achieve the appearance of passing traffic and streetlights by bringing the lights up and down on dimmers or panning them across the actors.

A

B

Figure 11.14 Rigging lights to moving vehicle. (A) Shotmaker truck towing a car. (B) A car on a process trailer. (Photos courtesy of Shotmaker Co., Valencia, CA.)

With fast film, the lighting need not consume a lot of power. A night scene could be very minimally lit using a couple of 12V fixtures (Kino Flos, stick-ups, Dedolights, or other 12V fixtures) running off of the car battery or a deep-cycle marine battery. In a pinch, I once liberated a headlight from the grip truck; bounced, diffused, and wrapped in blackwrap, it looked fantastic.

CHAPTER **12**

The Work World

This chapter gives a brief overview of labor standards that are considered fair and acceptable in the film industry, and in doing so explains how both union and nonunion productions conduct business. For union employees, the conditions of employment are spelled out in great detail in the union labor agreement. If a production company is a union signatory, the union represents the crew members, instituting standard minimum wage and overtime requirements, providing rules regarding turnaround, meals, number of crew members hired, and so on. Naturally, the union agreement represents the most favorable work conditions you are likely to find. Almost any nonunion deal will demand less of the producers. The union contract provides a yardstick by which nonunion labor arrangements can be measured; it is, therefore, a good starting point for this discussion.

The Unions

The largest and most powerful technician's union in the motion picture industry is the International Alliance of Theatrical and Stage Employees (IATSE, or IA). The National Association of Broadcast Employees and Technicians (NABET) once also represented film and television technicians, but NABET film technicians have been absorbed into the IA in New York and Los Angeles. NABET now represents mostly broadcasting technicians. Table 12.1 lists some union locals for the United States and Canada. All the major film studios and many independent producers are union signatories and have a standard three-year agreement with the IA. IA organizers work to organize nonunion shows and union business agents enforce contracts with signatories.

It can be difficult for a nonunion worker to start getting union work. It sometimes takes time, determination, and a certain amount of luck. Partly because of this, there is a large, experienced nonunion labor force, and roughly half of all films are made with nonunion crews. Whether union membership is needed in order to get

Table 12.1 Union Locals in the United States and Canada

State	City or Region	Type	Local
Arizona	Phoenix/Tucson	SM	IATSE Local 485
California	Los Angeles	MPSELT	IATSE Local 728
	San Jose	M	IATSE Local 134
	San Francisco	S	IATSE Local 16
	San Francisco		NABET Local 134
Colorado	Denver/Boulder	S	IATSE Local 7
	Colorado Springs	M	IATSE 62
Dist. of Columbia	Washington, D.C.	SM	IATSE Local 22
Florida	Miami/Orlando	SM	IATSE Local 477
Georgia	Atlanta	SM	IATSE Local 479
Hawaii	Honolulu	M	IATSE Local 665
Illinois	Chicago	SM	IATSE Local 476
Massachusetts	Boston (all New England)	SM	IATSE Local 481
Michigan	Detroit	SM	IATSE Local 38
Minnesota	Minneapolis (statewide)	SM	IATSE Local 490
Missouri	Saint Louis	S	IATSE Local 6
Nevada	Las Vegas	M	IATSE Local 720
New Mexico	Santa Fe	SM	IATSE Local 480
New York	New York	SM	IATSE Local 52
North Carolina	See South Carolina		
Ohio	Cleveland (statewide)	SM	IATSE Local 209
Oregon	Portland (Pacific NW)	SM	IATSE Local 488
Pennsylvania	Pittsburgh (Greater Pittsburgh)	SM	IATSE Local 489
South Carolina	Wilmington (Carolinas)	SM	IATSE Local 491
Texas	Houston (statewide)	SM	IATSE Local 484
Canada	Burnaby, B.C.	MPSPT	IATSE Local 891
	Toronto, Ont.	MPSPT	IATSE Local 873
			NABET Local 700

SM = Studio Mechanics
S = Stagehands
MPSELT = Motion Picture Studio Electrical Lighting Technicians
MPSPT = Motion Picture Studio Production Technicians
M = Mixed

work on features varies from town to town. For example, in Los Angeles and New York, there is a very strong nonunion presence, whereas in Chicago and San Francisco, it is next to impossible to find feature film work as a nonunion technician, although you can get commercial work.

Hollywood: Local 728

In most areas, set lighting technicians are included in the stagehands' or studio mechanics' local, along with grips, shop craftsmen, re-recording mixers, sound department personnel, video engineers, property personnel, and projectionists. Hollywood Local 728 is unique in that it is strictly a set lighting local.

In Los Angeles, a worker's name must be listed on the *Industry Experience Roster* in order to work under the basic labor agreement. The roster is provided to producers by the contract services department of the Association of Motion Picture and Television Producers (AMPTP). The roster lists union members from which producers can select their crew. To get on the experience roster you must have worked 30 days on a union show. This sounds like a Catch 22; however, there are two scenarios in which a nonunion worker can earn his 30 days and get on the experience roster.

1. If a worker is hired on a nonunion show whose employees vote to seek union representation and the show is organized by the union and the producers sign an agreement, that worker typically can count all of the days (retroactively to the beginning of his employment) as union days.
2. During the busiest times of the year, the union runs out of people, and the Local hall goes into *permit status*. At that time nonunion workers can be hired on permit.

Once a worker has accumulated 30 permit days within a one-year period, the worker applies to contract services, fills out CSATF paper work, takes a color blindness test, and, if eligible, his or her name is added to the experience roster. Once on the roster, the individual is eligible to work in LA and the applicant must join the union and pay the dues, before taking other union work. Each local office keeps a list of member availability. Union members are required to call in and report any work they take, including work on nonunion shows.

There is no written entrance test for Local 728, as there is for Local 52 in New York and some other locals. Rules for entrance vary from city to city.

Basic Agreement

The following are some of the current conditions provided in an IA *Basic Agreement* on the West Coast. They are included here as an example of the types of concerns workers have on any production. The rules may vary from one union local to another, and as signatories renew their contracts negotiations may change the current agreements, but the issues remain the same.

An Abbreviated Summary of Labor Agreements

Daily employee	Gaffer, best boy, and rigging gaffer, set electricians, 8 hrs. guaranteed. Wage shown in Table 12.2 under Schedule A.
Weekly employee	Gaffer, best boy, and rigging gaffer. Five consecutive days and at least 54 hrs., with at least nine hours of pay per day. Wage shown in Table 12.2 under Schedule B.
Studio	Shooting on premises.
Studio zone	Within 30 miles of central location. Reimbursed for mileage or travel time, or ride furnished to set. 10 hr. turnaround.
Nearby location	More than 30 miles away. Ride furnished. Go on the clock when you meet the van.
Distant location	Overnight necessary. 8 hr. turnaround; golden time after 14 hrs. elapsed; 6-day work week. Production pays for accommodations, meals, and all other out-of-pocket expenses. The production supplies trans- portation from the hotel to the set every day, and crew members go on the clock when they are picked up at the hotel, rather than when they arrive at the set, and they go off the clock when they are dropped off again.
Turnaround	Generally 9 hr. minimum, except where noted (distant location, studio zone).
Forced call	Less than required turnaround. Hours worked on forced call are added to the previous day's hours for the purpose of calculating overtime pay.

Base wage
  After 8 hr.
  After 12 hr.
	Shown in Table 12.2.
	Time and a half.
	Golden time. Double-time normally; 6th day triple-time; 7th day quadruple-time.

Meals	After every 6 hr. work; 30 to 60 minutes.
12-minute grace period	A 12-minute grace period allows the production to continue to shoot for 12 minutes beyond the 6-hr. limit with no penalty.
30-minute grace period	A 30-minute extension allows the production to finish a camera take that is in progress. No lighting or camera changes may be made. The extension is meant to be used when there is some sort of urgent extenuating circumstance, such as the need to get an expensive actor off the clock.
NBC contract and other alternative agreements	Special agreements for specific types of productions that were frequently formerly nonunion (e.g., NBC Agreement, HBO Agreement, etc.) Rules vary. Generally rate schedule is lower, as much as 24% lower for lighting technicians. Double-time pay starts after 14 hrs., instead of 12 hrs. Contractual holidays and vacation days not worked are unpaid, whereas under the basic agreement a percentage is paid, and there is no "drive to" pay.

Table 12.2 Sample Union Wage Table: Studio Minimum Rates

Classification	Schedule A: Daily employees (Time-and-a-half after 8 and/ or 40; minimum call 8 hrs.)	Schedule B: Weekly employees (Weekly guarantee. 54 cumulative hrs.; 5 consecutive days; minimum call 9 hrs.)	
	Per Hour	*Per Hour*	*Per Week*
Chief lighting technician (gaffer)	$24.69	$24.355	$1485.68
Assistant chief lighting technician	$22.33	$21.908	$1336.38
Chief rigging electric	$23.15	$21.908	$1336.38
Running repair (special operator)	$22.82		
Lighting technician	$21.32		
Entry level employee	$18.65		

Sample wage scale August 1, 1992 to July 31, 1993 for Local 728 in Los Angeles.

Lamp Specification Tables

The tables in this section offer lots of potentially helpful information about all types of lights. Beam angle and candle-power data allow you to calculate the beam diameter of any light at any distance. This is particularly helpful when choosing ellipsoidal spotlights. Knowing candle-power allows you to calculate footcandle intensity at any distance you choose. Here's how it works.

Calculating Field Diameter

Table A.12 lists specifications for various commonly used ellipsoidals. Included in this table (and in any manufacturer's catalogue) is the multiplier used to calculate field diameter at a given throw. For example, the Source Four 36° fixture has a multiplier of .65. If the throw is 20 ft., we can calculate the field diameter as follows:

$$\text{Distance x multiplier } = \text{ field diameter}$$

$$20 \text{ ft. x .65 } = 13 \text{ ft.}$$

For most other lights you can use the beam angle to look up the beam diameter at any distance using Table A.13.

Calculating Intensity

We can use Table A.14 to ascertain the light level of most fixtures at any distance. We can also calculate the intensity of a light at any distance using the inverse square law. To find the amount of light, divide the source candle-power given in candela (cd) (Table A.14) by the distance squared:

$$\frac{\text{Source cd}}{\text{D}^2 \text{ (feet)}} = \text{FC} \qquad \text{or} \qquad \frac{\text{Source cd}}{\text{D}^2 \text{ (meters)}} = \text{lux}$$

For example, a Source Four 36° fixture has a source intensity of 84,929 cd. The intensity at 20 ft. is therefore:

$$\frac{84,929}{(20)^2} = 212 \text{ FC}$$

You can use this equation to calculate the source intensity (cd) of a given fixture by measuring the FC level at a given distance, or to calculate the distance necessary to achieve a particular FC level from a given fixture.

$$\text{cd } = \text{ FC x D}^2$$

$$D = \sqrt{\frac{\text{fixture intensity (cd)}}{\text{light level (FC)}}}$$

Table A.1 Tungsten Fresnels

	Watts	Bulb ANSI code	Lens	Scrim (in.)	Chimera Ring Size (in.)
Altman					
300L	300	FKW	3"	5"	5"
650L	650	FRK	4.5"	6-5/8"	6-1/2"
1000L	1k	EGT	5"	7-3/4"	7-5/8"
Studio 1k	1k	EGT	7"	9"	9-5/8"
2000L	2k	CYX	7"	9"	9-5/8"
Studio 2k	2k	CYX	10"	13"	13-1/2"
5000L	5k	DPY	10"	13"	13-1/2"
Studio 5k	5k	DPY	12"	15-1/2"	16-1/8"
Arri					
300W	300	FKW	3.2"	5"	5"
650W	650	FRK	4.3"	6-5/8"	6-1/2"
1000W	1k	EGT	5.1"	7-3/4"	7-5/8"
Studio 1k	1k	EGT	6.9"	9"	9-5/8"
2000W	2k	CYX	6.9	9"	9-5/8"
Studio 2k	2k	CYX	10"	13"	13-1/2"
5000W	5k	DPY	10"	13"	13-1/2"
Studio 5k	5k	DPY	11.8"	15-1/2"	16-1/8"
Studio 10k	10k/12k	DTY[a]	16.7"	19-1/2"	20"
Cinemills					
20k	20k	20k	24"	29"	29"
DedoTech[b]					
DLH	100	FCR		3"	3"
	50	BRL			
	20	—			
DLHM	100	FCR		3"	3"
DLH-150	150	FCS		3"	3"
COOLH	250	ELC		3"	3"
Desisti					
Leonardo 1k	1k	EGT	6"	7.25"	7-3/8"
Piccolo 2k	2k	CYX	6"	7.25"	7-3/8"
Leonardo 2k	2k	CYX	10"	12"	12-3/8"
Piccolo 5k	5k	DPY	10"	12"	12-3/8"
Leonardo 5k	5k	DPY	12"	15.5"	15-3/4"
Leonardo 5k	5k	DPY	14"	15.5"	15-3/4"
Piccolo 10k	10k	DTY	14"	15.5"	15-3/4"
Leonardo 10k	10k	DTY	24"	29.75"	—
Super Leo 20k	20k	20k	24"	29.75"	—
Leonetti (Sunray)					
20k	20k	20k	24"	29"	29"
Mole Richardson					
Tiny Mole	200	FEV	2"	5"	3"
Mini Mole	200	FEV	3"	4-7/16"	4-1/2
Midget	200	FEV	4-15/36"	5-1/8	5-1/8
Betweenie	300	FKW	3"	5-1/8"	5-1/8"
Tweenie	650	DYS	4-1/2"	5-1/8"	5-1/8"
Tweeie II	650	FRK	4-1/2"	5-1/8"	5-1/8"
Baby Baby	1k	EGT	5"	7-3/16"	7-1/4"
Baby	1k	EGT	6"	6-5/8"	6-5/8"
Baby Junior	2k	EGT	6"	9"	9"

Table A.1 Tungsten Fresnels

	Watts	Bulb ANSI code	Lens	Scrim (in.)	Chimera Ring Size (in.)
Junior Solarspot	2k	CYX	9-7/8"	10-1/8	10-1/8"
8" Junior	2k	CYX	8"	9"	9"
Baby Senior	5k	DPY	9-7/8"	13-1/2"	13-1/2"
Senior Solarspot	5k	DPY	14"	15-1/2"	15-1/2"
Baby Tenner	10k	DTY	14"	18-1/2	18-1/2"
Tenner Solarspot	10k	DTY	20"	21"	21"
Big Eye	10k	DTY	24-3/4"	29"	29"
20k "Big Mo"	20k	20k	24-3/4"	29"	29"
LTM Peppers					
Pepper 100/200	100	ESR	2"	3"	3"
	200	FEV			
Pepper 200	200	FEV	3-1/8"	4-1/4"	4-1/4"
Pepper 300	300	FKW	3-1/8"	4-1/4"	4-1/4"
Pepper 420	420	EKB	3-1/8"	4-1/4"	4-1/4"
Pepper 650	650	FRK	4-3/8	5"	5"
Pepper 500/1k	500	EGN	5"	6-5/8"	7-1/4"
	1k	EGT			
20k Pepper	20k	20k	24"	29"	29"
Sachtler					
Director H	300	FKW	3"	5-1/4"	5-1/4"
Director C	500	FRG	3"	5-1/4"	5-1/4"
Director H	650	FRK	5"	7-3/4	7-3/4"
Director C	1k	c	5"	7-3/4"	7-3/4"
Director H	1k	EGT	6"	9"	9"
Director C	2k	d	6"	9"	9"
Director H	2k	CYX	8"	12	12
Director H	2k	CYX	10"	13.5"	13.5"
Director H	5k	DPY	10"	13.5"	13.5"
Director H	5k	DPY	12"	13.5"	13.5"
Director 10k	10k	DTY	—	—	—
Strand Quartz Color					
3" Mizar	200	FEV	3"	4-3/8"	4-1/4"
3" Mizar 300/500	300	FKW	3"	4-3/8"	4-1/4"
	500	FRK			
5" Bambino 1k	1k	EGT	5"	7-1/4"	7-1/4"
6" Polaris 1k	1k	EGT	6"	9" or 7-7/8"	7-5/8"
6" Bambino 2k	2k	CYX	6"	9"	7-5/8"
10" Castor 2k	2k	CYX	10"	12-5/8" 13-1/2"	12-3/4"
10" Bambino 5k	5k	DPY	10"	12-5/8" 13-1/2"	13-1/2"
12" Pollux 5k	5k	DPY	12"	16"	15-3/4
14" Vega 10k	10k	DTY	14"	16"	15-3/4
20" Draco 20k	20k	20k	20"	29"	29"

a Uses Koto 12k tungsten lamp and maximized reflector/lens system for output rivaling a 20k.

b All power supplies have selectable input voltage: 110, 120, 220, 230, or 240V AC and three-position switch selects output level.

c Uses special Phillips blue pinch 1k bulb with GY 9.5 base.

d Uses special Phillips blue pinch 2k bulb with G22 base.

Table A.2 Soft Lights

		Watts	Bulbs	ANSI code	Face Dimensions	Candle-power
Arri						
	Arrisoft 1000	1000	1	FCM	9.5 x 7.7	9200
	Arrisoft 2000	2000	2	FCM	8.2 x 17.1"	16,700
Desisti						
	Botticelli 2k	2000	2	FCM	21" x 1"	—
	Botticelli 4k	4000	4	FCM	32" x 21"	—
DN Labs						
	Spectra-flux 200T	100	1	GCC	6" x 6"	—
		200	1	GCB		—
Lowel						
	Softlight 2	2000	2	FCM	28" x 24"	—
LTM						
	400 Soft	400	1	FDA	4-3/4 x 6-7/8	1000
	1000 Soft	1000	1	FCM	11.5" x 17"	5000
	2000 Soft	2000	2	FCM	20.5" x 17"	10,080
	4000 Soft	4000	4	FCM	42" x 42"	18,000
Mole Richardson						
	Mini-Softlite	650	1	FAD	6-1/4" x 6-1/4"	2400
	750 Baby Soft	750	1	EJG	8" x 8"	3000
	1k Super Soft	1000	1	FCM	18" x 18"	5000
	2k Zip Baby Soft	2000	2	FCM	8" x 17-1/2"	10,080
	2k Super Soft	2000	2	FCM	24" x 24"	10,080
	4k Baby Soft	4000	4	FCM	18" x 18"	18,000
	4k Super Soft	4000	4	FCM	36" x 30"	24,320
	8k Super Soft	8000	8	FCM	36"x 30"	48,000
Strand						
	Arturo 1000/1500	1000	1	FFT	—	—
		1500	1	FDB	—	—
	Arturo 2000	2000	2	FFT	—	—
	Arturo 4000/6000	4000	4	FFT	—	—
		6000	4	FDB	—	—

Table A.3 Open Face Fixtures

		Watts	Bulbs	Scrim	Chimera Ring Size
Arri					
	Arrilite 600	600	DYS	5"	5-1/8"
		250	DYG		
	Arrilite 650	650	FAD	7-1/4"	7-1//4" *
	Arrilite 1000	1000	DXW	7-1/4"	7-1/4" *
	Arrilite 2000	2000	FEY	10"	10"
Desisti					
	Minilite 1000	1000	FHM	—	—
Lee Colortran					
	Mino Pro Broad	650	FAD	—	—

Table A.3   Open Face Fixtures (continued)

	Watts	*Bulbs*	*Scrim*	*Chimera Ring Size*
Mini-Broad	650	FAD	—	—
Broad	1000	FHM	—	—
Mini-lite Nook	1000	FHM	—	—
Set Light Nook	1000	FHM	—	—
Lowel				
Pro-light	125	FSH	Special	Special*
	250	GCA		
	200	GCB		
	100	GCC		
V-light	500	GDA	Special	Special*
Toto-light	300	EHZ	Special	Special*
	500	FCZ		
	750	EMD		
Omni-light	420	EKB	Special	Special*
	600	DYS		
DP Light	500	EHC	Special	Special*
	1000	FEL		
LTM				
Pepper 650 Flood	650	FRK	6"	6"
Mole Richardson				
Teenie Weenie	600	EKD	5-1/8"	5-1/8"
Teenie Mole	650	FAD	6-1/4"	6" *
Mickey-Mole	1000	DXW	7-3/16"	7-1/4"
Mighty	2000	FEY	10"	10"
1k Broad	1000	FHM	8-1/2" x 12"	—
2k Super Broad	2000	FFW	10-1/4" x 12"	—
650 Nooklite	650	FAD	—	—
1k Nooklite	1000	FCM	—	—
2k Nooklite	2000	FEY	—	—
1k Molette	1000	FCV	—	—
2k Molette	2000	BWG	—	—
Sachtler				
Reporter 20	20, 70	—	—	—
Reporter 50	30, 50	—	—	—
Reporter 100	100	—	—	—
Reporter 250	250	—	—	—
Reporter 300	150, 300	—	—	—
Reporter 650	650	—	—	—
Reporter 1000	1000	—	—	—
Strand Quartz Color				
Pulsar 600	600	DYS	—	Special*
Ianabeam 650 "Redhead"	650	FAD	7-1/4	Special*
Ianabeam 1000 "Redhead"	1000	DXW	7-1/4	Special*
Ianabeam 2000 "Blonde"	2000	FEY	10"	10-5/8"

* Fixture takes a dedicated nonstandard Chimera ring. See Chimera tables in Table H.2.

Table A.4   PAR Fixtures

	Watts	Bulb	Weight	Scrim
ETC				
Source Four Par	575	HPL575	7.5 lbs	7.5"
Mole Richardson				
Molepar	1000	PAR 64	4-3/4 lbs	10-1/8"
PAR CAN	1000	PAR 64	4-1/2 lbs	10"
Lee Colortran				
Cine-Queen	1000	PAR 64	—	9"

	Heads	Watts	Bulb	Weight
Mole Richardson				
Molefay	1 x 650	650	PAR 36	2-1/4 lbs
2-light	2 x 650	1300	PAR 36	9 lbs
4-light	4 x 650	2600	PAR 36	10-1/2 lbs
6-light	6 x 650	3600	PAR 36	17 lbs
9-light	9 x 650	5400	PAR 36	29-1/2 lbs
12-light	12 x 650	7800	PAR 36	26-1/2 lbs
5-light	5 x 650	3250	PAR 36	10 lbs
3-light obie	3 x 650	1950	PAR 36	4-1/2 lbs
6-light	6 x 1000	6000	PAR 64	45-1/2 lbs
9-light	9 x 1000	9000	PAR 64	63-1/2 lbs
24-light	24 x 1000	24000	PAR 64	131 lbs
Molecool	1 x 600	600	DYS	3-1/4 lbs
		250	DYG	
2-light	2 x 600	1200	DYS	9 lbs
9-light	9 x 600	5400	DYS	29-1/4 lbs
Ultra Light Mfg.				
24-lt. Dino	24 x 1000	24k	PAR 64	—
30-lt. Dino	30 x 1000	30k	PAR 64	—
Ultra Dino	36 x 1000	36k	PAR 64	190 lbs

Color temperature, beam angle, and intensity depend on the globe used. See bulb data in Appendix E.

Source Four Par uses interchangeable, rotatable lenses (Clear, VNSP, NSP, MFL, and WFL). Lumen output is equivalent to 1k PARs with smoother, rounder beam. Optional MCM reflector removes 90% of heat from beam.

Molepar accessories include intensifier and dichroic daylight conversion filter.

Table A.5 HMI Fresnels

	Globe	Lens	Scrim	Chimera Ring Size	Head Weight
Altman					
575 SE	575 SE	5"	7-3/4"	7-5/8"	16
1200 SE	1200 SE	7"	9"	9-5/8"	17
2500 SE	2500 SE	10"	13"	13-1/2"	38
4000 SE	4000 SE	12"	15-1/2"	16-1/8"	65
Arri					
200W	200	4.3"	5-1/4	—	5.5 lbs
200 SE	200 SE	4.3"	6-5/8"	6-1/2"	8 lbs
575W	575	6.9"	8.5"	8-1/2"	18 lbs
Compact 575W	575 SE	5.1"	7-3/4	7-5/8"	12 lbs
1200W	1200	11.8"	13"	12-3/4"	35 lbs
Compact 1200W	1200 SE	6.9"	9"	9-5/8"	20 lbs
2500W	2500	13.8"	16"	15-1/2"	66 lbs
Compact 2500W	2500 SE	10"	13"	13-1/2"	31 lbs
4000W	4000	19.7"	21"	21"	95 lbs
Compact 4000W	4000 SE	11.8"	15.5"	16-1/8"	49 lbs
6000W	6000	19.7"	21"	21"	96 lbs
Daylight 6000	6000	19.7"	21"	21"	85 lbs
Daylight 12000	12000	19.7"	21"	21"	137 lbs
Cinimills					
12k Silver Bullet	12k	24"	29"	29"	135 lbs
18k Silver Bullet	18k	24"	29"	29"	150 lbs
Desisti					
Rembrandt 200	200 SE	4.8"	6"	6"	5.29
Piccolo 575	575 SE	6"	7-1/4"	7-3/8"	15.21
Rembrandt 575	575	6"	7-1/4"	7-3/8"	—
Piccolo 1200	1200/SE	6"	7-1/4"	7-3/8"	18.74
Rembrandt 1200 SE	1200/SE	10"	12"	12-3/8"	27.78
Rembrandt 1200	1200	10"	12"	12-3/8"	—
Piccolo 2500	2500/SE	10"	12"	12-3/8"	33
Rembrandt 2500	2500	12"	15-1/2"	15-3/4"	—
Rembrandt 4000	4000	14"	15-1/2"	15-3/4"	—
Piccolo 6000	6000 SE	14"	15-1/2"	15-1/2"	—
Rembrandt 6000	6000	14"	15-1/2"	15-3/4"	—
Rembrandt 12k	12k	20"	24-1/4"	24-1/2"	117 lbs
Rembrandt 18k	18k	24"	—	26-1/2"	148 lbs
Mole Richardson					
575W Solarspot	575 SE	6"	6-5/8"	6-5/8"	11.25 lbs
1,200W Solarspot	1200W SE	8"	9"	9	20.25 lbs
2,500W Solarspot	2500W SE	9-7/8"	13-1/2"	12"	28 lbs
6,000W Solarspot	6000W SE	14"	18-1/2"	18-1/2"	31 lbs
12k Solar-arc Solarspot	12k	24-3/4"	29"	29"	150 lbs
18k Solar-arc Solarspot	18k	24-3/4"	29"	29"	125 lbs
LTM					
Bonzia 200 SE*	200 SE	3-1/8"	4-1/4"	4-1/4"	3.3 lbs
Luxarc 200	200	5"	6-5/8"	6-5/8"	6 lbs
Luxarc 575	575	7"	9"	9"	12 lbs
Luxarc 1200	1200	10"	12"	12"	22 lbs
Luxarc 2500	2500	12"	15-1/2"	15-3/4"	50 lbs

Table A.5 HMI Fresnels (continued)

	Globe	Lens	Scrim	Chimera Ring Size	Head Weight
Luxarc 4000	4000	14"	18-3/8"	18-1/2	58 lbs
Luxarc 6000	6000	20"	21-1/2"	21"	105 lbs
Super Lite 12k	12k	24"	29"	29"	125 lbs
Luxarc 18K	18k	24"	29"	29"	130 lbs
Super 12/18k	12k or 18k	24"	29"	29"	143 lbs
Sachler					
Director 125D	123W/SE	3"	5-1/4"	5-1/4"	4.4 lbs
Director 270D	250W/SE	5"	7-5/8"	7-5/8"	10-3/4 lbs
Director 575D	575 SE	6"	8-1/2"	8-1/2"	14 lbs
Director 1200D	1200SE	8"	12"	12"	—
Director 2500D	2500SE	10"	13.5"	13.5"	—
Director 4000C	4000SE	10"	13.5"	13.5"	—
Director 4000D	4000SE	12"	13.5"	13.5"	—
Strand Color Quartz					
575 Sirio	575	6"	9"	9"	24 lbs
1200 Sirio	1200	10"	12-3/4"	12-3/4"	44 lbs
2500 Sirio	2500	12"	16"	15-3/4"	58.5 lbs
Supernova 25/12	2.5k/1200 SE	10"	13-1/2"	13-1/2"	36 lbs
Spernova 40/25	4k or 2.5k SE	12"	16"	15-3/4"	43 lbs
4000 Sirio	4000	14"	16"	15-3/4"	72 lbs
6000 Sirio	6000	14"	16"	15-3/4"	68 lbs
12kW Sirio	12kW	20"	29"	29"	187 lbs
Sunray					
Sunray 12/18k Combo	12kw or 18 kw	24"	29"	29"	138 lbs

* Can operate on 30V battery with special DC electronic ballast.

Table A.6 HMI PAR and SE PAR Fixtures

	Globe	Scrim	Chimera Ring Size	Head Weight	Lens	Beam Angle	Candela
Arri							
Arrisun 5 PAR	575 PAR	—		11 lbs	Very narrow spot	14° x 8°	450,000
					Narrow spot	14° x 10°	400,000
					Medium flood	26° x 12°	150,000
					Wide flood	50° x 45°	25,000
Arrisun 1200W PAR	1200 PAR	—	10"	19 lbs	Very narrow spot	14° x 7°	1,800,000
					Narrow spot	11° x 8°	1,300,800
					Medium flood	22° x 10°	600,000
					Wide flood	54° x 19°	169,600
Arrisun 12 plus	1200 SE	13"	13-1/2"	25 lbs	Super spot	3.5°	5,625,000
					Spot	6.5°	2,5000,000
					Medium	12° x 20.5°	192,000
					Super wide	21° x 47°	110,000
					Frosted Fresnel	39°	53,250
Arrisun 40/25 2500W Bulb	2500 SE	15.5"	16-1/8"	43 lbs	Super spot	5°	8,750,000
					Spot	8.5	3,375,000
					Medium	11° x 20°	1,800,000
					Wide	11° x 44°	450,000
					Super wide	48°	200,000
					Frosted Fresnel	18°	202,500
Arrisun 40/25 4000W Bulb	4000 SE	15.5"	16-1/8"	43 lbs	Super spot	4.5°	10,500,000
					Spot	10°	4,500,000
					Medium wide	12° x 21°	2,150,000
					Wide	19° x 45°	600,000
					Super wide	50°	250,000
					Frosted Fresnel	22°	270,000
Arrisun 60	6000 SE	19.5"	—	59 lbs	Super spot	7°	14,900,000
					Spot	10°	7,175,000
					Medium	11° x 20°	3,375,000
					Wide	20° x 38°	1,225,000
					Super wide	42°	675,000
					Frosted Fresnel	37°	337,500

Table A.6 HMI PAR and SE PAR Fixtures (continued)

	Globe	Scrim	Chimera Ring Size	Head Weight	Lens	Beam Angle	Candela
LTM							
Cinepar 200S/E	200 SE	6-5/8"	6"	2.4 lbs	VNSP, NSP, MF, WF	—	—
Cinepar 200	200W PAR	6-5/8"	6"	4 lbs	NSP, M, WF, WF		
Cinepar 575 S/E	575 S/E	6-5/8"	6-5/8"	7 lbs	NSP , MF, SWF, FF	—	—
Cinepar 575	575 PAR	7-1/4"	7-1/4"	8 lbs	VNSP, M, WF , SWF		
Cinepar 1200 S/E	1200 SE	9"	9"	16 lbs	VNSP	4°	4,601,600
					MF	25° x 12°	490,800
					WF	54° x 21°	131,300
					SWF	53°	72,100
Cinepar 1200	1200 PAR	9"	9"	13 lbs	VNSP	12° x 6°	2,000,000
					NSP	12° x 8°	1,375,000
					MF	23° x 9°	805,100
					WF	54° x 22°	198,800
					SWF	64°	89,400
Cinepar 2500 S/E	2500/SE	13"	12-3/4"	32 lbs	VNSP	6°	5,832,000
					NSP	8°	2,592,000
					MF	27° x 11°	856,000
					WF	60° x 25°	222,400
					SWF	54°	124,800
Cinepar 4000 S/E	4000/SE	15-1/2"	15-3/4"	40 lbs	VNSP	5°	10,530,000
					M	23° x 10°	1,260,000
					WF	38° x 15°	540,000
					SWF	20°	261,000
					FF	33°	180,000
Cinepar 6000 S/E	6000S/E	19-1/2"	—	48.5 lbs	M, WF, SWF, FF	—	—

VNSP: very narrow spot; MF: medium flood; WF: wide flood; SWF: super wide flood; FF: frosted fresnel.

Table A.6 HMI PAR and SE PAR Fixtures (continued)

	Globe	Scrim	Chimera Ring Size	Head Weight
Cinimillis				
200W Wallylight	200PAR	7.25"	7-1/8"	11.5 lbs
200W SE	200 SE	7.25"	7-1/8"	6 lbs
575W SE	575 SE	7.25"	7-1/8"	12.5 lbs
1200W PAR	1200 PAR	10"	9"	16 lbs
1200W SE	1200 SE	10"	10-1/8"	16 lbs
2500W SE	2500 SE	13.5"	13-1/2"	24.5 lbs
4000W SE	4000 SE	13.5"	13-1/2"	24.5 lbs
6000W SE	6000 SE	13.5"	16-1/8"	—
Desisti				
Remington 200	200 SE	—	—	—
Caravaggio 575	575 PAR	—	7-3/8"	—
Caravaggio 1200	1200 PAR	—	—	19 lbs
Remington 2.5/4k	2500 SE			
	4000 SE	—	—	—
Remington Piccolo 6k	6000 SE	—	—	—
DN Labs				
575 Durapar PAR	575 PAR	7.5"	7-7/8"	10 lbs
575 Durapar SE	575 SE	10"	—	15 lbs
1200 Durapar PAR	1200 PAR	10"	10-1/8"	13 lbs
1200 Durapar SE	1200 SE	12"	12"	21 lbs
2500 Durapar SE	2500 SE	12"	12"	21 lbs
10kW Durapar				
(4-light cluster)	4 x 2500 SE	—	—	82 lbs
40kW Durapar				
(16-light cluster)	16 x 2500 SE	—	—	338 lbs
4000W Durapar	4000 SE	16"	15-3/4"	33 lbs
6000 SE Durapar	6000 SE	16"	15-3/4"	48 lbs
6000 DE Durapar	6000W DE	22" x 25"	—	65 lbs
12kW Durapar	12kW DE	22" x 25"	—	80 lbs
K 5600				
Joker 200*	200W SE	5"	5"	4.4 lbs
Joker 400	400W SE	6-5/8"	6-5/8"	5.2 lbs
Joker 1200	1200W SE	9"	9"	12 lbs
Mole Richardson				
200 Molepar	200 PAR	6-1/4"	6"	7.5 lbs
575 Molepar	575 PAR	7-3/16"	7-1/4"	10 lbs
1200 Molepar	1200 PAR	10-1/8"	10"	13 lbs
1,200 Molepar	1200 SE	10-1/8"	10"	15 lbs
2,500 Molepar	2500 SE	12"	12"	27 lbs
4,000W Molepar	4000W SE	13-1/2"	13-1/2"	28.5 lbs
6,000W Molepar	6000W SE	15-1/2"	—	39 lbs
Sachtler				
Production 575D	575 SE	6"	9"	14 lbs
Production 1200D	1200 SE	8"	9.5"	—

Table A.6 HMI PAR and SE PAR Fixtures (continued)

	Globe	Scrim	Chimera Ring Size	Head Weight
Sunray				
575 PAR	575 PAR	7-1/4" 12"**	7-3/8"	3 lbs
575 SE Par	575/SE	7-1/4" 12"**	7-3/8"	11 lbs
1200 PAR	1200 PAR	10" 15-1/2"**	10-1/8"	10 lbs
1200 SE Par	1200/SE	10" 15-1/2"**	10-1/8"	15 lbs
2500W SE	2500/SE	10" 15-1/2"**	10-1/8"	20 lbs
4000W SE	4000 SE	15-1/2" 21"**	15-1/2"	30 lbs
Strand Quartz Color				
Quasar 12	1200 PAR	10-3/16"	10-5/8"	19.8 lbs
Super Quasar 25/12	2500 SE or 1200 SE	10-3/16"	10-5/8"	34 lbs
Super Quasar 40/25	4000 SE or 2500 SE	12-5/8"	12-3/4"	44 lbs

* Can operate on 30V batteries with 200W Slimverter inverter.
** With intensifier.

Table A.7 HMI Sun Guns

	Globe	Scrim	Chimera Ring Size	Power Supply
Desisti				
Tiziano		—	6"	24-30 VDC Electronic Ballast 120VAC Mains Adaptor
Remington 200	200W SE	—	—	24-30 VDC Electronic Ballast 120VAC Mains Adaptor
DN Labs				
200 PAR	200 PAR	—	5-1/4"	—
LTM				
Sungun 200S/E	200W SE	5-7/8"	6"	DC Ballast: 30V electronic AC Ballast: 100-260V auto
Blue Torch 270	250W SE	5-7/8"	6"	DC Ballast: 24-30V AC Ballast: 110V
Bonzai 200 S/E	200W SE	4-1/2"	4-1/4"	DC Ballast: 20-30V AC Ballast: 120-250V
Sachtler				
Reporter 125D	123W SE	5-1/4"	5-1/4"	—
Reporter 270D	250W SE	7-5/8"	7-5/8"	—
Production 575D	575W SE	8-1/2"	8-1/2"	—
Production 1200D	1200W SE	12"	12"	—

Table A.8 Other HMI Fixtures

Description	Manufacturer	Name	Globe	Dimensions	Weight
Chickencoop	Cinemills	4000W/2500W	2500W DE 4000W DE	49" x 39"	55 lbs
Softlights	Desisti	Raffaello 575	575W DE	12-5/8" x 15"	20.5 lbs
	Desisti	Raffaello 1200	1200W DE	12-5/8" x 19"	24.5 lbs
	Desisti	Raffaello 2500	2500W DE	17"x 24-3/4"	50.2 lbs
	LTM	Softarc 575	575W DE	14" x 20-1/4"	18 lbs
	LTM	Sofarc 1200	1200W DE	19" x 30"	31 lbs
	DN Labs	Durapar 200T	—	—	—
Scoop	DN Labs	Spectra-Flux 1200	1200 SE	21" round	21 lbs
Bare bulb in Pyrex tube used for Chinese Lantern	K 5600	Bug Light	200W SE	Pyrex Tube	3.5 lbs
Open Face. 130° spread.	Desisti	Goya 1200 Shadowlight	1200W SE	—	—
Can be used in any orientation	Desisti	Goya 2500/4000 Shadowlight	2500 SE 4000 SE	20" x 22"	37 lbs

Table A.9 Mole Richardson Studio Arc Fixtures

	Grid Input Watts	Amps	Volts	Carbon Dimensions (in.)	In/hr.	Head Lens	Scrim	Weight
150	18k	150	120 DC	Pos .63 x 25 Neg 11/16 x 9	9" 4-1/2"	—	—	181 lbs
Baby Brute	27k	225	120 DC	Pos .63 x 22 Neg 17/32 x 6-3/4	20" 10	14"	18-1/2"	126 lbs
Litweight Brute	27k	225	120 DC	Pos .63 x 22 Neg 17/32 x 6-1/4	20 10	24-3/4"	29"	152 lbs
Brute	27k	225	120 DC	Pos .63 x 22 Neg 17/32 x 920	20 10	—	—	225 lbs
Titan	42k	350	120 DC	Pos .63 x 25 Neg 11/16 x 920	20 10	—	—	250 lbs

Table A.10 Fluorescent Fixtures

Fixture	Lamps	Lamp Length	Bulb Type	Dimensions of Face (in.)	Weight (lbs)	Ballast
Lowel						
Light Array	6	4 ft.	T-12	30 x 54	18	Detatchable, flicker-free
Mole Richardson						
Eight-tube, 18 in.	8	18 in.	T-12	16.4 x 19	25.25	Built-in, conventional
Four-tube, 4 ft.	4	4 ft.	T-12	21.75 x 55.25	42.74	Built-in, conventional
Leonetti Sunray						
Four-tube, 4 ft.	4	4 ft.	T-12	8 x 48	23	Flicker-free
Eight-tube, 4 ft.	8	4 ft.	T-12	16 x 48	36	Flicker-free
LTM						
Mini Moonlight	2	18 in.	Osram FT 36 DL/835 (3200K) Philips PL-L 36W/95 (5100K)	2 x 18	—	Built-in, flicker-free
Moonlight Single	6	18 in.	Osram FT 36 DL/835 (3200K) Philips PL-L 36W/95 (5100K)	18 x 18	25	Built-in, flicker-free
Moonlight Double	12	18 in.	Osram FT 36 DL/835 (3200K) Philips PL-L 36W/95 (5100K)	36 x 18	50	Built-in, flicker-free
Moonlight Triple	18	18 in.	Osram FT 36 DL/835 (3200K) Philips PL-L 36W/95 (5100K)	54 x 18	75	Built-in, flicker-free
Moonlight Quadruple	24	18 in.	Osram FT 36 DL/835 (3200K) Philips PL-L 36W/95 (5100K)	36 x 36	100	Built-in, flicker-free
Moonlight Sextuple	36	18 in.	Osram FT 36 DL/835 (3200K) Philips PL-L 36W/95 (5100K)	36 x 54	150	Built-in, flicker-free

Table A.11 Kino Flo Fixtures

Name	Length	Tubes	Ballast	Mount	Weight (lbs)	Amps	Volts	Lamp	Output at 6 ft. (fc)
Portable Fixture Systems									
Four Bank	4-ft.	4	Stnd, Slct, Dim	3/8 stud	10.5	5	117VAC	F40/T12	80
	2-ft	4	Stnd, Slct, Dim	3/8 stud	6.5	3.5	117 VAC	F20/T12	45
	15-in.	4	Stnd, Slct, Dim	3/8 stud	5	2.5	117 VAC	F14/T12	25
Two Bank	4-ft.	2	Stnd, Slct, Dim	3/8 stud	7	2.6	117 VAC	F40/T12	53
	2-ft.	2	Stnd, Slct, Dim	3/8 stud	4	1.8	117 VAC	F20/T12	23
	15-in.	2	Stnd, Slct, Dim	3/8 stud	3	1.4	117 VAC	F14/T12	14
Single	4-ft.	1	Stnd, Slct, Dim	3/8 stud	4	1.3	117 VAC	F40/T12	25
	2-ft.	1	Stnd, Slct, Dim	3/8 stud	2	0.9	117 VAC	F20/T12	10
	15-in.	1	Stnd, Slct, Dim	3/8 stud	1.5	0.7	117 VAC	F14/T12	6
Wall-O-Lite	4-ft.	10	Built-in	Jr. stud	47	12	117 VAC	F40/T12	180
Four Bank	8-ft.	4	Mega	—	—	—	117 VAC		—
	6-ft.	4	Mega	—	—	—	117 VAC		—
Two Bank	8-ft.	4	Mega	—	—	—	117 VAC		—
	6-ft.	4	Mega	—	—	—	117 VAC		—
Single	8-ft.	4	Mega, Slimline	—	—	—	117 VAC		—
	6-ft.	4	Mega, Slimline	—	—	—	117 VAC		—
12V DC Systems									
12V Single	4-ft.	1	12VDC Single	3/8 stud	-	4.5	12VDC	F40/T12	—
	2-ft.	1	12VDC Single	3/8 stud	-	2.6	12VDC	F20/T12	—
	15-in.	1	12VDC Single	3/8 stud	15 oz.	2.3	12VDC	F14/T12	—
Mini-flo	9-in.	1	Mini-flo 12VDC	—	8 oz.	.8	12VDC	F6/T5	—
Micro-flo	6-in.	—	Micro-flo 12VDC	—	—	—	12VDC		—
Micro-flo	4-in.	—	Micro-flo 12VDC	—	—	—	12VDC		—
Studio Fixtures									
Image 80	4-ft.	8	Built-in	Jr. stud	29	10	117 VAC	F40/T12	155
Image 40	4-ft.	4	Built-in	Jr. stud	14	5	117 VAC	F40/T12	78
Image 20	2-ft.	4	Built-in	Jr. stud	6	1.8	117 VAC	F20/T12	45
Trans-Panel Modules									
Trans-panel	4-ft.	12	Built-in	Hooks	50	2.1	117 VAC	F40/T12	—

Ballast types: Standard (Stnd), Select (Slct), Dimmable (Dim), Mega-ballasts and Slimline (8-ft. and 6-ft. lamps). 12VDC ballasts come with transformer for use with 120VAC or 220VAC service.

Table A.12 Ellipsoidal Reflector Spotlights

Fixture	Field Angle	Multiplier	Candle Power (cd)	Lamp	K	Watts	Weight (lbs.)	Gel Frame (in.)
Altman								
			Flat Field Data					
Shakespeare 50	50°	.93	27,500	FLK (HX600)	3200	575	18	6-1/4"
Shakespeare 40	40°	.73	43,500	"	"	"	18	6-1/4"
Shakespeare 30	30°	.54	104,000	"	"	"	18	6-1/4"
Shakespeare 20	20°	.35	119,000	"	"	"	18	6-1/4"
Shakespeare 10	10°	.17	265,000	"	"	"	30	6-1/4"
Shakespeare 1535Z	15°–35°	.26–.63	233k–58k	"	"	"	30	7-1/2"
Shakespeare 3055Z	30°–55°	.54–1.04	74k–23.5k	"	"	"	30	7-1/2"
ETC								
			Flat Field Data					
Source Four 450	50°	.93	34,866	HPL 575	3250	575	16	6-1/4"
Source Four 436	36°	.65	84,929	"	"	"	16.3	6-1/4"
Source Four 426	26°	.46	138,079	"	"	"	16	6-1/4"
Source Four 419	19°	.31	167,435	"	"	"	16	6-1/4"
Source Four 410	10.3	.178	800,300	"	"	"	16.3	12"
Source Four 405	6.8	.119	996,000	"	"	"	17.5	14"
Altman								
			Peak Field Data					
Micro-Elipse	—			MR-16 EYC/EYJ	3050	75	5	3-3/8"
3.5Q 3.5 x 5	48°	.89	12,000	EHD	3000	500	9	4-1/8"
3.5 x 6	38°	.69	15,200	"	"	"	9	4-1/8"
3.5 x 8	28°	.50	16,000	"	"	"	9	4-1/8"
3.5 x 10	23°	.41	17,200	"	"	"	9	4-1/8"
3.5 x 12	18°	.32	20,000	"	"	"	9	4-1/8"
4.5-1530 Baby zoom	15°–30°	.26–.54	88k–55k	EHF	3200	750	15	6-1/4"
4.5-2550 Baby zoom	25°–50°	.44–.93	80k–40k	"	"	"	15	6-1/4"
4.5-3060 Baby zoom	30°–60°	.55–1.15	50k–26k	"	"	"	15	6-1/4"

Table A.12 Ellipsoidal Reflector Spotlights (continued)

Fixture	Field Angle	Multiplier	Candle Power (cd)	Lamp	K	Watts	Weight (lbs.)	Gel Frame (in.)
360Q 4.5 x 6.5	56°	1.06	51,200	EHF	3200	750	13.5	7-1/2"
6 x 9	35°	.63	88,000	"	"	"	14	7-1/2"
6 x 12	25°	.44	152,000	"	"	"	15	7-1/2"
6 x 16	21°	.37	184,000	"	"	"	15	7-1/2"
6 x 22	11°	.19	216,000		"	"	15	7-1/2"
Altman			*Peak Field Data*					
1KL6-12	12°	.21	342,400	FEL	3200	1k	24	7-1/2"
1KL6-20	20°	.35	257,600	"	"	"	25	7-1/2"
1KL6-30	30°	.54	195,200	"	"	"	24	7-1/2"
1KL6-40	40°	.73	148,800	"	"	"	25	7-1/2"
1KL6-50	50°	.93	97,600	"	"	"	24	7-1/2"
1KL8-10	10°	.17	490,000	"	"	"	26	10"
1KJL 10-5	5°	.09	1,008,000	"	"	"	32	12"
1KL6-2040Z	20°–40°	.35–.73	275k–85k	"	"	"	28	7-1/2"
1KL8-1424Z	14°–24°	.25–.43	489k–262k	"	"	"	34	10"
Colortran			*Peak Field Data*					
5/50 Series 650-012	50°	.93	28,700	FEL	3200	1k		
5/50 Series 650-022	40°	.73	48,000	"	"	"		
5/50 Series 650-032	30°	.54	118,000	"	"	"		
5/50 Series 650-042	20°	.35	171,000	"	"	"		
5/50 Series 650-052	15°	.26	298,000	"	"	"		
5/50 Series 650-072	10°	.17	563,000	"	"	"		
5/50 Series 650-082	5°	.09	938,000	"	"	"		

Table A.12 Ellipsoidal Reflector Spotlights (continued)

Fixture	Field Angle	Multiplier	Candle Power (cd)	Lamp	K	Watts	Weight (lbs.)	Gel Frame (in.)
Colortran								
			Peak Field Data					
Mini-zoom 213-302	40°–65°	1.27–.73	32k–8.9k	FMR	3000	600		
Mini-zoom 213-312	25°–50°	.44–.93	49k–18.3k	"	"	"		
Mini-zoom 213-322	15°–30°	.26–.54	61k–44.5k	"	"	"		
Mini Ellipse 213-152	50°	.93	9,000	EVR	3000	500		
Mini Ellipse 213-152	40°	.73	16,500	"	"	"		
Mini Ellipse 213-152	30°	.54	24,000	"	"	"		
Ellipsoid 213-052	40°	.73	48,000	FEL	3200	1k		
Ellipsoid 213-062	30°	.54	118,000	"	"	"		
Ellipsoid 213-072	20°	.35	171,000	"	"	"		
Ellipsoid 213-092	12°	.21	298,000	"	"	"		
Ellipsoid 213-102	10°	.17	563,000	"	"	"		
Ellipsoid 213-112	5°	.09	938,000	"	"	"		
Ellipse Zoom 213-162	15°–35°	.26–0.63	206k–82k	"	"	"		
Strand								
			Peak Field Data					
Quartet PC	7.5°–55.5°	.13–1.05	64,000	FRK	3200	650	7.3	6"
Quartet 25	25°	.44	36,000	"	"	"	10.5	6"
Quartet 22/44	22°–44°	.39–.81	408,000	"	"	"	10.6	6"
Leko 15	15°	.26	190,800	FEL	3200	1k	17	7.5"
Leko 20	20°	.35	185,000	"	"	1k	13.2	7.5"
Leko 30	30°	.54	449,850	"	"	1k	13.2	7.5"
Leko 40	40°	.73	118,825	"	"	1k	13.2	7.5"
Leko 50	50°	.93	63,000	"	"	1k	13.2	7.5"
8" Leko	12°	.21	582,400	FEL	"	1k	22	10"
10" Leko	9°	.15	880,000	"	"	1k	26	11-3/4"
4-1/2" Variable Focus	25°–50°	.44–.93	24,698	EVR	"	500	15	6-1/4"

Table A.12 Ellipsoidal Reflector Spotlights (continued)

Fixture	Field Angle	Multiplier	Candle Power (cd)	Lamp	K	Watts	Weight (lbs.)	Gel Frame (in.)
6" Variable Focus	15°–40°	.26–.73	92,800	FEL	"	1k	27	7-1/2"
Cantata 11/26	11°–26°	.19–.46	265,000	FEL	"	1k	28	7-1/2"
Cantata 18/32	18°–32°	.32–.57	165,000	"	"	"	26.5	7-1/2"
Cantata 26/44	26°–44°	.46–.81	108,800	"	"	"	24	7-1/2 "
Optique 8/17	8°–17°	.17–.30	395,000	T–29	"	1200	28	7-1/2 "
Optique 15/42	15°–42°	.26–.77	119,790	"	"	"	28	7-1/2"
Alto 8/16 (2k)	8°–16°	.14–.28	595,200	CP92	"	2k	37.5	9.6"
Alto 14/32 (2k)	14°–32°	.25–.57	357,192	"	"	"	37.5	9.6"
Alto 20/38 (2k)	20°–38°	.35–.69	207,500	"	"	"	35	9.6"
Toccata 10/26	10°–26°	.17–.46	605,756	CP92	"	2k	45.2	9.6"
Toccata 15/38	15°–38°	.26–.69	348,480	"	"	"	43.56	9.6"

Lamp intensities for ETC Source Four and Altman Shakespeare fixtures are *cosine flat field* candle power. All others are *peak* candle power. Comparing the two is misleading because peak readings tend to exaggerate performance.

Altman 360Q lamps are manufactured with either a bi-pin base, or a mini-can base. The bi-pin bulb type is listed here.

Each fixture can take a variety of bulbs. The highest wattage bulb is shown here. See Table E.3 for bulb substitutions.

To determine beam width, multiply *multiplier* by distance.

To determine footcandle level, divide candle-power by distance squared, or use Table A.14.

Table A.13 Beam Diameter (in feet) at Various Distances

Beam Angle Degree	Multiplier	Distance in Feet												
		5	10	15	20	25	30	40	50	75	100	150	200	250
2	0.03	0.2	0.3	0.5	0.7	0.9	1.0	1.4	1.7	2.6	3.5	5.2	7.0	8.7
4	0.07	0.3	0.7	1.0	1.4	1.7	2.1	2.8	3.5	5.2	7.0	10.5	14.0	17.5
6	0.10	0.5	1.0	1.6	2.1	2.6	3.1	4.2	5.2	7.9	10.5	15.7	21.0	26.2
8	0.14	0.7	1.4	2.1	2.8	3.5	4.2	5.6	7.0	10.5	14.0	21.0	28.0	35.0
10	0.17	0.9	1.7	2.6	3.5	4.4	5.2	7.0	8.7	13.1	17.5	26.2	35.0	43.7
12	0.21	1.1	2.1	3.2	4.2	5.3	6.3	8.4	10.5	15.8	21.0	31.5	42.0	52.6
14	0.25	1.2	2.5	3.7	4.9	6.1	7.4	9.8	12.3	18.4	24.6	36.8	49.1	61.4
16	0.28	1.4	2.8	4.2	5.6	7.0	8.4	11.2	14.1	21.1	28.1	42.2	56.2	70.3
18	0.32	1.6	3.2	4.8	6.3	7.9	9.5	12.7	15.8	23.8	31.7	47.5	63.4	79.2
20	0.35	1.8	3.5	5.3	7.1	8.8	10.6	14.1	17.6	26.4	35.3	52.9	70.5	88.2
22	0.39	1.9	3.9	5.8	7.8	9.7	11.7	15.6	19.4	29.2	38.9	58.3	77.8	97.2
24	0.43	2.1	4.3	6.4	8.5	10.6	12.8	17.0	21.3	31.9	42.5	63.8	85.0	106.3
26	0.46	2.3	4.6	6.9	9.2	11.5	13.9	18.5	23.1	34.6	46.2	69.3	92.3	115.4
28	0.50	2.5	5.0	7.5	10.0	12.5	15.0	19.9	24.9	37.4	49.9	74.8	99.7	124.7
30	0.54	2.7	5.4	8.0	10.7	13.4	16.1	21.4	26.8	40.2	53.6	80.4	107.2	134.0
32	0.57	2.9	5.7	8.6	11.5	14.3	17.2	22.9	28.7	43.0	57.3	86.0	114.7	143.4
34	0.61	3.1	6.1	9.2	12.2	15.3	18.3	24.5	30.6	45.9	61.1	91.7	122.3	152.9
36	0.65	3.2	6.5	9.7	13.0	16.2	19.5	26.0	32.5	48.7	65.0	97.5	130.0	162.5
38	0.69	3.4	6.9	10.3	13.8	17.2	20.7	27.5	34.4	51.6	68.9	103.3	137.7	172.2
40	0.73	3.6	7.3	10.9	14.6	18.2	21.8	29.1	36.4	54.6	72.8	109.2	145.6	182.0
42	0.77	3.8	7.7	11.5	15.4	19.2	23.0	30.7	38.4	57.6	76.8	115.2	153.5	191.9
44	0.81	4.0	8.1	12.1	16.2	20.2	24.2	32.3	40.4	60.6	80.8	121.2	161.6	202.0
46	0.85	4.2	8.5	12.7	17.0	21.2	25.5	34.0	42.4	63.7	84.9	127.3	169.8	212.2
48	0.89	4.5	8.9	13.4	17.8	22.3	26.7	35.6	44.5	66.8	89.0	133.6	178.1	222.6
50	0.93	4.7	9.3	14.0	18.7	23.3	28.0	37.3	46.6	69.9	93.3	139.9	186.5	233.2
52	0.98	4.9	9.8	14.6	19.5	24.4	29.3	39.0	48.8	73.2	97.5	146.3	195.1	243.9

Table A.13 Beam Diameter (in feet) at Various Distances (continued)

Beam Angle Degree	Multiplier	Distance in Feet												
		5	10	15	20	25	30	40	50	75	100	150	200	250
54	1.02	5.1	10.2	15.3	20.4	25.5	30.6	40.8	51.0	76.4	101.9	152.9	203.8	254.8
56	1.06	5.3	10.6	16.0	21.3	26.6	31.9	42.5	53.2	79.8	106.3	159.5	212.7	265.9
58	1.11	5.5	11.1	16.6	22.2	27.7	33.3	44.3	55.4	83.1	110.9	166.3	221.7	277.2
60	1.15	5.8	11.5	17.3	23.1	28.9	34.6	46.2	57.7	86.6	115.5	173.2	230.9	288.7
62	1.20	6.0	12.0	18.0	24.0	30.0	36.1	48.1	60.1	90.1	120.2	180.3	240.3	300.4
64	1.25	6.2	12.5	18.7	25.0	31.2	37.5	50.0	62.5	93.7	125.0	187.5	249.9	312.4
66	1.30	6.5	13.0	19.5	26.0	32.5	39.0	52.0	64.9	97.4	129.9	194.8	259.8	324.7
68	1.35	6.7	13.5	20.2	27.0	33.7	40.5	54.0	67.5	101.2	134.9	202.4	269.8	337.3
70	1.40	7.0	14.0	21.0	28.0	35.0	42.0	56.0	70.0	105.0	140.0	210.1	280.1	350.1
72	1.45	7.3	14.5	21.8	29.1	36.3	43.6	58.1	72.7	109.0	145.3	218.0	290.6	363.3
74	1.51	7.5	15.1	22.6	30.1	37.7	45.2	60.3	75.4	113.0	150.7	226.1	301.4	376.8
76	1.56	7.8	15.6	23.4	31.3	39.1	46.9	62.5	78.1	117.2	156.3	234.4	312.5	390.6
78	1.62	8.1	16.2	24.3	32.4	40.5	48.6	64.8	81.0	121.5	162.0	242.9	323.9	404.9
80	1.68	8.4	16.8	25.2	33.6	42.0	50.3	67.1	83.9	125.9	167.8	251.7	335.6	419.5
82	1.74	8.7	17.4	26.1	34.8	43.5	52.2	69.5	86.9	130.4	173.9	260.8	347.7	434.6
84	1.80	9.0	18.0	27.0	36.0	45.0	54.0	72.0	90.0	135.1	180.1	270.1	360.2	450.2

Simply multiply distance times multiplier to get diameter at any distance.

Table A.14 Brightness (in footcandles) of Fixtures at Various Distances

Fixture	Approximate Candella Range	Footcandles at Various Distances — Distance in Feet														
		5	10	15	20	25	30	40	50	60	70	80	90	100	150	200
100W Pepper: Flood	1,875–2,500	75	19	8	5	3	2	1								
750 Zip Soft	2,500–3,200	100	25	11	6	4	3	2	1							
200W Pepper: Flood	3,200–3,750	128	32	14	8	5	4	2	1							
1k Soft	3,750–5,000	150	38	17	9	6	4	2	2	1						
300W Pepper: Flood	5,000–6,400 same as above	200	50	22	13	8	6	3	2	1						
200W HMI Fresnel: Flood	6,400–7,500	256	64	28	16	10	7	4	3	2	1					
650W Fresnel: Flood	7,500–10,000	300	75	33	19	12	8	5	3	2	2	1				
2k Soft	10,000–12,500	400	100	44	25	16	11	6	4	3	2	2	1	1		
	12,500–15,000	500	125	56	31	20	14	8	5	3	3	2	2	2		
4k Soft	15,000–20,000	600	150	67	38	24	17	9	6	4	3	2	2	2	1	
1k Baby Fresnel: Flood	same as above															
1k Mickey Mole: Flood	same as above															
575W HMI Fresnel: Flood	20,000–25,000	800	200	89	50	32	22	13	8	6	4	3	2	2	1	
2k Mighty Mole: Flood	25,000–30,000	1,000	250	111	63	40	28	16	10	7	5	4	3	3	1	
8k Soft	30,000–40,000	1,200	300	133	75	48	33	19	12	8	6	5	4	3	1	
2k Arrlite/Blonde: Flood	40,000–50,000	1,600	400	178	100	64	44	25	16	11	8	6	5	4	2	1
1k PAR 64: WF	same as above															
2k 8" Jr. Fresnel: Flood	50,000–60,000	2,000	500	222	125	80	56	31	20	14	10	8	6	5	2	1
1200W HMI Fresnel: Flood	60,000–80,000	2,400	600	267	150	96	67	38	24	17	12	9	7	6	3	2
5k Baby Senior Fresnel: Flood	80,000–100,000	3,200	800	356	200	128	89	50	32	22	16	13	10	8	4	2
1200W HMI PAR: SWF	100,000–120,000	4,000	1,000	444	250	160	111	63	40	28	20	16	12	10	4	2
10k Baby Tenner Fresnel: Flood	120,000–160,000	4,800	1,200	533	300	192	133	75	48	33	24	19	15	12	5	3
1k Mickey Mole: Spot	same as above															
2500W HMI Fresnel: Flood	same as above															
2500W HMI SE PAR: SWF	same as above															
1k PAR 64: MF	same as above															
4000W HMI Fresnel: Flood	160,000–200,000	6,400	1,600	711	400	256	178	100	64	44	33	25	20	16	7	4
1200W HMI PARI: WF	same as above															
4000W HMI SE PAR: FF	same as above															
2k Mighty Mole: Spot	same as above															
2500W HMI SE PAR: WF	200,000–240,000	8,000	2,000	889	500	320	222	125	80	56	41	31	25	20	9	5

Table A.14 Brightness (in footcandles) of Fixtures at Various Distances (continued)

Fixture	Approximate Candella Range	Footcandles at Various Distances — Distance in Feet														
		5	10	15	20	25	30	40	50	60	70	80	90	100	150	200
4000W HMI SE PAR: SWF	240,000–320,000	9,600	2,400	1,067	600	384	267	150	96	67	49	38	30	24	11	6
6000W HMI Fresnel: Flood	320,000–400,000	12,800	3,200	1,422	800	512	356	200	128	89	65	50	40	32	14	8
6000W HMI SE PAR: FF	same as above															
1k PAR 64: NSP	same as above															
20k Fresnel: Flood	400,000–480,000	16,000	4,000	1,778	1,000	640	444	250	160	111	82	63	49	40	18	10
12k HMI Fresnel: Flood	480,000–640,000	19,200	4,800	2,133	1,200	768	533	300	192	133	98	75	59	48	21	12
4000W HMI SE PAR: WF	same as above															
1k PAR 64: VNSP	same as above															
18k HMI Fresnel: Flood	640,000–800,000	25,600	6,400	2,844	1,600	1,024	711	400	256	178	131	100	79	64	28	16
1200W HMI PAR: MF	800,000–960,000	32,000	8,000	3,556	2,000	1,280	889	500	320	222	163	125	99	80	36	20
2500W HMI SE PAR: MF	same as above															
4000W HMI SE APR: MF	960,000–1,280,000	38,400	9,600	4,267	2,400	1,536	1,067	600	384	267	196	150	119	96	43	24
1200W HMI PAR: NSP	1,280,000–1,600,000	51,200	12,800	5,689	3,200	2,048	1,422	800	512	356	261	200	158	128	57	32
	1,600,000–1,920,000	64,000	16,000	7,111	4,000	2,560	1,778	1,000	640	444	327	250	198	160	71	40
1200W HMI PAR: VNSP	1,920,000–2,560,000	76,800	19,200	8,533	4,800	3,072	2,133	1,200	768	533	392	300	237	192	85	48
2500W HMI SE PAR: NSP	2,560,000–3,200,000		25,600	11,378	6,400	4,096	2,844	1,600	1,024	711	522	400	316	256	114	64
	3,200,000–3,840,000		32,000	14,222	8,000	5,120	3,556	2,000	1,280	889	653	500	395	320	142	80
	3,840,000–5,120,000		38,400	17,067	9,600	6,144	4,267	2,400	1,536	1,067	784	600	474	384	171	96
2500W HMI SE PAR: VNSP	5,120,000–6,400,000		51,200	22,756	12,800	8,192	5,689	3,200	2,048	1,422	1,045	800	632	512	228	128
	6,400,000–7,680,000		64,000	28,444	16,000	10,240	7,111	4,000	2,560	1,778	1,306	1,000	790	640	284	160
12kW HMI Fresnel: Spot	7,680,000–10,240,000		76,800	34,133	19,200	12,288	8,533	4,800	3,072	2,133	1,567	1,200	948	768	341	192
4000W HMI SE PAR: VNSP	>10,240,000			45,511	25,600	16,384	11,378	6,400	4,096	2,844	2,090	1,600	1,264	1,024	455	256
6000W HMI SE PAR: VNSP	>12,800,000			56,889	32,00	20,480	14,222	8,000	5,120	3,556	2,612	2,000	1,580	1,280	569	320
Overcast Day (ballpark)		1,800	1,800	1,800	1,800	1,800	1,800	1,800	1,800	1,800	1,800	1,800	1,800	1,800	1,800	1,800
Sunlight: Direct		6,400	6,400	6,400	6,400	6,400	6,400	6,400	6,400	6,400	6,400	6,400	6,400	6,400	6,400	6,400
Sunlight: Direct		8,000	8,000	8,000	8,000	8,000	8,000	8,000	8,000	8,000	8,000	8,000	8,000	8,000	8,000	8,000

Footcandle figures are based on the lower number in the candella range.

Candella ranges are in 1/3 stop increments.

Footcandle data represents the peak beam intensity. A reading at the beam edge is one-stop less than the peak beam reading.

Data is based on manufacturers marketing data and represents performance under ideal conditions (new bulb, clean new lens and reflector, no atmospheric interference).

Performance data varies with fixture design and manufacturer. These figures are meant to represent an average fixture of each type.

Cable Ampacity Tables

Table B.1   Ampacity of Cables: Type W and Entertainment Industry Stage Cable (EISC) Types SC, SCE, and SCT[a] (NEC Table 400-5(8))

	No. of Current-Carrying Wires in Cable		
Size of Cable	*1*	*2[b]*	*3[c]*
Cable rated at 90° C and 105° C			
4/0	405	361	316
3/0	350	313	274
2/0	300	271	237
1/0	260	234	205
2 AWG	190	174	152
4 AWG	140	130	114
6 AWG	105	99	87
8 AWG	80	74	65
Cable rated at 75° C			
4/0	360	317	277
3/0	310	275	241
2/0	265	238	208
1/0	230	207	181
2 AWG	170	152	133
4 AWG	125	*115*	101
6 AWG	95	88	77
8 AWG	70	65	57
Cable rated at 60° C			
4/0	300	265	232
3/0	260	230	201
2/0	225	199	174
1/0	195	173	*151*
2 AWG	140	128	112
4 AWG	*105*	96	84
6 AWG	80	72	63
8 AWG	60	*55*	48

Source: Reprinted with permission from NFPA 70-1993, The National Electrical Code®, Copyright © 1992, National Fire Protection Association, MA 02269. This reprinted material is not the complete and official position of the National Fire Protection Association on the referenced subject, which is represented only by the standard in its entirety.

[a]These amperage capacities are based on an ambient temperature of 30° C (86° F). They are allowable only where the individual conductors are not installed in raceways and are not in physical contact with one another, except in lengths not to exceed 24 in. where passing through the wall of an enclosure.

[b]See footnote b in Table B.2, p. 359.

[c]See footnote c in Table B.2, p. 359.

Table B.2 Amperage Capacities for Flexible Cords, Stingers, and Zip Cord[a]
(NEC Table 400-5 (A))

| | No. of Current-Carrying Wires | | |
AWG Size	2[b]	3[c]	*Asbestos[d]*
18	10	7	6
16	13	10	8
14	18	15	17
12	25	20	23
10	30	25	28
8	40	35	—
6	55	45	—
4	70	60	—
2	95	80	—

Source: Reprinted with permission from NFPA 70-1993, The National Electrical Code®, Copyright © 1992, National Fire Protection Association, MA 02269. This reprinted material is not the complete and official position of the National Fire Protection Association on the referenced subject, which is represented only by the standard in its entirety.

[a]These amperage capacities apply to the following types of cord: thermoset types C, E, EO, PD, S, SJ, SJO, SJOO, SO, SOO, SP-1, SP-2, SP-3, SRD, SV, SVO, and SVOO and thermoplastic types ET, ETT, ETLB, SE, SEO, SJE, SJEO, SJT, SJTO, SJTOO, SPE-1, SPE-2, SPE-3, SPT-1, SPT-2, SPT3, ST, STO, STOO, SRDE, SRDT, SVE, SVEO, SVT, SVTO, and SVTOO.

[b]The amperage capacities in this column apply to multiconductor cable in which two of the wires are current-carrying (such as a hot wire and a neutral wire, or two hot wires of a 240V single-phase circuit). The neutral wire of a balanced 240/120V single-phase circuit is not considered a current-carrying wire for the purpose of this table, with one exception: If the major portion of the load consists of electronic ballasts, electronic dimmers, or similar equipment, there are harmonic currents present in the neutral conductor and it shall be considered to be a current-carrying conductor. The green grounding wire is never considered to be a current-carrying wire.

[c]The amperage capacities in this column apply to multiconductor cable in which three of the wires are current-carrying wires (such as a three-wire three-phase-circuit, a balanced four-wire three-phase circuit, or a single-phase three-wire circuit derived from the neutral and two-phased legs of a wye-connected three-phase system). The neutral wire of a balanced four-wire three-phase circuit is only considered a current-carrying wire when there are harmonic currents present. A cord or cable with four or more current-carrying wires must be derated in accordance with NEC Section 400-5. Cords and cables in which four to six of the conductors are carrying current must be derated to 80% of the ampacities given in this table.

[d]This column gives the amperage capacities of asbestos cords (types AFC, AFPD, and AFPO), which are often used inside fixtures.

Table B.3 Minimum Size of Grounding Wires (NEC Table 250-95)

| | Gauge of Grounding Conductor | |
| *Rating of Overcurrent* | | *Aluminum and Copper-Clad* |
Protection of Cicuit (A)	*Copper Wire No.*	*Aluminum Wire No.*
15	14 AWG	12AWG
20	12 AWG	10 AWG
30	10 AWG	8 AWG
40	10 AWG	8 AWG
60	10 AWG	8 AWG
100	8 AWG	6 AWG
200	6 AWG	4 AWG
300	4 AWG	2 AWG
400	3 AWG	1 AWG
500	2 AWG	1/0
600	1 AWG	2/0
800	1/0	3/0
1000	2/0	4/0
1200	3/0	250 kcmil
1600	4/0	350 kcmil

Source: Reprinted.with permission from NFPA 70-1993, The National Electrical Code®, Copyright © 1992, National Fire Protection Association, Quincy, MA 02269. This reprinted material is not the complete and official position of the National Fire Protection Association on the referenced subject, which is represented only by the standard in its entirety.

Line Loss and Resistance Tables

Table C.1 Voltage Drop in Volts per 100 ft. for Various Cables

	Three-Phase			Single-Phase Circuits from 3-phase Feeders		Single-Phase and DC Circuits			
Amps per leg	4/0 Feeder	2/0 Feeder	#2 Banded	#2 Banded and "100A"	#6 "60A"	4/0 Feeder	2/0 Feeder	#2 Banded and "100A"	#6 "60A"
25	0.2	0.4	0.7	1.1	2.7	0.3	0.4	0.8	2.1
50	0.4	0.7	1.4	2.1	5.3	0.5	0.8	1.6	4.1
75	0.7	1.1	2.1	3.2	8.0	0.8	1.2	2.4	6.2
100	0.9	1.4	2.8	4.2	10.7	1.0	1.6	3.2	8.2
125	1.1	1.8	3.5	5.3		1.3	2.0	4.1	
150	1.3	2.1	4.2	6.3		1.5	2.4	4.9	
175	1.5	2.5	4.9	7.4		1.8	2.8	5.7	
200	1.8	2.8	5.6	8.4		2.0	3.2	6.5	
225	2.0	3.2				2.3	3.6		
250	2.2	3.5				2.5	4.1		
275	2.4	3.9				2.8	4.5		
300	2.6	4.2				3.1	4.9		
325	2.9					3.3			
350	3.1					3.6			
375	3.3					3.8			
400	3.5					4.1			

Table C.2 Resistance of Copper Wire

Size	Approx OD inches	Cross-sectional area (cmils)	Lbs per M/100 ft.	Ohms per M/100 ft.	ft./Ohm
4/0	0.528	211600	65.3	0.00509	19646
2/0	0.418	133100	41.1	0.00811	12330
2 AWG	0.292	66360	20.5	0.0162	6173
4 AWG	0.232	41740	12.9	0.0259	3861
6 AWG	0.184	26240	8.0	0.0410	2439
8 AWG	0.1285	16510	5.1	0.0640	1529
10 AWG	0.1019	10380	3.1	0.1018	981.9
12 AWG	0.0808	6530	20.0	0.1619	617.0
14 AWG	0.0641	4110	1.2	0.2575	389.0
16 AWG	0.0508	2580	.8	0.4094	244.0
18 AWG	0.0403	1620	.5	0.6510	154.0

Weights listed are of the copper itself, not the total weight or an insulated cable. Resistance at 25°C.

Flicker-Free Frame Rates

Table D.1　HMI Flicker-Free Frame
Rates at Any Shutter Angle: 60 Hz Power

Frames/Second	Optimal Shutter Angle
120.000	180
60.000	180
40.000	120
30.000	180
24.000	144
20.000	180
17.143	
15.000	
13.333	
12.000	180
10.909	
10.000	
9.231	
8.000	198
7.058	
6.000	
5.000	
4.000	
3.000	
2.000	
1.000	

Table D.3　Flicker-Free Frame Rates
at Any Shutter Angle: 50 Hz Power

Frame/Second	Optimal Shutter Angle
100.000	180
50.000	180
33.333	
25.000	180
20.000	144
16.666	
14.285	
12.500	
11.111	
10.000	
9.090	
8.333	
7.692	
7.142	
6.666	
5.000	
4.000	
3.125	
2.500	
2.000	
1.000	

Table D.2　Additional Flicker-Free
Frame Rates at Specific Shutter Angles:
60 Hz Power

Frames/Second	Shutter Angle
57.6	172.8
50	144
48	144
45	135
36	108
35	105
32	92 or 96
28	168
26	156
25	150
22	198 or 132
18	162
16	192 or 144

Table D.4　Additional Flicker-Free
Frame Rates at Specific Shutter Angles:
50 Hz Power

Frames/Second	Shutter Angle
48	172.8
40	144
36	129.6
32	115.2
30	108
28	108.8
26	187.2 or 93.6
24	172.8
22	158.4
18	194.4 or 129.6
16	172.8 or 115.2
12	172.8 or 129.6
8	172.8 or 144

Bulb Tables

Table E.1   Photo Floods, Mushroom Floods, MR-16s: Medium Screw Base Bulbs

Type	Bulb and Base Type	Volts	Watts	K Color	Life (hr)
Standard and Pear-shaped (PS) Photofloods					
PH-211	A-21 Medium	120	75	3200	100 hr
PH-212	A-21 Medium	120	150	3050	100 hr
PH-213	A-21 Medium	120	250	3400	3 hr
BBA (No 1)	A-21 Medium	120	250	3400	3 hr
BCA (B-1)	A-21 Medium	120	250	4800	3 hr
ECA	A-23 Medium	120	250	3200	20 hr
BAH	A-21 Medium	120	300	3200	20 hr
EBV (No 2)	PS-25 Medium	120	500	3400	6 hr
EBW (B-2)	PS-25 Medium	120	500	4800	6 hr
ECT	PS25/5 Medium	120	500	3200	60 hr
Mushroom Bulbs					
DAN (R-20)	R-20 Meduim	118	200	3400	4
BEP (R-30)	R-30 Medium	118	300	3400	4
EBR (R-30)	R-30 Medium	118	375	3400	4
DXH (PH/RFL-2)	R-40 Medium	118	375	3200	15
BFA (R-34)	R-40 Medium	118	375	3400	4
DXC (PH/RFL-2)	R-40 Medium	118	500	3400	6
EAL	R-40 Medium	120	500	3300	15
FAE	R-40 Medium	118	550	3400	10
MR-16 Bulbs Medium Screw Base					
FSA (NSP) or					
JDR120V75W NSP	MR-16, Medium	120	75	3000	—
FSB (MFL) or					
JDR120V75W MFL	MR-16, Medium	120	75	3000	—
FSD (WFL) or					
JDR120V75W WFL	MR-16, Medium	120	75	3000	—
FSC (NSP) or					
JDR120V100W NSP	MR-16, Medium	120	100	3000	—
FSE (MFL) or					
JDR120V75W MFL	MR-16, Medium	120	100	3000	—
FSF (WFL) or					
JDR120V75W WFL	MR-16, Medium	120	100	3000	—

The bulb type designation indicates type and size (in eighths of inches). For example, R-40 indicates it is a Reflector lamp with a 5-in. diameter (40/8 = 5). An R-30 bulb is 3-6/8 in. diameter, an MR-16 is 2-in. diameter, and so on.

The mushroom floods listed here are all 3000K or more. Mushroom floods also come in a wide variety of wattages that have lower color temperature, flood, and spot. R-40s, for example, come in 75W, 150W, and 300W.

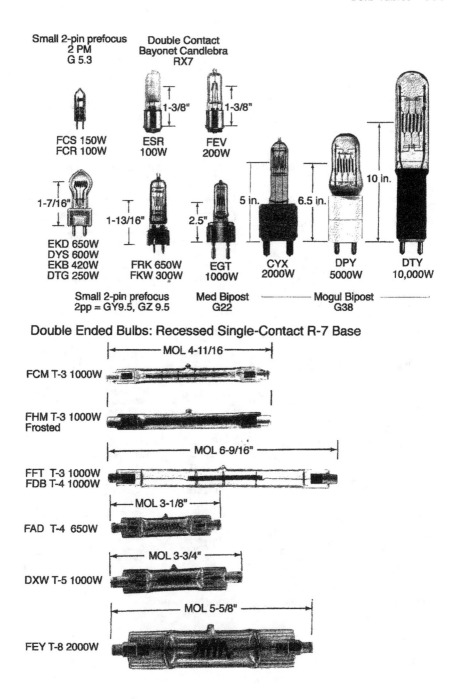

Figure E.1 Tungsten halogen lamps

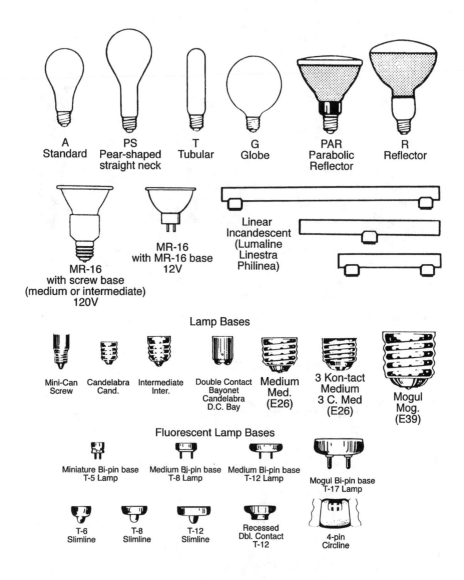

Figure E.2 Various types of practical bulbs and lamp bases

Table E.2 Fluorescent Lamps

Watts	Bulb	Diameter	Length	Description	Kelvin	Base
KF55 (Daylight) Lamps						
6	T5	5/8"	9"	F6T5/KF55	5500K	Mini Bipin
14	T12	1-1/2"	15"	FI4T12/KF55 SFC	"	Med. Bipin
20	T12	1-1/2"	24"	F20T12/KF55 SFC	"	"
30	T12	1-1/2"	36"	F30T12/KF55SFC	"	"
40	T12	1-1/2"	48"	F40T12/KF5S SFC	"	"
55	T12	1-1/2"	72"	F72T12/KF55/SL SFC	"	Single Pin
85	T12	1-1/2"	72"	F72T12/KF55/HO SFC	"	Med. Bipin
75	T12	1-1/2"	96"	F96T12/KF55/SL SFC	"	Single Pin
110	T12	1-1/2"	96"	F96T12/KF55/HO SFC	"	Med. Bipin
KF32 (Tungsten) Lamps						
6	T5	5/8"	9"	F6T5/KF32	3200K	Mini Bipin
14	T12	1-1/2"	15"	F14T12/KF32 SFC	"	Med. Bipin
20	T12	1-1/2"	24"	F20T12/KF32SFC	"	"
30	T12	1-1/2"	36"	F30T12/KF32 SFC	"	"
40	T12	1-1/2"	48"	F40T12/KF32SFC	"	"
55	T12	1-1/2"	72"	F72T12/KF32/SL SFC	"	Single Pin
85	T12	1-1/2"	72"	F72T12/KF32/HO SFC	"	Med. Bipin
75	T12	1-1/2"	96"	F96T12/KF32/SL SFC	"	Single Pin
110	T12	1-1/2"	96"	F96T12/KF32/HO SFC	"	Med. Bipin

Other Fluorescent Bulbs

Make and Name	Color Temp (°K)	Color Rendering Index	Minus-Green Correction Required
Duro Test Optima 32	3200	82	0–1/4
Duro Test Vita-Lite	5500	91	1/8–1/4
GE Chroma 50	5000	90	1/2
GE IF 27	3000	—	—
GTE Sylvania Design 50	5000	91	1/2
Warm White (WW)	3000	52	Full
Deluxe Warm White (WWX)	3000	77	Full
Cool White (CW)	4500	62	Full

Colored Fluorescent Bulbs

Bulb	Description
Super Blue	420 nm blue spike for blue screen opticals
Green	560 nm green spike for green screen opticals
Black Light	UV A stimulates luminescent materials
Red	Party colors
Pink	Party colors
Yellow	Party colors

Table E.3 Tungsten Bulb Specifications and Substitutions

Bi-pin Single-ended Tungsten Halogen Bulbs

Watts	ANSI Code	Color Temp (°K)	LCL	Finish	Volts	Bulb Life (hr)	Amps

100W and 200W Fresnels: Peppers, Midget, Tiny Mole, Mini Mole, etc.
Base: Double-contact bayonet candelabra RX7. Bulbs: B-12, G-16-1/2, T-4 and T-8.
Burn within 30 of vertical, base-down.

Watts	ANSI Code	Color Temp (°K)	LCL	Finish	Volts	Bulb Life (hr)	Amps
250	ESS	2950	1-3/8"	C	120	2000	2.1
200	**FEV**	**3200**	**1-3/8"**	**C**	**120**	**50**	**1.7**
200	BDJ	3200	1-3/8"	C	120	20	1.7
200	CCM	3075	1-3/8"	C	115-125	25	1.7
150	CGP	3075	1-3/8"	C	115-120	25	1.3
150	ETF	3000	1-3/8"	F	120	2000	1.3
150	ESP	2900	1-3/8"	C	120	1000	1.3
150	ETC	3000	1-3/8"	C	120	2000	1.3
100	**ESR**	**2850**	**1-3/8"**	**C**	**120**	**750**	**.5**
100	100Q/CL/DC	3000	1-3/8"	C	120	1000	.8
100	CEB	2975	1-3/8"	C	115-125	50	.8
75	CBX	2925	1-3/8"	C	115-125	50	.6
50	CAX	2875	1-3/8"	C	115-125	50	.4

100W and 150W Dedo.
Base: Small 2-pin : 2 PM = G 5.3 Bulb: T-3-1/2, T-4. Burn base down to horizontal

Watts	ANSI Code	Color Temp (°K)	LCL	Finish	Volts	Bulb Life (hr)	Amps
150	**FCS**	**3400**	**1.181"**	**C**	**24**	**100**	**6.25**
100	**FCR**	**3300**	**1.181"**	**C**	**12**	**50**	**8.3**
50	BRL	3300	1.181"	C	12	50	4.2

300W, 650W Fresnels: Tweenie II, Betweenie, 300W Pepper, etc.
Base: Small 2-pin prefocus: 2 PP = GY 9.5. GZ 9.5. Bulb: T-6. Burn with coil horizontal.

Watts	ANSI Code	Color Temp (°K)	LCL	Finish	Volts	Bulb Life (hr)	Amps
650	**FRK**	**3200**	**1 13/16"**	**C**	**120**	**200**	**5.4**
500	FRB	3200	1 13/16"	C	120	200	4.2
300	**FKW**	**3200**	**1 13/16"**	**C**	**120**	**200**	**2.5**

Small 1k Fresnels (special high seal temp bulb made for specially designed high-temp heads—Sachtler, Desisti).
Base: Small 2-pin prefocus GY9.5. Bulb: Phillips

Watts	ANSI Code	Color Temp (°K)	LCL	Finish	Volts	Bulb Life (hr)	Amps
1000	Blue Pinch	3200	1-13/16"	C	120	250	8.3

Old Style Tweenie, 420 Pepper, Teenie Weenie Open Face.
Base: 2-pin prefocus: 2 PP = GY 9.5. GZ 9.5. T-6 or T-7 bulb. Burn with coil horizontal.

Watts	ANSI Code	Color Temp (°K)	LCL	Finish	Volts	Bulb Life (hr)	Amps
650	**EKD-Q650/3CL2PP**	**3400**	**1-7/16"**	**C**	**120**	**25**	**5.4**
600	**DYS/DYV/BHC**	**3200**	**1-7/16"**	**C**	**120**	**75**	**5**
420	**EKB-Q420/4CL/2PP**	**3200**	**1-7/16"**	**C**	**120**	**75**	**2.5**
250	**DYG-Q250/4CL/2PP**	**3400**	**1-7/16"**	**C**	**30**	**15**	**5.3**
100	EYL	3300	1-7/16"	C	12	50	63

Table E.3 Tungsten Bulb Specifications and Substitutions (continued)

Watts	ANSI Code	Color Temp (°K)	LCL	Finish	Volts	Bulb Life (hr)	Amps
1k Fresnels							
Base: Medium bipost., G22. Bulb: T-6, T-7, T-20 or T-24. Burn within 45 of vertical base-down.							
1000	**EGT-Q1000T7/4CL**	**3200**	**2-1/2"**	**C**	**120**	**250**	**8.3**
1000	EGT	3200	2-1/2"	C	120	250	8.3
1000	EBB-1M24/13	3350	2-1/2"	C	120	12	8.3
750	EGR-Q750T7/4CL	3200	2-1/2"	C	120	200	6.3
750	EGR	3200	2-1/2"	C	120	200	6.3
750	DVH-750T24/16	3200	2-1/2"	C	120	50	6.3
500	EGN	3200	2-1/2"	C	120	100	4.2
500	DVG-500T20/63	3200	2-1/2"	C	120	50	4.2
Small 2k Fresnels (special high seal temp bulb made for specially designed high-temp heads—Sachtler, Desisti).							
Base: Medium Bi-post, G22. Bulb: T-8 Phillips							
2000	Blue Pinch	3200	2-1/2"	C	120	500	16.7
2k Fresnels							
Base: Mogul bipost., G38. Bulb: T-7, T-8, T-9 1/2, and T-48. Burn within 45 of vertica base down.							
2000	**CYX-Q2000T10/4**	**3200**	**5"**	**C**	**120**	**250**	**16.7**
1500	CXZ-Q1500T10/4CL	3200	5"	C	120	300	12.5
1000	CYV-Q1000T7/4CL/BP	3200	5"	C	120	200	5.3
5k Fresnel							
Base: Mogul bipost., G38. Bulb: T-17 and T-20. Burn base-down to horizontal.							
5000	**DPY-Q5000T20/4CL**	**3200**	**6-1/2"**	**C**	**120**	**500**	**41.6**
5000	DPY	3200	6-1/2"	C	120	500	41.6
10k and 12k Tungsten Fresnel							
Base: Mogul bipost, G38. Bulb: T-24. Burn within 45 of vertical base-down.							
10,000	**DTY**	**3200**	**10"**	**C**	**120**	**300**	**83.3**
12,000	**Koto 12k**	**3200**	**10"**	**C**	**120**	**—**	**100**
20k Fresnel							
Base: Mogul bipost., G38. Bulb: T32. Burn within 45 of vertical, base-down.							
20,000	KP200 208V	3200	13.937"	C	208	300	83.3
20,000	KP200 220V	3200	13.937"	C	220	300	83.3
20,000	**KP200 240V**	**3200**	**13.937"**	**C**	**240**	**300**	**83.3**
1k Molipso							
Base: medium prefocus, P28. Bulb: T-5 or T-6. Burn any position.							
1000	**EGJ-Q1000/4CL/P**	**3200**	**3-1/2"**	**C**	**120**	**500**	**8.3**
1000	EGM-Q1000/CL/P	3000	3-1/2"	C	120	2000	8.3
1000	EGJ	3200	3-1/2"	C	120	400	8.3
750	EGF-Q750/4CL/P	3200	3-1/2"	C	120	500	6.3
750	EGG-Q750/CL/P	3000	3-1/2"	C	120	2000	6.3
750	EGF	3200	3-1/2"	C	120	250	6.3
750	EGG	3000	3-1/2"	C	120	2000	6.3

Table E.3 Tungsten Bulb Specifications and Substitutions (continued)

Watts	ANSI Code	Color Temp (°K)	LCL	Finish	Volts	Bulb Life (hr)	Amps
2k Molipso							
Base: mogul bipost, G38. T-8 bulb. Burn any position.							
2000	**BWA-Q2000/4CL/**	**3200**	**5"**	**C**	**120**	**750**	**16.7**
2000	BWA	3200	5"	C	120	500	16.7
1k Molette, Ellipsoidal Spotlights							
Base: medium 2-pin. G9.5. T-4 or T-6 bulbs. Burn any position.							
1000	**FFL-Q1000/4CL**	**3200**	**2-3/8"**	**C**	**120**	**500**	**8.3**
1000	**FCV-Q1000/4**	**3200**	**2-3/8"**	**F**	**120**	**500**	**8.3**
1000	FEL	3200	2-3/8"	C	120	300	8.3
1000	FCV	3200	2-3/8"	F	120	300	8.3
750	EHF-Q750/4CL	3200	2-3/8"	C	122	300	6.3
750	EHF	3200	2-3/8"	C	120	300	6.3
750	EHG	3000	2-3/8"	C	120	2000	6.3
500	FHC/EHB	3200	2-3/8"	C	120	200	4.2
500	EHC/EHB-Q500/5CL	3150	2-3/8"	C	120	300	4.2
500	**EHD-Q500CL/TP**	**3000**	**2-3/8"**	**C**	**120**	**2000**	**4.2**
500	EHD	3000	2-3/8"	C	120	2000	4.2
2k Molette							
Base: mogul screw. T-8 bulb. Burn any position.							
2000	BWF-Q2000/4CL	3200	5-1/4"	C	120	750	16.7
2000	BWF	3200	5-1/4"	C	120	400	16.7
2000	**BWG**	**3200**	**5-1/4"**	**F**	**120**	**400**	**16.7**

Double-Ended Tungsten Bulbs

Watts	ANSI Code	Color Temp (°K)	MOL	Finish	Volts	Bulb Life (hr)	Amps
400W and 650W Soft Lights and Open Face Lights							
Base: Recessed Single-Contact R7S. 3-1/8" double-ended T-4 bulb. Burn any position.							
650	**FAD**	**3200**	**3-1/8"**	**C**	**120**	**100**	**5.4**
650	FBX	3200	3-1/8"	F	120	100	5.4
650	DWY	3400	3-1/8"	C	120	25	5.4
420	FFM	3200	3-1/8"	C	120	75	3.5
400	**FDA (400T4Q/4CL)**	**3200**	**3-1/8"**	**C**	**120**	**250**	**3.3**
400	EHR (400T4Q/CL)	2900	3-1/8"	C	120	2000	3.3
300	EHP (300T4Q/CL)	2900	3-1/8"	C	120	2000	2.5
1k Open Face, Mickey, 1k Arrilite							
Base: Recessed Single-Contact R7s. 3-3/4" double-ended T-3 bulb. Burn any position.							
1000	**DXW**	**3200**	**3-3/4"**	**C**	**120**	**150**	**8.3**
1000	FBY	3200	3-3/4"	F	120	150	8.3
1000	BRH	3350	3-3/4"	C	120	75	8.3
1000	DXN	3400	3-3/4"	C	120	75	5.0
600	FCB	3250	3-3/4"	C	120	75	5.0
500	FGD	3200	3-3/4"	C	120	100	4.2

Table E.3 Tungsten Bulb Specifications and Substitutions (continued)

Watts	ANSI Code	Color Temp (°K)	MOL	Finish	Volts	Bulb Life (hr)	Amps
1k Nook, 1k, 2k 4k and 8k Soft lights							
Base: Recessed Single-Contact R7Ss. 4 11/16" double-ended T-3 bulb. Burn horizontal ± 4°.							
1000	**FCM-Q1000T3/4CL**	**3200**	**4-11/16"**	**C**	**120**	**500**	**8.3**
1000	FCM-Q1000T3/4	3200	4-11/16"	F	120	500	8.3
1000	FCM	3200	4-11/16"	C	120	300	8.3
1000	**FHM**	**3200**	**4-11/16"**	**F**	**120**	**300**	**8.3**
750	EJG-Q750T3/4CL	3200	4-11/16"	C	120	400	8.3
750	EMD-Q750T3/4	3200	4-11/16"	F	120	400	6.3
750	**EJG**	**3200**	**4-11/16"**	**C**	**120**	**400**	**6.3**
500	FDF-Q500T3/4CL	3200	4-11/16"	C	120	400	4.2
500	FDN-Q500T3/4	3200	4-11/16"	F	120	400	4.2
500	EDF	3200	4-11/16"	C	120	400	4.2
500	EDN	3200	4-11/16"	F	120	400	4.2
500	Q500T3/CL	3000	4-11/16"	C	120	2000	4.2
500	Q500T3	3000	4-11/16"	F	120	2000	4.2
500	FCL	3000	4-11/16"	C	120	2600	4.2
500	FCZ	3000	4-11/16"	F	120	2600	4.2
300	EHM-Q300T2 1/2/CL	2980	4-11/16"	C	120	2000	2.5
300	EHZ-Q300T2 1/2	2950	4-11/16"	F	120	2000	2.5
2k Nook							
Base: Recessed Single-Contact R7s. 5-5/8" double-ended T-6 or T-8 bulb. Burn any position.							
2000	**FEY-Q2000T8/4CL**	**3200**	**5-5/8"**	**C**	**120**	**500**	**16.7**
2000	FEY (2MT8Q/4CL)	3200	5-5/8"	C	120	400	16.7
1000	FER/EHS-Q1000T4/6CL	3200	5-5/8"	C	120	500	8.3
1000	FER (1000T6Q/4CL)	3200	5-5/8"	C	120	500	8.3
1000	DWT-Q1000T6/CL	3000	5-5/8"	C	120	2550	8.3
1000	DWT (1000T6Q/CL)	3000	5-5/8"	C	120	2000	8.3
Cyc Strips							
Base: Recessed Single-Contact R7s. 6-9/16" double-ended T-3 or T-4 bulb. Burn horizontal ± 4°.							
1500	**FDB-Q1500T4/4CL**	**3200**	**6-9/16"**	**C**	**120**	**400**	**12.5**
1500	FGT-Q1500T4/4	3200	6-9/16"	F	120	400	12.5
1000	**FFT-Q1000T3/1CL**	**3200**	**6-9/16"**	**C**	**120**	**400**	**8.3**
1000	FGV-Q1000T3/1	3200	6-9/16"	C	120	400	8.3

LCL = Light Center Length, the distance from the center of the bulb's filament to the bottom of its base. If the wrong LCL is used, the filament will not be centered on the reflector and fixture performance will be greatly reduced.

MOL = Maximum Overall Length,the distance from the top of the lamp to the tip of the pins on the base, or from end to end for double-ended lamps. For double-ended lamps, MOL is necessary to match lamp to fixture size.

Interchangeability = Bulbs within each grouping in this table are interchangeable—they have the same base (type and dimensions) and the same LCL (or MOL in the case of double-ended lamps).

The most commonly used lamps for motion picture work are highlighted in bold print.

C = Clear finish

F = Frosted finish

Table E.4 PAR 64 Bulbs, 120V, EMEP Base (Extended Mogul End Prong)

Beam	*500W*		*1000W*		*1200W*
	2800K (2000 hrs)	*3000K (4000 hrs)*	*3200K (800 hrs)*	*5200K (200 hrs)*	*3200K*
Very narrow spot	—	—	FFN (VNSP) Q1000PAR64/1	—	GFC (VNSP)
Narrow spot	500PAR64NSP	1000PAR64QNSP	FFP (NSP) Q1000PAR64/2	FGM (NSP) Q1000PAR64/3D	GFB (NSP)
Medium flood	500PAR64MFL	1000PAR64QMFL	FFR (MFL) Q1000PAR64/5	FGN (MFL) Q1000PAR64/7D	GFA (MFL)
Wide flood	500PAR64WFL	1000PAR64QWFL	FFS (WFL) Q1000PAR64/6	—	GFE (WFL)
Extra wide flood	—	—	GFF (XWFL)	—	GFD (XWFL)

Table E.5 PAR 64 Lamp Performance Data for PAR 64 and Aircraft Landing Lights

ANSI Code	Volts	Watts	Base	Color Temp	Ave. Life (hr)	Beam	Beam Angle (degrees)	Candle Power
FFN	120	1000	EMEP	3200	800	VNSP	12 x 6	400,000
FFP	120	1000	EMEP	3200	800	NSP	14 x 7	330,000
FFR	120	1000	EMEP	3200	800	MFL	28 x 12	125,000
FFS	120	1000	EMEP	3200	800	WFL	48 x 24	40,000
GFF	120	1000	EMEP	3200	800	XWFL	—	—
GFC	120	1200	EMEP	3200	400	VNSP	10 x 8	540,000
GFB	120	1200	EMEP	3200	400	NSP	10 x 8	450,000
GFA	120	1200	EMEP	3200	400	MFL	24 x 13	160,000
GFE	120	1200	EMEP	3200	400	WFL	58 x 25	45,000
GFD	120	1200	EMEP	3200	400	XWFL	—	—
ACL (Aircraft Landing Light) Bulbs in PAR 64 size								
4559	28	600	Screw Terminal	—	25	VNSP	12 x 11	600,000
Q4559	28	600	Screw Terminal	—	100	VNSP	12 x 8	600,000
Q4559X	28	600	Screw Terminal	—	100	VNSP	11 x 7-1/2	600,000

Table E.6 PAR 36 Bulbs, 650W, 120V, Ferrule Base

Beam	5000K (35 hr)	3400K (30 hr)	3200K (100 hr)
Spot	—	FBJ Q650PAR36/3	—
Medium	FAY Q650PAR36/3D	DXK Q650PAR36/2	FCX Q650PAR36/7
Wide	—	—	FCW Q650PAR36/6

Gels and Diffusions

Table F.1   Kelvin Scale/MIRED Scale Conversion Table

Kelvin	0	100	200	300	400	500	600	700	800	900
2000	500	476	455	435	417	400	385	370	357	345
3000	333	323	313	303	294	286	278	270	263	256
4000	250	244	238	233	227	222	217	213	208	204
5000	200	196	192	189	185	182	179	175	172	169
6000	167	164	161	159	156	154	152	149	147	145
7000	143	141	139	137	135	133	132	130	128	127
8000	125	123	122	120	119	118	116	115	114	112
9000	111	110	109	108	106	105	104	103	102	101

Example: To find the MIRED value for a 6500 Kelvin source, look across from 6000, and down from 500. The MIRED value is 154.

Table F.2   Kelvin Conversion: Lee Color-Correction Conversion

Light Source Color (K)	CTO (Orange)				CTB (Blue)			
	Lee 223 Eighth	Lee 206 Quarter	Lee 205 Half	Lee 204 Full	Lee 218 Eighth	Lee 203 Quarter	Lee 205 Half	Lee 201 Full
2000	1901	1773	1642	1517	2075	2151	2370	2755
2300	1786	1672	1555	1443	1938	2004	2193	2519
2600	2433	2227	2024	1838	2725	2857	3257	4032
2900	2695	2445	2203	1984	3058	3226	3745	4808
3200	2959	2660	2375	2123	3401	3610	4274	5714
3500	3205	2857	2532	2247	3731	3984	4808	6711
3800	3460	3058	2688	2370	4082	4386	5405	7937
4400	3953	3436	2976	2591	4785	5208	6711	11111
5000	4425	3788	3236	2786	5495	6061	8197	15873
5600	4878	4115	3472	2959	6211	6944	9901	23810
6200	5348	4444	3704	3125	6993	7937	12048	41667
6800	5780	4739	3906	3268	7752	8929	14493	100000
7400	6211	5025	4098	3401	8547	10000	17544	
8000	6623	5291	4274	3521	9346	11111	21277	
9000	7299	5714	4545	3704	10753	13158	30303	

Table F. 3   Kelvin Conversion: Rosco Color-Correction Conversion

Light Source Color (K)	CTO (Orange)						CTB (Blue)						
	R-3410 Eighth	R-3409 Quarter	R-3408 Half	R-3411 3/4	R-3401 Sun 85	R-3407 Full	R-3216 Eighth	R-3208 Quarter	R-3206 Third	R-3204 Half	R-3203 3/4	R-3202 Full	R-3220 2 x CTB
2000	1923	1845	1721	1585	1585	1499	2049	2128	2217	2315	2500	2710	4115
2300	1805	1736	1626	1504	1504	1427	1916	1984	2062	2146	2304	2481	3610
2600	2469	2342	2146	1938	1938	1812	2681	2817	2976	3155	3509	3937	7813
2900	2740	2584	2347	2101	2101	1953	3003	3175	3378	3610	4082	4673	11364
3200	3012	2825	2545	2257	2257	2088	3333	3546	3802	4098	4717	5525	18182
3500	3268	3049	2725	2398	2398	2208	3650	3906	4219	4587	5376	6452	34483
3800	3534	3279	2907	2538	2538	2326	3984	4292	4673	5128	6135	7576	166667
4400	4049	3717	3247	2793	2793	2538	4651	5076	5618	6289	7874	10417	
5000	4545	4132	3559	3021	3021	2725	5319	5882	6623	7576	10000	14493	
5600	5025	4525	3846	3226	3226	2890	5988	6711	7692	9009	12658	20833	
6200	5525	4926	4132	3425	3425	3049	6711	7634	8929	10753	16393	33333	
6800	5988	5291	4386	3597	3597	3185	7407	8547	10204	12658	21277	62500	
7400	6452	5650	4630	3759	3759	3311	8130	9524	11628	14925	28571		
8000	6897	5988	4854	3906	3906	3425	8850	10526	13158	17544	40000		
9000	7634	6536	5208	4132	4132	3597	10101	12346	16129	23256	90909		

Table F.4 Kelvin Conversion: GAM Color-Correction Conversion

Light Source Color (K)	CTO (Orange)						CTB (Blue)					
	1555 Eighth	1552 Quarter	1549 Half	1546 3/4 CTO	1543 Full	1540 Extra CTO	1535 Eighth	1532 Quarter	1529 Half	1526 3/4 Blue	1523 Full	1520 Extra CTB
2000	1916	1852	1721	1585	1520	1294	2037	2110	2315	2577	2703	2817
2300	1799	1742	1626	1504	1445	1239	1905	1969	2146	2370	2475	2571
2600	2457	2353	2146	1938	1842	1520	2660	2786	3155	3663	3922	4167
2900	2725	2597	2347	2101	1988	1618	2976	3135	3610	4292	4651	5000
3200	2994	2841	2545	2257	2128	1709	3300	3497	4098	5000	5495	5988
3500	3247	3067	2725	2398	2252	1789	3610	3846	4587	5747	6410	7092
3800	3509	3300	2907	2538	2375	1866	3937	4219	5128	6623	7519	8475
4400	4016	3745	3247	2793	2597	2000	4587	4975	6289	8696	10309	12195
5000	4505	4167	3559	3021	2793	2114	5236	5747	7576	11364	14286	18182
5600	4975	4566	3846	3226	2967	2212	5882	6536	9009	14925	20408	29412
6200	5464	4975	4132	3425	3135	2304	6579	7407	10753	20408	32258	62500
6800	5917	5348	4386	3597	3279	2381	7246	8264	12658	28571	58824	500000
7400	6369	5714	4630	3759	3413	2451	7937	9174	14925	43478	200000	
8000	6803	6061	4854	3906	3534	2513	8621	10101	17544	76923		
9000	7519	6623	5208	4132	3717	2604	9804	11765	23256			

Table F.5 CTO Gels

Name	Rosco Cinegel	MIRED Shift	Lee	MIRED Shift	GAM	MIRED Shift	K Shift	Light Reduction (Stops)
Extra CTO	—	—	—	—	1540	+273	20,000K to 3200K 5500K to 2200K	1
Full CTO Full Straw	3407 3441	+167	204* 441	+159	1543	+163	6500K to 3200K 5500K to 2900K	2/3
Sun 85 85 Acrylic	3401 3761	+131	—	—	—	—	5500K to 3200K	2/3
3/4 CTO	3411	+130	285	—	1546	+130	5500K to 3200K	2/3
1/2 CTO 1/2 Straw 12 CTO Acrylic	3408 3442 3751	+81	205* 441	+109	1549	+81	5500K to 3800K	1/2
1/4 CTO 1/4 Straw	3409 3443	+42	206* 441	+64	1552	+40	5500K to 4500K	1/3
1/8 CTO 1/8 Straw	3410 3444	+20	223* 441	+26	1555	+22	5500K to 4900K	1/4

*Also available in 60-in. rolls

Table F.6 Neutral Density and ND/Daylight Correction Gels

Gel	Rosco Cinegel	MIRED Shift	Lee	MIRED Shift	GAM	K Shift	Light Reduction (Stops)
.15 ND	3415	0	298	0	1514	0	1/2
.3 ND Acrylic	3402 3762	0	209*	0	1515	0	1
.6 ND Acrylic	3403 3763	0	210*	0	1516	0	2
.9 ND Acrylic	3404 3764	0	211*	0	1517	0	3
1.2 ND	—	—	299	0	1518	0	4
CTO .3 ND	3405	+131	207	+159	1556	5500K to 3200K	1
CTO .6 ND	3406	+131	208	+159	1557	5500K to 3200K	2
CTO .9 ND	—	—	—	—	1558	5500K to 3200K	3

*Also available in 60-in. rolls.

Cinemills Corporation makes gels that share the same product numbers as Lee.

Table F.7 CTB Gels

Name	Rosco Cinegel	MIRED Shift	Lee	MIRED Shift	GAM	K Shift	Light Reduction (Stops)
Double Blue	3220	-257	200	—	—	2800K to 10,000K	4
Extra CTB	—	-150	—	—	1520	3200K to 6200K	1-3/4
Full CTB	3202	-131	201	-137	1523	3200K to 5700K	1-1/3
3/4 CTB	3203	—	281	—	1526	—	1-1/4
1/2 CTB	3204	-68	205	-78	1529	3200K to 4300K	1
1/3 CTB	3206	-49	—	—	—	3200K to 3800K	2/3
1/4 CTB	3208	-30	203	-35	1532	3200K to 3600K	2/3
1/8 CTB	3216	-12	218	-18	1535	3200K to 3400K	1/3

Cinemills Corporation makes gels that share the same product numbers as Lee.

Table F.8 Blue/Orange Correction: Colormeter LB Index (MIREDs) and Corresponding Camera Filters and Color Correction Gels

Colormeter LB reading (MIREDs)	Kodak Wratten Filter		Light Loss due to filter	Approximate equivalent gel	Kelvin Shift	
	Amber	Blue			from	to
−257	—	—	4	Double CTB	3200	10,000
−133	—	80A	2	Full CTB	3200	5500
−112	—	80B	1-2/3	—	3400	5500
−100	—	80C +82A	—	3/4 CTB	3200	4700
−90	—	82C + 82C	1-1/3	—	2490	3200
−81	—	80C	1	1/2 CTB	3800	5500
−77	—	82C + 82B	1-1/3	—	2570	3200
−66	—	82C + 82A	1	—	2650	3200
−56	—	80D	1/3	—	4200	5500
−55	—	82C + 82	1	1/3 CTB	2720	3200
−45	—	82C	2/3	—	2800	3200
−32	—	82B	2/3	1/4 CTB	2900	3200
−21	—	82A	1/3	1/8 CTB	3000	3200
−10	—	82	1/3	—	3100	3200
+9	81	—	1/3	—	3300	3200
+18	81A	—	1/3	—	3400	3200
+27	81B	—	1/3	1/8 CTO	3500	3200
+35	81C	—	1/3	—	3600	3200
+42	81D	—	2/3	1/4 CTO	3700	3200
+52	81EF	—	2/3	—	3850	3200
+81	85C	—	1/3	1/2 CTO	5500	3800
+112	85	—	2/3	—	5500	3400
+133	85B	—	2/3	3/4 CTO or Sun 85	5500	3200
+167	85B + 81C	—	2/3	Full CTO	5600	2900

Table F.9 Green/Magenta Correction: Colormeter CC Index and Corresponding Gels and Filters

Colormeter II Color Compensation	Colormeter III CC Filter Magenta	Colormeter III CC Filter Green	Gel Source With Gel Name	Rosco Cinegel No.	Lee Gel No.	GAM Gel No.	Compensation in f-Stops	Conversion
+18	40M	—	—	—	—	—	2/3	Removes Green
+13	30M	—	Full Minus Green	3308	247	1580	2/3	"
+8	20M	—	—	—	—	—	1/3	"
+6	15M	—	Half Minus Green	3313	248	1582	1/3	"
+4	10M	—	—	—	—	—	1/3	"
+3	7.5M	—	1/4 Minus Green	3314	249	1583	1/3	"
+2	5M	—	—	—	—	—	1/3	"
+1	3.5M	—	1/8 Minus Green	3318	279	1584	1/4	"
-1		3.5G	1/8 Plus Green	3317	278	—	1/4	Adds Green
-2		7.5G	1/4 Plus Green	3316	246	—	1/3	"
-4		10G	—	—	—	—	1/3	"
-5		15G	1/2 Plus Green	3315	245	1587	1/3	"
-7		20G	—	—	—	—	1/3	"
-10		30G	Full Plus Green	3304	244	1585	2/3	"
-13		40G	—	—	—	—	2/3	"
—	30M	—	Fluoro-Filter	3310	—	1590	1-2/3	Converts cool whites to 3200K
—	—	30G	Plus-green 50	3306	—	—	1-1/4	Converts 3200K source to match cool whites
—	—	30G	Fluorescent 5700	—	241	—	1-2/3	Converts 3200K source to 5700K (cool white fluorescents)
—	—	30G	Fluorescent 4300	—	242	—	1-1/2	Converts 3200K source to 4300K (white fluorescents)
—	—	30G	Fluorescent 3600	—	243	—	1-1/4	Converts 3200K source to 3600K (warm white fluorescents)

Table F.10   Theatrical Gel Colors

Gamcolor Gels					
The Great American Market		440	Very Light Straw	950	Purple
105	Antique Rose	450	Saffron	960	Medium Lavender
	(Minusgreen)	460	Mellow Yellow	970	Special Lavender
106	1/2 Antique Rose	470	Pale Gold	980	Surprise Pink
	(1/2 Minusgreen)	480	Medium Lemon	995	Orchid
107	1/4 Antique Rose	510	No Color Straw		
	(1/4 Minusgreen)	520	New Straw	**Lee Gels**	
108	1/8 Antique Rose	535	Lime (1/2 Plusgreen)	*Cosmetic Range*	
	(1/8 Minusgreen)	540	Pale Green (Plusgreen)	184	Cosmetic Peach
110	Dark Rose	570	Light Green Yellow	185	Cosmetic Burgundy
120	Bright Pink	650	Grass Green	186	Cosmetic Silver Rose
130	Rose	655	Rich Green	187	Cosmetic Rouge
140	Dark Magenta	660	Medium Green	188	Cosmetic Highlight
150	Pink Punch	680	Kelly Green	189	Cosmetic Silver Moss
155	Light Pink	685	Pistachio	190	Cosmetic Emerald
160	Chorus Pink	690	Bluegrass	191	Cosmetic Aqua Blue
170	Dark Flesh Pink	710	Blue Green		
180	Cherry	720	Light Steel Green	*Theatrical Colors*	
190	Cold Pink	725	Princess Blue	002	Rose Pink
195	Nymph Pink	730	Azure Blue	003	Lavender Tint
220	Pink Magenta	740	Off Blue	004	Medium Bastard
235	Pink Red	750	Nile Blue		Amber (HT)
245	Light Red	760	Aqua Blue	007	Pale Yellow (HT)
250	Medium Red XT	770	Christel Blue	008	Dark Salmon (HT)
260	Rosy Amber	780	Shark Blue	009	Pale Amber Gold (HT)
270	Red Orange	790	Electric Blue	010	Medium Yellow (HT)
280	Fire Red	810	Moon Blue	013	Straw Tint (HT)
290	Fire Orange	820	Full Light Blue	015	Deep Straw (HT)
305	French Rose	830	North Sky Blue	019	Fire (HT)
315	Autumn Glory	835	Aztec Blue	020	Medium Amber (HT)
320	Peach	840	Steel Blue	021	Gold Amber (HT)
323	Indian Summer	842	Whisper Blue (1/2 CTB)	022	Dark Amber (HT)
325	Bastard Amber	845	Cobalt	024	Scarlet (HT)
330	Sepia	847	City Blue (Extra CTB)	026	Bright Red (HT)
335	Coral (Extra CTO)	848	Bonus Blue	027	Medium Red (HT)
340	Light Bastard Amber	850	Primary Blue	035	Light Pink (HT)
343	Honey (Full CTO)	860	Sky Blue	036	Medium Pink (HT)
345	Deep Amber	870	Whinter White (1/8 CTB)	046	Dark Magenta (HT)
350	Dark Amber	880	Daylight Blue	048	Rose Pink
360	Amber Blush (1/2 CTO)	882	Southern Sky (Full CTB)	052	Light Lavender (HT)
363	Sand	885	Blue Ice (1/4 CTB)	053	Paler Lavender (HT)
364	Pale Honey (1/4 CTO)	888	Blue Bell (3/4 CTB)	058	Lavender (HT)
365	Warm Straw	890	Dark Sky Blue	061	Mist Blue (HT)
370	Spice (CTO/N.6)	905	Dark Blue	063	Pale Blue (HT)
375	Flame	910	Alice Blue	068	Sky Blue
380	Golden Tan (CTO/N.3)	920	Pale Lavender	079	Just Blue (HT)
385	Light Amber	930	Real Congo Blue	085	Deeper Blue (HT)
390	Walnut (CTO/N.9)	940	Light Purple	089	Moss Green (HT)
420	Medium Amber	945	Royal Purple	090	Dark Yellow Green
		948	African Violet		(HT)

HT = High temperature polycarbonate base.

101	Yellow	172	Lagoon Blue (HT)	21	Golden Amber
102	Light Amber	174	Dark Steel Blue	321	Soft Golden Amber
103	Straw	176	Loving Amber	22	Deep Amber
104	Deep Amber	179	Chroma Orange	23	Orange
105	Orange	180	Dark Lavender	24	Scarlet
106	Primary Red	181	Congo Blue (HT)	25	Orange Red
107	Light Rose	182	Light Red	26	Light Red
109	Light Salmon	183	Moonlight Blue	27	Medium Red
110	Middle Rose	192	Flesh Pink	30	Light Salmon Pink
111	Dark Pink	193	Rosy Amber	31	Salmon Pink
113	Magenta	194	Surprise Pink	32	Medium Salmon Pink
115	Peacock Blue (HT)	195	Zenith Blue (HT)	332	Cherry Rose
116	Medium Green Blue	196	True Blue	33	No Color Pink
	(HT)	197	Alice Blue (HT)	333	Blush Pink
117	Steel Blue	332	Follies Pink	34	Flesh Pink
118	Light Blue (HT)	332	Special Rose Pink	35	Light Pink
119	Dark Blue (HT)	343	Special Medium Lavender	36	Medium Pink
120	Deep Blue (HT)	344	Violet	37	Pale Rose Pink
121	Lee Green (HT)	353	Lighter Blue	337	True Pink
122	Fern Green (HT)	354	Special Steel Blue	38	Light Rose
124	Dark Green (HT)	363	Special Medium Blue	39	Skelton Exotic Sangria
126	Mauve		(HT)	339	Broadway Pink
127	Smoky Pink			40	Light Salmon
128	Bright Pink		**Roscolux Gel**	41	Salmon
129	Heavy Frost		*(in sheets and 24 in. rolls)*	42	Deep Salmon
130	Clear	00	Clear	342	Rose Pink
132	Medium Blue (HT)	01	Light Bastard Amber	43	Deep Pink
134	Golden Amber	02	Bastard Amber	44	Middle Rose
135	Deep Golden Amber	03	Dark Bastard Amber	344	Follies Pink
136	Pale Lavender	04	Medium Bastard Amber	45	Rose
137	Special Lavender	304	Pale Apricot	46	Magenta
138	Pale Green	05	Rose Tint	47	Light Rose Purple
139	Primary Green (HT)	305	Rose Gold	48	Rose Purple
141	Bright Blue (HT)	06	No Color Straw	49	Medium Purple
142	Pale Violet	07	Pale Yellow	349	Fisher Fuchia
143	Pale Navy Blue	08	Pale Gold	50	Mauve
144	No Color Blue	09	Pale Amber Gold	51	Surprise Pink
147	Apricot	10	Medium Yellow	52	Light Lavender
148	Bright Rose	310	Daffodil	53	Pale Lavender
151	Golt Tint	11	Light Straw	54	Special Lavender
152	Pale Gold	12	Straw	55	Lilac
153	Pale Salmon	312	Canary	355	Pale Violet
154	Pale Rose	13	Straw Tint	56	Middle Lavender
156	Chocolate	14	Medium Straw	57	Lavender
157	Pink	15	Deep Straw	357	Royal Lavender
158	Deep Orange	16	Light Amber	58	Deep Lavender
159	No Color Straw	316	Gallo Gold	358	Rose Indigo
161	Slate Blue	17	Light Flame	59	Indigo
162	Bastard Amber	317	Apricot	359	Medium Violet
164	Flame Red	18	Flame	60	No Color Blue
165	Daylight Blue	318	Mayan Sun	360	Clearwater
166	Pale Red	19	Fire	61	Mist Blue
170	Deep Lavender	20	Medium Amber	62	Booster Blue

63	Pale Blue	389	Chroma Green	624	Pink
363	Aquamarine	90	Dark Yellow Green	625	Pale Rose Pink
64	Light Steel Blue	91	Primary Green	626	Flesh Pink
364	Blue Bell	92	Turquoise	627	Rose Pink
65	Daylight Blue	93	Blue Green	631	Middle Rose
365	Cool Blue	94	Kelly Green	632	Salmon
66	Cool Blue	95	Medium Blue Green	638	Light Rose Purple
67	Light Sky Blue	395	Teal Green	639	Lilac
68	Sky Blue	96	Lime	641	Lavender
69	Brilliant Blue	97	Light Grey	642	Surprise Pink
70	Nile Blue	397	Pale Grey	644	Deep Lilac
71	Sea Blue	98	Medium Grey	645	Indigo
72	Azure Blue	99	Chocolate	647	Pale Blue
73	Peacock Blue			648	No Color Blue
74	Night Blue	**Rosco Cinecolor Gel**		649	Booster Blue
76	Light Green Blue	*(in 48 in. rolls)*		651	Light Steel Blue
376	Bermuda Blue	602	Bastard Amber	652	Azure Blue
77	Green Blue	603	Warm Rose	654	Daylight Blue
78	Trudy Blue	604	No Color Straw	657	Primary Blue
378	Alice Blue	605	Pale Gold	658	Medium Green Blue
79	Bright Blue	608	Warm Straw	659	Green Blue
80	Primary Blue	609	Straw	661	Medium Blue
81	Urban Blue	610	Light Flame	669	Pale Yellow Green
82	Surprise Blue	611	Rose Amber	671	Light Green
83	Medium Blue	612	Golden Amber	672	Moss Green
383	Sapphire Blue	613	Light Amber	673	Turquoise
84	Zephyr Blue	614	Flame	674	Primary Green
85	Deep Blue	615	Deep Straw	675	Light Blue Green
385	Royal Blue	617	Peach	676	Blue Green
86	Pea Green	618	Orange	677	Medium Blue Green
87	Pale Yellow Green	620	Deep Salmon	680	Light Grey
88	Light Green	621	Light Red	681	Medium Grey
388	Gaslight Green	622	Pink Tint	682	Chocolate
89	Moss Green	623	Light Pink		

Table F.11 Diffusion Materials

Types of Diffusion	Product No.	Light Reduction	Notes
Lee			
Full Tough Spun	214	2-1/2	Slight softening of field and beam edge.
Half Tough Spun	215	1-1/2	Slight softening of field and beam edge.
Quarter Tough Spun	229	3/4	Slight softening of field and beam edge.
Full Tough Spun	261	2	Flame retardant. Slight softening of field and beam edge.
3/4 Tough Spun	262	1-2/3	Flame retardant.
1/2 Tough Spun	263	1-1/3	Flame retardant.
3/8 Tough Spun	264	1	Flame retardant.
1/4 Tough Spun	265	3/4	Flame retardant.
216 White Diffusion	216	1-1/2	Very popular moderate/heavy diffusion. Available in 60" width.
1/2 216	250	3/4	Moderate beam spread and softening.
1/4 216	251	1/3	Moderate beam spread and softening.
1/8 216	252	1/8	Moderate beam spread and softening.
Blue Diffusion	217	1-1/2	Increases color temperature very slightly.
Daylight Blue Frost	224	2-1/4	CTB frost.
Neutral Density Frost	225	2	ND .6 frost.
Brushed Silk	228	3/4	Diffuses light in one direction only.
Hampshire Frost	253	1/4	Very light frost.
New Hampshire Frost	254	—	High-temperature polycarbonate base
Hollywood Frost	255	—	—
Half Hampshire	256	—	—
Quarter Hampshire	257	—	—
Heavy Frost	129	1-1/3	Flame retardant.
White Frost	220	1-1/3	Flame retardant.
Blue Frost	221	1-1/3	Flame retardant. Increases color temperature very slightly.
Grid Cloth	430	—	Heavy white fabric 52-in.width.
Light Grid Cloth	432	—	Lighter white fabric in 52-in. width.
Rosco			
Tough Spun	3006	2-1/2	Slight softening of field and beam edge.
Light Tough Spun	3007	1-2/3	Slight softening of field and beam edge.
1/4 Tough Spun	3022	1	Slight softening of field and beam edge.
Tough Frost	3008	2	Slight to moderate softening, moderate beam spread but with discernible beam center.
Light Tough Frost	3009	1-1/2	Slight to moderate softening, moderate beam spread but with discernible beam center.
Opal Tough Frost	3010	1	Popular light diffusion with slight to moderate softening, moderate beam spread but with discernible beam center.
Light Opal	3020	1/2	Slight to moderate softening, moderate beam spread but with discernible beam center.
Tough White Diffusion	3026	3-1/2	Like Lee 216. Dense diffusion with wide beam spread creating even field of shadowless light.
1/2 White Diffusion	3027	2-1/2	Like Lee 250. Moderately dense diffusion with wide beam spread.
1/4 White Diffusion	3028	1-1/2	Like Lee 251. Moderate diffusion with wide beam spread.

Table F.11 Diffusion Materials (continued)

Types of Diffusion	Product No.	Light Reduction	Notes
Tough Rolux	3000	2-1/2	Moderately dense diffusion with wide beam spread.
Light Tough Rolux	3001	—	Moderate diffusion with wide beam spread.
Grid Cloth	3030	5	Comes in 54 in. rolls. Very dense diffusion with very wide beam spread which creates soft shadowless light. Ideal for large area diffusion. Not tolerant of high heat.
Light Grid Cloth	3032	3-1/2	Smaller weave than grid cloth. Considerable softening. Comes in 54 in. rolls.
1/4 Grid Cloth	3034	2-1/2	Considerable softening. Comes in 54 in. rolls.
Silent Frost	3029	3	Diffusion made of a rubbery plastic that does not crinkle and rattle in the wind.
Hilite	3014	1	Quiet like silent frost. Comes in 54 in. rolls.
Soft Frost	3002	2	Quite like silent frost, denser than Hilite.
Wide Soft Frost	3023	2	In 72 in. width.
1/2 Soft Frost	3004	1/2	Quiet, light diffuser.
Tough Silk	3011	1-1/2	Considerable softening in one direction only.
Light Tough Silk	3015	1	Considerable softening in one direction only.
Tough Booster Silk	3012	—	Raises color temperature from 3200K to 3500K with silk softening characteristics.
Tough Booster Frost	3013	—	Raises color temperature from 3200K to 3800K with frost softening characteristics.
Full Blue Frost	3017	—	Raises color temperature from 3200K to daylight with frost softening characteristics.
GAM—The Great American Market			
Medium GAM Frost	10	—	Soft light, warm center, diffuse edge.
Light GAM Frost	15	—	Soft light, warm center, diffuse edge.
Full GAM Spun	32	2-1/2	Textural, warm center defined edge.
Medium GAM Spun	35	1-2/3	Textural, warm center defined edge.
Light GAM Spun	38	1	Textural, warm center defined edge.
Gamvel	45	3	Soft light with diffuse shadow line.
216 GAM White	55	—	Shadowless, white light. Heavy diffusion with no center or edge visible.
Medium GAM Silk	65	—	Spreads light predominantly in one direction.
Light GAM Silk	68	—	Spreads light predominantly in one direction.
Gam Fusion	10-10	1/4	Almost clear with no color shift.
Gam Fusion	10-20	1/4	Very light diffusion with no color shift.
Gam Fusion	10-30	1/2	Light diffusion with no color shift.
Gam Fusion	10-40	1/2	Medium-light diffusion with no color shift.
Gam Fusion	10-50	1	Medium diffusion with no color shift.
Gam Fusion	10-60	2	Medium-heavy diffusion with no color shift.
Gam Fusion	10-70	5	Heavy diffusion with no color shift.
Gam Fusion	10-75	5	Heavy diffusion with no color shift.
Gam Fusion	10-80	6	Very heavy diffusion with no color shift.
Gam Fusion	10-90	6	Fully diffuse with no color shift.

Light reduction values given here are manufacturers' approximate figures. The actual transmission will depend on the beam angle of the light and the distance from the diffusion.

APPENDIX **G**

Lighting Accessories

Ring sizes for all fixtures are listed in Appendix A. Table G.1 shows which banks correspond to which ring sizes. Table G.2 lists ordering numbers for lights requiring dedicated speed rings not given in Appendix A.

Table G.1 Chimera Light Bank Specifications

Chimera Type	Ring Sizes	Size	Dimensions (in.)	Depth (in.)
Video Pro	3–9"	Extra Small	16 x 22	12
		Small	24 x 32	18
		Medium	36 x 48	24
Quartz Bank	9–21"	Small	24 x 32	22
		Medium	36 x 48	29
		Large	54 x 72	38
Daylight Junior Bank	6-5/8–21"	Extra Small	16 x 22	21
		Small	24 x 32	30
		Medium	36 x 48	36
Daylight Bank	9–21"	Small	24 x 32	33
		Medium	36 x 48	40
		Large	54 x 72	48
Daylight Senior Bank	24-1/2–29"	Large	54 x 72	50

Table G.2 Ordering Numbers for Special Dedicated Speed Rings

Light Fixture	Video Pro	Daylight Junior Bank	Quartz Bank	Daylight Bank	Ring Frame Size (in.)
Lowel					
DP Light	9500AL				8
Tota-light	9510AL				8.5
Omni Light	9530AL				7.3
Pro-light	2945				5.9
V-light	2955				5.9
Quad DP Light			9011	9013	15.5
Triple Tota-light			9031	9033	13.5
Mole Richardson					
Baby 407	2970				6-5/8
Tennie-Mole 650	2990AL				8.5
Mickey 1k	9540	9542			8.5
Quad Mickey			9071	9073	15.5
Mighty 2k			9731	9733	13.5
Arri					
Arrilite 650, 800, and 1000W	2900				
Quad Arrilite			9051	9053	15.5
Strand Quartz Color					
Quad Ianebeam 650/1000			9061	9063	15.5
Reporter 200	9710				6.2
Sachtler					
Reporter 100H, 250H, 125D	9570				6.2
Reporter 270D, 650H	9580				7.5
Production 575	9590				7.5
Reporter 200, RL 250-300 DLF	9710				6.2

Table G.3 Dimmers

Dimmer	Model No.	Type	Ouput Voltage	Amps Per Chnl.	Total Amps	Input Power	Input Connector	Output Connector
Mole Richardson								
1200W Molestat	5241	Auto-transformer	0–140V AC	10A	10A	120V AC	Edison	Edison
1800W Molestat	5231	Auto-transformer	0–140V AC	15A	15A	120V AC	Edison	Edison
2.4kW DC Molelectronic	5321	Electronic	118V DC	20A	20A	120V DC	20A Bates	20A Bates
6kW DC Molelectronic	5331	Electronic	118V DC	50A	50A	120V DC	60A Bates	60A Bates
12kW DC Molelectronic	5351	Electronic	118V DC	100A	100A	120V DC	100A Bates	100A Bates
72kW DC 6-pack	53570	Electronic	118V DC	100A	600 amps 300A per leg	120/240V DC	Bus-bars	100A Bates
12kW AC Molelectronic	42590	Electronic	118V AC	100A	100A	120V AC	100A Bates	100A Bates
20kW AC Molelectronic	42450	Electronic	206/238V AC	100A @ 240V	100A per leg	208/240VAC	100A 250V Bates	100A 250V Bates
144kW AC 12-Pack	8881	Electronic	116V AC	100A	1200A, 400A per leg	208/240 VAC	Bus-bars, 4-wire + ground	100A Bates
1000W Plate Dimmer	504	Resistance	120V AC or DC	8.3A	8.3A	120V AC or DC	Full stage plug	Edison
2000W Plate Dimmer	503	Resistance	120V AC or DC	16.6A	16.6A	120V AC or DC	Full stage plug	Edison
3000W Plate Dimmer	5091	Reisistance	120V AC or DC	25A	25A	120V AC or DC	Mole Pin	Full stage plug
5000W Plate Dimmer	2301	Resistance	120V AC or DC	41.6A	41.6A	120V AC or DC	Full stage plug	Full stage plug
22,000W Plate Console	367	Resistance	120V AC or DC	2 41.6A 4 16.6A 4 8.3A	183.3A	120V AC or DC	2 Full stage plug	10 Full stage plugs
2–5k								
4–2k								
4–1k								
LTM								
1-Channel Pepper Pot		Triac	120V AC	8.3A	8.3A	120V AC	Edison	Edison
3-Channel Pepper Pot		Triac	120V AC	3–8.3A	25A	120V AC	As ordered	3 Edison
6-Channel Pepper Pot		Triac	120V AC	6–10A	60A	120V AC	As ordered	6 Edison

Table G.3 Dimmers (continued)

Dimmer	Model No.	Type	Output Voltage	Amps Per Chnl.	Total Amps	Input Power	Input Connector	Output Connector
20kW Dimmer	IA-925WA	Electronic	120 or 240V	100A @ 240V	100A @ 240V	120V AC or 240V	240V 100A Bates	240V 100A Bates
Strand								
20k Single	73118	Electronic	208V AC	83.3A @ 240V	83.3A per leg	120/208V AC	240V 100A Bates	240V 100A Bates
12k Single Analogue Multiplex	73115 73116	Electronic	120V AC	100A	100A	120V AC	100A Bates	100A Bates
6k Single Analogue Multiplex	73113 73114	Electronic	120V AC	50A	60A	120V AC	60A Bates	60A Bates
2.4k Single Analogue Multiplex	73111 73112	Electronic	120V AC	20A	20A	120V AC	20A Bates	20A Bates
CD80 Pack 24 1.2kW	—	Electronic	120V AC	24 10A	240A, 80A x 3 240A, 120A x 2	Three-phase Single-phase	Cam Lok	20A Bates
CD80 Pack 12 2.4kW	—	Electronic	120V AC	12 20A	240A, 80A x 3 240A, 120A x 2	Three-phase Single Phase	Cam Lok	20A Bates
CD80 Pack 24 2.4kW	—	Electronic	120V AC	24 20A	480A, 160A x 3 480A, 240A x 2	Three-phase Single-phase	Cam Loc	20A Bates
CD80 Pack 6 6kW	—	Electronic	120V AC	6 50A	300A, 100A x 3 300A, 150A x 2	Three-phase Single-phase	Cam Lok	60A Bates
CD80 Pack 6 12kW	—	Electronic	120V AC	6 100A	600A, 200A x 3	Three-phase only	Cam Lok	100A Bates
CD80 Rolling Rack 48 2.4kW	—	Electronic	120V AC	48 20A	960A, 160A x 6 960A, 320A x 3 960A, 320A x 3	Three-phase Three-phase Three-phase	2 sets Cam-lok or 1 set Posi-lok or 1 set Abbott	20A Bates or Socapex
CD80 Rolling Rack 24 6kW	—	Electronic	120V AC	48 20A	1200A,200A x 6 1200A, 400A x 3	Three-phase Three-phase	2 sets Cam-lok or 1 set Posi-lok or 1 set Abbott	60A Bates

Table G.3 Dimmers (continued)

Dimmer	Model No.	Type	Ouput Voltage	Amps Per Chnl.	Total Amps	Input Power	Input Connector	Output Connector
CD80 Rolling Rack 24 12kW	—	Electronic	120V AC	48 20A	2400A, 200A x 12 2400A, 400A x 6 2400A, 400A x 6	Three-phase Three-phase Three-phase	4 sets Cam-lok or 2 sets Posi-lok or 2 sets Abbott	100A Bates
Standard Variacs								
1k Variac		Auto-transformer	0-140V AC	8.3 A	8.3A	120V AC	Edison	Edison
2k Variac		Auto-transformer	0-140V AC	16.6A	16.6A	120V AC	Edison	Edison
5k Variac		Auto-transformer	0-140V AC	41.5A	41.5A	120V AC	60A Bates	60A Bates
Household Dimmers								
150W Socket Dimmer		Small Triac	120V AC	1.25A	1.24A	120V AC	Med screw base socket	Med Screw base socket
600W Household		Small Triac	120V AC	5.0A	5.0A	120V AC	Edison	Edison
1000W Household		Small Triac	120V AC	8.3A	8.3A	120V AC	Edison	Edison
Magic Gadgets								
Low Volt DC Dimmer		Transistor	0-24V DC	10A	10A @ 12 or 24V DC	24V DC	Screw terminals	Screw terminals
2k In-line Dimmer (w/flicker box input)		Triac	120V AC	16.6A	16.6A	120V AC	Edison	Edison
5k In-line Dimmer (w/flicker box input)		Dual SCR	120V AC	41.6A	41.6A	120V AC	60A Bates	60A Bates
10k In-line Dimmer (w/flicker box input)		Duel SCR	120V AC	83.3A	83.3A	120V AC	100A Bates	100A Bates
20k In-line Dimmer (w/flicker box input)		Duel SCR	220/240V AC	83.3A @ 240V	83.3A per leg	220 or 240V AC	100A, 240V Bates	100A, 240V Bates

All units are also available for foreign voltage.

Table G.4 Flicker Boxes

Device	Channels	Amps per chnl	Input Volts	Controls	Functions
Magic Gadgets—William A. McIntire Enterprises					
Shadowmaker	3-channel	16.6A	120V AC	3 high limit pots 3 low limit pots 1 speed pot 4 function switches Manual ON & OFF buttons	Manual dimmers, Full ON (test), All blink 5 chase sequences 2 lightning flashes 3 TV screen effects 2 candlelight, 2 firelight
Shadowmaker Programmable	3-channel	16.6A	120V AC	As above	User programable from Mac or PC
Flicker Dimmers 2k 5k 10k 20k	1-channel	16.6 41.6 83.3 83.3	120V AC 120V AC 120V AC 240V AC	1 speed pot 1 high limit pot 1 low limit pot 1 Dim/Off/Flicker	Manual dimmer or Flickers at random to levels between high and low settings.
Flicker Dimmer Progammable	1-channel	As above	As above	As above	User progammable from Mac or PC
Flicker 2D 2k 5k 10k 20k	1-channel	16.6A 41.6A 83.3A 83.3A	120V AC 120V AC 120V AC 240V AC	1 high limit pot 1 low limit pot 1 speed pot 4 function switches Manual ON & OFF buttons	4 TV/film, 6 firelight 2 lightning, 2 pulsating 1 blink, Full ON (test) or Manual dimmer
Flicker 3D	3-channel	Drives any number of 20A, 50A and 100A Magic Gadgets dimmers (Table G.3)	120V AC	1 speed pot 4 function switches Manual ON & OFF buttons	Full ON (test) Blink 5 chase sequences 2 lightning flashes 3 TV screen effects 2 candlelight 2 firelight
Flicker DC	1-channel	10A	0-24V DC	Same as 2D above	Same as 2D above
21D Sequencer	21-channel	Drives any number of 20-, 50-, & 100A Magic Gadgets dimmers (Table G.3)	120V AC	1 speed pot 5 function switches Manual ON & OFF buttons	Full ON (test) Blink 5 chase sequences 2 lightning flashes 3 TV screen effects 2 candlelight 2 firelight

Table G.4 Flicker Boxes (continued)

Device	Channels	Amps per chnl	InputVolts	Controls	Functions
Flicker Torch	1-channel	Battery-powered three 9-volt	27V DC	On/Off dimmer	Small flickering bulb for use in prop torch or lantern.
Lightning Stepper	3 inputs 9 outputs	Drives photo strobe packs	120V AC	None	None
Great American Market					
Flickermaster	1-channel	8.3A	120V AC 9 V battery	1 speed pot 1 dimmer pot 1 4-position selector (off, test, 0-100, 10-100)	Random flicker, Manual dimmer
SPE-5 Flickermaster	1-channel	16.6A	120V AC	1 speed pot 1 threshold pot 1 dimmer pot 1 4-position selector (off, test, 0-100, V-100), Flicker/Strobe Switch	Strobe Random flicker Manual dimmer
SPE-X3 Flickermaster	3-channel	16.6A	120V AC	3 channel On/Off 3 dimmer pots 3 delay pots 1 master speed pot 1 master dimmer Selector knob A/B toggle Memory set button 1 reverse/forward 1 chase/dark chase	Off, test, chase, random flicker, independent flicker, strobe, and 16 memory positions (recalls previous delay, dimmer and speed settings), manual dimmers. Retains memory settings between uses.

Equipment Manufacturers and Distributors

Abbott and Co., 1611 Cascada Dr., Marion, OH 43302. Electrical connectors.

Airstar, Lenix helium balloons. Contact Industrial Wholesale Electric Co., 1500 S. Griffith Ave., Los Angeles, CA 90021.

Altman Stage Lighting Company, Inc. 57 Alexander St., Yonkers, NY 10701. Tungsten and HMI fixtures, ellipsoidal and theatrical fixtures.

American Studio Equipment, 8922 Norris Ave., Sun Valley, CA 91352. Studio and grip equipment.

Arri, 617 Route 303, Blauvelt, NY 10913; 600 N. Victory Blvd., Burbank, CA 91502. Tungsten and HMI lights.

Automated Entertainment, P.O. Box 7309, Burbank, CA 91510-7309. Range of dichroic filters, blacklights, fully stocked theatrical rental house.

Backstage Studio Equipment, 8010 Wheatland Ave., Unit D, Sun Valley, CA 91352. Studio equipment.

Benjamin Electric Co., 1615 Staunton Ave., Los Angeles, CA 90021. Distribution boxes, deuce boards, studio distribution equipment.

Cam-Lok, 531 Fifth St., Unit E, San Fernando, CA 91340. Electrical connectors.

Carol Cable Co., Inc. Pawtucket, RI 02862. Cable.

Chimera Photographic Lighting, 1812 Valtec La., Boulder, CO 80301. Soft boxes.

Cinemills Corp., 3500 W. Magnolia Blvd., Burbank, CA 91505. HMI bulbs and lights, gel.

Clairmont Camera. 4040 Vineland Ave., Studio City, CA, 91604. Synchronous strobe system, camera rental.

Colortran Inc, 1015 Chestnut St, Burbank, CA 91506-9983. Ellipsoidal and theatrical fixtures.

Dedotec USA Inc., 410 Garibaldi Ave., Lodi, NJ 07644. Tungsten lights.

Desisti, Desmar Corp., 1109 Grand Ave., North Bergen, NJ 07147. Tungsten and HMI lights.

Di-Lite (Koto Luminous Corp.), Fujita Estate Building, 5th Floor, 4-8 Ueno 1-Chrome, Taito-ku, Tokyo, Japan 110. HMI bulbs.

DN Labs, 1430 Willamette St., Suite 18, Eugene, OR 97401. HMI lights.

Electronic Theatre Controls (ETC) 3030 Laura Ln., Middleton, WI 53562. Dimmer systems, ellipsoidal and par fixtures.

ExCel Wire and Cable Co., 108 Elm Ave., Tiffin, OH 44883. Cable.

Fisher Lights. 5528 Vineland Ave. North Hollywood, CA 91601. Large soft boxes for car photography, soft light crane light.

John Fluke Mfg. Co., Inc., P.O. Box 9090, Everett, WA 98206. Electrical meters.

General Electric, Nela Park, E. Cleveland, OH 44112. Tungsten and HMI bulbs.

Genie USA, 18340 N.E. 76th St., P.O. Box 69, Redmond, WA 98073-0069. Man lift.

Giddings Pace, Inc., 8001 Capwell Dr., Oakland, CA 94621. Underwater HMI lights.

Great American Market, 826 N. Cole Ave., Hollywood, CA 90038. Stick-up lights, flicker boxes, GAM gels, color changers.

Group 5 Engineering, 11620 Exposition Blvd., Los Angeles, CA 90064. Bates connectors.

High End Systems. 2217 West Braker Lane. Austin, TX 78758. Automated lights.

Hydro Image, Inc., 4121 Redwood Ave., Los Angeles, CA 90066. SeaPar underwater lights and cameras.

ILC Technology Inc., 399 Java Dr., Sunnyvale, CA 94089. HMI bulbs.

Innovision Optics. Santa Monica, CA. Fiber Optics lighting systems.

K 5600, 10434 Burbank Blvd, North Hollywood, CA 91601. HMI Joker fixtures and 200W Bug light and 200W inverter.

Kino Flo, Inc., 8824 Lankershim Blvd., Sun Valley, CA 91352. Fluorescent lights.

Lee Colortran, Inc., 1015 Chestnut St., Burbank, CA 91506; 40B Commerce Way, Totowa, NJ 07512. Lighting fixtures, Lee filters, color changers, studio distribution equipment.

Leelium Balloons Ltd., 266 Church Road, Northolt, London UB5 5AW, England. Helium balloons.

Leonetti (Sunray), 5609 Sunset Blvd., Hollywood, CA 90028. HMI and fluorescent fixtures.

Lightmaker, 28145 Ave. Crocker, Valencia, CA 91355. AC/DC and AC lightweight flicker-free ballasts.

Lightning Strikes, 6571 Santa Monica Blvd., Hollywood, CA 90038. Lightning effects lights.

Lowel-Light Manufacturing, Inc., 140 58th St., Brooklyn, NY 11220. Tungsten fixtures.

L.P. Associates, 6650 Lexington Ave., Hollywood, CA 90038. DCI lights and globes.

LTM Corp. of America, 11646 Pendleton St., Sun Valley, CA 91352-2501. Tungsten and HMI fixtures.

Magic Gadgets/William A. McIntire Enterprises, Box 4244, Portland, OR 97208. Dimmers, flicker effects boxes, various gadgets.

Matthews Studio Equipment, Inc., 2405 Empire Ave., Burbank, CA 91504. Studio equipment.

Meltric Corp., 6212 Ace Industrial Dr., Cundahy, WI 53110. Electrical connectors.

Minolta, 11150 Hope St., Cypress, CA 90630. Light meters.

Mole-Richardson Co., 937 N. Sycamore Ave., Hollywood, CA 90038-2384. Tungsten and HMI fixtures, studio equipment, distribution equipment, carbon arc lights.

Musco Mobile Lighting, Ltd., Hwy. 63 S., P.O. Box 73, Oskaloosa, IA 52577. Mobile lighting trucks.

Norms, 5219 Craner Ave., North Hollywood, CA 91601. Studio equipment.

Osram Corp., 110 Bracken Rd., Montgomery, NY 12549-9700; 7658 Haskell Ave., Van Nuys, CA 91406. HMI bulbs.

Peterson Systems International, 2350 E. Central Ave., Duarte, CA 91010. Cable crossovers.

Phillips Lighting Co., 200 Franklin Square Dr., P.O. Box 6800, Somerset, NJ 08875-6800. Bulbs.

Phoebus Manufacturing, 200 Third Street, San Francisco, CA 94107. Xenon follow spots and searchlights, electronic shutters, xenon projector and other specialty items.

Power Gems Corporation, 8010 Weatland Ave. G, Sun Valley, CA 91352; 6-7 Shearer Way, Agecroft Roud, Swinton, Manchester M27 8WA, England. Electronic HMI ballasts.

Rosco Laboratories, Inc., 36 Bush Ave., Port Chester, NY 10573. Gel.

Royal Electric, Inc., 95 Grand Ave., Pawtucket, RI 02862. Cable.

Sachtler, 55 N. Main St., Freeport, NY 11520. Tungsten and HMI fixtures.

Shotmaker, 28145 Ave. Crocker, Valencia, CA 91355. Custom tow vehicles.

Snorkelift, P.O. Box 4065, St. Joseph, MO 64504-4065. Telescoping boom platforms.

SpectraCine, Inc., 820 N. Hollywood Way, Burbank, CA 91505. Light meters.

Strand Lighting, Inc., 18111 S. Santa Fe Ave., P.O. Box 9004, Rancho Dominguez, CA 90021. Tungsten and HMI fixtures, ellipsoidal and threatrical fixtures, dimmer packs.

Strong International, Inc., 4350 McKinley St., Omaha, NE 68112. Xenon, HMI, and tungsten follow spots.

Studio Lighting, Inc., 13831 Herrick Ave., Sylmar, CA 91342. Space lights.

Sylvania, 500 N. State College Blvd., P.O. Box 14154, Orange, CA 92613-1554; 6505 E. Gayhart St., P.O. Box 2795, Los Angeles, CA 90051; 630 Fifth Ave., Suite 2670, New York, NY 10111. Tungsten and HMI bulbs.

Teatronics, 3100 McMillan Rd., San Luis Obispo, CA 93401. Dimmers.

Ultra Light Manufacturing Co., 6590 S. Bermuda Rd., Las Vegas, NV 89119. Tungsten lights and grip equipment.

Unilux, Inc., 290 Lodi St., Hackensack, NJ 07601. Strobe lighting system.

Union Connector, 300 Babylon Tnpk., Roosevelt, NY 11575. Distribution boxes, electrical connectors.

Ushio America, Inc., 20101 S. Vermont Ave., Torrance, CA 90502. Tungsten bulbs.

VEAM (a division of Litton Systems, Inc.), 100 New Wood Rd., Watertown, CT 06795. Electrical connectors.

Wildfire Inc. 11250 Playa Court, Culver City, CA 90230-6150. Ultraviolet light technology. Black light fresnel and theatrical fixtures, paints and accessories.

Wolfram, 30 Janis Way, Scotts Valley, CA 95066. HMI bulbs.

Xenotech, Inc., 11229 Vinedale Ave., Sun Valley, CA 91352. Xenon lights.

Young Generators, Inc., 6605 Cat Canyon La., Arroyo Grande, CA 93420. Generators.

APPENDIX I

World Power and Television Systems

Table I.1 Power and Television Systems Throughout the World

Country	Population (millions)	Language	Television Standard	Line Voltage	Line Frequency
Afghanistan	17.5	Pashtu/Persian	PAL	220	50
Algeria	20.6	Arabic/French	PAL	127/220	50
Angola	8.5	French/Portuguese	PAL	220	50
Antigua & Barbuda	0.077	English	NTSC	230	60
Argentina	28.9	Spanish/Castellano	PAL	220/225	50
Australia	16.25	English	PAL	240	50
Austria	7.6	German	PAL	220	50
Bahamas	0.22	English	NTSC	120/240	60
Babrain	0.4	Arabic/English	PAL	230/110	50/60
Bangladesh	100.0	Bengali	PAL	230	50
Barbados	0.252	English	NTSC	115/200/230	50
Belgium	9.9	Dutch/French	PAL	127/220	50
Benin	3.93	French	PAL	220	50
Bermuda	0.055	English	NTSC	120/240	60
Bolivia	6.4	Spanish	NTSC	115/230	50
Bophutatswana	1.7	English/Sitswana	PAL	220	50
Brazil	138.6	Portuguese	PAL	127/220	60
Brunei	0.3	Malay/English	PAL	230	50
Bulgaria	8.9	Bulgarian	SECAM	220	50
Burma	38.0	Burmese	NTSC	230	50
Burundi	4.46	French	Mono	220	50
Cameroon	9.564	English/French	PAL	220	50
Canada	25.6	English/French	NTSC	120/240	60
Canary Islands	0.14	Spanish	PAL	127/220	50
Central African Rep.	2.465	French/Sango	Mono	220	50
Chile	12.17	Spanish Castellano	NTSC	220	50
China	1000.0+	Chinese—regional	PAL	220	50
Colombia	27.5	Spanish	NTSC	120/240	60
Congo	1.77	French	SECAM	220	50
Costa Rica	2.9	Spanish	NTSC	120	60
Cuba	9.9	Spanish	NTSC	115/120	60
Curacao & Aruba	0.231	Dutch	NTSC	127/220	50
Cyprus	0.7	Greek/Turkish/English	PAL	240	50
Czechoslovakia	15.5	English/Czechoslovak	SECAM	220	50
Denmark	5.1	Danish	PAL	220	50
Djibouti	0.34	French/Arabic	SECAM	220	50
Dominican Rep.	5.8	Spanish	NTSC	110	60
Ecuador	9.25	Spanish	NTSC	110/120/127	60
Egypt	42.2	Arabic/English	SECAM	220	50
El Salvador	6.0	Spanish/English	NTSC	120/240	60
Ethiopia	33.9	Amharic/English	Mono	220	50
Finland	4.9	Finnish	PAL	220	50
France	55.4	French	SECAM	127/220	50
Gabon	0.7	French/Fang	SECAM	230	50

Table I.1 Power and Television Systems Throughout the World

Country	Population (millions)	Language	Television Standard	Line Voltage	Line Frequency
Gambia	0.7	English	Mono	230	50
Germany	77.4	German	PAL/SECAM	127/220	50
Ghana	12.68	English/Acan	PAL	250	50
Gibraltar	0.06	English	PAL	240	50
Greece	10.0	Greek	SECAM	220	50
Grenada	0.115	English	NTSC	230	50
Guadeloupe	0.328	French	SECAM	220	50/60
Guatemala	8.0	Spanish	NTSC	120/240	60
Guinea Rep.	6.0	French	SECAM	220	50
Haiti	5.2	French/Creole	SECAM	115/220/230	60
Honduras	4.1	Spanish	NTSC	110	60
Hong Kong	5.5	Cantonese/English	PAL	200	50
Hungary	10.6	Hungarian	SECAM	220	50
Iceland	0.245	Icelandic	PAL	220	50
India	750.0	Hindi/Urdu	PAL	230/250	50
Indonesia	160.0	Indonesian	PAL	127/220	50
Iran	43.0	Farsi/Kurdish/Arabic	PAL/SECAM	220	50
Iraq	15.0	Arabic/Kurdish	SECAM	220	50
Ireland	3.6	English	PAL	220	50
Israel	4.33	Hebrew/Yiddish/Arabic	PAL	230	50
Italy	57.2	Italian	PAL	127/220	50
Ivory Coast	9.3	French	SECAM	220	50
Jamaica	2.27	English/Spanish	NTSC	110/220	50
Japan	121.0	Japanese	NTSC	100/200/210	50/60
Jordan	3.5	Arabic/English	PAL	220	50
Kenya	19.0	English/Swahili	PAL	240	50
Korea (N)	19.63	Korean	SECAM/NTSC	220	60
Korea (S)	40.0	Korean	NTSC	100	60
Kuwait	1.7	Arabic/English	PAL	240	50
Laos	4.0	Lao	PAL	220	50
Lebanon	2.7	Arabic/French	SECAM	110/220	50
Lesotho	1.5	English	Mono	220	50
Liberia	2.1	English	PAL	120/240	60
Libya	3.5	Arabic/Italian/English	PAL	17/230	50
Luxembourg	0.366	French	PAL/SECAM	120/127/220	50
Macau	0.35	Portuguese/Cantonese/ English	PAL	110/220	50
Madagascar	9.5	Malagsy/French	PAL	127/220	50
Madeira	0.36	Portuguese	PAL	220	50
Malaysia	5.0	Malay	PAL	240	50
Mali	7.3	French	Mono	127/220	50
Malta	0.327	English	PAL	240	50
Mauretania	1.63	Hassaniya Arabic/French	SECAM	230	50
Mauritius	1.1	English/Creole	SECAM	230	50
Mexico	74.9	Spanish	NTSC	120/127/220	60
Mongolia	18.5	Mongol	SECAM	127/220	50
Morocco	21.0	Arabic/French	SECAM	115/127/220	50
Mozambique	13.5	Portuguese	PAL	220	50
Nepal	16.0	Nepali	PAL	220	50
Netherlands	14.5	Dutch	PAL	220	50
New Zealand	3.1	English	PAL	230/240	50
Nicaragua	2.8	Spanish	NTSC	120/240	60
Niger	2.8	French	Mono	220	50
Nigeria	9.4	English	PAL	220/230	50
Norway	4.2	Norwegian	PAL	230	50

Table I.1 Power and Television Systems Throughout the World

Country	Population (millions)	Language	Television Standard	Line Voltage	Line Frequency
Oman	1.5	Arabic/English	PAL	240	50
Pakistan	90.0	Urdu/English/Punjabi	PAL	230	50
Panama	1.9	Spanish/English	NTSC	120/240	60
Papua New Guinea	3.5	English	PAL	240	50
Paraguay	3.6	Spanish	PAL	220	50
Peru	19.69	Spanish	NTSC	225	60
Philippines	56.0	Filipino	NTSC	120/220/240	60
Poland	37.0	Polish	SECAM	220	50
Portugal	10.1	Portuguese	PAL	220	50
Puerto Rico	3.5	Spanish	NTSC	120/240	60
Qatar	0.29	Arabic/Farsi	PAL	240	50
Reunion	0.516	French	SECAM	220	50
Romania	22.6	Romanian	SECAM	220	50
Saudi Arabia	10.5	Arabic	SECAM	127/220	50
Senegal	6.3	French	SECAM	127	50
Seychelles	0.065	English/French	Mono	230	50
Sierra Leone	3.3	English	PAL	230	50
Singapore	1.5	Mandarin/English	PAL	230	50
Somalia	4.6	Arabic/Italian/English	Mono	110/220/230	50
South Africa	23.4	English/Afrikaans	PAL	220/230/250	50
Spain	38.8	Spanish	PAL	127/220	50
Sri Lanka	16.0	English/Sinhala/Tamil	PAL	230	50
St Vincent	0.138	English	NTSC	230	50
Sudan	20.66	Arabic	PAL	240	50
Suriname	0.372	Dutch/English	NTSC	115/127	50/60
Swaziland	0.7	English	PAL	230	50
Sweden	8.4	Swedish	PAL	220	50
Switzerland	6.5	French/German/Italian	PAL	220	50
Syria	10.0	Arabic/Kurdish	SECAM	115/220	50
Taiwan	20.0	Mandarin	NTSC	110/220	60
Tanzania	20.4	Swahili/English	PAL	230	50
Thailand	53.0	English/Thai	PAL	220	50
Togo	3.0	French	SECAM	220	50
Trinidad & Tobago	1.13	English	NTSC	115/230	60
Tunisia	6.84	Arabic/French	SECAM	220	50
Turkey	52.3	Turkish	PAL	220	50
Uganda	14.0	English	PAL	240	50
United Arab Emirates	1.2	Arabic/Farsi	PAL	220/240	50
United Kingdom	56.6	English	PAL	220/230/240	50
Uruguay	3.0	Spanish	PAL	220	50
USA	241.0	English	NTSC	120/208/240	60
USSR	280.0	Russian	SECAM	127/220	50
Venezuela	17.79	Spanish	NTSC	120/208/240	60
Vietnam	62.0	Vietnamese	SECAM	120/220	60
Virgin Islands	0.11	English	NTSC	110/220	60
Yemen Arab Rep.	7.7	Arabic	PAL	220	50
Yemen Dem. Rep.	2.1	Arabic	NTSC	250	50
Yugoslavia	22.6	Croatian	PAL	220	50
Zaire	31.6	French/English	SECAM	220	50
Zambia	6.26	English	PAL	230	50
Zimbabwe	7.8	English	PAL	225	50

Lighting Equipment Order Checklist

HMI Fresnels

To include: barn doors, 5-piece scrim set, gel frame, scrim box, magnetic ballast, 2 50-ft. head cables, ballast feeder cable

____ 18k Fresnel
____ 12k Fresnel
____ 6k Fresnel
____ 4k Fresnel
____ 2500 Fresnel
____ 1200 Fresnel
____ 575 Fresnel
____ 200 Fresnel

____ Electronic ballasts
____ 12k Clear glass lens

HMI Pars

To include: barn doors, 3 piece scrim set, gel frame, scrim box, 4- or 5-piece lens set, magnetic ballast, 2 50-ft. head cables, ballast feeder

____ 6k PAR
____ 4k PAR
____ 2500W PAR
____ 1200W PAR
____ 575W PAR
____ 400W Joker
____ 200W PAR

____ Electronic ballasts

Sun Guns

____ Sun Gun
____ 30V Nicad Belt-Battery
____ AC Power Supply

HMI Soft lights

To include: egg crate, magnetic ballast, 2 50-ft. head cables, ballast feeder

____ 6000 Soft
____ 2500 Soft
____ 1200 Soft
____ 575 Soft

____ Electronic ballasts

Tungsten Fresnels

To include: 5-piece scrim set, gel frame, scrim box or bag, 4-leaf barn doors, power feeder

____ 20k Fresnel w/ramp-up dimmer
____ 10k Studio Fresnel
____ 10k Big Eye Fresnel
____ 10k Baby Tenner
____ 5k Studio Fresnel
____ 5k Baby Senior
____ 2k 8" Junior Fresnel
____ 2k Baby Junior Fresnel
____ 2k Studio Junior Fresnel
____ 1k Studio Fresnel (407)
____ 1k Baby Baby Fresnel
____ 650W Fresnel
____ 420 Pepper
____ 300 Pepper
____ 200 Pepper
____ 200W Midget/Tiny/Mini
____ 100W Pepper

Dedos

____ 150W Dedo Kit
____ 100W Dedo Kit
____ 250W Dedo Cool Kit

Fresnel Accessories

____ Snoots
____ Focal Spots
____ Shutters
____ Chimera Banks
____ Chimera Speed Rings

Tungsten Softlights

To include: egg crate, power feeder

____ 8k Soft Light
____ 4k Softlight
____ 4k Zip Soft
____ 2k Super Soft
____ 2k Zip Soft
____ 1k Zip Soft
____ 750 Zip Soft
____ 400 Soft

Tungsten Open Face

To include: 5-piece scrim set, gel frame, scrim box or bag, 4-leaf barn doors

____ 2k Mighty Mole
____ 2k Blonde
____ 1k Mickey Mole
____ 1k Red Head
____ 650 Open Face
____ 2k Nook
____ 1k Nook
____ 650W Nook
____ 1k Molette
____ 2k Molette
____ Pinza (Med Screw Base)

Kits

____ R-40 Kit
____ Lowel Tape-up Kit
____ Stick-up Kit

Tungsten PARs

____ 1k Mole Par (w/ 3-piece scrim set, barn doors)
____ 1k Par Cans (w/ gel frame, bail block)
____ 6-lite PAR (6 PAR 64s)
____ Maxi-brute (9 PAR 64s)
____ Dino (24 PAR 64s)
____ Ultra Dino (36 PAR 64s)
____ VNSP PAR 64
____ NSP PAR 64
____ MFL PAR 64
____ WFL PAR 64
____ 9-light FAY
____ 6-light FAY
____ 4-light FAY
____ 2-light FAY
____ 1-light FAY
____ PAR 36 Dichroic
____ PAR 36 Tungsten MFL
____ PAR 36 Tungsten WFL

Tungsten Area Lights

____ Sky Pan (10k, 5k, or 2k)
____ Chicken Coop 6k
____ Space Light 6k
____ 2k Scoop Light
____ 1k Scoop Light

Ellipsoidal Spotlights

____ 2k Molipiso
____ 1k Molipso
____ 50° 1k 4.5 x 6 equivalent
____ 36° 1k 6 x 9 equivalent
____ 26° 1k 6 x 12 equivalent

____ 19° 1k 6 x 16 equivalent
____ 10° 1k 6 x 22 equivalent
____ 5° 1k 10 x 23 equivalent

____ Edison Pigtails
____ Bail Blocks

Other Theatrical Lights

____ Cyc Strip
____ Follow Spot
____ Beam Projector
____ Scene Machine

Fluorescents

____ Wall-o-light (10 bank)
____ 4-ft. Four bank
____ 4-ft. Double Bank
____ 4-ft. Single
____ 2-ft. Four bank
____ 2-ft. Double bank
____ 2-ft. Single
____ 15-in. Four bank
____ 15-in. Double bank
____ 15-in. Single
____ 8-ft tubes w/ Slimline Ballast
____ 6-ft tubes w/ Slimline Ballast
____ 12V Single 15-in. Kit
____ 12V Mini Flo 9-in. Kit
____ 12V Micro Flo 6-in. Kit
____ 12V Micro Flo 4-in. Kit

Xenons

____ 10k Xenon
____ 7k Xenon
____ 4k Xenon
____ 2k Xenon
____ 1k Xenon
____ 750W Xenon
____ 500W Xenon
____ 150W Xenon
____ 75W Xenon Flashlight

Stands

____ Cinevator, Molevator
____ Super Crank
____ Crank-o-vator
____ Low Crank Stand
____ Mombo Combo 4-riser Stand
____ Steal 3-Riser Junior Stand
____ Steal 2-riser Junior Stand
____ Aluminum 3-riser Junior
____ Aluminum 2-riser Junior
____ Junior Rolling Stand 3-riser
____ Junior Rolling Stand 2-riser
____ Low Boy Junior Stand

____ Steal 3-Riser Baby Stand
____ Steal 2-Riser Baby Stand
____ Baby Rolling Stand 3-riser
____ Baby Rolling Stand 2-riser
____ Low Baby Stand
____ Preemie Stand
____ Blade Stand
____ Low Blade Stand
____ Runway Base
____ Turtle Stand
____ T-bone
____ Wheel Set (3 pc)

Carts
____ Cable Cart
____ Doorway Dolly
____ Head Cart
____ Milk-crate cart
____ Work box

Dimmers
____ Control Console
____ CD80 (6 x 100A)
____ CD80 (6 x 60A)
____ CD80 (24 x 20A)
____ CD80 (24 x 15A)
____ 20k Stand Alone Dimmer
____ 12k Stand Alone Dimmer
____ 6k Stand Alone Dimmer
____ 5k Variac
____ 2k Variac
____ 1k Variac
____ 5k Plate Dimmer
____ 3k Plate Dimmer
____ 2k Plate Dimmer
____ 1k Plate Dimmer
____ 1k Hand dimmer
____ 650W Hand Dimmer

Distribution
____ 3-bar Spider Box
____ 4-bar Spider Box
____ 5-bar Spider Box
____ 600A Bull Switch 3-Phase
____ 400A Bull Switch Single Phase
____ 200A Bull Switch Single Phase
____ 900A Distro Box
____ 600A Distro Box
____ 400A Banded Box
____ Lug to Female Adaptors
____ Lug to Male Adaptors
____ Three-fers (pin)
____ Ground Squid (pin)
____ Female Suicide Pin Adaptor

____ Male Suicide Pin Adaptor
____ Cam-Loc T-splitter
____ Lug to Cam-Loc Jumper
____ 2-wire Pin to 100A 240V Bates Adaptor
____ 2-wire Pin to 100A Bates Adaptor
____ 3-wire Pin to 2 100A Bates Adaptor
____ 100A to 2 100A Bates Adaptor
____ 100A to 2 60A Bates Adaptor
____ 60A to 2 60A Bates Adaptor
____ 100A Lunch Box (5 duplex Edison
      outlets w/ circuit beakers)
____ 100A Gang Box (5 20A fused Edison)
____ 60A Gang Box
____ In-line Hertz Meter
____ Flicker Box
____ Cable Cross-overs
____ Tie-in Clamps

Cable
____ 4/0 100-ft.
____ 4/0 50-ft .
____ 4/0 25-ft .
____ 4/0 Jumper
____ 2/0 100-ft .
____ 2/0 50-ft.
____ 2/0 25-ft .
____ 2/0 Jumper
____ 50-ft #2 Grounding Cable
____ 50-ft #2 Banded (three-wire plus ground)
____ 50-ft #2 Banded (four-wire plus ground,
      three-phase)
____ Banded Jumper 10-ft
____ 100A 100-ft. Bates Extension
____ 100A 50-ft. Bates Extension
____ 100A 25-ft. Bates Extension
____ 60A 100-ft. Bates Extension
____ 60A 50-ft. Bates Extension
____ 60A 25-ft. Bates Extension
____ 50-ft. Stinger
____ 25-ft. Stinger
____ Socapex 150-ft. (6 20A dimmer circuits)
____ Socapex 100-ft.
____ Socapex 50-ft.
____ Socapex Break-out
____ Socapex Break-in

Generator
____ 46 Amp EX 5500 Honda
____ 350 A
____ 450A
____ 750A
____ 1000A
____ 1200A
____ 1400A

Expendables Checklist

Gel and Diffusion

Orange
____ roll Extra CTO
____ roll full CTO
____ roll Sun 85
____ roll 3/4 CTO
____ roll half CTO
____ roll quarter CTO
____ roll eighth CTO
____ roll full Straw
____ roll half Straw
____ roll quarter Straw
____ roll eighth Straw

Blue
____ roll Extra CTB
____ roll full CTB
____ roll 3/4 CTB
____ roll half CTB
____ roll quarter CTB
____ roll eighth CTB

Magenta
____ roll full minus-green
____ roll half minus-green
____ roll quarter minus-green
____ roll eighth minus-green

Green
____ roll full plus-green
____ roll half plus-green
____ roll quarter plus-green
____ roll eighth plus-green

Neutral Density and ND CTO
____ ND .3
____ ND .6
____ ND .9
____ ND 1.2
____ 85 ND .3
____ 85 ND .6
____ 85 ND .9

Diffusion
____ roll 216
____ roll 250
____ roll 251
____ roll opal

____ roll grid cloth
____ roll light grid
____ 1000H Velum

Other Gels
____ Other color correction (e.g., CID,
         SCI, Y1, Fluorofilter)
____ Heat shield
____ Cosmetic colors
____ Party colors
____ Party gel sheets

Bulbs

3200K
____ PH 211 75W (100 hrs)
____ PH 212 150W (100 hrs)
____ ECA 500W (60 hrs)
____ MR-16 75W narrow spot
____ MR-16 100W narrow spot
____ ECA 250W (20 hrs)

3400K
____ PH 213 (250W) (3 hrs)
____ No. 1 BBA 250W (3 hrs)
____ No. 2 EBV 500W (6 hrs)

4800K
____ 60W (blue)
____ 100W (blue)
____ No 1 BCA 250W (3 hrs)
____ EBW 500W (6 hrs)

Other Bulbs
____ 75 W R-40 flood
____ 150 W R-40 flood
____ 300 W R-40 flood
____ EAL 500W R-40 flood (3200K)
____ 25W Softwhite household
____ 40W Softwhite household
____ 60W Softwhite household
____ 75W Softwhite household
____ 100W Softwhite household
____ 12" 35W 1613 Linestra (Osram)
____ 20" 60W 1614 Linestra (Osram)
____ 40" 150W 1106 Linestra (Osram)
____ Socket 661 Linestra (Osram)
____ 60W or 100W blue

___ 60W or 100W red
___ 60W or 100W green
___ 60W or 100W clear
___ 40W candella base make-up table bulbs

Fluorescents

___ 4-ft. Optima 32
___ 4-ft. Vita-lite
___ 8-ft. Optima 32
___ 8-ft. Vita-lite

Tape

___ 2" gaffers tape (gray)
___ 2" gaffers tape (black)
___ 2" gaffers tape (white)
___ Black 2" paper tape
___ Photo black 2" paper tape (matte black)
___ White 1" camera tape
___ Electrical tape (Bk, Bl, Rd, Gr, Wt)
___ 1/2" snot tape
___ 3/4" snot tape

Hardware

___ Bags clothes pins
___ Trick line (black) #4
___ Mason line (white) #4
___ Hanks sash cord #6
___ Hank sash cord #8
___ Hank sash cord #10
___ Box large garbage bags
___ 12" rolls blackwrap
___ 24" rolls blackwrap
___ 36" rolls blackwrap
___ Bottle pure isopropyl alcohol
___ Clean lint-free rags
___ Roll bailing wire
___ Box cotter pins
___ Box Sharpie markers
___ Box pens
___ Rubber matting (by the ft.)

___ Roll Visqueen
___ Refracil (by the yard)
___ Crutch tips 1-1/4"
___ Crutch tips 3/4"
___ Bungy cords (36", 24", 18", 12")
___ S-hooks

Electrical

___ Box 20A cartridge fuses
___ Box 60A fuses
___ AA batteries
___ 6V meter batteries
___ A-76 meter batteries
___ 9V batteries
___ Spare Mag light bulbs
___ Cube taps (w/ground)
___ Ground lifters
___ Roll zip cord (18/2) 250' black
___ Roll zip cord (18/2) 250' white
___ Roll red/black #12 wire (twisted pair)
___ Roll red/black #14 wire (twisted pair)
___ Porcelain sockets (med. screw base)
___ In-line taps female Edison
___ Add-a-tap male Edison
___ Add-a-tap female Edison
___ Plug-in switch (Edison in/out)
___ Hubble female Edison
___ Hubble male Edison
___ Box wire nuts
___ In-line dimmers 1000W
___ In-line dimmers 600W
___ Socket dimmers (screw base)
___ Medium screw base extension
___ 6" swivel screw base extension
___ 9" swivel screw base extension
___ Pig nose adapters (screw base to Edison)
___ Mogul to medium screw base adaptors
___ Medium to candella screw base adaptor
___ Candella to medium base adaptor

Glossary*

A   Ampere.

Abbott   A manufacturer of single-conductor connectors used on feeder cable.

Abby Singer   The second to last shot of the day. The shot before the *martini*.

above-the-line costs   Production costs of the producer, director, writer, and principal actors.

AC   (1) Alternating current. (2) Camera assistant.

ace   A 1k Fresnel light.

AD   *See* assistant director.

adaptor   A device used to convert from one type of connector to another.

ammeter   A meter for measuring amperage.

ampacity   Amperage capacity of cable, connectors, etc.

amperage (I)   A unit of current. One ampere will flow through a resistance of 1 ohm under a pressure of 1 volt.

ampere-hour   A quantity of electricity equal to the number of amperes times the number of hours of charge that a battery can deliver.

AMPTP   Association of Motion Picture and Television Producers.

anode   A negative electrode.

ANSI   American National Standards Institute. Three-letter ANSI codes are used to identify light bulbs (e.g., EGT is a 1k bulb).

apple box   A reinforced plywood box used on the set for many purposes, including to raise an actor who is too short or to raise furniture. Apple boxes come in four sizes: full, half, quarter, and pancake.

arc light   Any light that makes light by forming an arc, including arc discharge lights such as HMIs. On the set, *arc light* is normally understood to mean a carbon arc light.

ASA   (1) American Standards Association (now the ANSI). (2) The exposure index (EI) rating of a film emulsion, also referred to as ISO.

aspect ratio   The ratio of the width to the height of the film frame. The standard aspect ratios are 1.33:1 (television), 1.66:1 (high-definition television and European theatrical film standard), 1.85:1 (American theatrical film standard), and 2.36:1 (Anamorphic 35mm).

assistant director (AD)   The person who runs the set. The AD is responsible for coordinating the actions of the many departments so that everyone is ready when the time comes to roll cameras.

AWG   American Wire Gauge.

baby   A 1k Fresnel lighting fixture manufactured by the Mole-Richardson Co.

baby stand   A stand with a 5/8 in. stud.

baby stud   A 5/8 in. mounting stud that mates with a 5/8 in. receptacle.

backdrop   A scenic painting or enlarged photograph transparency used outside set windows and doors when filming in a studio.

---

* Entries that have an asterisk are taken from *Practical Electrical Wiring* by Herbert P. Richter and W. Creighton Schwann. New York: McGraw-Hill, 1990.

bail   U-shaped part of a lighting fixture that attaches the fixture to the stand.

ballast   A device required to operate any discharge light, such as HMI, fluorescents, and xenon lights. The ballast provides the ignition charge and then acts as a choke, regulating the power to maintain the arc.

banded cable   Several single-conductor cables banded together at intervals, forming one bundle.

barn doors   Metal shields on a ring that mounts to the front of a lighting fixture. Barn doors are used to shape and control the beam of light.

base   (1) The basket on the underside of a fixture. (2) The base of a bulb is the porcelain part. (3) The lamp socket is also sometimes called the *base*.

Bates   A common name for three-pin connectors (20A, 30A, 60A, 100A, and 100A/220V).

batten   Usually refers to 1 × 3 lumber. May also refer to pipe on which lights, scenery, curtains, blacks, and borders can be hung.

battery belt   A battery pack, usually containing nickel-cadmium batteries, mounted in a leather belt that can be worn around the waist during mobile shooting.

bead board   Styrofoam used to make soft bounce light.

beam angle   The diameter of the beam angle is defined as the area of the light field that is 50% or more of the peak intensity of the beam.

beam projector   A theatrical lighting fixture that provides relatively strong, parallel rays of light.

beaver board   A nail-on plate mounted to a pancake.

below-the-line costs   The production costs of all members of the crew, but not the producer, director, writer, and principal actors.

best boy   The assistant chief lighting technician, or second electrician. The best boy is the gaffer's chief assistant.

big eye   A 10k incandescent fixture with an extra large lens (Mole-Richardson).

black wrap   A thick, durable black foil used on hot lights to control spill and to shape the beam.

blackbody radiator   A theoretical incandescent source used in defining the concept of color temperature. The spectral power and color distribution of a blackbody source depend only on temperature.

blonde   An Ianero 2k open-face fixture.

boom operator   The sound person who operates the microphone boom and affixes microphones to the talent.

branch circuit   As defined by the NEC, circuits that are downstream of the last overcurrent protection.

branchaloris   A branch of a tree or bush held in front of a light to create a moving or stationary foliage pattern.

broad   A nonfocusing, wide-angle lighting fixture, typically using a double-ended bulb, installed in a rectangular fixture with a silver reflector.

Brute   A 250A carbon arc light manufactured by Mole-Richardson.

bull switch   A main switch used on the main feeder or on subfeeder lines.

bump   A feature on a dimmer console — an instantaneous change in stage levels from one set of intensities ("look") to another.

bus bar   Copper bars (1/4 in. thick) to which lug connectors are attached.

butterfly set   A frame used to support a net or silk over the top of the action. The silk reduces and softens direct sunlight.

C   Celsius (temperature scale).

C-47   A common, wooden spring-type clothes pin.

C-74 A clothespin inverted to be used as a scrim-puller.

c-clamp A large C-shaped clamp with a baby stud or junior receptacle welded to it that is used to mount lights to beams.

C-stand A multipurpose stand used for setting flags and nets. Short for *Century stand*.

cable crossover A special rubber ramp used to protect cable from being damaged by being run over and to protect pedestrians from tripping over cable.

call sheet A sheet distributed by the production department before the end of each day that indicates the scenes that are to be shot on the following day, the call time of all cast and crew members, special travel instructions, special equipment that will be used, and general notices to the cast and crew.

Cam-Lok A type of single-conductor connector used for feeder cable.

can A permanently installed panelboard bus bar in a sound stage.

candela (cd) A unit of light intensity derived from brightness and distance. cd = FC × feet^2 or, in Europe: cd = lux × meters^2.

carbon arc light A very bright DC lighting fixture that creates light by igniting an arc flame between two carbon electrodes.

cathode A positive electrode.

catwalk A metal or wooden walkway above a sound stage.

CC *See* color compensation.

CCT Correlated color temperature.

celo cuke A wire mesh painted with a random pattern and placed in front of a light to throw a subtle pattern.

chain vice grip A mounting device that uses a bicycle chain and vice grip to create a tight clamp around pipes, poles, or tree limbs.

channel Device controlling a dimmer or group of dimmers. In a simple system there is a slider for each channel. On most current control systems, channels are numbers, accessed by numeric keypad. Multiple dimmers may be controlled by a single channel to which they are *patched*.

chaser lights A linear string of lights similar to those on a theater marquee. The lamps are wired in three, four, or five circuits; equally spaced lights are connected to the same circuit, which can be sequentially energized, creating the effect of light chasing along the line of lights.

cheater An Edison plug adaptor that allows three-prong grounded plugs to be plugged into a two-prong ungrounded outlet found in older buildings. Also called a *ground lifter*, *ground plug adaptor*, or *two-to-three adaptor*.

chiaroscuro A strongly contrasting treatment of light and shade in drawing and painting. Translated from the Italian, the word means "half-revealed."

chicken coop An overhead suspended light box that provides general downward ambient or fill light. Also called a *coop*.

chief lighting technician *See* gaffer.

chimera A specially designed, lightweight, collapsible soft box manufactured by Chimera Photographic Lighting.

CID *See* compact indium discharge.

cinevator stand A heavy-duty stand used for the largest types of lights. The mechanism that raises and lowers the light is driven by an electric motor.

circuit When talking about dimmer circuits refers to everything downstream of the dimmer, from the dimmer's output connector to the lighting fixtures themselves.

circuit breaker An overcurrent protection switch. It trips and disconnects a circuit if the current drawn exceeds the rating of the circuit breaker.

clothesline cable A cable hanging in the air at a level at which someone could trip on it or run into it. Cable should instead be routed so that it runs along the ground away from traffic areas.

Cmil Cross-sectional area of cable in circular mil.

color chart A chart of standard colors filmed at the head of a roll of film as a color reference for the lab.

color compensation (CC) A reading gained from a color meter indicating the amount of green or magenta gel needed to neutralize off-color hues, usually present in fluorescent lights.

color temperature A temperature expressed in degrees Kelvin (K) that defines the color makeup of light emitted by a source, such as the sun or a filament lamp, which has a continuous color spectrum.

combo stand A junior stand with a 1-1/8 in. receptacle used to hold reflector boards and larger lights.

compact indium discharge (CID) A 5500K gas discharge globe often used in sun guns.

compact source iodine (CSI) A type of gas discharge bulb similar to an HMI.

condor A vehicle with a telescoping boom arm used as a platform to position lights 30 to 120 ft. in the air.

continuity (1) Script continuity (the job of the script supervisor): the task of making sure that all the details of the scene remain consistent from take to take and from angle to angle. Shots may be filmed hours and even weeks apart, but they will be cut back to back in the final film. (2) Electrical continuity: the unbroken flow of electricity through various conductors.

continuity tester A device that runs a small amount of voltage through a conductor and lights a small bulb or makes a sound if the conductor is continuous.

continuous load An electrical load that is to be delivered continuously for more than three hours.

continuous spectrum The color makeup of light from a source, such as an incandescent bulb or natural daylight, which includes all the wavelengths of light without spikes or holes anywhere across the spectrum of colors.

contrast ratio The ratio of the intensity of the key light plus the fill light to the intensity of the fill light alone.

cookie *See* cucaloris.

cool the lights To turn the lights off.

crank-up stand A heavy-duty stand that provides a crank to raise and lower heavy lights.

CRI Color rendering index.

cribbing Blocks of wood used to level dolly track.

Croney cone A cone-shaped attachment fitted with diffusion that fits on the front of a light to soften and control the beam.

crossfade A fade that contains both an up-fade and down-fade. Also may refer to any fade where the levels of one cue are replaced by the levels of another cue.

crowder hanger A fixture mount that fastens to the top of a set wall and provides two studs.

crystal-controlled A crystal-based circuit that maintains a camera's frame rate very precisely. A wild camera has no crystal control.

CSI *See* compact source iodine.

CTB gel A blue gel that corrects a tungsten source to daylight.

CTO gel An orange gel that corrects a daylight source to tungsten.

cube tap A device that allows three Edison plugs to plug into one Edison socket.

cucaloris A wooden cutout pattern placed in front of a light to create a pattern.

cue The process of recalling a *preset* from its memory location (in a dimmer console) and putting the result on stage.

cue light A flashing or rotating light positioned outside the set to warn people when the camera is rolling.

cup blocks Wooden blocks with concave indents. Cup blocks are placed under the wheels of light stands to prevent them from rolling.

current The rate of flow of electricity measured in amperes.

cutter A long, thin flag used to make cuts in the light.

cyc strip A strip of open-face fixtures used to light a cyclorama. The lights are often wired in two, three, or four separate circuits to provide individual control of different colors.

cyclorama A seamless hanging or set piece, usually white, often curved where it meets the floor. It is used to create a limbo background, having no discernible horizon or texture.

day rate The wage for a day's work.

daylight Light commonly considered to have a color temperature of 5500K to 6000K. Daylight-balanced film renders colors naturally when lit with 5600K light.

DC *See* direct current.

dead-man pedal A floor pedal that must be pressed by the operator's foot in order to operate or drive a Snorkelift. The dead-man pedal is a safety device to prevent runaways.

Dedolight A small, special light fixture with a wide range of beam angle adjustment.

deferred pay Payment for the crew's work made in lieu of salary when and if the production turns a profit.

delta-connected system A system that provides four-wire, three-phase and three-wire, single-phase current with 120V, 208V, and 240V current from four wires. The voltage between each leg must be carefully measured to determine which is the high leg (the leg that gives 208V).

depth of field The depth of the scene that will be in focus on the screen. Depth of field varies with the camera's aperture, focal length, and distance from the subject and the film format.

deuce A 2k Fresnel light.

deuce board A fused AC/DC distribution box having two high-amperage contactors that can be controlled from remote switches.

dichroic filter A filtering lens used on some tungsten lights to convert tungsten to about 4800K.

diffusion Material used in front of lighting fixtures to soften the light they produce.

dike A dichroic filter lens.

dikes Wire cutters.

dimmer The device controlling power to a circuit and lighting fixtures. Two lights on one dimmer circuit cannot be separately controlled.

direct current (DC) Current that does not alternate polarity. Batteries and DC generators create DC.

director of photography (DP) The person in charge of the lighting and camera departments. The DP has direct creative control of the image.

discontinuous spectrum A light source with a discontinuous spectrum, such as a standard fluorescent bulb, that does not emit light evenly across the color spectrum, but instead has spikes at particular wavelengths and emits little or no light at others, resulting in poor color rendering.

distant location A location that is far enough from the production's town of origin that the crew must stay overnight.

distribution box An electrical box with circuit protection, used to stepdown cable size and connector size and to provide a variety of sizes of outlets for subfeeders, stage extensions, and various sizes of lights.

dog collar A short length of aircraft cable used to secure lights hung above the set. The collar is fitted with a loop at one end and a leash clip or carabiner at the other.

dolly grip The grip in charge of laying dolly track and executing dolly moves and crane moves.

doorway dolly A small, steerable, flat-bed dolly with large inflated tires, frequently used to move cable and large lights.

dot A very small, circular flag, net, or silk used to alter only a small portion of the beam of light.

douser The mechanism on a follow spot used to make a quick blackout without the operator having to extinguish the light itself. On a carbon arc follow spot, the douser protects the lens while the arc is struck.

down-fade The portion of a fade that involves only channels that are decreasing in level.

DP *See* director of photography.

dress a light To neaten up the light or cable.

duck bill A vice grip with a baby stud on the handle and two 6 sq. in. plates welded to the jaws. Used to mount foamcore and bead board on a C-stand.

dummy load *See* ghost load.

duvetyn Thick, black cloth used to block light.

E Electromotive force, measured in volts.

ears The metal brackets on the front of a light that hold the barn doors and scrims.

Edison plug and socket A typical household plug and socket with two parallel blades and a U-shaped grounding pin. Also called a *U-ground parallel-blade plug.*

egg crate An accessory for a soft light fixture that cuts stray light and narrows the beam angle.

electrician Common name for a lighting technician.

18% gray Medium gray used to determine exposure.

electromotive force Voltage.

electronic ballast A solid-state ballast. The term *electronic ballast* is synonymous with flicker-free square-wave ballast (HMI), or high frequency (fluorescent).

ellipsoidal reflector spotlight (ERS) A spotlight of fixed or adjustable focal length that has framing shutters and a projection gobo slot and produces a long, narrow throw of light. Also called a *Leko.*

Elvis A gold lamé stretched on a frame and used to bounce light.

emulsion The photochemical substance on a piece of film that captures the image.

equipment grounding The grounding of non–current-carrying parts of equipment via a green grounding wire.

expendables Supplies, such as tape, that are used up during the course of a production.

eye light A light used to create a twinkle of light in the eye of the subject.

F Fahrenheit (temperature scale).

f-stop A scale used to set the aperture of the camera.

fade A gradual change in stage levels from one set of intensities ("look") to another.

fall-off The diminishing intensity of light from one position to another.

FAR cyc A lighting fixture that lights a cyclorama.

FAY An incandescent PAR light with dichroic coating that creates daylight-colored light.

FC *See* foot-candle.

feeder cable Large single-conductor cable used to run power from the power source to the set.

field The area that is at least 10% of the maximum candle power of a beam of light.

field angle The angle from the light fixture to the opposite edges of the field.

filament The tungsten coil inside a bulb that glows when voltage is applied to it, creating light.

fill light Soft light used to reduce the darkness of the shadow areas.

finger A very small rectangular flag, net, or silk used to make minute cuts of the beam of light.

first team The director and actors.

fixture A luminaire, light, lamp, instrument, head, or lantern.

flag Black duvetyn cloth stretched over a metal frame and used to shape and cut light.

flag box A wooden box in which flags, nets, and silks are stored.

FLB filter A filter used on the camera to remove the green hue of fluorescents.

flex arm A small jointed arm used to hold fingers and dots.

flicker box An electrical circuit box used to simulate the flickering of a flame or television screen. A flicker box randomly increases and decreases the intensity of the lighting fixtures.

flicker-free An HMI or fluorescent ballast that provides a square-wave or high-frequency signal that eliminates light-level pulsation when filmed at any shutter speed.

flood The spread of the beam from a fixture that is broad and relatively weak.

foamcore A white, glossy card material reinforced with 1/4 in. Styrofoam and used to bounce light.

focal length The distance from a lens at which an image comes into focus (the focal point). For camera lenses, it is usually expressed in millimeters. A long lens has a very narrow angle of view and a short depth of field. A short lens has a wide angle of view and greater depth of field.

focal spot An accessory that mounts on a Fresnel fixture, essentially changing the fixture into an ellipsoidal spotlight.

follow spot A high-power, narrow-beam spotlight suitable for very long throws. It is designed to follow performers on stage.

foot-candle (FC) An international unit of illumination. One foot-candle equals the intensity of light falling on a sphere placed 1 ft. away from a point source of light of 1 candela. One footcandle equals 1 lumen per sq. ft. *See also* lux.

foot-lambert An international unit of brightness. One foot-lambert equals the uniform brightness of a perfectly diffusing surface emitting or reflecting light at a rate of one lumen per sq. ft.

forced call When less than the minimum turnaround time is given between wrap on one day and call on the following day.

format The film or video medium and the aspect ratio of the image.

4-by cart A cart for moving and storing 4 × 4 ft. frames, flags, nets, bounce boards, and so on.

4-by floppy A 4 × 4 ft. flag with an additional flap that folds out to make a 4 × 8 ft. flag.

fps Frames per second.

frequency The number of cycles per second of alternating current, measured in hertz.

Fresnel (1) A type of lens that has the same optical effect as a plano-convex lens but has reduced weight and heat retention. (2) The light fixture that uses a Fresnel lens.

furniture clamp An adjustable clamp used for mounting lights.

furniture pad A packing blanket used to protect floors, deaden sound, soften a fall, and so on.

fuse An overcurrent device that uses an alloy ribbon with a low melting point. The circuit is broken when the current exceeds the rating of the fuse.

gaffer The head of the lighting crew. The gaffer works directly under the director of photography.

gaffer's tape   Heavy, fabric-based tape that rips cleanly in the direction of the weave. It is used for securing cables and lights on the set.

gamma   A graph line that describes a film emulsion's reaction to tonal gradation and its innate contrast. Also called *D log E curve* or *characteristic curve.*

gang box   An outlet box that provides Edison outlets and plugs into a larger connector, such as a 60A Bates or a 100A stage box.

gator grip   A baby stud on a spring-loaded clamp with rubber jaws, used for mounting light-weight fixtures to doors, poles, furniture, and so on.

gel   Polyester-based colored gelatin used to color a beam of light.

generator   The power plant used to create power on location. Motion picture generators are sound-baffled and provide bus bars or other common feeder connectors.

genny   *See* generator.

GFCI, GFI   *See* ground fault interrupter.

ghost load   A load that is not used to light the set and is placed on a circuit to balance the various legs of power or to bring the load on a resistance-type dimmer up to its minimum operating wattage. Also called *dummy load* and *phantom load.*

globe   A bulb.

gobo arm   The arm of a C-stand.

gobo head   The metal knuckle that attaches the gobo arm to a C-stand.

golden time   Premium overtime pay after 12 hours of work (14 hours when on a distant location). Golden time is normally double the regular hourly rate.

gray scale   A chart showing gradations of gray from white to black.

greens   The wooden catwalk suspended above the set in a sound stage.

grid   (1) A transformer unit used with a carbon arc light. (2) The structure of metal pipes suspended above the stage floor for hanging lighting fixtures.

grid clamp   A clamp that attaches to grid pipe.

grid cloth   A white nylon diffusion fabric with a grid-like weave.

griffolyn   Nylon-reinforced plastic tarp material. Griffolyns are typically black on one side and white on the other; they are used as a bounce for fill. Also called *griff.*

grip   A crew member responsible for the nonelectrical aspects of lighting and rigging, and for the camera dolly and other camera platforms.

grip clip   A metal spring clamp.

grip helper   A metal arm that mounts to a junior stand. A gobo head angles down and out from the stand to which a 4-by frame can be attached in front of the fixture.

grip truck   The lighting truck that houses the lights and grip equipment during location shooting.

ground fault interrupter (GFI)   A special type of circuit protection. There are a number of different types of GFIs. One type compares the outgoing current of a circuit to the returning current. If it detects a difference in the two (indicating a ground fault), it trips a switch to disconnect the circuit.

ground lifter   *See* cheater.

ground row   Cyclorama lights placed along the ground at the base of the cyc. A mask normally hides the lights from view.

grounded wire   The grounded, white, current-carrying wire of an AC circuit. Do not confuse this term with the green *grounding wire.*

grounding star   A mole-pin connector to which a number of grounding leads can be attached.

grounding wire   The green, non-current-carrying equipment grounding wire of an AC circuit.

halogen cycle   The cycle by which halogen in a bulb returns tungsten deposits to the filament, preventing blackening on the inner wall of the bulb.

head   A light fixture.

head cable   The cable running from the ballast of a lighting fixture to the head.

hi boy   An extra tall stand.

HID   High-intensity discharge. A type of street lamp.

high leg   The 208V leg of a delta-connected three-phase system.

high roller   An extra tall rolling stand, often used to fly an overhead frame.

high-key   A bright lighting style with low contrast and bright highlights.

HMI   *See* mercury medium-arc iodide.

honey wagon   The trailer that houses the lavatories used when shooting on location.

hot spot   (1) The beam center. (2) A shiny spot or glare reflection that is distracting to the eye.

house lights   The permanent lighting in the audience area of a theater or sound stage.

housing   The metal casing that surrounds the bulb and reflector of a lighting fixture.

Hz   Hertz (cycles per second).

I   Current, measured in amperes.

IA, IATSE   International Alliance of Theatrical and Stage Employees.

IBEW   International Brotherhood of Electrical Workers.

impedance (Z)   A measure, in ohms, of the opposition to current flow in an AC circuit. Impedance includes resistance, capacitive reactance, and inductive reactance.*

incandescent   Any type of electric light that creates light by making a metallic filament (usually tungsten for film lights) glow by applying current to it.

incident light meter   A light meter that reads the light falling onto the face of the meter.

inductance   A measure, in henrys, of the opposition to current change in an AC circuit (causing current to lag behind voltage). Inductance is exhibited by turns of wire with or without an iron core.

infrared (IR)   Wavelengths above the highest visible wavelength of light, felt as heat.

inky   A 100W or 200W Fresnel fixture manufactured by Mole-Richardson Co.

instrument   In the theater, a lighting fixture.

intermittent duty   Operation for alternate intervals of load, no load, and rest.

IR   *See* infrared.

iris   The mechanism on a follow spot that adjusts the diameter of the beam.

ISO   *See* ASA.

J-box   A junction box. The term usually refers to an Socapex HMI head cable junction box used to connect an extension head cable to the existing head cable.

jockey boxes   Metal storage containers on the underside of a truck. Jockey boxes usually store sandbags, cable, and so on.

juicer   A set lighting technician.

junior   A 2k Fresnel fixture.

junior stand   A stand with a 1-1/8 in. junior receptacle.

junior stud   A 1-1/8 in. stud.

K   Kelvin (temperature scale).

k   One thousand.

Kelvin   A unit of measurement of temperature (0K = –273°C). In set lighting, the term refers to the color temperature (color makeup) of light and not to its physical temperature.

key light   The main source lighting the subject.

kick-out   The accidental unplugging of a light.

kicker   A side backlight.

kit rental   An additional fee a technician charges for the use of his or her own tools, equipment, and hardware. Also called *box rental.*

knuckle   The part of a C-stand gobo head that grips the flag.

ladder   A metal ladder-like structure, suspended from above or mounted to a wall, that provides a position from which to hang lights. Ladders are often used in theaters to position a stack of lights in the wings.

lantern   A lighting fixture (British theater).

layout board   Cardboard sheets, 4 × 8 ft., commonly used to protect floors.

Leko   Leko is a trademark of Strand's ellipsoidal reflector spotlight.

light-balancing (LB) scale   Scale used on Minolta color meters.

Lightmaker   A manufacturer of flicker-free AC and AC/DC ballasts.

Linnabach projector   A simple small-point-source lamp mounted inside a black box that projects cut-out shapes or transparencies onto a cyclorama. The images are slightly diffuse shadows.

louvers   Thin, parallel strips with a black finish arranged in a grid pattern that is placed in front of a soft light source. Louvers reduce spill light and direct the light in one direction.

low boy   A very short stand.

low-key   A dark, shadowy lighting style.

lug   An extremely heavy-duty brass connector that bolts feeder cables to bus bars, deuce boards, and spiders. Also called *sister lugs.*

lumen   A unit of light (flux).

luminaire   A light fixture.

lux   An international unit of light intensity used primarily in Europe. One lux equals one lumen per square meter. One foot-candle equals 10.764 lux. lux = cd/meters^2.

MacBeth   A blue glass conversion filter used on some open-face lights. Converts tungsten sources to daylight.

mafer clamp   An all-purpose grip clamp (cam screw tightening) that can receive a number of different mounting attachments, such as a baby stud or a flex arm.

magic hour   The hour of light after sunset, during which the western sky creates a warm-colored soft light.

make first, break last   A rule of thumb when connecting single-conductor cables. The grounding connection must be made first, before any of the other wires. When disconnecting the cables, the grounding wire connection should be broken last.

martini   The last shot of the day.

matth pole   A pole that braces against two opposite walls to provide a structure from which to hang a lightweight fixture.

meal penalty   The fee paid by the production company (on union films) when shooting continues beyond six hours without breaking for a meal.

meat ax   An arm mounted to the pipe of a catwalk or to the basket of a boom platform that provides a way to place a flag in front of a fixture.

Meltric   A five-pin, heavy-duty connector used in some power distribution systems.

memory   On a dimmer console, the storage location for preset information

mercury medium-arc iodide (HMI)   A type of gas discharge bulb with a color temperature of 5600K and high efficiency of more than 90 lumens per watt.

Mickey   A 1k open-face fixture manufactured by Mole-Richardson.

Midget   A 200W wide-beam Fresnel fixture manufactured by Mole-Richardson.

Mini   (1) A 100W or 200W Fresnel fixture manufactured by Mole-Richardson, or a miniature soft light manufactured by LTM. (2) Girlfriend of Mickey manufactured by Walt Disney.

minusgreen gel   A magenta gel used to take the green out of fluorescent light.

MIRED   One million times the reciprocal of the Kelvin rating of a given light source. The MIRED scale is used to determine the color shift of a given gel when used with any source. Short for *microreciprocal degree.*

mole-pin   A 0.5 in. slip pin used as a distribution system connector.

MOS   A scene filmed without recording sound.

mountain leg   The leg of a three-leg stand that extends to allow the stand to remain upright on uneven ground.

MT-2   A color-correction gel used on carbon arc lights with a Y-1 gel to correct the color temperature of a white flame arc to 3200K.

multiline spectrum   The spectral energy distribution graph of an HMI light. Instead of a continuous line across the color spectrum, the color makeup is created by numerous single spikes.

Musco Light   A very powerful mobile lighting truck.

NABET   National Association of Broadcast Employees and Technicians.

nanometer (nm)   A unit of length used to measure the wavelengths of the colors of light. One nanometer equals one-billionth of a meter.

ND   *See* neutral-density.

NEC   National Electrical Code.

net   A black honeycomb netting material sewn onto a rod frame that is used to reduce the intensity of part or all of a light's beam.

neutral-density (ND)   A gel or filter that reduces light transmission without altering the color of the light.

NFPA   National Fire Protection Association.

nook light   A small, lightweight open-face fixture that typically uses a double-ended bulb and a V-shaped reflector.

offset   A piece of grip hardware used to hang a light out to the side of a stand.

ohm (Ω)   A unit of electrical resistance equal to the resistance through which 1V will force 1A.

opal   A popular, thin diffusion.

open-face light   A fixture that has no lens, only a bulb mounted in front of a reflector.

OSHA   Occupational Safety and Health Administration.

overcurrent device   A circuit breaker or fuse.

overhead set   A large frame with one of several types of material stretched across it, including a solid, single net, double net, silk, or griffolyn.

O-zone   The open spaces between the perms, in the rafters of a sound stage. Only rigging grips are typically allowed to work in the O-zone using safety lines.

PA   *See* production assistant.

paddle   The male plug that is plugged into a stage box.

pancake   A 3/4 in. piece of plywood matching the dimensions of the large side of an apple box.

paper method   A method of calculating the amperage of 120V fixtures by dividing the wattage by 100.

PAR can   A rugged fixture used often in rock-and-roll concerts. A PAR can is simply a PAR globe mounted in a cylindrical can that provides a slot for colored gel.

parabolic reflector   A reflector shaped like a parabola, giving it a focal point from which all light rays will be reflected outward in a parallel beam.

parallel circuit   The connection of two or more fixtures across the same conductors of a circuit such that current flow through each is independent of the others.[*]

parallels   A small, easy-to-assemble scaffold platform.

party gel   Colored gels, also called *effects gel* or *theatrical gel*

patch   Historically, the process of physically connecting circuits to dimmers. Now usually refers to electronic assignment of dimmers to channels. "Patch" does not refer to the assignment of channels to cues or submasters.

Peppers   A line of small, lightweight tungsten lights manufactured by LTM in sizes of 100W, 200W, 300W, 420W, 500W, 650, 1000W, and 20k.

perms   Permanent catwalks near the high ceilings of sound stages.

phantom load   *See* ghost load.

phase   (1) An energized single conductor, usually ungrounded and never the neutral.* (2) The positioning of an AC cycle in time, relative to the phases of the other hot legs. Most electrical services are either single-phase or three-phase services.

photoflood   A bulb, typically with a standard medium screw base that has a color temperature of 3200K to 3400K

piano board   Originally, a portable dimmer switchboard or road board. This term has come to be used for many types of portable dimmer switchboards.

pigeon plate   A baby nail-on plate.

pins   Any of several types of connectors. Mole-pins and *.515* pins are single-conductor slip pins used on feeder cable. Three-pin connectors, commonly called *Bates connectors*, are also sometimes called *pins*.

pipe clamp   A clamp used to hang a light from an overhead pipe.

plano-convex   A lens that is flat on one side and convex on the other. Light comes from the flat side and converges or diverges as it passes though the lens, in proportion to the lamp's distance to the lens.

plate dimmer   A resistance-type dimmer commonly used with DC circuits.

plugging box   A stage box. May also refer more generally to any outlet box.

plusgreen gel   A gel used to add green to lights to match their color to that of fluorescent bulbs.

pocket   Outlets for stage circuits, often located under a protective trapdoor; for example, floor pockets, wall pockets, and fly pockets.

polarity   The orientation of the positive and negative wires of a DC circuit or the hot and neutral wires of an AC circuit. A polarized plug cannot be plugged in with reversed polarity.

pole cats   Lighting support equipment consisting of extendible metal tubes that wedge between two walls or between floor and ceiling to which lights can be mounted.

power   The total amount of work, measured in watts. The term is also generally understood as electricity, or juice.

power factor   In AC, the ratio of the actual or effective power in watts to the apparent power in volt-amperes, expressed as a percentage. Inductive loads cause the current to lag behind the voltage, resulting in a power factor of less than 100%.*

practical lamp   A lamp, sconce, or fixture that is shown in the scene.

prefocus base   The type of lamp base.

prelight or **prerig**   To rig in advance. During production, the grip and electrical crew may form a second crew or bring in a second crew to work ahead, rigging the sets that are to be shot during the following days.

preset   Of a dimmer console — a predefined set of intensities for a set of channels, stored in memory for later replay.

primary colors   For light, red, blue, and green. When the primary colors of light are projected onto a white surface, the area where all three colors intersect should theoretically make white light.

prime fixture   A focusable, open-face fixture.

Priscilla   A silver lamé stretched on a frame and used to bounce light.

producer   The person who oversees the production of the film or television show from the very beginning — obtaining the script, raising money, finding the backing to produce the show — to the very end — selling the finished film in domestic and world markets, trying to maximize its sales and profitmaking potential. The producer is the ultimate authority on all money-related decisions and most others. Everyone on the production works for the producer.

production assistant (PA)   An assistant in the production department who performs any number of menial and administrative tasks.

PSA   Public service announcement.

quick-on plugs and sockets   Low-amperage, parallel-blade, no-ground Edison plugs and sockets that are designed to be quick and convenient to wire.

R   Resistance, measured in ohms. *See* resistance.

rag   The cloth part of an overhead set.

rain tent   A tent to cover lights and electrical equipment in case of precipitation.

reactance (X)   A measure, in ohms, of the opposition to AC due to capacitance (X_C) or inductance (X_L).

receptacle   A female connector or female mounting hardware.

rectifier   An electrical unit that converts AC to DC.

redhead   A 1k open-face fixture.

reflected light meter   A light meter that reads the amount of light reflected by the scene into the meter. A standard reflected meter has a relatively wide angle of view and averages the areas of light and dark to give the reading. *See* also spot meter.

reflectors   Silver-covered boards typically used to bounce light, usually sunlight. Also called *shiny boards*.

resistance (R)   A measure, in ohms, of the opposition to current flow in a conductor, device, or load. In DC, volts ÷ amperes = ohms of resistance. For AC, *see* impedance.

rheostat   A resistance dimmer.

rigging bible   A set of diagrams showing the power layout of a studio's sound stages.

rigging gaffer   The gaffer in charge of designing and installing the cabling and electrical distribution for a large set.

rim   A backlight that makes a rim around the head and shoulders of the subject from the perspective of the camera.

Ritter fan   A large effects fan used to blow snow and rain and to give the appearance of wind or speed.

safety   A wire, chain, cable, or rope looped around the bail of a light to prevent it from falling should it come loose from its stud.

sandbag   A sand-filled bag used to stabilize stands and equipment by adding dead weight or counterweight.

scale   The minimum pay scale set forth by the labor union representing the crew or cast.

scene machine   A lighting unit that projects an image on a screen, usually from the back. The image can be made to move by scrolling through the machine or to rotate by using adjustable-speed motors. Scene machines are often used to create moving clouds across the cyclorama in theatrical productions.

scissor arc   A special carbon arc machine used to create a lightning effect.

scissor clip   A device that provides a means of hanging lights from a false ceiling, such as those found in many modern commercial buildings.

scissor lift   A self-propelled electric lift.

scoop   A lighting fixture that consists of a large 1k or 2k bulb mounted in a reflector. Scoops are used for general area light.

scosh   A very small amount, as in "Flood it out a scosh."

scrim   A circle of wire mesh, which slides into the ears on the front of a fixture and reduces the intensity of the light. A single dims the light about a half-stop. A double dims it about one stop. A half-single or double affects only half of the beam.

second team   The stand-ins used as models during lighting.

secondary colors   The colors formed by combining two primary colors. Also called *complementary colors*.

Senior   A 5k incandescent Fresnel fixture manufactured by Mole-Richardson Co.

series circuit   Connection of two or more devices or loads in tandem so that the current flowing through one also flows through all the others.*

service   Electrical service. This term can refer to the types of circuits installed, for example, single-phase, three-wire service.

service entrance   The main panelboard into which the power lines running to a building terminate.

shock   The sensation or occurrence of an electrical circuit being completed through a person's body.

short   A film of 30 minutes or less. Directors and students often shoot a short as a resumé or promotional piece to demonstrate their abilities or to help them move into a new area.

short circuit   Unwanted current flow between conductors.

Shotmaker   A customized tow vehicle for shooting moving car scenes.

show card   Thick card stock, usually white on one side and black on the other, used to bounce light.

shutter   In a motion picture camera, a butterfly-type device that spins in front of the aperture plate.

shutters   Venetian blind–like metal slats that are mounted on a fixture in place of barn doors for use as a douser.

silicone spray   A dry lubricant used on dolly track.

silk   Silk fabric used to soften and cut the intensity of light. It is used in all sizes, from very small dots and fingers to very large 20 × 20 ft. overheads.

Silver Bullet   A 12k or 18k HMI light manufactured by Cinemills Corp.

single-phase   A type of alternating current typically used in circuits that have two hot wires and one neutral.

sister lugs   *See* lug.

sky pan   A large, soft light fixture used for general fill, comprising a 2k, 5k, or 10k bulb and a large pan-shaped reflector.

snoot   A black metal cylinder or cone mounted on the ears of a fixture to narrow the beam.

Snorkelift   A telescoping-boom vehicle similar to the Condor.

snot tape   Sticky adhesive substance used to attach gel to a frame.

Socapex cable   Multi-wire cable connector used (1) on HMI head feeder, and (2) on multicircuit cable for dimmer circuits.

soft box   A device used to create very soft, diffuse light.

soft light   A light fixture with a large, curved, white reflector surface that bounces light onto the scene. No direct light is used. The large aperture and reflected light creates light with soft shadows that is often used as fill light.

solid   A black "rag" stretched on a frame and used to cut light.

sound mixer   The person who operates the audio recording machine, usually a DAT or Nagra tape recorder.

space light A large silked cylinder that hangs above the set to create soft ambient illumination.

spark A nickname for set lighting technician.

SPD Spectral power distribution (graph).

specular An adjective used to describe hard light emitted by a point source.

spider box A cable splicing box used to join lug feeder cables. The cable's lug connectors bolt to copper bus bar plates.

spot A beam that is focused into a narrow, relatively strong beam of light.

spot meter A type of reflected meter having a very narrow angle of acceptance (1° to 20°) used to determine the light value of a specific point on the set.

square wave A type of AC created by an electronic ballast that renders HMI lights flicker-free.

squeezer A dimmer.

stage box A distribution box with pockets that accept a male paddle connector. Stage boxes are normally referred to by the number of pockets they have: one-hole, two-hole, four-hole, or six-hole boxes.

stage extension A high-amperage extension cable; it has a paddle on one end and a one-hole or two-hole box at the other.

staging area The area on the sound stage or location selected as a temporary place to keep the lighting equipment and carts.

stick-up An extremely small, lightweight fixture that can be taped to the wall.

stinger An extension cord; officially, a hot extension cord.

stop An f-stop or a t-stop.

strain relief A rope tie used to reduce strain at the point at which a cable attaches to its connector.

streaks and tips Cans of hair color that are often handy for darkening reflective surfaces.

strike (1) To dismantle a set or to take down and put away a piece of equipment. (2) When referring to an HMI, to strike the light can mean to turn it on.

strobe light A light that creates short, bright, regular flashes of light at an adjustable speed.

studio zone In California, the area within 30 miles of a specific point in Hollywood. Labor rules are different inside and outside of this zone.

submaster A controller (usually a linear slider) on a dimmer board that allows manual control of groups, effects, cues, or channels.

suicide pin An adaptor with two male ends.

swing A crew member who performs the tasks of both grip and electrician, as needed.

system grounding The grounding of the service equipment and the current-carrying, neutral white wire to the transformer and to earth.

t-bone A metal T-shaped base with a junior receptacle, used to place larger lights at ground level.

t-stop The aperture setting of a zoom lens after compensation for light lost in the numerous optical elements of the lens.

taco cart A special cart that carries grip equipment, such as C-stands, apple boxes, wedges, mounting hardware, and grip expendables.

tag line A line dropped from aloft and used to hoist equipment into a catwalk, green beds, or Condor.

talent On-camera people and animals, usually actors, not necessarily talented ones.

three-fer A connector that provides three female connectors from one male connector.

three-phase A type of alternating current that has three hot legs. The alternating voltage cycle of each leg is a third of a cycle apart.

three-riser A stand that has three extensions.

throw The distance at which a fixture can effectively light a subject.

tie-in The connection of distribution cables to a facility's service panel box.

Titan A 350A carbon arc light manufactured by Mole-Richardson.

tracing paper Thin, translucent paper used to white out windows.

transformer A device with no moving parts and two or more insulated windings on a laminated steel core that is used to raise or lower AC voltage by inductive coupling. Volt-amperes into the primary coil and volt-amperes out of the secondary coil arc the same, less the small current necessary to magnetize the core.[*]

tree A tall stand or tower that has horizontal pipes on which lights can be hung. Used a great deal in theater and concert lighting.

trombone Fixture-mounting hardware that hooks over the top of the set, drops down the set wall, is adjustable, and provides a baby or junior stud or receptacle to which a light is mounted.

truss A metal structure designed to support a horizontal load over an extended span. Trusses are used largely in concert lighting to support lighting fixtures aloft.

tungsten color temperature A color temperature of 3200K.

tungsten halogen lamp A lamp designed to maintain an almost constant color temperature and a high lumen output throughout its life. The halogen cycle is a regenerative process that prevents the blackening of the inside of the bulb.

turnaround The time between the time you go off the clock on one day and call time on the next.

turtle stand A squat junior stand that enables a large light to be positioned at ground level.

tweco clamp An electrical clamp consisting of two saw-tooth jaws that clamp together by turning the threaded screw base.

Tweenie A 650W Fresnel light manufactured by Mole-Richardson Co.

twist-lock A connector for which the plug inserts into the socket and then twists, locking the plug to the socket.

216 A popular, relatively heavy diffusion.

type W cable Cable that is manufactured to meet the requirements of NEC Articles 520 and 530 regarding portable entertainment cable. It is abrasion, oil, solvent, and ozone resistant and flame tested.

U-ground A standard Edison plug with a U-shaped grounding pin.

UL Underwriter Laboratories.

ultraviolet (UV) The wavelengths of light below the shortest visible wavelength. UV-A is black light. UV-B radiation can cause skin burns and eye damage as well as skin cancer if not filtered.

Unilux A manufacturer of strobe lighting equipment that can be synchronized to a motion picture camera shutter.

up-fade The portion of a fade that involves only channels that are increasing in level.

UV *See* ultraviolet

V *See* volt

VA *See* volt-ampere.

variac An autotransformer dimmer.

VEAM connector VEAM Litton is a manufacturer of connectors, including multipin HMI head feeder connectors and single conductor feeder cable connectors.

velum *See* tracing paper.

visqueen   Plastic material used to protect equipment from precipitation.

volt (V)   A unit of electrical force. One volt is required to force 1A of electricity though a resistance of 1Ω (ohm).

volt-ampere (VA)   Voltage times amperage. In DC, volts × amps = watts, but in AC, inductance and capacitance in the circuit may introduce reactance, causing a discrepancy between watts and volt-amperes.

voltage drop   The difference in voltage between two points in a circuit due to the intervening impedance or resistance.

voltmeter   A meter used to measure voltage potential between two points in a circuit.

W   *See* watt.

wall sled   A fixture-mounting device that hangs from the top of the set wall and rests against the wall.

wall spreader   Hardware that mounts to either end of a piece of lumber, creating a span from one wall to another from which lights can be hung.

watt (W)   A unit of electrical power, the product of voltage and amperage.

wedge   A triangular wooden block used to level dolly track.

welding cable   A flexible electrical cable once widely used for power distribution. Welding cable can no longer be used legally, except as a grounding wire.

western dolly   A large flat-bed camera platform with large inflated tires that steer at one end. A western dolly can be useful for moving lights and cable.

wet cell battery   A car battery.

wiggy   A continuity or resistance-testing device.

woof   Stop.

wrap   The process of taking down lights and coiling cable that begins after the last shot of the day has been completed successfully.

wye-connected system   A common type of three-phase transformer arrangement. Voltage reads 208V between any two of the hot legs and 120V between a hot leg and the neutral white leg.

xenon lights   An extremely bright type of arc discharge light that has a color temperature of 5600K. Because the arc is very small, the light can be channeled into a very narrow shaft of extremely bright light.

Y-1   A type of gel that converts a white carbon arc to normal daylight color balance.

Y-connected system   *See* wye-connected system.

yoke   *See* bail.

zip cord   Two-wire, 18AWG electric lamp cord.

zip light   A small soft light.

zone system   Ansel Adams' system of eleven gradations of gray from pure black to pure white. The zones are numbered in Roman numerals from 0 to X. There is a one-stop difference from zone to zone.

Φ   Phase.

Ω   Resistance (ohms).

Bibliography

The following publications were consulted in the writing of this book. Each is an excellent reference for further reading in specific areas.

Carlson, Verne, and Sylvia E. Carlson. *Professional Lighting Handbook*, 2nd ed. Boston: Focal Press, 1991.

Carter, Paul. *Backstage Handbook: An Illustrated Almanac of Technical Information*. New York: Broadway Press, 1988.

Detmers, F., ed. *American Cinematographer Manual*. Hollywood, CA: American Society of Cinematographers Press, 1989.

Fitt, B., and J. Thornley. *Lighting by Design*. Boston: Focal Press, 1992.

Goodell, Gregory. *Independent Feature Film Production: A Complete Guide from Concept to Distribution*. New York: St. Martin's Press, 1982.

Local 728, International Alliance of Theatrical and Stage Employees. *Working Manual for Studio Electrical Technicians*. Hollywood, CA: IATSE.

Maikiewicz, Kris. *Cinematography*. New York: Prentice Hall, 1973.

Matthews Studio Equipment Inc. *Matthews 1992 Product Catalog*. Burbank, CA, 1992.

Mole-Richardson Co. *Mole-Richardson Co. Catalog*. Hollywood, CA, 1990.

Moody, James L. *Concert Lighting: Techniques, Art and Business*. Boston: Focal Press, 1989.

National Fire Protection Association. *National Electrical Code*. Quincy, MA: NEPA, 1991.

Pilbrow, Richard. *Stage Lighting*. New York: Drama Book Publishers, 1970.

Richter, Herbert P., and Creighton W. Schwan. *Practical Electrical Wiring*. New York: McGraw-Hill, 1990.

Samuelson, David W. *Motion Picture Camera and Lighting Equipment: Choice and Technique*, 2nd ed. Boston: Focal Press, 1986.

Schaefer, John P. *An Ansel Adams Guide: Basic Techniques of Photography*. Boston: Little, Brown, 1992.

Strand Lighting, *CD80 Digital Pack, Users Manual*. Rancho Domingues, CA, Revision Date 9/28/92.

Sylvania GTE. *Lighting Handbook for Television, Theater and Professional Photography*, 8th ed. Danvers, MA: Sylvania, 1989.

Additional References for Further Reading

Periodicals

American Cinematographer. ASC Holding Corporation, 1782 N. Orange Drive, Hollywood, CA 90028

Lighting Dimensions. Lighting Dimensions Associates, 135 Fifth Avenue, New York, NY 10010-7193

Books

Brown, Blain. *Motion Picture and Video Lighting*. Boston: Focal Press, 1992.

Glerum, Jay. *Stage Rigging Handbook*. Carbondale, IL: Southern Illinois University Press, 1989.

Hirshfeld, Gerals. *Image Control*. Boston: Focal Press, 1993.

Lowell, Ross. *Matters of Light and Depth*. Philadelphia, PA: Broad Street Books, 1992.

McCandles, Stanley. *A Method of Lighting the Stage*. New York: Theater Arts Books, 1958.

Schaefer, Dennis, and Larry Salvato. *Masters of Light: Conversations with Contemporary Cinematographers*. Berkeley and Los Angeles, CA: University of California Press, 1984.

Uva, Michael. *The Grip Book*. Michael C. Uva, 1988.

Wilson, Anton. *Cinema Workshop*. Hollywood, CA: ASC Holding Co., 1983.

Index